Fodor's 12th Edition

Philadelphia and the Pennsylvania Dutch Country

S0-CFC-448

Fodor's Travel Publications • New York, Toronto, London, Sydney, Auckland
www.fodors.com

CONTENTS

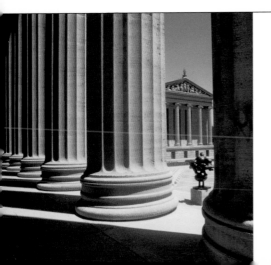

MAPS

Circled letters in text correspond to letters on the photographs. For more information on the sights pictured, turn to the indicated page number Ⓐ＞ on each photograph.

DESTINATION PHILADELPHIA AND THE PENNSYLVANIA DUTCH COUNTRY

William Penn was on to something good when he founded Philadelphia more than 300 years ago. His City of Brotherly Love has entered the 21st century as a treasury of America's most sacred historical landmarks, a bastion of genteel cultural institutions, a professional sports powerhouse, and a marvelous host of festivals and special events. This big city with a small-town feel is dedicated to preserving its history; yet it's always ready to make room for another innovative restaurant or hip new enclave. And if you stray into the nearby countryside you'll find yourself in lovely little towns, amid bucolic landscapes and the powerfully evocative fields of some of the nation's most momentous battles.

SPIRIT
OF 1776

As you meander down the cobbled lanes of old Philadelphia, the sense of history is palpable—as loud and clear as the clap of the bell that "proclaimed liberty throughout all the land and unto all the inhabitants thereof." The chambers of the first U.S. Congress, the country's first bank, its oldest residential street . . . one after another, these historic places transport you back in time to the heady days that witnessed the emergence of a nation.

Ⓐ **29**

ⒸＩＩＩ⟩35

The Ⓐ**Liberty Bell,** famously cracked and silenced forever, is enshrined under glass not far from Ⓓ**Independence Hall,** where America's founding fathers gathered to sign the Declaration of Independence, the document that so eloquently declares a commitment to life, liberty, and the pursuit of happiness for all. At the Ⓒ**Betsy Ross House,** you can peek into the small rooms where the Quaker lady may or may not have sewn the first Stars and Stripes. Even if she pulled her needle and thread through material a little less emblematic, the house provides a satisfying glimpse of life in Colonial Philadelphia. Among the pews of Ⓑ**Christ Church** is one that was once occupied by George Washington, who served most of his presidency in

Ⓓ⟩28

what was then the largest and most important city in the colonies. In Philadelphia, history even leaves its mark on an event as quotidian as a meal—at Ⓔ**City Tavern** you can partake of the same fare that pleased the palates of hardworking early patriots.

Ⓔ⟩90

7

Thanks in part to the distinct personalities of its numerous neighborhoods, Philadelphia often feels more like a cluster of small towns than a metro-polis—even though it's the fifth-largest city in the nation and home to some 1.6 million souls. On occasions like the twice-annual ©**Mummers Parade,** mounted by neighborhood clubs from throughout the city, these personalities gel into a flamboyant whole. The enclaves, however can be as bohemian as Ⓕ**South Street,** the boundary line between tony Soc-

NEIGHBORHOODS

iety Hill and down-to-earth Southwark, or as genteel as ⒹRittenhouse Square, a particularly favored greensward surrounded by Victorian brownstones and swank hotels in the heart of upper-crust Philly. The patrician ⒺPhiladelphia Museum of Art stands guard over the working-class Fairmount neighborhood, which contains the Rodin Museum, the best collection of the sculptor's work outside France, and architecturally varied and whimsical ⒶBoathouse Row on the Schuylkill River. At ⒷPenn's Landing, in the backyard of the Old City and Society Hill, you can see the spot where the founding father stepped ashore in 1682, now a Delaware riverfront park that, like so much of the city, would make the old boy proud.

DINING

There was a time when even the staunchest civic booster would have trouble using "Philadelphia" and "fine food" in the same sentence, unless, of course, talk didn't stray far beyond hoagies and cheese steaks. But in this city known for its revolutionary spirit, innovative chefs have been wielding kitchen utensils with the zeal of a patriot's quill. Venture into any neighborhood, from Center City to Manayunk, and you're likely to stumble upon some temple of gastronomy, the most sacred being ©**Le Bec-Fin.** You'll also notice that residents of this most American of cities enjoy whetting their appetites at places that fuse ingredients and cooking styles, such as French-Asian inspired ®**Susanna Foo.** Even so, the beloved cheese steak has not fallen from grace, as proven by the round-the-clock crowds at Geno's Steaks and its arch rival ®**Pat's King of Steaks,** across the way in South Philly.

Ⓐ 75

Ⓑ 94

Ⓒ 96

SIDE TRIPS

The names of George Washington, Andrew Wyeth, and Pierre-Samuel du Pont echo through the countryside west of the city. The first president and his beleaguered army spent the winter of 1777-78 at Ⓐ**Valley Forge,** where a national park pays tribute to their valor. Artist Andrew Wyeth captured the bucolic spirit of the Brandywine Valley, where a Colonial barn houses the Ⓑ**Chaddsford Winery** and a Civil War–era gristmill is home to the Brandywine River Museum. Prominent families such as the du Ponts brought

Ⓑ▷163

the valley a touch of high life, filling their mansions at Winterthur and Nemours with fine furnishings and planting a lavish botanical wonder at Ⓒ**Longwood Gardens.**

Ⓒ▷164

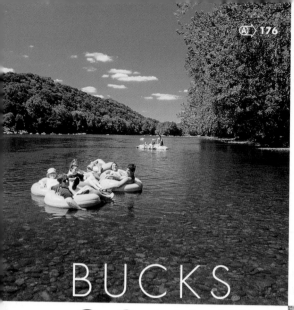

Ⓐ 176

A lazy float down the Ⓐ**Delaware River** is a fitting way to get in touch with the easy-living and idyllic landscapes of Bucks County. Back on land there is copious evidence of the artistic fervor that gave the county its moniker "the genius belt." You can visit the farmhouse of author Pearl S. Buck, the storybook castle of Henry Chapman Mercer, and the American-art museum endowed by novelist James Michener. Later, catch a show at the

BUCKS
COUNTY

Ⓑ 187

Ⓑ**Bucks County Playhouse** and stay overnight at inns that were once the country retreats of dramatic luminaries George S. Kaufman and Oscar Hammerstein. Stop by New Hope and Doylestown, where every building seems to be a national historic landmark (and holds an antiques shop or an art gallery). At its heart, though, and some say at its best, Bucks County is a place where rural beauty steals the show; at Ⓒ**Tinicum Park,** where you can pause for a picnic, it's evident in abundance.

Ⓒ 192

LANCASTER COUNTY, HERSHEY & GETTYSBURG

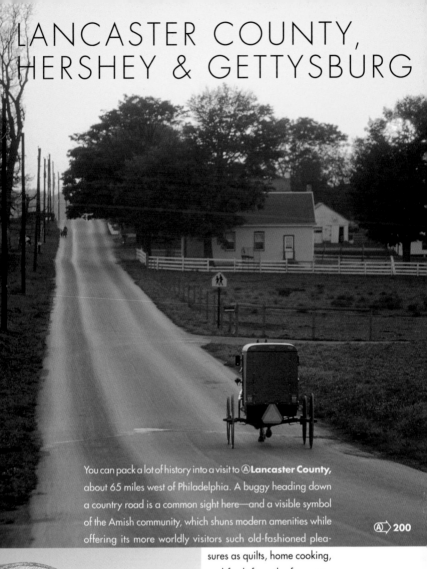

You can pack a lot of history into a visit to Ⓐ**Lancaster County,** about 65 miles west of Philadelphia. A buggy heading down a country road is a common sight here—and a visible symbol of the Amish community, which shuns modern amenities while offering its more worldly visitors such old-fashioned plea-sures as quilts, home cooking, and fresh-from-the-farm pro-duce. At Ⓑ**Gettysburg National Military Park,** another hour west, museums and mon-uments honor the 51,000 sol-diers who died in the Civil War's bloodiest battle. For a lighter note, head to ©**Hershey;** even the streetlights in this town—turned–theme park mimic foil-wrapped confections.

Ⓐ ⟩ **200**

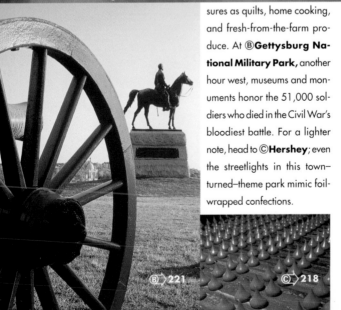

Ⓑ ⟩ **221**

© ⟩ **218**

FODOR'S
CHOICE

Even with so many special places in the Philadelphia area, Fodor's writers and editors have their favorites. Here are a few that stand out.

QUINTESSENTIAL PHILADELPHIA

Ⓖ **Barnes Foundation.** This Merion mansion holds one of the world's finest collections of Impressionist and post-Impressionist art, including 65 works by Matisse, 66 Cézannes, and 175 Renoirs. ☞ p. 64

Boathouse Row at night. Hundreds of tiny white lights outline the dozen or so houses along the Schuylkill River just beyond the Philadelphia Museum of Art. ☞ p. 71

Fourth of July celebration. This spectacular 10-day birthday party—the Sunoco Welcome America Festival—includes several nights of fireworks, an illuminated boat parade, outdoor concerts with superstar talent, and the awarding of the Philadelphia Liberty Medal to world leaders. ☞ p. 261

Independence National Historical Park. Start at the Visitor Center and follow the redbrick road past a dozen stirring sites, including Independence Hall and the Liberty Bell. History buff or not, you'll probably experience a few quivers. ☞ p. 29

Lunch in Rittenhouse Square. Grab a bench at the city's toniest downtown park. With majestic elms, Victorian statues, and playing children, it seems to have sprung from the brush of Mary Cassatt. ☞ p. 60

Philadelphia Museum of Art. *Rocky* fans may have the urge to run up the steps. Go ahead, indulge! Then go inside and discover one of the world's great art collections. ☞ p. 66

QUINTESSENTIAL DUTCH COUNTRY

Back-country roads. To see the Amish farms and roadside stands, drive the rural roads between Routes 23 and 340. ☞ p. 200

Ⓒ **Family-style eating.** The all-you-can-eat restaurants, like Good 'N Plenty, don't have menus—they just keep the Pennsylvania Dutch food coming. ☞ p. 209

Farmers' markets. For the best "sweets and sours" and chowchow, head for the Central Market in downtown Lancaster or the Green Dragon Farmers Market and Auction, in Ephrata. ☞ p. 203

BRANDYWINE VALLEY

Ⓑ **Brandywine River Museum.** A converted 19th-century gristmill on the banks of the Brandywine showcases the art of three generations of the Wyeth family. ☞ p. 163

Ⓗ **Longwood Gardens.** The valley's No. 1 attraction has more than 1,000 acres of flowers, trees, color, and beauty, 365 days a year. ☞ p. 164

Winterthur Museum and Gardens. An unrivaled collection of American decorative arts from 1640–1860 fills Henry Francis du Pont's nine-story mansion. The gardens are particularly lovely in spring. ☞ p. 165

AFTER HOURS

Delaware River waterfront. You can club-hop by river taxi to more than a dozen nightspots near the Ben Franklin Bridge. ☞ p. 126

Ⓕ **Lights of Liberty.** When the sun goes down, the streets around Independence Hall become a stage set for a dazzling sound-and-light show (April through October) that brings to life early U.S. history. ☞ p. 30

Manayunk. This old mill neighborhood has been transformed into a trendy dining and shopping mecca. ☞ p. 80

South Street. From art galleries to tattoo parlors, South Street—the stretch between Front and 7th streets—is, as the song says, "the hippest place in town." ☞ p. 46

LODGING

Four Seasons. Philly's poshest hotel has the best restaurants, service, and—if you get a room overlooking the fountains in Logan Circle—the most romantic views. $$$$ ☞ p. 120

The Rittenhouse. You'll be pampered at this elegant small hotel that makes the best of its swank Rittenhouse Square setting. $$$$ ☞ p. 116

Ⓓ **Westin Philadelphia.** The Westin has brought its impressive standards of luxury to a space once occupied by the Ritz-Carlton. $$$$ ☞ p. 117

Ⓔ **Penn's View Inn.** Urban charm and a fine Italian restaurant distinguish this Old City inn. $$–$$$ ☞ p. 115

DINING

Fountain Restaurant. Its classy setting in the Four Seasons and outstanding contemporary fare consistently draw locals and visitors alike. $$$$ ☞ p. 103

Le Bec-Fin. *Formidable!* The most prestigious restaurant in town, the Bec is internationally renowned for its impeccable service, elegance, and the soufflés of owner Georges Perrier. $$$$ ☞ p. 96

Striped Bass Restaurant and Bar. At this see-and-be-seen spot, the food (all seafood) is delicious, and so is the stunning setting in a former brokerage house. $$$$ ☞ p. 100

Ⓐ **Jake's.** Fine contemporary crafts decorate a stellar eatery in Manayunk; the scallops are a taste of perfection. $$$–$$$$ ☞ p. 107

Overtures. This stylish, creative restaurant serves good-value French-inspired fare. $$–$$$$ ☞ p. 92

1 EXPLORING PHILADELPHIA

As the city that gave us the Declaration of Independence and the Twist, William Penn's principles of peace and purity and the soft pretzel, Philadelphia can be both significant and lighthearted. It delivers all the art and cultural treasures you'd expect from the nation's fifth-largest city (and more), plus more chapters of American history than you'll find anywhere else—packaged in an appealingly quirky town with a friendly feel.

By Joyce
Eisenberg

Updated by
Robert
DiGiacomo

ON THE WHOLE I'D RATHER BE IN PHILADELPHIA." W. C. Fields may have been joking when he wrote his epitaph, but if he were here today, he would eat his words. They no longer roll up the sidewalks at night in Philadelphia. A construction boom, a restaurant renaissance, and cultural revival have helped transform the city. For more than a decade there has been a new optimistic mood, aggressive civic leadership, and national recognition of what the locals have long known: Philadelphia can be a very pleasant place to live—a city with an impressive past and a fascinating future. For many observers, Philadelphia really *is* the only civilized big city in America.

FROM BENJAMIN FRANKLIN TO GRACE KELLY

Philadelphia is a place of contrasts: Grace Kelly and Rocky Balboa; Le Bec-Fin—one of the nation's finest French haute cuisine restaurants—and the fast-food heaven of Jim's Steaks; Independence Hall and the Mario Lanza Museum; 18th-century national icons with 21st-century-style skyscrapers soaring above them. The world-renown Philadelphia Orchestra performs in a stunning new concert hall—the focal point of efforts to transform Broad Street into a multicultural Avenue of the Arts. Along the same street, 25,000 Mummers dressed in outrageous sequins and feathers historically have plucked their banjos and strutted their stuff to the strains of "Oh, Dem Golden Slippers" on New Year's Day. City residents include descendants of the staid Quaker founding fathers, the self-possessed socialites of the Main Line (remember Katharine Hepburn and Cary Grant in *The Philadelphia Story*?), and the unrestrained sports fans, who are as vocal as they are loyal.

Historically speaking, Philadelphia is a city of superlatives: the world's largest municipal park; the best collection of public art in the United States; the widest variety of urban architecture in America; and according to some experts, the greatest concentration of institutions of higher learning in the country.

A CITY OF NEIGHBORHOODS

In addition, Philadelphia is known as a city of neighborhoods (109 by one count). Shoppers haggle over the price of tomatoes in South Philly's Italian Market; families picnic in the parks of Germantown; street vendors hawk soft pretzels in Logan; and all over town kids play street games such as stickball, stoopball, wireball, and chink. It's a city of neighborhood loyalty: ask a native where he's from and he'll tell you: Fairmount, Fishtown, or Frankford, rather than Philadelphia. The city's population is less transient than that of other large cities; people who are born here generally remain, and many who leave home to study or work eventually return. Although the population is close to 1.6 million, its residents are intricately connected; on any given day, a Philadelphian is likely to encounter someone with whom he grew up. The "it's-a-small-world" syndrome makes people feel like they belong.

THE PHILADELPHIA STORY

William Penn founded the city in 1682 and chose to name it Philadelphia—Greek for "brotherly love"—after an ancient Syrian city, site of one of the earliest and most venerated Christian churches. Penn's Quakers settled on a tract of land he described as his "greene countrie towne." After the Quakers, the next wave of immigrants to arrive were Anglicans and Presbyterians (who had a running conflict with the "stiff Quakers" and their distaste for music and dancing). The new residents forged traditions that remain strong in parts of Philadelphia today: united families, comfortable houses, handsome furniture, and good education. From these early years came the attitude Mark Twain summed up as: "In Boston, they ask: 'What does he know?' In New York, 'How much does he make?' In Philadelphia, 'Who were his parents?' "

The city became the queen of the English-speaking New World from the late 1600s to the early 1800s. In the latter half of the 1700s Philadelphia was the largest city in the Colonies, a great and glorious place. So, when the delegates from the Colonies wanted to meet in a centrally located, thriving city, they chose Philadelphia. They convened the First Continental Congress in 1774 at Carpenters' Hall. The rest, as they say, is history. It is here that the Declaration of Independence was written and adopted, the Constitution was framed, the capital of the United States was established, the Liberty Bell was rung, the nation's flag was sewn by Betsy Ross (though scholars debate this), and George Washington served most of his presidency.

GETTING YOUR BEARINGS

Today you will find Philadelphia's compact 2-square-mi downtown (William Penn's original city) between the Delaware and the Schuylkill (pronounced *skoo*-kull) rivers. Thanks to Penn's grid system of streets— laid out in 1681—the downtown area is a breeze to navigate. The traditional heart of the city is Broad and Market streets (Penn's Center Square), where City Hall now stands. Market Street divides the city north and south; 130 South 15th Street, for example, is in the second block south of Market Street. North–south streets are numbered, starting with Front (1st) Street, at the Delaware River, and increasing to the west. Broad Street is the equivalent of 14th Street. The diagonal Benjamin Franklin Parkway breaks the rigid grid pattern by leading from City Hall out of Center City into Fairmount Park, which straddles the Schuylkill River and the Wissahickon Creek for 10 mi.

Although Philadelphia is the fifth-largest city in the nation (1.6 million people live in the city, 5.8 million in the metropolitan area), it maintains a small-town feel. It's a cosmopolitan, exciting, but not overwhelming city, a town that's easy to explore on foot yet big enough to keep surprising even those most familiar with it.

AROUND INDEPENDENCE HALL

The Most Historic Square Mile in America

Any visit to Philadelphia, whether you have one day or several, should begin in the city area that comprises Independence National Historical Park. Philadelphia was the birthplace of the United States, the home of the country's first government, and nowhere is the spirit of those miraculous early days—the boldness of conceiving a brand-new nation—more palpable than along the cobbled streets of the city's most historic district.

In the late 1940s, before civic-minded citizens banded together to save the area and before the National Park Service stepped in, the Independence Hall neighborhood was crowded with factories and run-down warehouses. Then the city, state, and federal government took interest. Some buildings were restored, and others were reconstructed on their original sites; several attractions were built for the 1976 Bicentennial celebration. In recent years, a flurry of construction once again is transforming the area, with several notable buildings—including an expanded visitor center, a more attractive home for the Liberty Bell, and a new national museum to celebrate the U.S. Constitution. Today the park covers 42 acres and holds close to 40 buildings. Urban renewal in Independence Mall plaza and in Washington Square East (So-

Downtown Philadelphia

Poplar St.
TO MANAYUNK
Parrish St.
Brown St.
Aspen St.

28th St.
27th St.
26th St.
25th St.
24th St.
23rd St.

George St.
Vineyard St.
Corinthian Ave.

TO GERMANTOWN,
TEMPLE UNIVERSITY,
CHESTNUT HILL
Parrish St.

Rte. 611
Ridge Ave.

Fairmount Ave.
Mt. Vernon St.

North St.
Wallace St.

19th St.

Fairmount Park

Green St.
Brandywine St.
Spring Garden St.
Hamilton St.

Philadelphia Museum of Art

Benjamin Franklin Parkway

Rodin Museum

Buttonwood St.

18th St.

Broad St.

Buttonw

76
30

Schuylkill River

Center City and Along the Parkway

Callow

676 30

Franklin Institute

Logan Circle

17th St.

Race St.

Pe
Conve
Reading

23rd St.

Cherry St.

Academy of Natural Sciences

Arch St.

19th St.

Parkway

Suburban Station

JFK Plaza

30th St. Station

John F. Kennedy Blvd.

Market-Frankford Subway

Subway-Surface

Market St.
Ludlow St.

City Hall

University City

30th St.

Airport Train (R1)

TO U.
OF PENN.

TO AIRPORT

76

Schuylkill River

21st St.

Chestnut St.
Sansom St.
Walnut St.

Rittenhouse Square

20th St.

Locust St.

Spruce St.

19th St.

Pine St.

Lombard St.

24th St.
25th St.

Center City

16th St.

Locust St.

15th St.

Broad St. (Ave. of the Arts)

Juniper St.

Broad St. Subway

N

0   440 yards
0   400 meters

Schuylkill Ave.

Grays Ferry Ave.

22nd St.
23rd St.

South St.
Pemberton St.
Fitzwater St.

Bainbridge St.

Christian St.

Webster St.

Carpenter St.

Catharine St.
TO SPORTS STADIUMS

Rte. 611

KEY

- - - - Market-Frankford Subway
——— Broad St. Subway
– – – Subway-Surface Subway
——— Airport Train

Poplar St.

9th St.
Franklin St.
Marshall St.
Lawrence St.
Oriana St.
Wildey St.
Germantown Ave.
Market St.
Penn St.
95

Brown St.
American St.
2nd St.

Fairmount Ave.

Green St.
Spring Garden St.

8th St.
7th St.
5th St.

Clay St.

Ridge Ave.

Broad St. Subway

...ood St.

...hill St.

10th St.

Willow St.

6th St.

Callowhill St.

Front St.

Vine St.

30

Ben Franklin Br.

Franklin Square

30 676

...nnsylvania ...ation Center and Terminal Market

Chinatown

Race St.

U.S. Mint

Christopher Columbus Blvd. (formerly Delaware Ave.)

Delaware River

Arch St.

Old City

Market East Station

Filbert St.

7th St.

Independence

National

Historical Park   Market St.

Front St.

Penn's Landing

The Historic Area

Chestnut St.

Independence Hall

Independence Square

2nd St.
Front St.

Ferry Dock
TO CAMDEN, NJ

13th St.

11th St.

Sansom St.

Walnut St.

Washington Square

Locust St.

4th St.
3rd St.

Society Hill

Spruce St.

Quince St.

Historic Area and Penn's Landing

Pine St.

9th St.
8th St.

Lombard St.

South St.

5th St.

95

12th St.

Bainbridge St.

7th St.

Fitzwater St.

South Philadelphia and Southwark

Fitzwater St.

TO WALT WHITMAN BRIDGE
↓

Christian St.

Catharine St.

Queen St.

ciety Hill) have ensured that Independence Hall will never again keep unsightly company. The city's most historic area is now also one of its loveliest.

The best time to visit Independence National Historic Park is on America's birthday; expect big crowds, though. Here, in America's birthplace, the city throws a weeklong party known as Sunoco Welcome America! From June 27 to July 4, there are more than 50 free events, including parades (the Mummers and an illuminated boat procession), outdoor concerts, historical reenactments, elaborate fireworks, and the awarding of the prestigious Philadelphia Liberty Medal to a world leader. If you visit anytime in summer, there are plays, musicals, parades, and more; town criers dressed in 18th-century garb perform short vignettes about life in Colonial America. The town criers dispense maps and schedules of their performances. For information on the entertainment schedule, call **Historic Philadelphia, Inc.** (☎ 800/764–4786).

The Independence Visitor Center, Independence Hall, and the Liberty Bell Pavilion are open daily year-round from 9 to 5, later in summer. Other park buildings are also open daily, although their hours may vary from season to season, depending on park staffing and the number of visitors. The 24-hour hot line at the visitor center will give you current hours plus a schedule of park programs; for Web information on park sites, visit www.nps.gov/inde and click the "in depth" button. Except as noted, all attractions run by Independence National Historical Park are free. You can easily explore the park on your own; in each building a knowledgeable park ranger can answer all your questions. On spring weekends and in summer, the rangers lead a variety of walking tours; some are specifically for families. In winter, if there's adequate staffing, the rangers give entertaining talks in various buildings. Inquire about these in the morning at the information desk of the visitor center.

If you are planning a trip in 2002 or early 2003, take note: a number of construction projects are transforming Independence Mall. These include a new pavilion for the Liberty Bell, just 200 yards away from the old site, scheduled to be completed by early 2003. This change of scene will allow you to view the bell with a clear view of Independence Hall in the background and to linger longer by the bell without being shooed on by rangers who are ready to address the next group. A new museum, the National Constitution Center, at 6th and Arch streets, is under construction for a mid-2003 opening. The new Independence Visitor Center, on 6th Street between Market and Arch streets, has replaced the former facility at 3rd and Chestnut streets.

Numbers in the text correspond to numbers in the margin and on the Historic Area and Penn's Landing map.

A Good Walk

This walk back in time will immerse you in Colonial history. The best place to orient yourself is at the **Independence Visitor Center** ① on 6th Street between Market and Arch. A block to the north is the contemporary **National Constitution Center** ②. Directly across Market Street is the gathering area for the new **Liberty Bell Pavilion** ③, an angled glass building with fine sightlines of Independence Hall. Cross Chestnut Street to **Independence Square,** site of **Independence Hall** ④, where the Declaration of Independence was signed; tours begin in the courtyard alongside **Old City Hall** ⑤, home of the U.S. Supreme Court from 1791 to 1800. Just in front of it is **Philosophical Hall,** home of the country's oldest learned society. Independence Hall is flanked on the other side by **Congress Hall** ⑥, which holds the restored chambers of the first U.S.

Congress. Next, cross 5th Street to the cobblestoned L[...] where you'll see **Library Hall** ⑦, a reconstruction of the firs[...] brary in the United States. Just before 4th Street on the l[...] Parthenon look-alike, the **Second Bank of the United States** ⑧ its portrait gallery of Colonial Americans; its entrance is on Che[...] Street. Crossing 4th Street, follow a redbrick path to the Carpent[...] Court; **Carpenters' Hall** ⑨, with its displays of 18th-century tools, [...] on your right. On your left is **Pemberton House,** now a bookstore and gift shop. Behind the bookstore is the **New Hall Military Museum** ⑩; it contains a variety of weapons and uniforms. Leave Carpenters' Court and continue on the redbrick path alongside manicured lawns and ancient oaks and maples east to 3rd Street, site of the **First Bank of the United States** ⑪, a handsome example of Federal architecture.

Walk north on 3rd Street, cross Chestnut Street, and turn left to the **National Liberty Museum** ⑫; the exhibits here celebrate diversity and honor Nobel Peace Prize winners. Your next stop, particularly if you have children in tow, should be **Franklin Court** ⑬. Just past the National Liberty Museum, turn right through the gates and walk down the cobblestone path. Head into the underground museum that celebrates the achievements of Benjamin Franklin, and visit the Colonial-era print shop and post office. Exit on Market Street and turn left. Walk several blocks, passing the Liberty Bell and the visitor center, and turn left on 7th Street. On your right, you'll see the reconstructed **Declaration House** ⑭, where Thomas Jefferson wrote his rough draft of the Declaration of Independence, and the **Balch Institute for Ethnic Studies** ⑮, with its library and exhibits on immigration and ethnicity, as well as a branch of the Free Library of Philadelphia. Across 7th Street is the **Atwater Kent Museum** ⑯, which chronicles the city's history. Next to the museum is a walkway under the Rohm and Haas Building. You'll pass the sculpture-fountain *Milkweed Pod*. Installed in 1959, it was one of the first examples of Philadelphia's law requiring public buildings to spend 1% of construction costs for art. At 6th Street turn right and walk south almost to Walnut Street to the **Curtis Center** ⑰; peek into the lobby to see the spectacular glass mosaic mural by Maxfield Parrish and Louis Comfort Tiffany.

If you have more time and energy, continue east on Walnut Street. On the corner of 4th and Walnut streets is the **Todd House** ⑱, the simply furnished home of Dolley Madison, which has a lovingly maintained 18th-century garden; it stands in contrast with the lavishly furnished **Bishop White House** ⑲, at 3rd and Walnut streets. Follow Walnut a half block east to see the **Philadelphia Merchant's Exchange,** the city's commercial center for part of the 19th century. Around the corner at 2nd, between Walnut and Sansom, is **Welcome Park** ⑳, marking the spot where William Penn once lived.

TIMING

If you've put on your walking shoes and are good at negotiating the cobblestones, you can wander through this compact area in about two hours. But the city's atmospheric historic district warrants a slower pace. Budget a full day here. An early start lets you reserve timed tickets for a tour of the Todd and Bishop White houses and adjust your schedule to catch some of the special events on the visitor center's daily schedule. Allow about 40 minutes for the Independence Hall tour and another hour each at Franklin Court and the Todd and Bishop White houses. Allow 30 minutes each at Declaration House and the visitor center, where it's a good idea to see the film *Independence* before you set out. From April through October, you might want to dine in the area and then catch the Lights of Liberty walking sound-and-light

The Historic Area and Penn's Landing

220 yards
200 meters

N

KEY

- - - - Market-Frankford Subway

Arch St.

Commerce St.

Market-Frankford Subway

TO DISNEYQUEST

Market St.

Independence National Historic Park

Ludlow St.
The Bourse
Ranstead St.

Ranstead St.

Chestnut St.

Pemberton House

Philosophical Hall

Independence Square

Sansom St.

Walnut St.

Washington Square

Willings Al

Locust St.

SOCIETY HILL

Marshalls Ct.

St. Joseph's Way

Spruce St.

Cypress St.

Cypress St.

Panama St.

Pine St.

23
rary Street,
Public li-
't is the
with
nut
s'

Race St.

Bread St.

Cherry St.

(23)

(22)

Front St.

(24)

Arch St.

OLD CITY

Mascher St.

Cuthbert

St.

Filbert St.

American St.

Church St.

(21)

3rd St.

2nd St.

Church St.

Market St.

Front St.

Delaware Expwy.

Strawberry St.

Black Horse Alley

Letitia

Penn's
Landing

(30)

(12)

Bank St.

Chestnut St.

95

(11)

Ionic St.

Gatzmer St.

Sansom St.

(31)

(32)

**Philadelphia
Merchant's
Exchange**

(20)

Christopher Columbus Blvd. (formerly Delaware Ave.)

Ferry Dock

(33)

(19)

Walnut St.

(34)

Chancellor St.

Dock St.

ey

St. James Pl.

(43)

Dock St.

Locust St.

Spruce St.

3rd St.

American St.

Phillip St.

2nd St.

(35)

(36)

(42)

Delancey St.

Front St.

TO SOUTH STREET

Pine St.

(41)

↓

(37)

Pier 5

Delaware River

Pier 3

show. In summer, when Independence Hall is open until 8, you could visit it last and then head for the show.

Sights to See

16 **Atwater Kent Museum.** Philadelphia's official history museum, the Atwater Kent is dedicated to telling the Philadelphia story from the city's founding more than 300 years ago until today. Started in 1938 by Atwater Kent, a wealthy inventor, radio magnate, and manufacturer, the museum houses more than 100,000 objects—everything from textiles to toys—that illustrate what everyday life was like for generations of Philadelphians. It occupies an elegant 1826 Greek Revival building designed by John Haviland, who was also the architect of the Eastern State Penitentiary. The museum owns a sizable collection of works by Norman Rockwell, the most well-known American illustrator of the 20th century, including the artist's 324 covers for the *Saturday Evening Post.* ⊠ *15 S. 7th St.,* ☎ *215/922–3031,* WEB *www.philadelphiahistory. org.* ☞ *$3, free Sun. until noon.* ☉ *Wed.–Mon. 10–5.*

15 **Balch Institute for Ethnic Studies.** More a research center than a museum, the Balch Institute has a 60,000-volume library on immigration history and ethnicity that is open to the public several days a week. Changing exhibitions examine contemporary issues of ethnic and racial identity; recent shows have included "Refuge: The Newest New Yorkers," "Ethnic Weddings," and "Italian-American Traditions." A branch of the Free Library of Philadelphia, with extensive children's and gay and lesbian collections, is also located here. ⊠ *18 S. 7th St.,* ☎ *215/ 925–8090,* WEB *www.balchinstitute.org.* ☞ *$3.* ☉ *Exhibitions, Mon.– Sat. 10–4; library, Tues., Thurs., and Sat. 10–4.*

19 **Bishop White House.** Built in 1786, this restored upper-class house embodies Colonial and Federal elegance. It was the home of Bishop William White (1748–1836), rector of Christ Church, first Episcopal bishop of Pennsylvania, and spiritual leader of Philadelphia for 60 years. White, a founder of the Episcopal church after the break with England, was chaplain to the Continental Congress and entertained many of the country's first families, including Washington and Franklin. The second-floor study contains much of the bishop's own library. Unlike most houses of the period, the bishop's house had an early form of flush toilet. The house tour is not recommended for small children, who may be bored. ⊠ *309 Walnut St.,* ☎ *215/597–8974,* WEB *www.nps.gov/inde/ bishop-white.html.* ☞ *$2; purchase tickets at the visitor center for one of the daily 1-hr tours that include the Todd House and the Bishop White House.* ☉ *Apr.–Oct., tours daily at 10, noon, and 2; open house (no tickets required) at 2:45. Nov.–Mar., hours vary; check the Web site or visitor center.*

9 **Carpenters' Hall.** This handsome, patterned red-and-black brick building dating from 1770 was the headquarters of the Carpenters' Company, a guild founded to support carpenters, who were both builders and architects in this era, and to aid their families. In September 1774 the First Continental Congress convened here and addressed a declaration of rights and grievances to King George III. Today re-creations of Colonial settings include original Windsor chairs and candle sconces and displays of 18th-century carpentry tools. The Carpenters' Company still owns and operates the building. ⊠ *320 Chestnut St.,* ☎ *215/ 597–8974,* WEB *www.nps.gov/inde/carpenters-hall.html.* ☞ *Free.* ☉ *Jan.–Feb., Wed.–Sun. 10–4; Mar.–Dec., Tues.–Sun. 10–4.*

6 **Congress Hall.** Formerly the Philadelphia County Courthouse, Congress Hall was the meeting place of the U.S. Congress from 1790 to 1800—one of the most important decades in our nation's history.

Here the Bill of Rights was added to the Constitution; Alexander Hamilton's proposals for a mint and a national bank were enacted; and Vermont, Kentucky, and Tennessee became the first new states after the original Colonies. On the first floor is the House of Representatives, where President John Adams was inaugurated in 1797. On the second floor is the Senate chamber, where in 1793 George Washington was inaugurated for his second term. Both chambers have been authentically restored. ⊠ *6th and Chestnut Sts.,* ☎ *215/597–8974,* WEB *www.nps.gov/inde/congress-hall.html.* ⊒ *Free.* ⊙ *Daily 9–5.*

⑰ Curtis Center. The lobby of the Curtis Publishing Company building has a great treasure: a 15- by 50-ft glass mosaic mural, *The Dream Garden,* based on a Maxfield Parrish painting. It was executed by the Louis C. Tiffany Studios in 1916. The work's 260 colors and 100,000 pieces of opalescent hand-fired glass laced with gold leaf make it perhaps the finest Tiffany mural in the world. Privately owned by the estate of a local art patron, the mural was put up for sale for $9 million in 1998, but after public outcry the Philadelphia Historical Commission voted to designate it a "historic object," the first such designation in the city's history, and that stopped the sale. ⊠ *6th and Walnut Sts.,* ☎ *215/238–6450.* ⊒ *Free.* ⊙ *Weekdays 9–5, Sat. 10–1, enter from 7th St.*

⑭ Declaration House. In a second-floor room that he had rented from bricklayer Jacob Graff, Thomas Jefferson (1743–1826) drafted the Declaration of Independence in June 1776. The home was reconstructed for the Bicentennial celebration; the bedroom and parlor in which Jefferson lived that summer were re-created with period furnishings. The first floor has a Jefferson exhibition and a seven-minute film, *The Extraordinary Creation.* The display on the Declaration of Independence shows some of the changes Jefferson made while writing it. You can see Jefferson's original version—which would have abolished slavery had the passage not been stricken by the committee that included Benjamin Franklin and John Adams. ⊠ *7th and Market Sts.,* ☎ *215/597–8974,* WEB *www.nps.gov/inde/declaration-house.html.* ⊒ *Free.* ⊙ *Hours vary; check Web site or inquire at visitor center.*

⑪ First Bank of the United States. A fine example of Federal architecture, the oldest bank building in the country was headquarters of the government's bank from 1797 to 1811. Designed by Samuel Blodget, Jr. and erected in 1795–1797, the bank was an imposing structure in its day, exemplifying strength, dignity, and security. Head first to the right, to the north side of the structure, to find a wrought-iron gateway topped by an eagle. Pass through it into the courtyard, and you magically step out of modern-day Philadelphia and into Colonial America. Before you do so, check out the bank's pediment. Executed in 1797 by Clodius F. Legrand and Sons, its cornucopia, oak branch, and American eagle are carved from mahogany—a late-18th-century masterpiece that has withstood acid rain better than the bank's marble pillars. ⊠ *120 S. 3rd St.* ⊙ *Interior closed to the public.*

☚ ⑬ Franklin Court. In 1763, at the age of 57, Benjamin Franklin (1706–1790) built his first permanent home in Philadelphia, in a courtyard off Market Street. This underground museum on the site of the house is an imaginative tribute to a Renaissance man: scientist and inventor (of bifocals and the lightning rod), philosopher and writer, savvy politician and successful businessman. Franklin, publisher of *Poor Richard's Almanac,* helped draft the Declaration of Independence and negotiate the peace with Great Britain. He also helped found Pennsylvania Hospital, the University of Pennsylvania, the Philadelphia Contributionship, and the American Philosophical Society.

In the courtyard adjacent to the museum, architect Robert Venturi erected a steel skeleton of Franklin's former home. You can peek through "windows" into cutaways to see wall foundations, outdoor privy wells, and other parts of his home that were uncovered during excavations. Within the museum the accomplishments of the statesman, diplomat, scientist, inventor, printer, and author are brought to life. Dial-a-quote to hear his thoughts or pick up a telephone and listen to what his contemporaries really thought of him. There is also an informative 20-minute film on Franklin's life. At the Market Street side are several houses, now exhibition halls, that Franklin had rented in addition to his main home. In one, you can see how Franklin fireproofed the building: his interest in fireproofing led him to experiment with kite flying and lightning (remember the delightful rendition of those experiments in Disney's animated cartoon *Ben and Me?*). Here, too, you'll find a restoration of a Colonial-era print shop and a post office. Don't forget to get a letter hand-stamped with a "B. FREE FRANKLIN" cancellation. ✉ *314–322 Market St., or enter from Chestnut St. walkway,* ☎ *215/597–8974,* WEB *www.nps.gov/inde/Franklin_Court.* ◻ *Free.* ◷ *Mar.–Nov., daily 9–5; Dec.–Feb., 10–4.*

★ ❹ **Independence Hall.** The birthplace of the United States, this redbrick building with its clock tower and steeple is one of our nation's greatest icons. America's most historic building was constructed in 1732–1756 as the Pennsylvania State House. What happened here between 1775 and 1787 changed the course of American history—and the name of the building to Independence Hall. The delegates to the Second Continental Congress met in the hall's Assembly Room in May 1776, united in anger over the blood that had been shed when British troops fired on citizens in Concord, Massachusetts. In this same room George Washington was appointed commander in chief of the Continental Army, Thomas Jefferson's eloquent Declaration of Independence was signed, and later the Constitution of the United States was adopted. Here the first foreign minister to visit the United States was welcomed; the news of Cornwallis's defeat was announced, signaling the end of the Revolutionary War; and, later, John Adams and Abraham Lincoln lay in state. The memories this building holds linger in the collection of polished muskets, the silver inkstand used by delegates to sign the Declaration of Independence, and the "Rising Sun" chair in which George Washington sat. (After the Constitution was adopted, Benjamin Franklin said about the sun carving on the chair, "I have the happiness to know that it is a rising and not a setting sun.")

In the **East Wing**—attached to Independence Hall by a short colonnade—you can embark on free tours that start every 15 to 20 minutes and last 35 minutes. Admission is first-come, first-served; you may have to wait. The **West Wing** of Independence Hall contains an exhibit of the national historical park's collection of our nation's founding documents: the final draft of the Constitution, a working copy of the Articles of Confederation, and the first printing of the Declaration of Independence.

In front of Independence Hall, next to the statue of George Washington, note the plaques marking the spots where Abraham Lincoln stood on February 22, 1861, and where John F. Kennedy delivered an address on July 4, 1962. Each year on July 4, the Philadelphia Liberty Medal is presented here to a world leader. With Independence Hall in front of you and the Liberty Bell behind you, this is a place to stand for a moment and soak up a sense of history. ✉ *Chestnut St. between 5th and 6th Sts.,* ☎ *215/597–8974,* WEB *www.nps.gov/inde/indep-hall. html.* ◻ *Free.* ◷ *Sept.–June, daily 9–5; July–Aug., daily 9–8.*

① Independence Visitor Center. The new 47,500 square-
being a gateway to Independence National Historica'
the city's official visitor center. On hand are park
questions and distribute maps and brochures on park sites
historic locations. There's also a fully staffed concierge and trip pla
ning desk, which will provide information on other attractions, from
the Philadelphia Museum of Art to the Philadelphia Zoo, as well as a
reservation and ticketing service. Before you set off on a walking tour,
acquaint yourself with Colonial American history by watching the founding fathers come to life in the 30-minute movie *Independence*, one of
the films being shown in the center's three theaters. There are also a
coffee bar and an excellent bookstore, where you can stock up on books,
videos, brochures, prints, wall hangings, and souvenirs about historic
figures and events. The most popular items are the tiny Liberty Bell
reproductions. An atrium connects the visitor center to a renovated underground parking facility.

To see two of the city's famous historic homes—the Bishop White and
Todd houses—you'll need to stop at the information desk to purchase
a ticket ($2) and reserve a spot on one of the hour-long tours. ⊠ *6th
St., between Market and Arch,* ☎ *215/965–7676 or 800/537–7676,*
WEB *www.independencevisitorcenter.com.* ⊙ *Sept.–June daily 9–5; July–
Aug. daily 9–6.*

Independence Square. On July 8, 1776, the Declaration of Independence was first read here in public. Although the square is not as imposing today, it still has great dignity. You can imagine the impact the
reading had on the Colonists. ⊠ *Bounded by Walnut and Chestnut
Sts. and 5th and 6th Sts.*

★ ③ Liberty Bell. The bell fulfilled the biblical words of its inscription when
it rang to "proclaim liberty throughout all the land unto all the inhabitants thereof," beckoning Philadelphians to the State House yard
to hear the first reading of the Declaration of Independence. Ordered
in 1751 and originally cast in England, the bell cracked during testing
and was recast in Philadelphia by Pass and Stow two years later. To
keep it from falling into British hands during the Revolution—they would
have melted it down for ammunition—the bell was spirited away by
horse and wagon to Allentown, 60 mi to the north. The bell is the subject of much legend; one story says it cracked when tolled at the funeral of Chief Justice John Marshall in 1835. Actually, the bell cracked
slowly over a period of years. It was repaired but cracked again in 1846
and was then forever silenced. It was called the State House Bell until
the 1830s, when a group of abolitionists adopted it as a symbol of freedom and renamed it the Liberty Bell.

After being housed in Independence Hall for more than 200 years, the
bell was moved to a glass-enclosed pavilion for the 1976 Bicentennial,
that for many seemed an incongruous setting for such a historic ob-
ject. In 2002, the bell will move once again to another glass-enclosed
pavilion with redbrick accents. This time, great care has been taken to
improve access to the bell and the view of its former home at Independence Hall, which will be seen against the backdrop of the sky—
rather than 20th-century buildings. The new Liberty Bell complex
houses a bell chamber, an interpretive exhibit area with historic displays and memorabilia, and a covered area for waiting in line. ⊠ *6th
and Chestnut Sts.,* ☎ *215/597–8974,* WEB *www.nps.gov/inde/liberty-
bell.html.* ⊠ *Free.* ⊙ *Sept.–June, daily 9–5; July–Aug., daily 9–8.*

NEED A
BREAK?

Enter the **Bourse** (⊠ 5th St. across from the Liberty Bell Pavilion, ☎
215/625–0300) and you're in another century. The skylighted Great

Hall, with its Corinthian columns, marble, wrought-iron stairways, and Victorian gingerbread details, has been magnificently restored. Built in 1895 as a stock exchange, it now houses shops and a food court, where you can grab a cup of cappuccino or a Philly cheese steak.

⑦ Library Hall. This 20th-century building is a reconstruction of Franklin's Library Company of Philadelphia, the first public library in the Colonies. Home of the library of the American Philosophical Society, one of the country's leading institutions for the study of science, it is basically a research facility for scholars. Its vaults contain such treasures as a copy of the Declaration of Independence handwritten by Thomas Jefferson, William Penn's 1701 Charter of Privileges, and journals from the Lewis and Clark expedition of 1803–06. The library's collection also includes first editions of Newton's *Principia Mathematica,* Franklin's *Experiments and Observations,* and Darwin's *On the Origin of Species.* The lobby has fascinating changing exhibitions that showcase the society's collection. ✉ *105 S. 5th St.,* ☎ *215/440–3400,* WEB *www.amphilsoc.org/about/libhall.htm.* 🎫 *Free.* ☼ *Weekdays 9–5.*

★ ☾ Lights of Liberty. A nighttime multimedia extravaganza, billed as the "world's first walkable sound-and-light show," takes place in five acts throughout Independence National Historical Park. The one-hour show, which dramatizes the events that led up to the American Revolution, takes you back to British Philadelphia in 1763 at Franklin Court, the site of Ben Franklin's home, and culminates in the grand finale at Independence Hall on July 8, 1776, with the first public reading of the Declaration of Independence. You wear 3-D sound wireless headsets and view high-definition five-story projections on the area's historic buildings. The show features special effects and a stirring musical score recorded by the Philadelphia Orchestra. Narration is available in German, Japanese, Spanish, Italian, and English; Walter Cronkite, Ossie Davis, and Charlton Heston tell the tale; Whoopi Goldberg narrates a children's version. The walking distance is a half mile, and wheelchairs are available. There are six shows per hour; call for reservations and schedule. ✉ *PECO Energy Liberty Center, 6th and Chestnut Sts.,* ☎ *215/542–3789 or 877/462–1776,* WEB *www.lightsofliberty.org.* 🎫 *$17.76; $50 family package with 2 adult and 2 children's tickets.* ☼ *Apr.–Oct., daily, from just after dark, weather permitting.*

❷ National Constitution Center. Scheduled to open in mid-2003, this 132,000-square-ft museum will bring the U.S. Constitution alive through a series of highly interactive exhibits tracing the development and adoption of the nation's landmark guiding document. The heart of the sprawling museum, "The Story of We the People," takes you from the American Revolution through the Constitution's ratification to major events in the nation's constitutional history. Later, you can play the role of a Supreme Court justice deciding an important case, and walk among the framers in Signers Hall, where you can decide whether to add your signature to the list of founding fathers. Exhibits at the $132 million facility are being designed by Ralph Appelbaum Associates, the firm that designed the highly regarded U.S. Holocaust Memorial Museum in Washington, D.C. ✉ *525 Arch St.,* ☎ *215/923–0004,* WEB *www.constitutioncenter.org.* ☼ *Daily 9–5.*

⑫ National Liberty Museum. Using interactive exhibits, video, and works of art, the museum aims to combat bigotry in the United States by putting a spotlight on the nation's rich traditions of freedom and diversity. Galleries celebrate outstanding Americans, including 19 Nobel Peace Prize winners, as well as heroes from around the world. The museum's collection of glass art is symbolic of the fragility of peace; its highlight is Dale Chihuly's 20-ft-tall red glass sculpture, "Flame of Liberty." Sandy Skoglund's colorful Jelly Bean People is a reminder that we're all the same inside regardless of the color of our skin. ✉ *321 Chestnut St.,* ☎ *215/925–2800,* WEB *www.libertymuseum.org.* ☞ *$5.* ☼ *Tues.– Sun., 10–5.*

⑩ New Hall Military Museum. The original of this reconstructed 1790 building briefly served as headquarters for the U.S. Department of War. On display are Revolutionary War uniforms, medals, and authentic weapons, including powder horns, swords, and a 1763 flintlock musket. Dioramas depict highlights of the Revolutionary War. The building also houses a Marine Corps memorial. ✉ *Chestnut St. east of 4th St.,* ☎ *215/597–8974,* WEB *www.nps.gov/inde/new-hall.html.* ☞ *Free.* ☼ *Daily 10–4.*

❺ Old City Hall. Independence Hall is flanked by Congress Hall to the west and Old City Hall to the east: three distinctive Federal-style buildings erected to house the city's growing government. But when Philadelphia became the nation's capital in 1790, the just-completed city hall was lent to the federal government. It housed the U.S. Supreme Court from 1791 to 1800; John Jay was the Chief Justice. Later, the boxlike building with a peaked roof and cupola was used as the city hall. Today an exhibit presents information about the early days of the federal judiciary. ✉ *5th and Chestnut Sts.,* ☎ *215/597–8974,* WEB *www.nps.gov/ inde/old-city-hall.html.* ☞ *Free.* ☼ *Daily 9–5.*

Pemberton House. "America's National Parks" store sells books, videos, and souvenirs, plus Civil War, Revolutionary War, and Constitution memorabilia. ✉ *316 Chestnut St.,* ☎ *215/597–8019.* ☼ *Daily 9–5.*

Philadelphia Merchant's Exchange. Designed by the well-known Philadelphia architect William Strickland and built in 1832, this impressive Greek Revival structure served as the city's commercial center for 50 years. It was both the stock exchange and a place where merchants met to trade goods. In the tower a watchman scanned the Delaware River and notified merchants of arriving ships. The exchange stands behind Dock Street, a cobblestone thoroughfare closed to traffic. The building is not open to the public. ✉ *3rd and Walnut Sts.*

Philosophical Hall. This is the headquarters of the American Philosophical Society, founded by Benjamin Franklin in 1743 to promote "useful knowledge." The members of the oldest learned society in America have included Washington, Jefferson, Lafayette, Emerson, Darwin, Edison, Churchill, and Einstein. Erected between 1785 and 1789 in what has been called a "restrained Federal style" (designed, probably, to complement, not outshine, adjacent Independence Hall), Philosophical Hall is brick with marble trim and has a handsome arched entrance. The society's library is across the street in Library Hall. ✉ *104 S. 5th St.,* ☎ *215/440–3400,* WEB *www.amphilsoc.org.* ☼ *Wed.–Fri. noon–5.*

❽ Second Bank of the United States. When Second Bank President Nicholas Biddle held a design competition for a new building, he required all architects to use the Greek style; William Strickland, one of the foremost architects of the 19th century, won. Built in 1824, the bank, with its Doric columns, was based on the design of the Parthenon and helped establish the popularity of Greek Revival architecture in the United States. The interior banking hall, though, was Roman, with a dramatic, barrel-vault ceiling. Housed here are portraits of prominent Colonial Americans by noted artists such as Charles Willson Peale, William Rush, and Gilbert Stuart. Don't miss Peale's portrait of Jefferson: it's the only one that shows him with red hair. The permanent exhibition, *Portraits of the Capital City,* has a life-size wooden statue of George Washington by William Rush; a mural of Philadelphia in the 1830s by John A. Woodside Jr.; and the only known likeness of William Floyd, a lesser-known signer of the Declaration of Independence. In March 2002, the Second Bank will close for renovations for one year; during this time, a portion of the portrait collection is expected to be moved to the First Bank of the United States. ✉ *420 Chestnut St.,* ☎ *215/597–8974,* WEB *www.nps.gov/inde/second-bank.html.* ☞ *$2.* ☉ *Sept.–June, daily 10–4; July–Aug., daily 10–5.*

⑱ **Todd House.** Built in 1775 by John Dilworth, Todd House has been restored to its 1790s appearance, when its best-known resident, Dolley Payne Todd (1768–1849), lived here. She lost her husband, the Quaker lawyer John Todd, to the yellow fever epidemic of 1793. Dolley later married James Madison, who became the fourth president. Her time as a hostess in the White House was quite a contrast to her years in this simple home. There's an 18th-century garden next to Todd House. ✉ *4th and Walnut Sts.,* ☎ *215/597–8974,* WEB *www.nps.gov/ inde/todd-house.html.* ☞ *$2; purchase tickets at the visitor center for one of the daily 1-hr tours that include the Todd House and the Bishop White House.* ☉ *Apr.–Oct., tours daily at 10, noon, and 2; open house (no tickets required) at 2:45. Nov.–Mar., hours vary; check Web site or inquire at visitor center.*

⑳ **Welcome Park.** In the park, on a 60-ft-long map of Penn's Philadelphia carved in the pavement, sits a scale model of the Penn statue that tops City Hall. The wall surrounding the park displays a time line of William Penn's life, with information about his philosophy and quotations from his writings. The park was the site of the slate-roof house where Penn lived briefly and where he granted the Charter of Privileges in 1701. (The *Welcome* was the ship that transported Penn to America.) Written by Penn, the Charter of Privileges served as Pennsylvania's constitutional framework until 1776; the Liberty Bell was commissioned to commemorate the charter's 50th anniversary. The City Tavern, across the street, marks the site where George Washington once dined. It is still open for historically correct lunches and dinners. ✉ *2nd St. just north of Walnut St.*

OLD CITY
Living "North of Market"

In Colonial days, the rich folks in residential Society Hill spoke in hushed tones of those who lived "north of Market," for this area, between Front and 5th streets and Chestnut and Vine streets, was the city's commercial district for industry and wholesale distributors, filled with wharves and warehouses and taverns. It also held the modest homes of the craftsmen and artisans who resided here. Old City (as it became known some 40 years ago, to distinguish it from the national park area) is aptly named: it is one of the city's oldest and most historic neighborhoods, home to Elfreth's Alley; the Betsy Ross House; and Christ Church, where George Washington and John Adams came (across the tracks!) to worship at services. There's evidence of the Quaker presence here, too, in the Arch Street Meeting House.

Today Old City is Philadelphia's trendiest neighborhood, a local version of New York's SoHo. Many cast-iron building facades remain, though the old warehouses, with telltale names such as the Sugar Refinery and the Hoopskirt Factory, now house well-lighted loft apartments popular with artists and architects. There are small theaters—the Painted Bride, the Arden Theatre Company—and numerous art galleries and boutiques. In the past few years, more restaurant have opened here than in any other part of the city. The Old City Arts Association hosts a festive, popular event the first Friday of each month—known, appropriately enough, as First Friday—when the galleries throw open their doors during evening hours.

Numbers in the text correspond to numbers in the margin and on the Historic Area and Penn's Landing map.

A Good Walk

A walk through Old City begins at 2nd and Market streets, location of the impressive **Christ Church** ㉑, attended by George and Martha Washington, among other notables. Continuing north on 2nd Street for a block and passing Arch Street, you'll come to a tiny Colonial street on the right, **Elfreth's Alley** ㉒; two houses are open to the public. Head back to 2nd Street, turn right (north), and a few footsteps will take you to the **Fireman's Hall Museum** ㉓, with exhibits on the history of fire fighting. If you then follow 2nd Street back to Arch and turn right (west), you'll find the most popular residence in Philadelphia, the **Betsy Ross House** ㉔.

A bit farther along, between 321 and 323 Arch Street, you can peer into the gated **Loxley Court** and its 18th-century houses and then cross the street to the Society of Friends' **Arch Street Meeting House** ㉕. Just ahead one block is the **Christ Church Burial Ground,** final resting place for Ben Franklin and other signers of the Declaration of Independence. Across 5th Street is the **Free Quaker Meeting House,** built for Friends who had been disowned by their pacifist meetings for participating in the Revolutionary War. Diagonally across Arch Street stands the **United States Mint** ㉖, where you can watch coins being made. If you're up for an adventure—and a hearty 1¾-mi walk (each way)—you could cross the Benjamin Franklin Bridge. The walkway entrance is about two blocks north of the Mint, on 5th Street. Otherwise, turn left (south) on 5th Street, cross Arch Street, and walk until you find a redbrick courtyard, entrance to the modern building that houses both the **National Museum of American Jewish History** ㉗ and **Mikveh Israel** ㉘, the oldest Jewish congregation in Philadelphia. Walking two blocks west on Arch Street to 7th Street brings you to the **African American Museum** ㉙, with displays that illuminate the black experience through the centuries. At this point you might want to follow 7th Street (on foot or by bus) five blocks north to the residence and exhibits at the Edgar Allan Poe National Historic Site.

TIMING

If possible, set aside four or five hours on a Sunday for your visit to Old City. You could attend the 9 AM service at Christ Church, as George and Martha Washington did, and then join the 10:30 Quaker meeting at the Arch Street Friends Meeting House, where William Penn worshiped. Try to avoid scheduling a Monday visit, when two of the top sights—the Betsy Ross House and Elfreth's Alley—are closed. On a weekday it's worth your while to see the coin-making operation at the Mint. If you detour to the Poe House, allow another two hours. You can take this walk in any kind of weather and at any time of year since the neighborhood is a small one.

Sights to See

㉙ **African American Museum in Philadelphia.** Permanent and changing exhibits are dedicated to the history, fine art, artifacts, crafts, and culture of African-Americans in the United States—with a focus on

WILLIAM PENN AND HIS LEGACY

BORN IN LONDON in 1644 into a nobleman's family, William Penn was truly a rebel with a cause. He attended Oxford University, studied law, and tried a military career (in emulation of his father, an admiral in the British Navy). It was at Oxford that Penn first heard Quaker preachers professing that each life is part of the Divine spirit, and that all people should be treated equally, even royalty. At age 23, Penn joined the Religious Society of Friends (Quakers), who at the time were considered religious zealots.

Penn was imprisoned in the Tower of London a few times for his heretical pamphlets, but he was spared worse persecution because of his father's support of King Charles II. He petitioned the king to grant him land in the New World for a Quaker colony; he was given a 45,000-square-mi tract along the Delaware River in payment of a debt Charles owed to his late father. Indeed, the king named the land Pennsylvania in honor of the admiral.

On Penn's first visit to his colony, from 1662 to 1664, he began his "Holy Experiment," establishing his haven for Quakers. His early laws guaranteed religious freedom and an elected government. He bought land from the Native Americans and established a peace treaty with them that lasted for 70 years.

Penn was called back to England in 1684 and remained there until 1699, caring for his ill wife, Gulielma Maria Springett, who would die without ever seeing his beloved Pennsylvania. Penn was suspected of plotting with the former Catholic King, James II, to overthrow the current Protestant monarchy of William and Mary, who revoked his charter in 1692 for 18 months.

Penn made his second trip to America with his second wife, Hannah Callowhill Penn, in 1699. The couple moved into **Pennsbury Manor** along the upper Delaware River, where, while preaching about a life of simplicity, he lived in luxury. Penn issued a new frame of government, the Charter of Privileges, which became a model for the U.S. Constitution. He had to return to England yet again in 1701; there he was consumed by the political and legal problems of his colony, a term in prison for debt, and then illness. Penn died before he could return to Pennsylvania. After his death, his wife honored him by assuming the governorship for nine years.

Although Penn spent only four of his 74 years in Pennsylvania, his legacy is profound. As a city planner, he mapped out a "greene countrie towne" with broad, straight streets. He positioned each house in the middle of its plot, so that every child would have green grass and play space; he named its streets—Walnut, Spruce, Chestnut—for trees, not for men. His original city plan has survived—and his statue looks out over it from atop City Hall. As a reformer, Penn replaced dungeons with workhouses, established the right of a jury to decide a verdict without harassment by a judge; provided schools where boys—and girls—could get a practical education; and limited the death penalty to two offenses—murder and treason—rather than the 200 mandated by English criminal law.

The **Arch Street Meeting House** (✉ 4th and Arch Sts.), on land Penn set aside as a Quaker burial ground, still holds weekly meetings for worship; they are open to the public, as is a museum honoring Penn. **Welcome Park** (✉ 2nd St. just north of Walnut), has a time line of Penn's life and a map of Penn's Philadelphia carved in the pavement.

Philadelphia and Pennsylvania. Past exhibitions have showcased African-American female sculptors, slavery artifacts, and sports in Philadelphia. The museum's gift shop stocks the area's widest selection of books on black culture, history, fiction, poetry, and drama, along with African textiles and sculpture and African-American jewelry, prints, and tiles. Opened in the Bicentennial year of 1976, this is the first museum of its kind funded and built by a city. ⊠ *701 Arch St.*, ☏ *215/574–0380*, WEB *www.aampmuseum.org.* ⊡ *$6.* ☉ *Tues.–Sat. 10–5, Sun. noon–5.*

㉕ **Arch Street Meeting House.** Constructed in 1804 for the Philadelphia Yearly Meeting of the Society of Friends, this building of simple lines is still used for that purpose, as well as for biweekly services. The largest Friends meeting house in the world, it was built to hold 3,000 people. When a contemporary architect measured the space, he determined that each of those folks would have only 18 inches to sit in. Today the meeting house can accommodate about 800 21st-century-size behinds. Among the most influential members in the 19th century was Lucretia Mott (1793–1880), a leader in the women's suffrage, anti-war, and anti-slavery movements. A small museum in the meeting house presents a series of dioramas and a 14-minute slide show depicting the life and accomplishments of William Penn (1644–1718), who gave the land on which the meeting house sits to the Society of Friends. Quaker guides give tours year-round. ⊠ *4th and Arch Sts.*, ☏ *215/627–2667*, WEB *www.archstreetfriends.org.* ⊡ *$1 minimum donation requested.* ☉ *Mon.–Sat. 10–4; services Wed. at 7 pm and Sun. at 10:30 AM.*

OFF THE
BEATEN PATH

BENJAMIN FRANKLIN BRIDGE – When the bridge opened in 1926, its 1,750-ft main span made it the longest suspension bridge in the world. Paul Cret, architect of the Rodin Museum, was the designer. A blue paint job and a lighting system that shows off its contours have made the bridge more handsome than ever. You can get an excellent view of riverfront Philadelphia by walking or bicycling across the smooth, resurfaced walkway; the south walkway has the best view. Cars, trucks, and trains zoom past, and brisk winds make your face tingle as you cross the Delaware River, 150 ft below. Start the 1¾-mi walk (one-way) from either the Philadelphia side, two blocks north of the U.S. Mint, or the Camden, New Jersey, side. ⊠ *5th and Vine Sts.*, ☏ *215/218–3750.* ⊡ *Free.* ☉ *Daily 6 am–around 6 pm.*

★ ☚ ㉔ **Betsy Ross House.** It's easy to find this little brick house with the gabled roof: just look for the 13-star flag displayed from its second-floor window. Whether Betsy Ross, also known as Elizabeth Griscom Ross Ashbourn Claypoole (1752–1836)—who worked in her family's flag making and upholstery business—actually lived here and whether she really made the first Stars and Stripes is debatable. Nonetheless, the house, built about 1760, is a splendid example of a Colonial Philadelphia home and is fun to visit. Owned and maintained by the city, the eight-room house overflows with artifacts such as a family Bible and Betsy Ross's chest of drawers and reading glasses. The small rooms hold period pieces that reflect the life of this hardworking Quaker (who died at the age of 84, outliving three husbands). You may have to wait in line here, as this is one of the city's most popular attractions. The house, with its winding narrow stairs, is not accessible to people with disabilities. Alongside the house is brick-paved Atwater Kent Park, with a fountain, benches, and the graves of Betsy Ross and her third husband, John Claypoole. ⊠ *239 Arch St.*, ☏ *215/686–1252*, WEB *www. ushistory.org/betsy/flaghome.html.* ⊡ *$2 donation requested.* ☉ *Tues.– Sun. 10–5.*

NEED A
BREAK?
Mulberry Market (✉ 236 Arch St., ☎ 215/592–8022) is a great little market stocked floor to ceiling with goodies, from freshly baked breads and steaming coffee to deli sandwiches and cereal. You can pick up anything you might need for a picnic or to stock your hotel room. The small restaurant in the rear is open daily from 7 AM to 10 or 11 PM.

㉑ **Christ Church.** The Anglicans of the Church of England built a wooden church on this site in 1697. When they outgrew it, they erected a new church, the most sumptuous in the Colonies, designed by Dr. John Kearsley and modeled on the work of famed English architect Sir Christopher Wren. The symmetrical, classical facade with arched windows, completed in 1754, is a fine example of Georgian architecture; the church is one of the city's treasures. The congregation included 15 signers of the Declaration of Independence. The bells and the soaring 196-ft steeple, the tallest in the Colonies, were financed by lotteries run by Benjamin Franklin. Brass plaques mark the pews of George and Martha Washington, John and Abigail Adams, Betsy Ross, and others. Two blocks west of the church is Christ Church Burial Ground. ✉ *2nd St. north of Market St.,* ☎ *215/922–1695,* WEB *www.christchurchphila.org.* ✆ *Mar.–Dec., Mon.–Sat. 9–5, Sun. 1–5; Jan.–Feb., Wed.–Sat. 9–5, Sun. 1–5; services Sun. 9 and 11, Wed. noon.*

NEED A
BREAK?
Metropolitan Bakery (✉ 126 Market St., ☎ 215/928–9528) offers up a tantalizing array of artisan breads, brownies, and jumbo cookies, as well as coffee drinks and juices. You can also sit down inside or out—weather permitting—and enjoy a changing menu of sandwiches on fresh-sliced bread.

Christ Church Burial Ground. Weathered gravestones fill the resting place of five signers of the Declaration of Independence and other Colonial patriots. The best-known is Benjamin Franklin; he lies alongside his wife, Deborah, and their son, Francis, who died at age four. According to local legend, throwing a penny onto Franklin's grave will bring you good luck. Although you can no longer walk through the cemetery, you can toss your penny from outside the iron gate. ✉ *5th and Arch Sts.,* ☎ *215/922–1695.*

OFF THE
BEATEN PATH
EDGAR ALLAN POE NATIONAL HISTORIC SITE – One of America's most original writers, Edgar Allan Poe (1809–1849), lived here from 1843 to 1844; it is the only one of his Philadelphia residences still standing. During that time some of his best-known short stories were published: "The Telltale Heart," "The Black Cat," and "The Gold Bug." You can tour the three-story brick house; to evoke the spirit of Poe, the National Park Service deliberately keeps it empty. An adjoining house has exhibits on Poe and his family, his work habits, and his literary contemporaries; there is also an eight-minute film and a small Poe library and reading room. A statue of a raven helps set the mood. Special programs include Poetry Month tours (usually March or April) and popular "ghostly" tours in October (reservations required). The site, easily reached from the African-American Museum, is five blocks north of Market Street. SEPTA Bus 47 travels on 7th Street to Spring Garden Street, where you should disembark. ✉ *532 N. 7th St.,* ☎ *215/597–8780,* WEB *www.nps.gov/edal.* ✆ *Free.* ✆ *June–Oct., daily 9–5; Nov.–May, Wed.–Sun. 9–5.*

★ ㉒ **Elfreth's Alley.** The alley, the oldest continuously occupied residential street in America, dates to 1702. Much of Colonial Philadelphia resembled this area, with its cobblestone streets and narrow two- or three-story brick houses. These were modest row homes, most built for rent, lived in by craftsmen, such as cabinetmakers, silversmiths, pewterers, and their families. They also housed captains and others who made their living in the city's busy shipping industry. The earliest houses (two stories) have pent eaves; taller houses, built after the Revolution, show the influence of the Federal style. The Elfreth's Alley Museum includes two homes that have been restored by the Elfreth's Alley Association: Number 124, home of a Windsor chair maker, and Number 126, a Colonial dressmaker's home, with authentic furnishings and a Colonial kitchen. On the second weekend in June residents celebrate Fete Days, when about 20 of the 30 homes are open to the public for tours hosted by guides in Colonial garb. On the second Friday evening in December, homeowners again welcome visitors for a candlelight Christmas tour. Both of these special events require advance tickets. ⊠ *Front and 2nd Sts. between Arch and Race Sts.,* ☎ *215/574–0560,* WEB *www.elfrethsalley.org.* ⌨ *Alley free; museum $2.* ☉ *Jan., Sat. 10–4, Sun. noon–4; Feb.–Dec., Tues.–Sat. 10–4, Sun. noon–4.*

☙ ❷❸ **Fireman's Hall Museum.** Housed in an authentic 1876 firehouse, this museum traces the history of fire fighting, from the volunteer company founded in Philadelphia by Benjamin Franklin in 1736 to the professional departments of the 20th century. The collection includes early hand- and horse-drawn fire engines, such as an 1815 hand pumper and a 1907 three-horse Metropolitan steamer; fire marks (18th-century building signs marking them as insured for fire); uniforms; and other memorabilia. ⊠ *147 N. 2nd St.,* ☎ *215/923–1438.* ⌨ *Free; donations welcome.* ☉ *Tues.–Sat. 9–4:30.*

Free Quaker Meeting House. This was the house of worship for the Free "Fighting" Quakers, a group that broke away from the Society of Friends to take up arms against the British during the Revolutionary War. The building was designed in 1783 by Samuel Wetherill, one of the original leaders of the group, after they were disowned by their pacifist brothers. Among the 100 members were Betsy Ross (then Elizabeth Griscom) and Thomas Mifflin, a signer of the Constitution. After the Free Quaker group dissolved (many left to become Episcopalian), the building was used as a school, library, and warehouse. The meeting house, built in the Quaker plain style with a brick front and gable roof, has been carefully restored. ⊠ *500 Arch St.,* ☎ *215/597–8974.* ☉ *Closed to the public.*

Loxley Court. One of the restored 18th-century houses in this lovely court was once home to Benjamin Loxley, a carpenter who worked on Independence Hall. The court's claim to fame, according to its residents, is as the spot where Benjamin Franklin flew his kite in his experiment with lightning; the key tied to it was the key to Loxley's front door. ⊠ *321–323 Arch St.*

❷❽ **Mikveh Israel.** Nathan Levy, a Colonial merchant whose ship, the *Myrtilla,* brought the Liberty Bell to America, helped found this Jewish congregation in 1740, making it the oldest in Philadelphia and the second oldest in the United States. The original synagogue was at 3rd and Cherry streets; the congregation's current space (1976) is in the Sephardic style (following Spanish and Portuguese Jewish ritual) and occupies the same building as the ☞ **National Museum of American Jewish History.** The synagogue's Spruce Street Cemetery (about eight blocks away, beyond Old City) dates from 1740 and is the oldest surviving Jewish site in Philadelphia. It was the burial ground for the Spanish-Portuguese Jewish community. Among those buried here are Nathan Levy; Haym Salomon, a financier of the American Revolution; and Rebecca Gratz, the inspiration for the character Rebecca in Sir Walter Scott's novel *Ivanhoe.* ⊠ *Synagogue: 44 N. 4th St.,* ☎ *215/922–5446.* ☉ *Mon.–Thurs. 10–5, Fri. 10–3, Sun. noon–5. Services Mon. and Thurs. 7:15 AM,*

Fri. evening, Sat. 9 AM and evening. To arrange a tour, call the National Museum of American Jewish History. ✉ *Cemetery: Spruce St. between 8th and 9th Sts.,* ☎ *215/922–5446,* WEB *www.mikvehisrael.org.* ⊙ *Guide present July–Aug., Mon.–Thurs. 10–4; Sept.–June, visiting arrangements can be made through synagogue office.*

㉗ National Museum of American Jewish History. Established in 1976, this small museum is the only one in the nation dedicated exclusively to collecting, preserving, and interpreting artifacts pertaining to the American Jewish experience. It presents exhibits and programs exploring not only Jewish life but also issues of American ethnic identity, history, art, and culture. A powerful permanent exhibition, *Creating American Jews,* tells the history of this community through diaries, letters, and oral histories. The museum shares a building with **Mikveh Israel** synagogue. ✉ *55 N. 5th St.,* ☎ *215/923–3811,* WEB *www.nmajh.org.* ✉ *$3.* ⊙ *Mon.–Thurs. 10–5, Fri. 10–3, Sun. noon–5.*

㉖ United States Mint. The first U.S. mint was built in Philadelphia at 16th and Spring Garden streets in 1792, when the Bank of North America adopted dollars and cents instead of shillings and pence as standard currency; the current mint was built in 1971. On the self-guided tour, which takes about 45 minutes, you can see blank disks being melted, cast, and pressed into coins, which are then inspected, counted, and bagged. The visitors' gallery has an exhibition of medals from the nation's wars, including the Medal of Honor, the Purple Heart, and the Bronze Star. Seven Tiffany glass tile mosaics depict coin making in ancient Rome. A shop in the lobby sells special coins and medals—in mint condition. ✉ *5th and Arch Sts.,* ☎ *215/408–0114,* WEB *www.usmint.gov.* ✉ *Free.* ⊙ *Sept.–Apr., weekdays 9–4:30; May–June, Mon.–Sat. 9–4:30; July–Aug., daily 9–4:30. Coinage machinery operates weekdays only.*

SOCIETY HILL AND PENN'S LANDING
Enduring Grace and the Waterfront City

During the 18th century Society Hill was—as it still is today—Philadelphia's showplace. A carefully preserved district, it is easily the city's most photogenic neighborhood, filled with hidden courtyards, delightful decorative touches such as chimney pots and brass door knockers, wrought-iron foot scrapers, and other remnants from the days of horse-drawn carriages and muddy, unpaved streets. Here time has not quite stopped but meanders down the cobblestone streets, whiling away the hours.

A trove of Colonial- and Federal-style brick row houses (homes with common sidewalls), churches, and narrow streets, Society Hill stretches from the Delaware River to 6th Street, south of Independence National Historical Park. Those homes built before 1750 in the Colonial style generally have 2½ stories and a dormer window jutting out of a steep roof. The less heavy, more graceful houses built after the Revolution were often in the Federal style, popularized in England during the 1790s.

Here lived the "World's People," wealthier Anglicans who arrived after William Penn and loved music and dancing—pursuits the Quakers shunned when they set up their enclave in Old City, north of Market Street, in a less desirable commercial area. The "Society" in the neighborhood's moniker refers, however, to the Free Society of Traders, a group of business investors who settled here on William Penn's advice.

Today many Colonial homes in this area have been lovingly restored by modern pioneers who began moving into the area 40 years ago and rescued Society Hill from becoming a slum. Inspired urban renewal efforts have transformed vast empty factory spaces into airy lofts; new town houses were carefully designed to blend in with the old. As a result, Society Hill is not just a showcase for historic churches and mansions but a living, breathing neighborhood.

Before setting out to explore Society Hill, you may want to tour Philadelphia's nearby waterfront, with attractions that include a maritime museum and historic marine vessels. You can take a ferry across the Delaware River to Camden's attractions, which include an aquarium, a children's garden, and the USS *New Jersey*. Those who don't wish to enjoy this waterside detour should jump ahead in the following walk to Head House Square.

Numbers in the text correspond to numbers in the margin and on the Historic Area and Penn's Landing map.

A Good Walk

Begin your waterfront visit at **Penn's Landing** ㉚, a riverfront promenade with a maritime museum, historic ships, and restaurants. To get there, cross the Walnut Street Bridge at Front Street, which deposits you at the **Independence Seaport Museum** ㉛, with its engaging interactive exhibits and nautical artifacts. You can catch a passenger ferry right in front of the museum from April to mid-November. It crosses the Delaware River to Camden, New Jersey, in about 10 minutes, leaving you a few steps from the **New Jersey State Aquarium** ㉜, the **Camden Children's Garden** ㉝ and the **Battleship New Jersey** ㉞.

On your return you'll see the tall masts of the 1883 fishing ship *Gazela of Philadelphia,* docked next to the museum—when it's in port. A five-minute stroll south along the river brings you to two historic ships well worth a visit. Descend the steep metal ladder into the **USS *Becuna*** ㉟. Arise from the depths of this submarine and cross the gangplank for a decidedly different shipboard experience on Commodore Dewey's flagship, the **USS *Olympia*** ㊱. If you have a car, before you head to Society Hill you could take a detour to visit Ft. Mifflin and the John Heinz National Wildlife Refuge at Tinicum, both near the airport.

Your next stop is Society Hill. Backtrack half a block north on Columbus Boulevard to cobblestone Dock Street and turn left—right will land you in the Delaware River. Just ahead are the Society Hill Towers, three high-rise apartment buildings designed in the early '60s by I. M. Pei. These, along with the Society Hill Townhouses at 3rd and Locust streets, were the winning entries in a design competition for housing that would symbolize the renewal of Society Hill. Today the tall buildings seem out of scale with the rest of the neighborhood. At the dead end turn left. You'll be walking along 38th Parallel Street; in the park to your left is Philadelphia's Vietnam Veterans Memorial. Turn right (west) on Spruce Street and left (south) on 2nd Street to Delancey Street. On summer weekends you may want to continue a few blocks farther on 2nd Street to **Head House Square** ㊲, a Colonial marketplace that hosts a crafts and fine arts fair. Just one block ahead is **South Street,** with its funky shops, bookstores, restaurants, and bars. Otherwise, walk west along Delancey Street, lined with some of the city's prized Colonial homes.

On your right at 4th Street is the freestanding **Physick House** ㊳, with its superb Federal and Empire furnishings. In the next few blocks, you'll see three of the city's historic churches. Follow 4th Street half a block south to Pine Street and turn right (west) toward 6th Street. Between Pine and Lombard streets, on what has been renamed Richard Allen Avenue, is **Mother Bethel African Methodist Episcopal Church** ㊴. Head east on Pine Street; on your right, just before 4th Street, is **Old Pine Street Presbyterian Church** ⑩. This, and **St. Peter's Episcopal Church** ㊶, which dominates most of the next block, were designed by Robert Smith. St. Peter's slim belfry tower is six stories high, topped by a wooden steeple. On the northwest corner of 3rd and Pine streets is the **Thaddeus Kosciuszko National Memorial** ㊷, honoring the Polish general who fought in the Revolution.

Turn left (north) on 3rd Street. Within a few blocks, you'll come across the brownstones of **Bouvier's Row** (Nos. 258–262), once owned by Jacqueline Kennedy Onassis's ancestors. A few doors up is the brick Georgian **Powel House** ㊸, filled with fine 18th-century furniture. Continue north on 3rd Street to Willings Alley (opposite the former Old St. Paul's Church). Turn left and then right into the courtyard of **Old St. Joseph's Church** ㊹, the city's first Catholic church. Walk up the alley to 4th Street and then a half block south to **Old St. Mary's Church** ㊺, another early Catholic church. Following 4th Street back north brings you to the nation's oldest fire-insurance company, the **Philadelphia Contributionship for the Insurance of Houses from Loss by Fire** ㊻. Turn left on Walnut Street to 6th Street, and you'll come upon tree-shaded **Washington Square,** one of the five in Penn's original city plan. On the east side of the square is the **Athenaeum** ㊼ research library and gallery. If you have an interest in medicine, walk two blocks south and two more west to Pennsylvania Hospital, the nation's oldest.

TIMING

You could easily spend a whole day here, with the bulk of your time allotted to Penn's Landing. If your kids are in tow, you'll want to allow an hour and a half for the Independence Seaport Museum and its historic boats and another two or three hours for the ferry ride and visit to the aquarium, followed by a tour of the Battleship New Jersey. You'll need about one hour to walk through Society Hill, more if you tour the Powel and Physick houses. If walking is your main interest, save this excursion for a warm day, because it can be quite windy along the waterfront. The prime time for this walk? A summer Sunday, when Penn's Landing bustles with festivals and Head House Square turns into an open-air fine arts and crafts market.

Sights to See

㊼ **Athenaeum.** Housed in a national landmark Italianate brownstone dating from the mid-1800s and designed by John Notman, the Athenaeum is a research library specializing in architectural history and design. Its American Architecture Collection has close to a million items. The library, founded in 1814, contains significant materials on the French in America and on early American travel, exploration, and transportation. Besides books, the Athenaeum has notable paintings and period furniture; changing exhibits are presented in the gallery. ⊠ *219 S. 6th St.,* ☎ *215/925–2688,* ᴡᴇʙ *www.philaathenaeum.org.* ⊡ *Free.* ☉ *Gallery, weekdays 9–5; tours and research by appointment only.*

㉞ **Battleship New Jersey.** The World War II–era USS *New Jersey,* one of the most decorated battleships in the history of the U.S. Navy, was set to open in late 2001 as a floating museum following a $35 million renovation. Docked in Camden, New Jersey, south of the Tweeter Center, the ship's current berth is across the Delaware River from the Philadelphia Naval Shipyard, which built and launched it in 1942. A two-hour guided tour takes visitors around the upper and lower decks of the ship, which was involved in a long list of Pacific operations, including the Marshalls, Iwo Jima, and Okinawa. ⊠ *Beckett St., at the Delaware River, Camden, NJ,* ☎ *856/966–1652,* ᴡᴇʙ *www.battleshipnewjersey.org.*

Bouvier's Row. Three of the Victorian brownstones on a stretch of 3rd Street near Spruce Street, often called Bouvier's Row, were once owned by the late Jacqueline Kennedy Onassis's ancestors. Michel Bouvier, her great-great-grandfather—the first of the family to come from France—and many of his descendants lie in the family vault at Old St. Mary's Church, a few blocks away on 4th Street. ⊠ *258–262 S. 3rd St.*

㉝ Camden Children's Garden. Located adjacent to the New Jersey State Aquarium on the Camden waterfront, this delightful 4-acre garden is an interactive horticultural playground with theme exhibits. You can smell, hear, touch, and even taste some of the elements in the Dinosaur, Butterfly, Picnic, and World's Kitchen gardens. The Storybook Gardens include a Three Little Pigs Garden, the Giant's Garden from "Jack in the Beanstalk," and a Frog Prince Grotto; there's also a maze, carousel, train ride and treehouse. To get here, drive or take the ferry from Penn's Landing. ⊠ *3 Riverside Dr., Camden, NJ,* ☎ *856/365–8733,* WEB *www.camdenchildrensgarden.com.* 🎫 *$5.* ☉ *Apr.–Sept., weekdays 9:30–5:30, weekends 10–5; Oct.–Mar. daily 9:30–4:30.*

Camden Waterfront. The city of Camden has been sprucing up its waterfront and building attractions to lure visitors across the Delaware River. The lineup includes the **New Jersey State Aquarium,** the **Camden Children's Garden,** the **Battleship New Jersey,** and Campbell's Field, a minor league park where the Camden Riversharks play ball. The indoor-outdoor Tweeter Center amphitheater hosts concerts (big names like Paul Simon, Backstreet Boys, and Dave Matthews Band), Broadway theatrical productions, and family entertainment. The world's largest four-masted tall ship, the Moshulu, doubles as a restaurant; it will be berthed at Camden's Pier 1, north of the aquarium, beginning in spring 2002. Camden and Philadelphia are linked by the **RiverLink Ferry;** in spring 2003, they will also be connected by the Delaware River Aerial Tram, whose eight-passenger gondolas will make the trip in five minutes. ⊠ *Along the Delaware River in Camden, New Jersey,* ☎ *856-757-9400,* WEB *www.camdenwaterfront.com.*

OFF THE **FT. MIFFLIN –** Within this 49-acre National Historic Landmark, you can
BEATEN PATH see cannons and carriages, officers' quarters, soldiers' barracks (which contain an exhibition called *Defense of the Delaware*), an artillery shed, a blacksmith shop, a bomb shelter, and a museum. Because of its Quaker origins, Philadelphia had no defenses until 1772, when the British began building Ft. Mifflin. It was completed in 1776 by Revolutionary forces under General Washington. In a 40-day battle in 1777, 300 Continental defenders held off British forces long enough for Washington's troops to flee to Valley Forge. The fort was almost totally destroyed but was rebuilt in 1798 from plans by French architect Pierre Charles L'Enfant, who also designed the plan for Washington, DC. In use until 1962, the fort has served as a prisoner-of-war camp, an artillery battalion, and a munitions dump. Special events include Civil War Garrison Days in October and a reenactment of the siege of Ft. Mifflin held in November. From Penn's Landing you can easily hop on I-95 to reach the fort; call for directions. ⊠ *Island and Hog Island Rds., on the Delaware River near Philadelphia International Airport,* ☎ *215/685-4192,* WEB *www.fortmifflin.org.* 🎫 *$5.50.* ☉ *Apr.–Nov., Wed.–Sun. 10–4; tours at 11 and 2.*

Gazela of Philadelphia. Built in 1883 and formerly named *Gazela Primeiro,* this 177-ft square-rigger is the last of a Portuguese fleet of cod-fishing ships. Still in use as late as 1969, it is the oldest and largest wooden square-rigger still sailing. As the Port of Philadelphia's ambassador of goodwill, the *Gazela* sails up and down the Atlantic Coast from May to October to participate in harbor festivals and celebrations. It is also a school ship and a museum. An all-volunteer crew of 35 works on ship maintenance from November to April, while it's in port. ⊠ *Penn's Landing at Market St.,* ☎ *215/336–0199.* ☉ *Call ahead; tours can be arranged when the ship is in port.*

㊲ Head House Square. This open-air Colonial marketplace, extending from Pine Street to Lombard Street, is a reminder of the days when people went to central outdoor markets on designated days to buy food directly from the farmers. It was first established as New Market in 1745. George Washington was among those who came here to buy butter, eggs, meat, fish, herbs, and vegetables. The Head House, a boxy building with a cupola and weathervane, was built in 1803 as the office and home of the market master, who tested the quality of the goods. Today, on summer weekends, the square is home to a crafts and fine arts fair featuring the work of more than 30 Delaware Valley artists. There are free children's workshops on Sundays from 1 to 3. ⊠ *2nd and Pine Sts.,* ☎ *215/790–0782.* ☉ *Memorial Day–Sept., Sat. noon–11 PM, Sun. noon–6.*

NEED A
BREAK?

At **Xando-Cosi** (⊠ 215 Lombard St., at Head House Sq., ☎ 215/925–4910), s'mores aren't just for savoring around the campfire. This funky cafe, part of a chain, serves up its tabletop version with the traditional fixings—marshmallows, graham crackers and Hershey bars—and a sterno substituting for a roaring blaze. You can also enjoy a latte or cup of hot chocolate while relaxing on the comfy couches.

★ ♻ ㉛ Independence Seaport Museum. Philadelphia's maritime museum houses many nautical artifacts, figureheads, and ship models as well as interactive exhibits that convey just what the Delaware and Schuylkill Rivers have meant to the city's fortunes over the years. You can climb in the gray, cold wooden bunks used in steerage, unload cargo from giant container ships with a miniature crane, weld and rivet a ship's hull, or even hop in a scull and row along the Schuylkill. Enter the museum by passing under the three-story replica of the Benjamin Franklin Bridge. ⊠ *211 S. Columbus Blvd.,* at Walnut St., ☎ *215/925–5439,* WEB *seaport.philly.com.* ⌨ *$8 includes museum and USS Olympia and USS Becuna; free Sunday, 10 am–noon.* ☉ *Daily 10–5.*

OFF THE
BEATEN PATH

JOHN HEINZ NATIONAL WILDLIFE REFUGE AT TINICUM – More than 280 species of ducks, herons, egrets, geese, gallinules, and other birds have been spotted at this 1,200-acre preserve. Among the resident earthbound animals are turtles, foxes, muskrats, deer, raccoons, weasels, and snakes. Facilities in this freshwater tidal marsh, the largest remaining in Pennsylvania, include 8 mi of foot trails, an observation blind, an observation deck, boardwalks through the wet areas, and a canoe launch into the 4½-mi stretch of Darby Creek that runs through the preserve (the best way to see it). An environmental education center has a library, classrooms, and permanent and changing exhibits on wetlands, natural history, and regional wildlife. Bird-watchers can prepare for their visit by calling 215/567–2473 for recent sightings. The refuge is convenient to I-95, which you can pick up from Penn's Landing. Call for directions. ⊠ 86th St. and Lindbergh Blvd., ☎ 215/365–3118, WEB heinz.fws.gov. ⌨ Free. ☉ Refuge, daily 8–sunset; visitor center, daily 8:30–4.

㊴ Mother Bethel African Methodist Episcopal Church. Society Hill holds a notable landmark in the history of African-Americans in the city. In 1787, Richard Allen led fellow blacks who left St. George's Methodist Church as a protest against the segregated worship. Allen, a lay minister and former slave who had bought his freedom from the Chew family of Germantown, purchased this site in 1791. It is believed to be the country's oldest parcel of land continuously owned by African-Americans. When the African Methodist Episcopal Church was formed in 1816, Allen was its first bishop. The current church, the fourth on the site, is an example of the 19th-century Romanesque Revival style, with broad arches and a square corner tower, opalescent stained-glass windows, and stunning woodwork. The earlier church buildings were the site of a school where Allen taught slaves to read and also a stop on the Underground Railroad. Allen's tomb and a small museum are on the lower level. ⊠ *419 Richard Allen Ave. (S. 6th St. between Pine and Lombard Sts.),* ☏ *215/925–0616,* WEB *www.motherbethel.org.* ⌦ *Free; donation requested.* ☉ *Museum and guided tours, Tues.–Sat. 10–3.*

★ ⊙ ㉜ **New Jersey State Aquarium.** This marvel across the Delaware River in Camden combines entertainment, science education, and cutting-edge technology with more than 4,000 aquatic animals representing some 500 species. *Ocean Base Atlantic* has a 760,000-gallon open ocean tank (one of the country's largest) with sharks, stingrays, sea turtles, 1,400 fish, and a diver who during demonstrations can answer your questions via a "scubaphone." Promoting the concept of the global habitat, *COOL* (Conservation, Outreach and Observation Lab) is home to all manner of exotic creatures—the toco toucan, the four-eyed butterfly fish, and the 3-ft-long beaver-like coypu—from the Caribbean and Central and South America. There are also daily seal shows, dive demonstrations, live animal talks, and theater presentations. To get here, drive or take the ferry from Penn's Landing. ⊠ *1 Riverside Dr., Camden, NJ,* ☏ *856/365–3300,* WEB *www.njaquarium.org.* ⌦ *$12.95, includes admission to Camden's Children Garden.* ☉ *Mid-Apr.–mid-Sept., daily 9:30–5:30; mid-Sept.–mid-Apr., weekdays 9:30–4:30, weekends 10–5.*

㊵ **Old Pine Street Presbyterian Church.** Designed by Robert Smith in 1768 as a simple brick Georgian-style building, Old Pine is the only remaining Colonial Presbyterian church and churchyard in Philadelphia. Badly damaged by British troops during the Revolution, it served as a hospital and then a stable. In the mid-19th century, its exterior had a Greek Revival face-lift that included Corinthian columns. In the 1980s, the interior walls and ceiling were stenciled with thistle and wave motifs, a reminder of Old Pine's true name—Third, Scots, and Mariners Presbyterian Church, which documented the congregation's mergers. The beautifully restored church is painted in soft shades of periwinkle and yellow. In the churchyard are the graves of 100 Hessian soldiers from the Revolution—and of Eugene Ormandy, former conductor of the Philadelphia Orchestra. Jazz Vespers are held here the third Sunday of each month at 5 PM. ⊠ *412 Pine St.,* ☏ *215/925–8051,* WEB *www. libertynet.org/oldpine.* ⌦ *Free.* ☉ *Mon., Wed.–Fri. 8–5; Tues. 10–5; Sat., call ahead.*

㊸ **Old St. Joseph's Church.** In 1733, a tiny chapel was established by Jesuits for Philadelphia's 11 Catholic families. It was the first place in the English-speaking world where Catholic mass could be legally celebrated, a right granted under William's Penn 1701 Charter of Privileges, which guaranteed religious freedom. But freedom didn't come easy; on one occasion Quakers had to patrol St. Joseph's to prevent a Protestant mob from disrupting the service. The present church, built in 1839, is the third on this site. The late 19th-century stained-glass windows are notable. ⊠ *321 Willings Alley,* ☏ *215/923–1733,* WEB *www.oldstjoseph. org.* ☉ *Daily 11–4; from 1 to 4, stop at the rectory for admittance.*

㊺ **Old St. Mary's Church.** The city's second-oldest Catholic church, circa 1763, became its first cathedral when the archdiocese was formed in

1808. A Gothic-style facade was added in 1880; the interior was re-done in 1979. The stained-glass windows, a ceiling mural of St. Mary, and brass chandeliers that hung in the Founders Room of Independence Hall until 1967 are highlights. Commodore John Barry, a Revolutionary War naval hero, and other famous Philadelphians are buried in the small churchyard. ⊠ *252 S. 4th St.,* ☎ *215/923–7930,* WEB *www.ushistory. org/tour/tour_stmary.htm.* ☉ *Mon.–Sat. 9–4:45; mass Sat. 5 PM, Sun. 9 and 10:30 AM.*

③⓪ Penn's Landing. The spot where William Penn stepped ashore in 1682 is the hub of a 37-acre riverfront park that stretches from Market Street south to Lombard Street. Walk along the waterfront and you'll see scores of pleasure boats moored at the marina and cargo ships chugging up and down the Delaware. Philadelphia's harbor, which includes dock-ing facilities in New Jersey and Delaware, is one of the world's largest freshwater ports. Attractions include the **Independence Seaport Museum;** the **USS** *Olympia,* Commodore Dewey's flagship; and the **USS** *Be-cuna,* a World War II submarine. The development of this area—an am-bitious effort to reclaim the Delaware River waterfront—began in 1967 and has started in earnest once again. The Hyatt Regency Hotel opened here in late 2001; works in progress include an aerial tram with ac-companying laser light show that will connect Camden and Philadel-phia's waterfronts (scheduled to open spring 2003), and a Family Entertainment Center, with a multiscreen movie theater and dozens of restaurants and shops. Philadelphia's waterfront is the scene of the an-nual Memorial Day Jam on the River, July 4th fireworks, as well as jazz and big band concerts, ethnic festivals, children's events, and more. While construction is underway, those events have been moved from Penn's Landing to Festival Pier, at Columbus Boulevard and Spring Garden Street. The **RiverLink Ferry** links Penn's Landing with the attractions on the Camden waterfront. ⊠ *On the Delaware River from Market St. to Lom-bard St.,* ☎ *215/923–4992,* WEB *www.pennslandingcorp.com.*

OFF THE
BEATEN PATH

PENNSYLVANIA HOSPITAL – Inside the fine 18th-century original buildings of the oldest hospital in the United States are the nation's first medical library and first surgical amphitheater (an 1804 innovation, with a sky-light). The hospital also has a portrait gallery, early medical instruments, art objects, and a rare-book library with items dating from 1762. The art-work includes the Benjamin West painting *Christ Healing the Sick in the Temple.* Dr. Thomas Bond thought of the idea of a community hospital to improve care for the poor and enrolled Benjamin Franklin in his vision. The Pennsylvania Assembly agreed to put up £2,000 if those interested in a hospital could do the same: it took Franklin only a month and a half to raise the money. Today Pennsylvania Hospital is a full-service modern medical center four blocks southwest of the Athenaeum. Pick up a copy of "Pennsylvania Hospital: A Walking Tour" at the Welcome Desk just off the 8th Street entrance. ⊠ *8th and Spruce Sts.,* ☎ *215/829–3000,* WEB *www.pahosp.com.* ⊠ *Free.* ☉ *Weekdays 9–5; call 215/829–3270 to arrange a guided group tour for 10 or more.*

④⑥ Philadelphia Contributionship for the Insurance of Houses from Loss by Fire. The Contributionship, the nation's oldest fire insurance com-pany, was founded by Benjamin Franklin in 1752; the present Greek Revival building with fluted marble Corinthian columns dates from 1836 and has some magnificently elegant salons (particularly the boardroom, where a seating plan on the wall lists Benjamin Franklin as the first incumbent of seat Number One). The architect, Thomas U. Walter, was also responsible for the dome and House and Senate wings of the U.S. Capitol in Washington, DC. This is still an active business, but a small museum is open to the public. ⊠ *212 S. 4th St.,* ☎ *215/627–1752,* WEB *www.ushistory.org/tour/tour_contrib.htm.* ◻ *Free.* ☉ *Weekdays 10–3.*

★ ㊳ **Physick House.** Built in 1786, this is one of two remaining freestanding houses from this era in Society Hill (you will see plenty of the famous Philadelphia row houses here). It is also one of the most beautiful homes in America, with elegantly restored interiors and some of the finest Federal and Empire furniture in Philadelphia. Touches of Napoléon's France are everywhere: the golden bee motif woven into upholstery; the magenta-hue Aubusson rug (the emperor's favorite color); and stools in the style of Pompeii, the Roman city rediscovered at the time of the house's construction. Upstairs in the parlor, note the inkstand that still retains Benjamin Franklin's fingerprints. The house's most famous owner was Philip Syng Physick, the "Father of American Surgery" and a leading physician in the days before anesthesia. His most celebrated patient was Chief Justice John Marshall. The garden planted on three sides of the house is filled with plants common during the 19th century: complete with an Etruscan sarcophagus, a natural grotto, and antique cannon, it is considered by some to be the city's loveliest. ⊠ *321 S. 4th St.,* ☎ *215/925–7866,* WEB *www.physickhouse. org.* ◻ *$3.* ☉ *Sept.–May, Thurs.–Sat. 11–2; June–Aug., Thurs.–Sat. noon–4, Sun. 1–4; guided tours on the hr.*

★ ㊸ **Powel House.** The 1765 brick Georgian house purchased by Samuel Powel in 1769 remains one of the most elegant homes in Philadelphia. Powel—the "Patriot Mayor"—was the last mayor of Philadelphia under the Crown and the first in the new republic. The lavish home, a former wreck saved from demolition in 1930, is furnished with important pieces of 18th-century Philadelphia furniture. A mahogany staircase from Santo Domingo embellishes the front hall, and there is a signed Gilbert Stuart portrait in the parlor. In the second-floor ballroom, Mrs. Powel—the city's hostess-with-the-mostest—served floating islands and whipped syllabubs to distinguished guests (including Adams, Franklin, and Lafayette) on Nanking china that was a gift from George and Martha Washington. Today the ballroom can be rented for parties and special events. ⊠ *244 S. 3rd St.,* ☎ *215/627–0364,* WEB *www. powelhouse.org.* ◻ *$3.* ☉ *Thurs.–Sat. noon–5, Sun. 1–5.*

RiverLink Ferry. This passenger ferry makes a 12-minute trip across the Delaware River; it travels back and forth between the Independence Seaport Museum at Penn's Landing and Camden's waterfront attractions, including the New Jersey State Aquarium, the Camden Children's Museum, and the Battleship New Jersey. You'll get a picturesque view of Philadelphia's skyline and the Ben Franklin Bridge. Besides its daytime schedule, the ferry runs express service two hours before and one hour after Tweeter Center concerts and Camden Riversharks baseball games. ⊠ *Penn's Landing near Walnut St.,* ☎ *215/925–5465,* WEB *www. riverlinkferry.org.* ◻ *$5 round-trip.* ☉ *Apr.–mid-Nov., daily. Departs from Camden every 40 min. from 9:40–5:40, from Phila. every 40 min. from 10–5:20.*

★ ㊶ **St. Peter's Episcopal Church.** Founded by members of Christ Church in Old City who were living in newly settled Society Hill, St. Peter's has been in continuous use since its first service on September 4, 1761. William White, rector of Christ Church, also served in that role at St. Peter's until his death in 1836. The brick Palladian-style building was designed by Scottish architect Robert Smith, who was responsible for Carpenters' Hall and the steeple on Christ Church. William Strickland's simple steeple, a Philadelphia landmark, was added in 1842. Notable features include the grand Palladian window on the chancel wall, high-back box pews that were raised off the floor to eliminate drafts, and the unusual arrangement of altar and pulpit at either end of the main aisle. The design has been called "restrained," but what is palpable on a visit is the silence and grace of the stark white interior. In the churchyard lie Commodore John Hazelwood, a Revolutionary War hero, painter Charles Willson Peale, and seven Native American chiefs who died of smallpox on a visit to Philadelphia in 1793. ⊠ *313 Pine St.,* ☎ *215/925–5968,* WEB *www.stpetersphila.org.* ⊙ *Weekdays 9–4, Sat. 11–3, Sun. 1–3. A guide is on hand weekends to answer questions; tours can be arranged by calling ahead on weekdays.*

South Street. Philadelphia's most bohemian neighborhood is crammed with craft shops and condom stores, coffee bars and tattoo parlors, ethnic restaurants, and New Age book shops. At night it's crammed with people—those who hang out, and those who come to watch them, giving South Street the offbeat, off-color feel of Greenwich Village mixed with Bourbon Street. To some, it's still "the hippest street in town," as the Orlons called it in their 1963 song, although flower children have been replaced by teens with pierced eyebrows, and the crowds can get rowdy, especially late on weekend nights. ⊠ *South St. from Front St. to about 10th St., Lombard St. to Bainbridge St.,* WEB *www.ushistory.org/tour/tour_south.htm.*

㊷ Thaddeus Kosciuszko National Memorial. A Polish general who later became a national hero in his homeland, Kosciuszko came to the United States in 1776 to help fight in the Revolution; he distinguished himself as one of the first foreign volunteers in the war. The plain three-story brick house, built around 1776, has a portrait gallery; you can also view a six-minute film (in English and Polish) that portrays the general's activities during the Revolution. ⊠ *301 Pine St.,* ☎ *215/597–8974,* WEB *www.nps.gov/thko.* ☜ *Free.* ⊙ *June–Oct., daily 9–5; Nov.–May, Wed.–Sun. 10–5.*

�35 USS *Becuna.* You can tour this 318-ft-long "guppy class" submarine, which was commissioned in 1944 and conducted search-and-destroy missions in the South Pacific. The guides—all World War II submarine vets—tell amazing stories of what life was like for a crew of 88 men, at sea for months at a time, in these claustrophobic quarters. Then you can step through the narrow walkways, climb the ladders, and glimpse the torpedoes in their firing chambers. Children will love it, but it's fascinating for adults, too. ⊠ *Penn's Landing at Spruce St.,* ☎ *215/922–1898,* WEB *www.geocities.com/Athens/Acropolis/7612/ becuna.html.* ☜ *$8 includes admission to USS Becuna, USS Olympia, and the Independence Seaport Museum. The ticket booth by the boats is closed seasonally; tickets must be purchased at the museum on weekdays mid-Nov.–mid-Apr.* ⊙ *Daily 10–5.*

㊱ USS *Olympia.* Commodore George Dewey's flagship at the Battle of Manila in the Spanish-American War is the only remaining ship from that war. Dewey entered Manila Harbor after midnight on May 1, 1898. At 5:40 AM, he told his captain, "You may fire when ready, Gridley," and the battle began. By 12:30 the Americans had destroyed the entire Spanish fleet. The *Olympia* was the last ship of the "New Navy" of the 1880s and 1890s, the beginning of the era of steel ships. You can tour the entire restored ship, including the officers' staterooms, engine room, galley, gun batteries, pilothouse, and conning tower. ⊠ *Penn's Landing at Spruce St.,* ☎ *215/922–1898,* WEB *www.spanamwar.com/ olympia.htm.* ☜ *$8 includes admission to USS Olympia, USS Becuna, and the Independence Seaport Museum. The ticket booth by the boats is closed seasonally; tickets must be purchased at the museum on weekdays mid-Nov.–mid-Apr.* ⊙ *Daily 10–5.*

Washington Square. This leafy area resembling a London square has been through numerous incarnations since it was set aside by William Penn. From 1705 until after the Revolution, the square was lined on three sides by houses and on the fourth by the Walnut Street Prison. The latter was home to Robert Morris, who went to debtors' prison after he helped finance the Revolution. The square served as a burial ground for victims of the 1793 yellow fever epidemic and for 2,600 British and American soldiers who perished during the Revolution. The Square holds a Tomb of the Unknown Soldier, erected to the memory of unknown Revolutionary War soldiers. By the 1840s the square had gained prestige as the center of the city's most fashionable neighborhood. It later became the city's publishing center. During recent renovations to improve landscaping and repave walkways, construction workers were surprised to unearth a number of bones. ⊠ *Between 6th and 7th Sts. and Walnut and Locust Sts.*

CENTER CITY
City Hall and Environs

For a grand introduction to the heart of the downtown area, climb the few steps to the plaza in front of the Municipal Services Building at 15th Street and John F. Kennedy Boulevard. You'll be standing alongside a 10-ft-tall bronze statue of the late Frank L. Rizzo waving to the people. Rizzo, nicknamed the "Big Bambino," was the city's police commissioner, two-term mayor (in the 1970s), and a five-time mayoral candidate. He shaped the political scene just as the buildings that surround you—City Hall, the PSFS Building, the Art Museum, the skyscrapers at Liberty Place, Oldenburg's *Clothespin,* and more—shape its architectural landscape.

The story behind this skyline begins with Philadelphia's historic City Hall, which reaches to 40 stories and was the tallest structure in the metropolis until 1987. No law prohibited taller buildings, but the tradition sprang from a gentleman's agreement not to build higher. In May 1984, when a developer proposed building two office towers that would break the 491-ft barrier, it became evident how entrenched this tradition was: the proposal provoked a public outcry. The traditionalists contended the height limitation had made Philadelphia a city of human scale, given character to its streets and public places, and showed respect for tradition. The opposing camp thought that a dramatic new skyline would shatter the city's conservative image and encourage economic growth. After painstaking debate the go-ahead was granted. In short order, the midtown area became the hub of the city's commercial center, Market Street west of City Hall became a district of high-rise office buildings, and the area became a symbol of the city's ongoing transformation from a dying industrial town to a center for service industries. Here, too, are a number of museums, the excellent Reading Terminal Market and the convention center, and Chinatown.

Numbers in the text correspond to numbers in the margin and on the Center City and Along the Parkway map.

A Good Walk

Ask most locals where "downtown" or "Center City" is, and you'll find they agree that Victorian **City Hall** ① is at its heart. Take the elevator up to the tower for an incomparable bird's-eye view of the city. Leave City Hall by the north exit and cross John F. Kennedy Boulevard to the **Masonic Temple** ②, with its ornate interiors and collection

Center City and Along the Parkway

Green St.

Brandywine St.

Spring Garden St.

25

*Eakins
Oval*

Fairmount Park

Hamilton St.

24

Benjamin Franklin Parkway

Park Towne Pl.

24th St.

20th St.

Schuylkill River

Vine St. Expwy.

30

676 **30**

76

Winter St.

22

Spring St.

Race St.

23

Cherry St.

Appletree St.

23rd St.

Arch St.

Cuthbert St.

**30th St.
Station**

John F. Kennedy Blvd.

Market-Frankford Subw

Market St.

Ranstead St.

Airport Train (R1)

30th St.

Chestnut St.

Sansom St.

21st St.

20th St.

Walnut St.

Locust St.

Manning St.

Spruce St.

76

26th St.

25th St.

24th St.

23rd St.

22nd St.

Delancey Pl.

11

Schuylkill River

Pine St.

Lombard St.

Broad St. Subway

Ridge Ave.

Spring Garden St.

Nectarine St.
Buttonwood St.

18th St.

Callowhill St.
Carlton St.
Wood St.

Broad St.

Broad St. Subway

Vine St.

20

19th St.

Logan
Circle

18

17th St.

16th St.

15th St.

19

**Pennsylvania
Convention Center**

8

21

Race St.

Cherry St.

3

7

19th St.

Arch St.

Suburban
Station

JFK
Plaza

2

Filbert St.

Commerce St.

6

Commerce St.

ay

Subway-Surface

Market St.

1

5

4

Ludlow St.

Ranstead St.

Chestnut St.

18th St.

Sansom St.

Moravian St.

17th St.

15th St.

Broad St. (Ave. of the Arts)

Juniper St.

13th St.

12th St.

11th St.

Walnut St.

9

Rittenhouse
Square

10

15

Quince St.

Locust St.

14

16 **17**

Spruce St.

13

19th St.

12

N

Pine St.

Broad St. Subway

KEY
—— Airport Train
—— Broad St. Subway
---- Market-Frankford Subway
-- -- Subway-Surface Subway

0   440 yards

0   Lombard St.   400 meters

of Masonic items. Two blocks north on Broad Street, at Cherry Street in a striking Victorian Gothic building, is the **Pennsylvania Academy of the Fine Arts** ③, filled with paintings by such artists as Winslow Homer and Andrew Wyeth. Head west on Cherry Street one block to 15th Street, turn left, and walk south three blocks to Market Street. This walk will take you from the classics to the avant-garde: Claes Oldenburg's 45-ft-high, 10-ton steel *Clothespin.* (From here you can take public transportation to a few of the city's more distant sites—the Insectarium, the American-Swedish Historical Museum, and Bartram's Garden—or you can drive to Bryn Athyn Cathedral.)

Two blocks west of the sculpture are **Liberty Place One and Two** ④; the food court between them makes a great stop for lunch. Exit the building at 16th and Chestnut; three blocks east at 13th Street is **Lord & Taylor** ⑤, formerly the John Wanamaker store, famous for its eagle statue and its nine-story grand court. Walk over to Market Street, turn right, and go one block to 12th Street. Here is the **Philadelphia Saving Fund Society (PSFS) Building,** an early (1930) skyscraper, now an upscale Loews Hotel. On the same block, SEPTA's headquarters holds the **Transit Museum.** Two blocks north on 12th Street is the **Reading Terminal Market** ⑥, filled with vendors of all kinds of food. Across Arch Street is the **Pennsylvania Convention Center** ⑦, which houses a terrific collection of contemporary art. Walking two blocks east on Arch Street brings you to the 40-ft-tall Chinese Friendship Gate, the unofficial entrance to the restaurants and stores of **Chinatown** ⑧.

TIMING

To get a feel for the city at work, save this walk for a weekday, when the streets are bustling (on weekends the area can be quite deserted). Besides, the City Hall Observation Tower is open weekdays only, and both the Reading Terminal Market and the Masonic Temple, two don't-miss spots, are closed Sunday. You could complete this walk in 45 minutes, but if you want to sightsee, reserve about half a day, with an hour each at the Masonic Temple, City Hall Tower, and the Pennsylvania Academy of the Fine Arts. If you get an early start, you can finish with lunch at the Reading Terminal Market.

Sights to See

OFF THE BEATEN PATH

AMERICAN-SWEDISH HISTORICAL MUSEUM – The Swedes settled the Delaware Valley in the mid-1600s before William Penn, but few traces remain other than Gloria Dei (Old Swedes') Church in Southwark and this museum. Modeled after a 17th-century Swedish manor house, the museum has 14 galleries that trace the history of Swedes in the United States. The John Ericsson Room honors the designer of the Civil War ironclad ship the *Monitor,* and the Jenny Lind Room contains memorabilia from the Swedish Nightingale's American tour of 1848–1851. Other rooms display handmade costumed Swedish peasant dolls, crafts, paintings, and drawings. To get here, you can pick up the subway just below the *Clothespin* sculpture, at 15th and Market streets. ✉ *1900 Pattison Ave.,* ☎ *215/389-1776,* WEB *www.americanswedish.org. Take Broad St. subway south to Pattison Ave. Cross Broad St., walk 5 blocks west through the park to the museum.* ✆ *$5.* ⊙ *Tues.–Fri. 10–4, weekends noon–4.*

BARTRAM'S GARDEN – Begun in 1728 by the pioneering botanist John Bartram (1699–1777), America's oldest surviving botanical garden has remained relatively unchanged while the surrounding areas have altered dramatically. The 44-acre oasis is tucked into a heavily industrialized and depressed corner of southwest Philadelphia. With stone columns and carvings by Bartram himself, the 18th-century farmhouse on the grounds reflects his unique vision of classical and Colonial architecture; it's a National Historic Landmark. The self-trained Bartram became botanist to King George III, traveling throughout the Colonies and returning with many unusual species. He corresponded and exchanged plants with botanists around the world. The gardens include the nation's oldest Gingko tree, a fragrant flower garden, and a riverside meadow. The trails extending to the Schuylkill River are part of the National Recreation Trails System. You can catch the subway in front of the *Clothespin,* at 15th and Market streets. Note that you can get a map to tour the gardens only when the house is open. ⊠ *54th St. and Lindbergh Blvd.,* ☎ *215/729–5281,* WEB *www.bartramsgarden.org. 20-min ride on the No. 36 Trolley from 15th and Market Sts., then right to the entrance.* ☑ *$3 for house tour; garden free.* ☉ *Garden, daily 10–5. House, Mar.–Dec., Tues.–Sun. noon–4; tours at 12:10, 1:10, 2:10 and 3:10.*

BRYN ATHYN CATHEDRAL – At one of the most beautiful spots in the Philadelphia area, atop a hill overlooking the Pennypack Valley, stands a spectacular cathedral built in 12th-century Romanesque and 14th-century Gothic styles. The cathedral is the episcopal seat of the Church of the New Jerusalem, a sect based on the writings of the Swedish scientist and mystic Emanuel Swedenborg (1688–1772). The main patrons of the church are descendants of John Pitcairn, an industrialist who made his fortune in paint and plate glass. Construction of the cathedral began in 1914 and went on for decades. It was built according to the medieval guild system: all materials—wood, metal, glass, stone—were brought to craftspeople at the site, and everything was fashioned by hand. The stained glass includes two colors, striated ruby and cobalt blue, found nowhere else in the Americas. From Center City, go north on Broad Street to Route 611, right on County Line Road, and south on Route 232 to the second traffic light; the cathedral will be on your right. ⊠ *Rte. 232, Huntingdon Pike at Cathedral Rd., Bryn Athyn, 15 mi north of Center City,* ☎ *215/947–0266,* WEB *www.brynathyncathedral.org.* ☑ *Free.* ☉ *Tues.–Sun. 1–4; guides offer 30–minute tours (sometimes preempted by special events); visitors also welcome at services Sun. 9:30 and 11.*

GLENCAIRN – The former home of Raymond and Mildred Pitcairn, this neo-Romanesque building sits on a hill near Bryn Athyn Cathedral, the construction of which Raymond had supervised. The home is now a museum focusing on the history of religion. On display are art and artifacts representing ancient Egyptian, medieval European, Islamic, and Native American cultures, among others. ⊠ *1001 Cathedral Rd., Bryn Athyn,* ☎ *215/938–2600,* WEB *www.glencairnmuseum.org.* ☑ *$5.* ☉ *Open for tours by appointment, Mon.–Fri., 9–5; and for self-guided tours on selected second Sundays, 2–5.*

❽ **Chinatown.** Centered on 10th and Race streets two blocks north of Market Street, Chinatown serves as the residential and commercial hub of the city's Chinese community. Chinatown has grocery stores, souvenir and gift shops, martial arts studios, a fortune cookie store, bilingual street signs, and red-and-green pagoda-style telephone booths, and more than 50 restaurants. Over the past 20 years, Chinatown's population has become more diverse, reflecting the increase in immigration from other parts of Southeast Asia. As a result, the dining options are more varied; there now are restaurants serving authentic Vietnamese, Thai, Cambodian, and Burmese cuisine. One striking Chinatown site is the **Chinese Friendship Gate,** straddling 10th Street at Arch Street. This intricate and colorful 40-ft-tall arch—the largest authentic Chinese gate outside China—was created by Chinese artisans, who brought their own tools and construction materials. The citizens of Tianjin, Philadelphia's sister city in China, donated the building materials, including the ornamental tile. From February to May you can celebrate Chinese New Year with a 10-course banquet at the **Chinese Cultural Center** (✉ 125 N. 10th St., ☎ 215/923–6767). The center occupies an 1831 building of the Beijing Mandarin-palace style. ✉ *9th to 11th Sts., Arch to Vine Sts.* WEB *www.enjoychinatown.com.*

....

NEED A
BREAK?

For a savory or sweet Chinese snack, stop at the **Hong Kong Bakery** (✉ 915 Race St., ☎ 215/925–1288). Sample the "Hong Kong Hotdog," a smallish weiner encased in puff pastry (try it with mustard), or a sweet egg custard tart. Some of the items in the case defy description, but if you're feeling adventurous, try one or more. They're cheap (usually under $1) and you might just find a new taste thrill.

....

★ ❶ **City Hall.** Topped by a 37-ft bronze statue of William Penn, City Hall was Philadelphia's tallest building until 1987; you can study the trappings of government and also get a panoramic of the city here. With 642 rooms, it is the largest city hall in the country and the tallest masonry-bearing building in the world: no steel structure supports it. Designed by architect John McArthur Jr., the building took 30 years to build (from 1871 to 1900) and cost taxpayers more than $23 million. The result has been called a "Victorian wedding cake of Renaissance styles." Placed about the facade are hundreds of statues by Alexander Milne Calder, who also designed the statue of William Penn at the top. Calder's 27-ton cast-iron statue of Penn is the largest single piece of sculpture on any building in the world.

Not only the geographic center of Penn's original city plan, City Hall is also the center of municipal and state government. Many of the magnificent interiors—splendidly decorated with mahogany paneling, gold-leaf ceilings, and marble pillars—are patterned after the Second Empire salons of part of the Louvre in Paris. On a tour each weekday at 12:30, you'll see the mayor's ornate reception room, Conversation Hall, the Supreme Court of Pennsylvania, and the City Council chambers (Room 400). You can attend these often heated City Council meetings, held each Thursday morning at 10.

To top off your visit, take the elevator from the 7th floor up the tower to the observation deck at the foot of William Penn's statue for a 30-mi view of the city and surroundings. The elevator holds only six people per trip and runs every 15 minutes; the least crowded time is early morning. ✉ *Broad and Market Sts. (tour office: East Portal, Room 121),* ☎ *215/686–1776; 215/686–2840 for tour information,* WEB *www.geocities.com/Athens/Delphi/2115.* ⌨ *Free; donations welcome.* ⏱ *Tower: weekdays 9:30–4:15; 90-min. building tour including tower, weekdays at 12:30.*

Clothespin. Claes Oldenburg's 45-ft-high, 10-ton steel sculpture stands in front of the Center Square Building. Lauded by some and scorned by others, this pop art piece contrasts with the traditional statuary so common in Philadelphia. ✉ *15th and Market Sts.*

....

OFF THE
BEATEN PATH

INSECTARIUM – Even if you hate bugs, you'll love this ugly, yet beautiful collection of more than 1 million creepy crawlers—tarantulas, giant centipedes, scorpions, assassin bugs, and metallic beetles that look like pieces of gold jewelry. About 25% of the insects are alive; the rest are mounted. The 18,000-square-ft museum recently acquired the largest butterfly and moth collection in North America, with 63,000 mounted specimens. Don't forget to check out the amazing bug gift shop. It's easier to drive here than to take public transportation; call the museum for directions, although you can pick up the subway in front of the *Clothespin.* ✉ *8046 Frankford Ave., Northeast Philadelphia,* ☎ *215/338–3000,* WEB *www.insectarium.com. By public transit: from 15th and Market St. station take the Market-Frankford subway to end (Bridge St.); transfer to SEPTA Bus 66 to Welsh Rd.* ⬚ *$5.* ◷ *Mon.–Sat. 10–4.*

❹ **Liberty Place One and Two.** One Liberty Place is the 945-ft, 63-story office building designed by Helmut Jahn that propelled Philadelphia into the "ultra-high" skyscraper era. Built in 1987, it became the tallest structure in Philadelphia. The art deco–style structure, vaguely reminiscent of New York's Chrysler Building, is visible from almost everywhere in the city. In 1990 the adjacent 58-story tower, **Two Liberty Place,** opened. It held the elegant Ritz-Carlton Hotel, which became the equally elegant St. Regis; now it's the Westin Philadelphia. Zeidler Roberts designed this second building. ✉ *One Liberty Place, 1650 Market St.;* ✉ *Two Liberty Place, 1601 Chestnut St.*

NEED A
BREAK?

The **Shops at Liberty Place** (✉ 1625 Chestnut St., between Liberty One and Liberty Two, ☎ 215/851–9055) houses a large international food court on the second level, above the upscale boutiques. You'll find anything from salad to sushi to those familiar Philly cheese steaks.

❺ **Lord & Taylor.** The former John Wanamaker department store, this building is almost as prominent a Philadelphia landmark as the Liberty Bell. Wanamaker began with a clothing store in 1861 and became one of America's most innovative and prominent retailers. The massive building, which occupies a city block with grace, was designed by the noted Chicago firm of D. H. Burnham and Company. Its focal point is the nine-story grand court with its 30,000-pipe organ—the largest ever built—and a 2,500-pound statue of an eagle, both remnants of the 1904 Louisiana Purchase Exposition in St. Louis. "Meet me at the Eagle" remains a popular way for Philadelphians to arrange a rendezvous. Happily, the current owners have kept the eagle and continue the famous Christmas sound-and-light show and the organ performances. ✉ *13th and Market Sts.,* ☎ *215/241–9000,* WEB *www.lordandtaylor.com.* ◷ *Mon., Tues., Thurs., Fri. 10–7; Wed. 9–8; Sat. 10–7; Sun. noon–5; organ concerts Mon.–Sat. at 11:15 and 5:15.*

★ ❷ **Masonic Temple.** The temple is one of the city's architectural jewels, but it remains a hidden treasure even to many Philadelphians. Historically, Freemasons were skilled stoneworkers of the Middle Ages who possessed secret signs and passwords. Their worldwide fraternal order—the Free and Accepted Masons—included men in the building trades, plus many honorary members; the secret society prospered in Philadelphia during Colonial times. Brother James Windrim designed this elaborate temple as a home for the Grand Lodge of Free and Accepted Masons of Pennsylvania. The trowel used here at the laying of the cornerstone in 1868, while 10,000 brothers looked on, was the same one that Brother George Washington used to set the cornerstone of the U.S. Capitol. The temple's ornate interior consists of seven lavishly decorated lodge halls built to exemplify specific styles of architecture: Corinthian, Ionic, Italian Renaissance, Norman, Gothic, Oriental, and Egyptian. The Egyptian room, with its accurate hieroglyphics, is the most famous. The Temple also houses an interesting museum of Masonic items, including Benjamin Franklin's printing of the first book on Freemasonry published in America and Brother George Washington's Masonic Apron, which was embroidered by Madame Lafayette, wife of the famous marquis. ✉ *1 N. Broad St.,* ☎ *215/988–1917,* WEB *www.pagrandlodge.org/tour/mtemple.html.* ⬚ *Free.* ◷ *45-min. tours*

FLORAL FANTASY

I T TAKES ONE WEEK; 7,000 Belgian blocks; 3,500 volunteers; thousands of plumbers, carpenters and electricians; more than a million plants; and 50 tractor-trailer loads of mulch to transform the Pennsylvania Convention Center into the annual **Philadelphia Flower Show** (☎ 215/988–8899, WEB www.theflowershow.com), the world's largest indoor horticultural event. But the exhibitors—nursery owners, landscapers, and florists from the region and from Africa, Japan, and Europe—spend the better part of a year planning their displays. The astonishing, fragrant results of their efforts arrive in the city as a touch of spring in early March.

It's a fitting tribute to William Penn that Philadelphia hosts this extravaganza, for this was Penn's "greene countrie town," which he laid out on a grid punctuated with tree-lined streets, pocket parks, small squares, and large public parks. It's also appropriate that this city gave root to the Pennsylvania Horticultural Society (PHS), the nation's first such organization. In 1829, two years after its founding, the society hosted its first show at the Masonic Hall in an 82-by-69-ft exhibition space; 25 society members showed off their green thumbs.

Today the show fills 10 acres of exhibition space at the convention center and spills throughout the area as local restaurants, hotels, and attractions offer special deals. (The show's Web site may have discounts and coupons.) Along with the more than 60 major exhibits, amateur gardeners contribute over 2,000 entries in 330 competitive categories—from pressed plants and miniature settings to spectacular jewelry designs that use flowers. There are free cooking and gardening demonstrations, lectures, and an area where you can try out the latest gardening gadgets. Hundreds of vendors sell plants, birdhouses, topiaries, watering systems, botanical prints, and more.

Each year, the show has a theme, and the show's designers think big—*very* big. Highlights from "The Art of Gardening," 1999's theme, included re-creations of four of the many formal gardens maintained by the National Trust for Historic Preservation, including the Kykuit gardens at the Rockefeller mansion in New York state, and a prehistoric landscape with "living fossils" of horsetail, gingko, and ferns, presided over by an apatosaurus.

If you've made reservations, you can rest your weary feet during **Afternoon Tea at the Flower Show** (☎ 215/988–8899), a proper English tea served at 12:30 and 3:45; it's $26 in addition to the show admission ($18–$24). For a more substantial lunch break, you can head across the street to the **Reading Terminal Market** (✉ 12th and Arch Sts.), which has more than 80 stalls, shops, and lunch counters. Or walk two blocks east to the many restaurants of **Chinatown** (✉ 9th to 11th Sts., Arch to Vine Sts.)

Many people plan trips to Philadelphia around the show, so be sure to make reservations early. (In recent years, attendance has neared 300,000, with 40% of the crowd from out of town.) Wear good walking shoes, check your coat, and bring spending money for the many horticultural temptations. To avoid crowds, which can be daunting, arrive after 4 on weekdays and stay until the 9:30 closing, or show up when the doors open on weekend mornings, at 10.

Sept.–June, weekdays 10, 11, 1, 2, and 3, Sat. 10 and 11; July–Aug., weekdays 10, 11, 1, 2, and 3.

★ ❸ **Pennsylvania Academy of the Fine Arts.** This High Victorian Gothic structure is a work of art in itself. Designed in 1876 by the noted, and sometimes eccentric, Philadelphia architects Frank Furness and George Hewitt, the multicolor stone-and-brick exterior is an extravagant blend of columns, friezes, and Richardsonian Romanesque and Moorish flourishes. The interior is just as lush, with rich hues of red, yellow, and blue and an impressive staircase. The nation's oldest art school and museum (founded in 1805) displays a fine collection that ranges from the Peale family, Gilbert Stuart, Benjamin West, and Winslow Homer to Andrew Wyeth and Red Grooms. *Fox Hunt* by Winslow Homer, *The Artist in His Museum* by Charles Willson Peale, and *Interior with Doorway* by Richard Diebenkorn are just a few notable works. The permanent collection is supplemented by constantly changing exhibitions of sculpture, paintings, and mixed-media artwork. The academy faculty has included Thomas Sully, Thomas Eakins, and Charles Willson Peale; the latter is one of the school's founders. Art classes are now held a block away at 1301 Cherry Street. ⊠ *118 N. Broad St., at Cherry St.,* ☎ *215/972–7600,* WEB *www.pafa.org.* ⌨ *$5; free Sun. 3–5.* ◷ *Tues.–Sat. 10–5, Sun. 11–5.*

❼ **Pennsylvania Convention Center.** Opened in June 1993 with galas, parties, and Vice President Al Gore cutting the ribbon, the convention center has helped rejuvenate Philadelphia's economy and fuel a hotel boom. It's big: with 313,000 square ft, the area of the main exhibition hall equals seven football fields. And it's beautiful: the 1.9 million square ft of space are punctuated by the largest permanent collection of contemporary art in a building of its kind. Many city and state artists are represented in the niches, nooks, and galleries built to house their multimedia works. To see the architectural highlight of the building—the Reading Terminal's magnificently restored four-story-high Victorian train shed, which has been transformed into the Convention Center's Grand Hall—enter the building through the century-old Italian Renaissance headhouse structure on Market Street between 11th and 12th Streets and ride up the escalator. The Headhouse is also home to Philadelphia's Hard Rock Cafe. ⊠ *1101 Arch St.,* ☎ *215/ 418–4735,* WEB *www.paconvention.com.* ⌨ *Free.* ◷ *45-min. tours by appointment only subject to convention schedules.*

Philadelphia Saving Fund Society (PSFS) Building. In 1930, architects George Howe and William Lescaze wowed the world with their design for the PSFS Building, one of the city's first skyscrapers. This was America's first skyscraper to embrace modernism's International style; 70 years later, the structure is still modern-looking. The architects installed custom-designed Cartier clocks in every elevator lobby and even designed the wastebaskets. Loews Hotels has turned the 33-story National Historic Landmark into a handsome 585-room hotel while maintaining its architectural integrity. The company preserved another distinguishing feature: the 27-ft-high red neon PSFS sign on the roof. ⊠ *1200 Market St.,* ☎ *215/627–1200,* WEB *www.loewshotels.com/ philadelphia.*

★ ❻ **Reading Terminal Market.** The market is nothing short of a historical treasure and a food heaven to Philadelphians and visitors alike. One floor beneath the former Reading Railroad's 1891 train shed, the sprawling market has more than 80 food stalls and other shops, selling items from hooked rugs and handmade jewelry to South American and African crafts. Here, amid the local color, you can sample Bassett's ice cream, Philadelphia's best; down a cheese steak, a bowl of snapper soup, or a soft pretzel; or nibble Greek, Mexican, and Indian specialties. From Wednesday through Saturday the Amish from Lancaster County cart in their goodies, including Lebanon bologna, shoofly pie, and scrapple. Many stalls have their own counters with seating; there's also a central eating area. If you want to cook, you can buy a large variety of fresh food from fruit and vegetable stands, butchers, fish stores, and Pennsylvania Dutch markets. The entire building is a National Historic Landmark, and the train shed is a National Engineering Landmark. ⊠ *12th and Arch Sts.,* ☎ *215/922–2317,* WEB *www.readingterminalmarket.org.* ◷ *Mon.–Sat. 8–6.*

Transit Museum. Located, appropriately enough, in the headquarters of the Southeastern Pennsylvania Transportation Authority (SEPTA), this small museum showcases the history and development of public transportation in the region and its impact on social, political, and economic life. On display is a 1947 President's Conference Car trolley, along with transit memorabilia and archival photographs from the 1930s to 1960s. The gift shop has model trucks and trains, four-tone train whistles, and transit-related books and games. ⊠ *Concourse level, 1234 Market St.,* ☎ *215/580–7168,* WEB *www.septa.org/store/museum.html.* ▨ *Free.* ◷ *Mon.–Fri. 10–5, Sat. 10–3.*

RITTENHOUSE SQUARE
Living the Good Life

Rittenhouse Square, at 18th and Walnuts streets, has long been one of the city's swankiest addresses. The square's entrances, plaza, pool, and fountains were designed in 1913 by Paul Cret, one of the people responsible for the Benjamin Franklin Parkway. The square was named in honor of one of the city's 18th-century stars: David Rittenhouse, president of the American Philosophical Society and a professor of astronomy at the University of Pennsylvania. The first house facing the square was erected in 1840, soon to be followed by other grand mansions. Almost all the private homes are now gone, replaced by hotels, apartments, and cultural institutions, and elegant restaurants and stylish cafés dot the neighborhood. The former home of banker George Childs Drexel was transformed into the Curtis Institute, alma mater of Leonard Bernstein and Gian Carlo Menotti. The former Samuel Price Wetherill mansion is now the Philadelphia Art Alliance, sponsor of exhibitions, drama, dance, and literary events.

The area south and west of the square is still largely residential and lovely, with cupolas and balconies, hitching posts and stained-glass windows. You can also find some small shops and two fine museum/library collections tucked in: the Civil War Library and Museum and the Rosenbach Museum and Library. In the heart of the city there are green places, too. Peek in the streets behind these homes or through their wrought-iron gates, and you'll see well-tended gardens. On Delancey Place, blocks alternate narrow and wide. The wide blocks had the homes of the wealthy, while the smaller ones held dwellings for servants or stables (today these carriage houses are prized real estate). When he saw 18th Street and Delancey Place, author R. F. Delderfield, author of *God Is an Englishman,* said, "I never thought I'd see anything like this in America. It is like Dickensian London." Today the good life continues in Rittenhouse Square. Annual events include the Rittenhouse Square Flower Show and the Fine Arts Annual, an outdoor juried art show.

Four blocks south of the square is the Avenue of the Arts, also known as Broad Street. "Let us entertain you" could be the theme of the ambitious cultural development project that has transformed North and South Broad Street from a commercial thoroughfare to a performing arts district. Dramatic new performance spaces have been built, old landmarks have been refurbished, and South Broad Street has been spruced up with landscaping, cast-iron lighting fixtures, and decorative sidewalk paving.

Numbers in the text correspond to numbers in the margin and on the Center City and Along the Parkway map.

A Good Walk

The lovely residential area around **Rittenhouse Square** ⑨ is dotted with small museums. A walk through this neighborhood logically begins at the square itself, on Walnut Street between 18th and 19th streets. East of the square are the former Barclay Hotel, celebrated for decades as the city's most fashionable hotel; the Philadelphia Art Alliance (✉ 251 S. 18th St.), housed in an 1890s mansion, with galleries open to the public; the environmentally smart Sheraton Rittenhouse Square; and the **Curtis Institute of Music** ⑩, whose talented students give free public recitals. West of the square you'll find a branch of the Free Library of Philadelphia, the Rittenhouse Hotel, and the Church of the Holy Trinity, presided over in the mid-19th century by Reverend Phillips Brooks, who achieved renown as the lyricist of *O Little Town of Bethlehem.*

Leave the square on its south side and continue south on 19th Street to **Delancey Place,** then turn right and take a look at this urban residential showcase with its grand houses. The 2000 block of Delancey wins the prize: at Number 2010 is the **Rosenbach Museum and Library** ⑪, a local gem, with paintings, manuscripts, and rare books. Heading east a block south of Delancey, you'll find the **Civil War Library and Museum** ⑫, at 18th and Pine streets. Back at Rittenhouse Square, an elegant tea time can be had in the tearoom at the Rittenhouse Hotel.

From Rittenhouse Square head east on Spruce Street four blocks to the **Kimmel Center for the Performing Arts** ⑬, the dramatic new home of the Philadelphia Orchestra and other arts groups. Turn left on Broad Street, which has been rechristened the **Avenue of the Arts,** and walk one block to the **Academy of Music** ⑭, the orchestra's former home. As you walk along the west side of Broad between Spruce and Walnut streets, notice the more than 30 plaques in the sidewalk honoring some of those who contributed to Philadelphia's cultural history. Where else could Frankie Avalon and Dizzy Gillespie rub shoulders with Anna Moffo and Eugene Ormandy? A block north of the venerable Academy of Music is another grande dame of South Broad Street, the former Bellevue Stratford Hotel, now the **Park Hyatt Philadelphia at the Bellevue** ⑮. As you continue up Broad Street, you'll pass a French Renaissance–style building, the **Union League of Philadelphia.** Cross Broad Street, double back to Locust Street and walk east. Within the first block you come across two renowned collections, the **Library Company of Philadelphia** ⑯ and the **Historical Society of Pennsylvania** ⑰. It you have any time or energy remaining, you could walk three blocks east to 10th and Locust streets to see Thomas Eakins's masterpiece, *The Gross Clinic,* in Thomas Jefferson University's Alumni Hall.

TIMING

This is one of the city's loveliest neighborhoods for strolling. Two hours would allow you enough time to wander through the Rittenhouse Square area and visit the Rosenbach Museum and Library (get there before 2:45). Add at least another hour for a stroll along South broad Street, including afternoon tea or a cold lemonade at the Ritz-Carlton.

Sights to See

⑭ Academy of Music. The only surviving European-style opera house in America is the current home of the Opera Company of Philadelphia and the Pennsylvania Ballet; for the past century, it was home to the Philadelphia Orchestra. Designed by Napoleon Le Brun and Gustav Runge and completed in 1857, the building has a modest exterior; the builders ran out of money and couldn't put marble facing on the brick, as they had intended. The brick hides a lavish, neo-Baroque interior modeled after Milan's La Scala opera house, with gilt, carvings, murals on the ceiling, and a huge Victorian crystal chandelier. Tours are occasionally given on designated weekdays at 2 by reservation. ⊠ *Broad and Locust Sts.,* ☎ *215/893–1999 for box office; 215/893–1935 for tours,* WEB *www.academyofmusic.org.*

Avenue of the Arts. Broad Street, the city's main north-south thoroughfare, has been reinvented as a performing arts district. Although most of the cultural institutions are situated along South Broad Street from City Hall to Spruce Street, the avenue's cultural, education, and arts organizations span as far south as Washington Avenue in South Philadelphia and as far north as Dauphin Street in North Philadelphia. Joining the Merriam Theater and the University of the Arts on South Broad Street are the Wilma Theater, a 300-seat theater for this innovative company; a cabaret-style theater for the Philadelphia Clef Club of Jazz and the Performing Arts; the intimate Philadelphia Arts Bank at the University of the Arts, and the Prince Music Theater, a venue for musical theater and film. The newest venue is the Kimmel Center for the Performing Arts, at Broad and Spruce streets, which includes a 2,500-seat concert hall, specifically designed for the Philadelphia Orchestra, and a recital hall. On North Broad Street, the Pennsylvania Academy of the Fine Arts has completed structural renovations; the Apollo of Temple, Temple University's multipurpose sports and concert complex, has opened; and the Freedom Theatre, the state's oldest African-American theater, has built a new auditorium in its majestic Italianate mansion. ⊠ *Broad St.,* WEB *www.avenueofthearts.org.*

⑫ Civil War Library and Museum. The museum is one of the country's premier collections of Civil War memorabilia pertaining to the Union. Artifacts include two life masks of Abraham Lincoln; dress uniforms and swords that belonged to generals Grant and Meade; plus many other weapons, uniforms, and personal effects of Civil War officers and enlisted men. The library has more than 12,000 volumes about the war. ⊠ *1805 Pine St.,* ☎ *215/735–8196,* WEB *www.netreach.net/~cwlm.* 💲 *$5.* ☉ *Thurs.–Sat. 11–4:30.*

⑩ Curtis Institute of Music. Graduates of this tuition-free school for outstanding students include Leonard Bernstein, Samuel Barber, Ned Rorem, and Anna Moffo. The school occupies four former private homes; the main building is in the mansion that belonged to banker George W. Childs Drexel. Built in 1893 by the distinguished Boston firm of Peabody and Stearns, it is notable for Romanesque and Renaissance architectural details. Free student and faculty concerts are given from October through May at 8, usually on Monday, Wednesday, and Friday evenings; there's also an opera, alumni recital, and symphony orchestra series. ⊠ *1726 Locust St.,* ☎ *215/893–5261 for recital hot line; 215/893–7902 for Curtis ticket office,* WEB *www.curtis.edu.*

Delancey Place. This fine residential area southwest of Rittenhouse Square was once the address of Pearl S. Buck (⊠ 2019 Delancey Pl.) and Rudolf Serkin. At one corner (⊠ 320 S. 18th St.) there is an interesting old sea captain's house. At Number 2010 is the **Rosenbach Museum and Library.** Cypress Street, just north of Delancey Place, and

Panama Street (especially the 1900 block, one block south of Delancey) are two of the many intimate streets lined with trees and town houses characteristic of the area.

OFF THE
BEATEN PATH

THE GROSS CLINIC – Most art historians would put Thomas Eakins's magnificent medical painting *The Gross Clinic* (1875) on the list of top 10 American paintings; you can view it in Eakins Gallery in the alumni hall of Thomas Jefferson University. Eakins depicts Dr. Samuel D. Gross, Jefferson's celebrated surgeon and teacher, presiding over an operation for osteomyelitis in an amphitheater under a skylighted roof. His assistants are removing the bone, while the patient's mother stands off to the side. It's a dramatic piece in size (96 by 78 inches), composition (the light streaming into the murky room), and subject matter. Eakins, who studied anatomy at Jefferson Medical College, also painted portraits of two prominent professors, which are also on display here. The alumni hall is three blocks east of the Historical Society of Pennsylvania; request entry at the alumni hall information desk. ⊠ *Jefferson Alumni Hall, 1020 Locust St.,* ☎ *215/503–7926,* WEB *jeffline.tju.edu/CWIS/Eakins.* ☞ *Free.* ☉ *Mon.–Sat. 10–4.*

⑰ Historical Society of Pennsylvania. More than 500,000 books, 300,000 graphic works, and 15 million manuscript items are housed in this superlative special collections library with an emphasis on Colonial, early national, and Pennsylvania history. Founded in 1824, the society also owns one of the largest family history libraries in the nation. This is the place to go to trace your family roots. Notable items from the collection include the Penn family archives, President Buchanan's papers, a printer's proof of the Declaration of Independence, and the first draft of the Constitution. The library is open to anyone over 13 years old. ⊠ *1300 Locust St.,* ☎ *215/732–6200,* WEB *www.hsp.org.* ☞ *$6 for use of library.* ☉ *Tues., Thurs., Fri. 9:30–4, Wed. 1–8, Sat. 10–4.*

⑬ Kimmel Center for the Performing Arts. Intended to make a contemporary design statement in this Colonial city, the Kimmel Center for the Performing Arts evokes Philadelphia's traditional redbrick structures, while providing architectural oomph with its dramatic vaulted glass roof. The 450,000 square-ft facility by architect Raphael Viñoly includes the 2,500-seat, cello-shaped Verizon Hall; the more intimate 650-seat Perelman Theater; a cafe and restaurant; a gift shop; rooftop terrace; and a public plaza. Together, with the venerable Academy of Music, it comprises the Regional Performing Arts Center. Making their home at the Kimmel are the Philadelphia Orchestra, Philadanco, Philadelphia Chamber Music Society, Concerto Soloists Chamber Orchestra, and American Theater Arts for Youth. ⊠ *Broad and Spruce Sts.,* ☎ *215/790–5810 or 215/893–1999,* WEB *www.rpac.org.*

⑯ Library Company of Philadelphia. Founded in 1731, this is one of the oldest cultural institutions in the United States and the only major Colonial American library that has survived virtually intact, despite having moved from building to building. You can stop by and read the rare books, although nothing circulates. Ben Franklin and his Junto, a group of people who read and then discussed philosophical and political issues, started the Library Company; they also founded the American Philosophical Society. From 1774 to 1800 it functioned as the de facto Library of Congress, and until the late 19th century it was the city library. Ten signers of the Declaration of Independence were members, among them Robert Morris, Benjamin Rush, and Thomas McKean. The 400,000-volume collection includes 200,000 rare books. Among the first editions—many acquired when they were first published—are Melville's *Moby Dick* and Whitman's *Leaves of Grass.* The library is particularly rich in Americana up to 1880, black history to 1915, the history of science, and women's history. Changing exhibits showcase the library's holdings. ⊠ *1314 Locust St.,* ☎ *215/546–3181,* WEB *www.librarycompany.org.* 🖼 *Free.* ⊙ *Weekdays 9–4:45.*

⑮ Park Hyatt Philadelphia at the Bellevue. Though its name has been changed many times, this building will always be "the Bellevue" to Philadelphians. The hotel has had an important role in city life, much like the heroine of a long-running soap opera. The epitome of the opulent hotels characteristic of the early 1900s, the Bellevue Stratford was the city's leading hotel for decades. It closed in 1976 after the first outbreak of Legionnaires' disease, which spread through the building's airconditioning system during an American Legion convention. Reopened as the Fairmont several years later, the hotel failed to regain its luster and closed again in 1986. When renovations were completed in 1989, this magnificent building debuted as home to a number of upscale shops (the Shops at the Bellevue), restaurants, and a food court, as well as the luxurious Hotel Atop the Bellevue. Although the hotel has been renamed, its character seems to have remained the same. ⊠ *Broad and Walnut Sts.,* ☎ *215/893–1776,* WEB *www.hyatt.com.*

NEED A BREAK?
> For a most civilized break from touring, enter the luxurious world of the Ritz-Carlton's soaring Rotunda (⊠ 10 Avenue of the Arts, ☎ 215/735–7700). Here, surrounded by white marble columns and soothed with live music from a piano or harp, you can relax on an overstuffed sofa and enjoy a cool drink, afternoon tea, or a cocktail.

⑨ Rittenhouse Square. Once grazing ground for cows and sheep, Philadelphia's most elegant square is reminiscent of a Parisian park. One of William Penn's original five city squares, the park was named in 1825 to honor David Rittenhouse, 18th-century astronomer, clock maker, and the first director of the United States Mint. Many of Philadelphia's movers, shakers, and celebrities have lived here. Extra paths were made for Dr. William White, a leader in beautifying the square, so he could walk directly from his home to the exclusive Rittenhouse Club across the square and lunch with the likes of Henry James. Until 1950 town houses bordered the square, but they have now been replaced on three sides by swank apartment buildings and hotels. Some great houses remain, including the celebrated former residence of Henry P. McIlhenny (on the southwest corner), once home to one of the world's great art collections, now on view at the Philadelphia Museum of Art. If you want to join the office workers who have lunch-hour picnics in the park, you'll find scores of restaurants and sandwich shops along Walnut, Sansom, and Chestnut streets east of the square. The term "Rittenhouse Row" has recently been coined to describe the greater Rittenhouse Square area, bordered by Pine, Market, 21st, and Broad streets. ⊠ *Walnut St. between 18th and 19th Sts.,* WEB *www.rittenhouserow.org.*

NEED A BREAK?
> A block north of Rittenhouse Square is **Pronto** (⊠ 103 S. 18th St., ☎ 215/564–2772), which features a fantastic selection of prepared foods, salads, and sandwiches, perfect for a quick lunch or snack. You'll smell the mouthwatering aroma down the block. It's take-out only, but claim a bench in nearby Rittenhouse Square for the best alfresco seat in town.

★ **⑪ Rosenbach Museum and Library.** This 1863 three-floor town house, and a recently purchased adjoining building, are filled with Persian rugs and 18th-century British, French, and American antiques (plus an entire living room that once belonged to poet Marianne Moore), but the real treasures are the artworks, books, and manuscripts here. Amassed by Philadelphia collectors Philip H. and A. S. W. Rosenbach, the collection includes paintings by Canaletto, Sully, and Lawrence; drawings by Daumier, Fragonard, and Blake; book illustrations ranging from medieval illuminations to the works of Maurice Sendak; the only known copy of the first edition of Benjamin Franklin's *Poor Richard's Almanack;* and the library's most famous treasure—the original manuscript of James Joyce's *Ulysses.* The library has more than 130,000 manuscripts and 30,000 rare books. ⊠ *2010 Delancey Pl.,* ☎ *215/732–1600,* WEB *www. rosenbach.org.* ⊠ *$5.* ☉ *Sept.–July, Tues.–Sun. 11–4. Guided 75-min. tour as visitors arrive; last tour at 2:45.*

Union League of Philadelphia. An elegant double staircase sweeps from Broad Street up to the entrance of this 1865 French Renaissance–style building; within lies a bastion of Philadelphia conservatism. The Union League is a private social club founded during the Civil War to support the Union—in a big way. The club contributed $100,000, then a huge sum. ⊠ *140 S. Broad St.,* WEB *www.unionleague.org.* ☉ *Closed to the public.*

THE BENJAMIN FRANKLIN PARKWAY

Museums and Marvels

The Benjamin Franklin Parkway is the city's Champs-Elysées, home to many great cultural institutions. Alive with colorful flowers, flags, and fountains, this 250-ft-wide boulevard stretches northwest from the John F. Kennedy Plaza to the Kelly (East) and West River drives. It is crowned by a Greco-Roman temple on a hilltop—the Philadelphia Museum of Art. French architects Jacques Greber and Paul Cret designed the parkway in the 1920s. Today a distinguished assemblage of museums, institutions, hotels, and apartment buildings line the road, competing with each other in grandeur.

Here you'll find the Free Library of Philadelphia and the Family Court, housed in buildings whose designs are both copied from the palaces on Paris's Place de la Concorde. A newer addition is the Four Seasons Hotel, though its dignified design has made it look like a local institution since the day it opened. A grand processional path, the parkway occasionally lets down its hair as the route for city parades and the site of many festivals and events, including the Thanksgiving and Columbus Day parades and the First Union U.S. Pro Cycling championship.

Numbers in the text correspond to numbers in the margin and on the Center City and Along the Parkway map.

A Good Walk

Begin at John F. Kennedy Plaza, on the west side of City Hall, site of the LOVE sculpture. If you'd prefer not to walk the length of the Benjamin Franklin Parkway, you could pick up one of Philadelphia Trolley Works's trolley buses here; the 90-minute narrated tour of the city includes stops at the parkway museums. Or, providing you called ahead for reservations, you could board SEPTA Bus 44 to Merion, home of the Barnes Foundation, with its Impressionist and Postimpressionist paintings. From the plaza walk northwest on the parkway about four blocks to **Logan Circle** ⑱ and its lovely fountain sculpture. Next visit the Italian Renaissance–style **Cathedral of Saints Peter and Paul** ⑲, at 18th Street.

Walking counterclockwise around Logan Circle, you'll see twin marble Greek Revival buildings off to your right. The nearer of the two is the city's Family Court; the other is the **Free Library of Philadelphia** ㉐. Cross Logan Circle to see the dinosaur exhibition and more at the **Academy of Natural Sciences** ㉑. From the academy walk west on Race Street to 20th Street and tour the hands-on exhibits at the **Franklin Institute Science Museum** ㉒. If it's a warm day, head outside to the **First Union Science Park,** a play-and-learn area just behind the museum on 21st Street. If you have children under the age of seven, don't miss the interactive displays at the **Please Touch Museum** ㉓, just a half block south on 21st Street. If your kids are older and if you and they appreciate the macabre, it's worth walking a few blocks south to see the Mutter Museum's collection of skulls and specimens.

Head back to the north side of the parkway and walk northwest. On your right is the Youth Study Center (a detention center for juvenile offenders) with two striking tableaux depicting families. At the next corner, guarded by a bronze cast of the famous sculpture *The Thinker,* is the **Rodin Museum** ㉔. Just ahead, atop Faire Mount, the plateau at the end of Franklin Parkway, is the **Philadelphia Museum of Art** ㉕, with its world-class collections. Before you see the beauty at the art museum, you could choose to tour the "beast." Half a mile north at 22nd Street and Fairmount Avenue is Eastern State Penitentiary, a former prison that is now an offbeat attraction. From there, following Fairmount Avenue west toward the higher numbers is the quickest route back to the art museum.

TIMING

The parkway is at its most colorful in spring, when the trees and flowers are in bloom. Leave early in the morning and plan to spend an entire day—and possibly the evening—in this area. On Wednesday you can cap off your day of culture with dinner and entertainment at the Philadelphia Museum of Art. If it's a Friday or Saturday, save the Franklin Institute for mid-afternoon, head out to dinner in the neighborhood, and return for a film on the giant screen of the Omniverse Theater, followed by a rock-and-roll laser light show in Fels Planetarium (the last show is at midnight). How much time you spend at each museum depends on your interests; be aware that the art museum and the Rodin Museum are closed on Monday.

Sights to See

㉑ **Academy of Natural Sciences.** The world-famous dioramas of animals from around the world displayed in their natural habitats give this natural history museum an old-fashioned charm; the latest discoveries give it drawing power. The most popular attraction is Dinosaur Hall, with reconstructed skeletons of a Tyrannosaurus rex and the latest paleontological find—the giganotosaurus, the biggest meat-eating dinosaur ever discovered. Dinosaur Hall, completely revamped in 1998, features fossils dating as far back as 160 million years ago. Other drawing cards are Living Downstream, an interactive watershed model with multimedia kiosks for visitors to play a role-playing game called Tough Choices; The Big Dig, where you can dig for real fossils; and the live butterflies that flutter all around you in a tropical rain forest setting. Outside-In is an interactive children's nature museum where kids can crawl through a log, investigate a real bee hive, and touch a tarantula. If you're keeping track of Philadelphia firsts, note that the academy, the oldest science research institution in the Western Hemisphere and a world leader in the fields of natural science research, education, and exhibition, was founded in 1812; the present building dates from 1868. ✉ *19th St. and Benjamin Franklin Pkwy.,* ☎ *215/299–1000,* WEB *www.acnatsci.org.* ✇ *$9.* ☉ *Weekdays 10–4:30, weekends 10–5.*

OFF THE
BEATEN PATH

BARNES FOUNDATION – It used to be pretty much a secret that one of the world's greatest collections of Impressionist and Postimpressionist art— 175 Renoirs; 66 Cézannes (including his *Card Players*); 65 Matisses; plus masterpieces by van Gogh, Degas, Picasso, and others—was on view in the little town of Merion, 8 mi west of Center City. That was the way Albert C. Barnes wanted it. The son of a Philadelphia butcher who made millions by inventing Argyrol (used to treat eye inflammations), Barnes considered his art collection an educational tool, and until a 1961 court order the collection was open only to students of the educational institution he had chartered. Now that the trustees of Lincoln University have taken over, Barnes's public-be-damned attitude is a thing of the past. Thanks to a successful worldwide tour of the collection (which allowed the trustees to renovate Barnes's French Renaissance–style mansion), the secret is out. The Gauguins, Tintorettos, and Degases are displayed as they have always been: wallpapered floor to ceiling and cheek by jowl with household tools, Amish chests, and New Mexican folk icons (a Matisse and an antique door latch shared similar aesthetics, according to Barnes). Reservations are required and should be made at least 60 days in advance as admissions—and hours—are limited. ⊠ *300 Latches La., Merion,* ☎ *610/667–0290,* WEB *www.barnesfoundation.org.* 🎫 *$5.* ☉ *Sept.– June, Fri.–Sun. 9:30–5; July–Aug., Wed.–Fri. 9:30–5. SEPTA's Ardmorebound 44 bus runs from 15th St. and Kennedy Blvd. to Old Lancaster Rd. and N. Latches La., ½ block from the museum; or take SEPTA's R-5 train from 30th Street Station to the Merion Station stop, turn right on Merion Rd. and left on Latches La. and walk ½ mi to the museum.*

⑲ Cathedral of Saints Peter and Paul. This is the basilica of the archdiocese of Philadelphia and the spiritual center for the Philadelphia area's 1.4 million Roman Catholics. Topped by a huge copper dome, it was built between 1846 and 1864 in the Italian Renaissance style. Many of the interior decorations were done by Constantino Brumidi, who painted the dome of the U.S. Capitol. Six Philadelphia bishops and archbishops are buried beneath the altar. ⊠ *18th and Race Sts.,* ☎ *215/561– 1313.* ☉ *Daily 7–5. Masses weekdays 7:15, 8, 12:05, 12:35; Sat. 12:05, 5:15; Sun. 8, 9:30, 11, 12:15, 5.*

OFF THE
BEATEN PATH

EASTERN STATE PENITENTIARY HISTORIC SITE – Designed by John Haviland and built in 1829, Eastern State was at the time the most expensive building in America; it influenced penal design around the world and was the model for some 300 prisons from China to South America. The massive hulk, with 30-ft-high, 12-ft-wide walls and a hub-and-spoke floor plan, was created to promote a revolutionary and controversial concept: the reform of prisoners through solitary confinement, in accordance with the Quaker belief that if prisoners had light from heaven (in their private exercise yard), the word of God (the Bible), and honest work, they would reflect and repent. Charles Dickens came to America in 1842 to see Niagara Falls and Eastern State; he became its most famous detractor, insisting that solitary confinement was cruel. Before it closed in 1971, the prison was home to Al Capone, Willie Sutton, and Pep the Dog, who killed the cat that belonged to a governor's wife. The guides on the hourly tours of the unrestored structure (you must wear hard hats) tell terrific anecdotes and take you on a visit to Death Row. The penitentiary, just a half mile north of the Rodin Museum, hosts changing art exhibitions, Haunted House tours around Halloween, and a Bastille Day celebration the Sunday before July 14, with a reenactment of the storming of the Bastille. ⊠ *22nd St. and Fairmount Ave.,* ☎ *215/236–3300,* WEB *www.easternstate.org.* 🎫 *$7; children under 7 not allowed.* ☉ *Early May–Memorial Day and Labor Day–Oct.,*

HIGH SOCIETY ON THE MAIN LINE

"OLD MAIDS NEVER WED And Have Babies Period." With this mnemonic, Philadelphians were taught to remember the westward-bound stops along the main line of the Pennsylvania Railroad: Overbrook, Merion, Narberth, Wynnewood, Ardmore, Haverford, Bryn Mawr, and after unnamed others, Paoli.

In March 1823, the Pennsylvania legislature passed a charter for the construction of this, the state's first railroad, linking Philadelphia to Columbia via Lancaster, a distance of 82 miles. After the Civil War, genteel suburbs sprung up around the stations. The gracious estates with endless lawns and towering maples, the debutante balls and cricket clubs, were the province of wealthy Philadelphia families, like that of Nicholas Biddle, president of the Second Bank of the United States, and financier Anthony J. Drexel, founder of Drexel University. Philadelphia's social elite were attracted by what was touted as the benefits of healthy, yet cultivated, country living. The 1939 film *Philadelphia Story*, a depiction of Main Line society life, starred Katharine Hepburn, a graduate of **Bryn Mawr College,** (✉ 101 N. Merion Ave., Bryn Mawr), the first college for women that offered B.A. degrees. Founded in 1885 and modeled after Cambridge and Oxford colleges, Bryn Mawr introduced the "collegiate gothic" style of architecture to the United States. Nearby is the **Baldwin School** (✉ 701 W. Montgomery Ave., Bryn Mawr), which Miss Florence Baldwin began in 1888 as a prep school for the college. The Baldwin campus includes a five-story 1892 chateau-style structure designed by Philadelphia architect Frank Furness. Furness also built the massive Victorian redbrick clubhouse at the **Merion Cricket Club** (✉ Montgomery Ave. and Gray's La., Haverford). In the early 1900s the club drew crowds of 25,000 spectators to its matches; today its Great Lawn also hosts croquet matches and tennis events.

The main attraction of the Main Line is undoubtedly the **Barnes Foundation,** home to Albert C. Barnes' staggering collection of Impressionist and Postimpressionist art, considered to be one of the world's finest. The opulent **Chanticleer** (✉ 786 Church Rd., Wayne, ☎ 610/687–4163, WEB www.chanticleergarden.org) is a 31-acre pleasure garden circling a country estate; even the old tennis court has been transformed into a garden. There are woodland and water gardens, a Tropical Teacup exotic garden, and a Ruin Garden set among the remains of one of the family homes on the property. Chanticleer is open April through October, Wednesday through Saturday 10–5 (until 8 Friday, June through August); admission is $5.

Centuries before the socialites arrived, the Welsh Quakers settled on the Main Line on land granted by William Penn. Penn is said to have worshipped at the **Merion Friends Meeting** (✉ 615 Montgomery Ave., Merion, ☎ 610/664–4210), which is among the oldest Friends meeting houses in America. It was built between 1695 and 1704 in a Welsh-inspired architectural style. (Meetings for worship are Sunday at 11.) If you're lucky, Mother Divine herself will lead you on a fascinating tour of the well-preserved **Woodmont** (✉ 1622 Spring Mill Rd., Gladwyne, ☎ 610/525–5598), headquarters of Father Divine's Peace Mission Movement, a progressive religious and social movement that was in its heyday in the 1930s. Father Divine is buried in a mausoleum on the grounds of this striking 1892 Gothic manor house, a National Historic Landmark that was built by a steel baron for a million dollars. Woodmont is free and open Sunday 1–5 April through October, with weekday tours by appointment. Modest dress is required.

weekends 10–5; Memorial Day–Labor Day, Wed.–Sun. 10–5; guided tours on the hr.

First Union Science Park. A cooperative venture between the Franklin Institute Science Museum and the Please Touch Museum, the park presents interactive displays in an outdoor setting—which means children get a chance to run around and play while they learn. Swings demonstrate the laws of gravity and energy, and golf illustrates physics in motion. ⊠ *21st St. between Winter and Race Sts.* ⌖ *Free with admission to the Franklin Institute or the Please Touch Museum.* ⊙ *First Sat. in May–last Sun. in Oct., daily 9–4:30.*

★ ☽ ㉒ **Franklin Institute Science Museum.** Founded over 175 years ago to honor Benjamin Franklin, the institute is a science museum that is as clever as its namesake, thanks to an abundance of dazzling hands-on exhibits. To make the best use of your time, study the floor plan before you begin exploring. You can sit in the cockpit of a T-33 jet trainer, trace the route of a corpuscle through the world's largest artificial heart (15,000 times life size), and ride to nowhere on a 350-ton Baldwin steam locomotive. The many exhibits cover energy, motion, sound, physics, astronomy, aviation, ships, mechanics, electricity, time, and other scientific subjects. You'll also find a working weather station and the world's largest pinball machine. In **Franklin–He's Electric** you'll see the museum namesake's actual lightning rod and explore the areas that fascinated him, from optics, aquatics, and electricity to meteorology, music, and medicine. **The Sports Challenge** conveys the physics, physiology, and material science behind your favorite sport through such activities as simulating surfing, climbing a rock wall, and comparing your sneaker size to Shaquille O'Neal's size 22s or your dress size to skater Tara Lipinski's petite costume. The **Fels Planetarium** has shows about the stars, space exploration, comets, and other phenomena, plus laser light shows choreographed to rock-and-roll favorites on Friday and Saturday nights (the last show's at midnight). The **Mandell Center** includes the Cyberzone computer lab with 20 computers linked to the Web; Material Matters, a chemistry lesson; and the Tuttleman IMAX Theater, with a 79-ft domed screen and a 56-speaker high-tech sound system; recent movies include "Michael Jordan to the MAX," "Dolphins," and "Journey Into Amazing Caves." One don't-miss: the 30-ft statue of Benjamin Franklin. ⊠ *20th St. and Benjamin Franklin Pkwy.,* ☎ *215/448–1200; 215/448–1388 for laser show hot line,* WEB *www.fi.edu.* ⌖ *Ticket packages range from $9.75 to $14.75.* ⊙ *Daily 9:30–5. The Mandell Center and Omniverse Theater remain open until 9 Fri.–Sat.*

㉓ **Free Library of Philadelphia.** Philadelphia calls its vast public library system the "Fabulous Freebie." Founded in 1891, the central library has more than 1 million volumes. With its grand entrance hall, sweeping marble staircase, 30-ft ceilings, enormous reading rooms with long tables, and spiral staircases leading to balconies, this Greek Revival building looks the way libraries should. With more than 12,000 musical scores, the Edwin S. Fleisher Collection is the largest of its kind in the world. Tormented by a tune whose name you can't recall? Hum it to one of the Music Room's librarians, and he or she will track it down. The Department of Social Science and History has nearly 100,000 charts, maps, and guidebooks. The Newspaper Room stocks papers (back issues are on microfilm) from all major U.S. and foreign cities, some dating all the way to Colonial times. The Rare Book Room is a beautiful suite housing first editions of Dickens, ancient Sumerian clay tablets, illuminated medieval manuscripts, and more modern manuscripts, including Poe's *Murders in the Rue Morgue* and "The Raven."

With 100,000 books for children from preschool to eighth grade, the Children's Department houses the city's largest collection of children's books in a made-for-kids setting. Historical collections include copies of the Hardy Boys and Nancy Drew series, over which adults wax nostalgic. The foreign-language collection has children's books in more than 50 languages. The department also sponsors story hours and film festivals. ✉ *19th St. and Benjamin Franklin Pkwy.*, ☎ *215/686–5322,* WEB *www.library.phila.gov.* ☉ *Mon.–Thurs. 9–9, Fri. 9–6, Sat. 9–5, Sun. 1–5; late May–Sept., closed Sun.; tours of Rare Book Room weekdays at 11.*

NEED A BREAK?   Lunch in a supermarket? **Fresh Fields Whole Foods Market** (✉ 2001 Pennsylvania Ave., ☎ 215/557–0015) is no ordinary grocer, but an upscale, specialty market stocking mainly organic and natural foods. There are plenty of prepared salads and entrees for takeout and a bright café to enjoy them in. Note: Pennsylvania Avenue is located one block north of the Parkway.

⑱ Logan Circle. One of William Penn's five squares, Logan Circle was originally a burying ground and the site of a public execution by hanging in 1823. It found a fate better than death, though. In 1825 the square was named for James Logan, Penn's secretary; it later became a circle and is now one of the city's gems. The focal point of Logan Circle is the **Swann Fountain** of 1920, designed by Alexander Stirling Calder, son of Alexander Milne Calder, who created the William Penn statue atop City Hall. You'll find many works by a third generation of the family, noted modern sculptor Alexander Calder, the mobile- and stabile maker, in the nearby **Philadelphia Museum of Art.** The main figures in the fountain symbolize Philadelphia's three leading waterways: the Delaware and Schuylkill rivers and Wissahickon Creek. Around Logan Circle are some examples of Philadelphia's magnificent collection of outdoor art, including *General Galusha Pennypacker,* the Shakespeare Memorial (*Hamlet and the Fool,* by Alexander Stirling Calder), and *Jesus Breaking Bread.*

OFF THE BEATEN PATH   **MUTTER MUSEUM –** Skulls, antique microscopes, and a cancerous tumor removed from President Grover Cleveland's mouth in 1893 form just part of the unusual medical collection in the Mutter Museum, in the College of Physicians of Philadelphia, a few blocks south of the Please Touch Museum. The museum has hundreds of anatomical and pathological specimens, medical instruments, and organs removed from patients, including a piece of John Wilkes Booth's neck tissue. The collection contains 139 skulls; items that belonged to Marie Curie, Louis Pasteur, and Joseph Lister; and a 7'6"skeleton, the tallest on public exhibition in the United States. ✉ *19 S. 22nd St.,* ☎ *215/563–3737,* WEB *www. collphyphil.org.* ✍ *$8.* ☉ *Daily 10–5.*

★ ㉕ Philadelphia Museum of Art. The city's premier cultural attraction is one of the country's leading museums. Actually, one of the greatest treasures of the museum is the building itself. Constructed in 1928 of Minnesota dolomite, it's modeled after ancient Greek temples but on a grander scale. The museum was designed by Julian Francis Abele, the first African-American to graduate from the University of Pennsylvania School of Architecture. Covering 10 acres, it has 200 galleries and a collection of more than 300,000 works. You can enter the museum from the front or the rear; choose the front, and you can run up the 99 steps made famous in the movie *Rocky* (Rocky ran up only 72). From the expansive terrace look up to the pediment on your right, at a group of 13 glazed multicolor statues of classical gods. After passing Jacques Lipchitz's statue *Prometheus Strangling the Vulture,* climb the last flight of steps; before entering the museum, turn around to savor the impressive view down the parkway.

Once inside, you'll see the grand staircase and Saint-Gaudens's statue of *Diana;* she formerly graced New York's old Madison Square Garden. The museum has several outstanding permanent collections: the John G. Johnson Collection covers Western art from the Renaissance to the 19th century; the Arensberg and A. E. Gallatin collections contain modern and contemporary works by artists such as Brancusi, Braque, Matisse, and Picasso. Famous paintings in these collections include Van Eyck's *St. Francis Receiving the Stigmata,* Rubens's *Prometheus Bound,* Benjamin West's *Benjamin Franklin Drawing Electricity from the Sky,* van Gogh's *Sunflowers,* Cézanne's *The Large Bathers,* and Picasso's *Three Musicians.* Two important recent acquisitions are a John Singleton Copley painting, *Portrait of Mr. and Mrs. Thomas Mifflin,* and a marble bust of Ben Franklin by Jean-Antoine Houdon.

The enigmatic Marcel Duchamp, whose varied creations influenced many 20th-century artists, is a specialty of the house; the museum has the world's most extensive collection of his works, including the world-famous *Nude Descending a Staircase* and *The Bride Stripped Bare by Her Bachelors, Even.* Among the American art worth seeking out is a fine selection of the works by 19th-century Philadelphia artist Thomas Eakins, including *The Concert Singer* and some notable portraits. The most spectacular "objects" in the museum are entire structures and great rooms moved lock, stock, and barrel from around the world: a 12th-century French cloister, a 16th-century Indian temple hall, a 16th-century Japanese Buddhist temple, a 17th-century Chinese palace hall, and a Japanese ceremonial teahouse. Among the other collections are costumes, Early American furniture, and Amish and Shaker crafts. An unusual touch—and one that children especially like—is the Kienbusch Collection of Arms and Armor.

Pick up a map of the museum at either of the two entrances and wander on your own, or you can select from a variety of guided tours. You'll have at least one or two special exhibitions to choose from, too. About once a year, the museum hosts blockbuster exhibits, which require the purchase of advance tickets. Recent shows have included, "Van Gogh: Face to Face," "Delacroix: The Late Work," "Cèzanne," and "From Cézanne to Matisse: Great French Paintings from The Barnes Foundation." Every Wednesday evening, the museum throws a themed party including music, entertainment, films, tours, lectures, storytelling, demonstrations, poetry readings, food, and drink. The museum has a fine restaurant and a suprisingly good cafeteria. ✉ *26th St. and Benjamin Franklin Pkwy.,* ☎ *215/763–8100; 215/684–7500 for 24-hr taped message,* WEB *www.philamuseum.org.* ▤ *$8; free Sun. 10–1.* ☉ *Tues., Thurs.–Sun. 10–5, Wed. and Fri. 10–8:45.*

🖐 ㉓　**Please Touch Museum.** Philadelphia's children's museum, one of the country's best, is designed for youngsters ages 1–7. Highlights include Alice's Adventures in Wonderland, a 2,300-square-ft re-creation of Wonderland that encourages children to develop problem-solving and literacy skills; Sendak, an interactive exhibit of oversize settings and creatures from books by celebrated author-illustrator Maurice Sendak; and SuperMarket Science, with large shopping and kitchen play settings and a lab where science and math-related demonstrations are held. The museum also has a child-size television studio, an exhibit on transportation, a farm-theme area for toddlers, and interactive theater shows. The museum is planning to move to a new, larger facility on the Delaware River waterfront in spring 2004; it will be part of the planned Family Entertainment Center. ✉ *210 N. 21st St.,* ☎ *215/963–0667,* WEB *www.pleasetouchmuseum.org.* 🎫 *$8.95.* ⊙ *Sept.–June, daily 9–4:30; July–Aug., daily 9–6.*

★ ㉔ **Rodin Museum.** This jewel of a museum holds the best collection outside France of the work of sculptor Auguste Rodin (1840–1917). You'll pass through Rodin's *Gates of Hell*—a 21-ft-high sculpture with more than 100 human and animal figures—into an exhibition hall where the sculptor's masterworks are made even more striking by the use of light and shadow. Here are the French master's *The Kiss, The Burghers of Calais,* and *Eternal Springtime.* A small room is devoted to one of Rodin's most famous sitters, the French novelist Balzac. Photographs by Edward Steichen showing Rodin at work round out the collection. The museum occupies a 20th-century building designed by French architects Jacques Greber and Paul Cret. ✉ *22nd St. and Benjamin Franklin Pkwy.,* ☎ *215/763–8100,* WEB *www.rodinmuseum. org.* 🎫 *$3 donation requested.* ⊙ *Tues.–Sun. 10–5.*

FAIRMOUNT PARK
The Emerald City

Stretching from the edge of downtown to the city's northwest corner, Fairmount Park is the largest landscaped city park in the world. With more than 8,500 acres and 2 million trees (someone claims to have counted), the park winds along the banks of the Schuylkill River—which divides it into west and east sections—and through parts of the city. Quite a few city dwellers consider the park their backyard. On weekends the 4-mi stretch along Kelly Drive is crowded with joggers, bicycling moms and dads with children strapped into kiddie seats atop the back wheel, hand-holding senior citizens out for some fresh air, collegiate crew teams sculling along the river, and budding artists trying to capture the sylvan magic just as Thomas Eakins once did.

Fairmount Park encompasses natural areas—woodlands, meadows, rolling hills, two scenic waterways, and a forested 5½-mi gorge. It also contains tennis courts, ball fields, playgrounds, trails, exercise courses, several celebrated cultural institutions, and some historic Early American country houses that are operated by the Philadelphia Museum of Art and open to visitors. Philadelphia has more works of outdoor art than any other city in North America, and more than 200 of these works—including statues by Frederic Remington, Jacques Lipchitz, and Auguste Rodin—are scattered throughout Fairmount Park. Some sections of the park that border depressed urban neighborhoods are neglected, but it's better maintained along the Schuylkill.

The park was established in 1812 when the city purchased 5 acres behind Faire Mount, the hill upon which the Philadelphia Museum of Art now stands, for waterworks and public gardens. Through private bequests and public purchases (which continue today), it grew to its present size and stature.

The following tour highlights many of the park's treasures. You can tour by car (get a good city map), starting near the Philadelphia Museum of Art. Signs help point the way, and the historic houses have free parking. Before you set out, call **Park House Information** (☎ 215/684–7926), to find out which historic houses are open that day and what special events are planned. Another option is to take the narrated tour given by Philadelphia Trolley Works (board it at the Philadelphia Museum of Art or at John F. Kennedy Plaza, at 16th Street and John

Fairmount Park

TO EAST
FALLS BRIDGE

**Laurel Hill
Cemetery** ▪

TO THE
WISSAHICKON

I-76

13

US 13

Lehigh Ave.

Strawberry
Mansion Br.

Monument Rd.

Ford Rd.

Chamounix Dr.

Schuylkill Expwy.

West River Dr.

Cumberland St.

Ridge Ave.

Dauphin St.

31st St.

29th St.

9

8

7

*East Park
Reservoir*

Diamond St.

Kelly Dr.

33rd St.

Reservoir Dr.

13

Sedgley Ave.

Montgomery Ave.

Glenwood Ave.

Oxford Ave.

Belmont Ave.

I-76

10

11

12

North Concourse Dr.

South Concourse Dr.

13

15

Schuylkill River

6

14

16

Thompson St.

Girard Ave.

Cambridge St.

30

Girard Ave.

41st St.

40th St.

30

17

30

Zoological Ave.

13

4

5

3

Brown St.

48th St.

Lancaster Ave.

Parrish St.

39th St.

Mantua Ave.

I-76

30

34th St.

33rd St.

31st St.

2

1

N

0 _____ 1 mile

0 _____ 1 km

13

30

F. Kennedy Boulevard). The trolley bus visits many of these sites, and you can get on and off all day for $10. Also, the Philadelphia Museum of Art has a two-hour guided tour of three park houses. For tickets, call 215/235–7469.

Numbers in the text correspond to numbers in the margin and on the Fairmount Park map.

A Good Drive

Your visit can start where the park began, at **Faire Mount** ①. If it's a nice day, you could begin this outing with a short walk before you set off by car. Park behind the art museum and walk down the stairs. To your right is the museum's Azalea Garden, designed in the English romantic style. Straight ahead, overlooking the Schuylkill River, is the **Fairmount Waterworks** ②, an elegant group of Greek Revival buildings. A few steps north of the Waterworks you'll see the Victorian structures of **Boathouse Row** ③; watch for rowers on the river here, too. Walking north along Kelly Drive, alongside the river, you soon reach the **Ellen Phillips Samuel Memorial Sculpture Garden** ④, with works by 16 artists.

Now's the time to walk back to your car for a driving tour of East Fairmount Park. Follow Kelly Drive to the end of Boathouse Row; turn right up the hill to a Federal-style country house, **Lemon Hill** ⑤. Head back to Kelly Drive, turn right, pass through the rock archway, and turn right again at the equestrian statue of Ulysses S. Grant. The first left takes you to **Mt. Pleasant** ⑥, a Georgian mansion. Continue along the road that runs to the right of the house (as you face it) past Rockland, a handsome Federal house that's currently closed. At the dead end turn left onto Reservoir Drive. You'll pass the redbrick Georgian-style Ormiston, also closed. Take the next left, Randolph Drive, to another Georgian house, **Laurel Hill** ⑦, on Edgely Drive, which becomes Dauphin Street. Just about 10 ft before reaching 33rd Street, turn left on Strawberry Mansion Drive, and you're at **Woodford** ⑧, which has an interesting collection of household goods. A quarter mile northwest of Woodford stands the house that gave its name to the nearby section of Philadelphia, **Strawberry Mansion** ⑨. It has furniture from three periods of its history.

If you're a fan of historic cemeteries, you can visit Laurel Hill Cemetery before you cross the river to West Fairmount Park. Drive back down the driveway of Strawberry Mansion, turn left at the stop sign, and follow the narrow road as it winds right to the light. Turn left onto Ridge Avenue and follow it to the entrance gate, which sits between eight Greek columns. To skip the cemetery and continue your tour, proceed down the Strawberry Mansion driveway to the stop sign, turn left, and follow the road as it loops down and around to the Strawberry Mansion Bridge. Cross the river and follow the road; when it splits, stay left. You'll come to Chamounix Drive, a long straightaway. Turn left and then left again on Belmont Mansion Drive for a fine view from **Belmont Plateau** ⑩. Follow Belmont Mansion Drive down the hill. Where it forks, stay to the left, cross Montgomery Drive, and bear left to reach the **Horticulture Center** ⑪ with its greenhouse and garden. Loop all the way around the Horticulture Center to visit the serene **Japanese House** ⑫ and its waterfall and gardens.

Drive back around the Horticulture Center and continue through the gates to Montgomery Drive. Turn left and then left again at the first light (Belmont Avenue). Turn left again on North Concourse Drive. On your left is **Memorial Hall** ⑬, a building from the 1876 Centennial Exposition. The two towers just ahead are part of the **Smith Civil War**

Memorial ⑭. Turn left just past them to see furniture from over the centuries at **Cedar Grove** ⑮. Just south of Cedar Grove, atop a hill sloping down to the Schuylkill, is a Federal mansion, **Sweetbriar** ⑯. Continue past the house, make the first left, and turn left again at the stop sign onto Lansdowne Drive. Follow the signs straight ahead to the **Philadelphia Zoo** ⑰. If you enjoy hiking, you could continue on to the Wissahickon, in the northwest section of Fairmount Park.

TIMING

Any time but winter is a fine time to explore the great outdoors in Fairmount Park. In spring the cherry blossoms are lovely; in fall the changing leaves blaze with color. In winter you can explore the indoors, on Christmas tours of the historic houses. Hikers, bikers, and joggers will enjoy a recreational trail that connects Bartram's Garden in Southwest Philadelphia with Valley Forge National Historical Park west of the city. If you leave the driving to the Philadelphia Trolley Works, your narrated tour will take just 40 minutes. If you drive, after you've explored Kelly Drive on foot, you'll need about two hours. Add another 20–30 minutes for each historic house you tour. Because each property keeps its own quirky schedule, it's hard to choose one day that's best for seeing the interiors, although a summer weekend is your best bet. Animal lovers can spend half a day at the Philadelphia Zoo.

Sights to See

⑩ **Belmont Plateau.** Literally the high point of your park tour, Belmont Plateau has a view from 243 ft above river level. In front of you lie the park, the Schuylkill River winding down to the Philadelphia Museum of Art, and—4 mi away—the Philadelphia skyline. ⊠ *Belmont Mansion Dr., West Fairmount Park.*

❸ **Boathouse Row.** These architecturally varied 19th-century buildings— in Victorian Gothic, Gothic Revival, and Italianate styles—are home to the rowing clubs that make up the "Schuylkill Navy," an association of boating clubs organized in 1858. The view of the boathouses from the west side of the river is splendid—especially at night, when they're outlined with hundreds of small lights. The row's newest addition, Lloyd Hall, has a gymnasium, bicycle and skate rentals in season, and a two-story café overlooking the river. ⊠ *Kelly Dr., East Fairmount Park.*

⑮ **Cedar Grove.** Five styles of furniture—Jacobean, William and Mary, Queen Anne, Chippendale, and Federal—reflect the accumulations of five generations of the Paschall-Morris family. The house stood in Frankford, in northeastern Philadelphia, for 180 years before being moved to this location in 1927. ⊠ *Lansdowne Dr. off N. Concourse Dr., West Fairmount Park,* ☎ *215/235–7469,* WEB *www.philamuseum. org/collections/parkhouse.* ☞ *$2.50.* ☉ *Tues.–Sun. 10–5.*

❹ **Ellen Phillips Samuel Memorial Sculpture Garden.** Bronze and granite sculptures by 16 artists stand in a series of tableaux and groupings on riverside terraces. Portraying American themes and traits, they include *The Quaker,* by Harry Rosen; *Birth of a Nation,* by Henry Kreis; and *Spirit of Enterprise,* by Jacques Lipchitz. ⊠ *Kelly Dr., East Fairmount Park.*

❶ **Faire Mount.** This is now the site of the Philadelphia Museum of Art. In 1812 a reservoir was built here to distribute water throughout the city.

★ ❷ **Fairmount Waterworks.** Designed by Frederick Graff, this National Historic Engineering Landmark built in 1815 was the first steam-pumping station of its kind in the country. The notable assemblage of Greek

Revival buildings—one of the city's most beautiful sights—has undergone a $23 million renovation. The revamped Fairmount Water Works, located just behind the Philadelphia Museum of Art, houses an upscale restaurant and casual pub in its former engine house, an interpretive center, an art gallery, and an information center. On weekends there's an outdoor marketplace with crafts, flowers, souvenirs, and pastries; musicians, jugglers, and mimes provide free entertainment on the deck of the New Mill House. The decks reopened in 2001; the restaurant and other attractions are scheduled to debut in the spring of 2002. ✉ *Waterworks Dr., off Kelly Dr.,* ☎ *215/685–0000,* WEB *www.parkalacarte.com.*

⑪ **Horticulture Center.** On the Horticulture Center's 22 wooded acres are a butterfly garden, a greenhouse where plants and flowers used on city property are grown, and a pavilion in the trees for bird-watching from the woodland canopy. Don't miss the whimsical *Seaweed Girl* fountain in the display house. The center stands on the site of the 1876 Centennial Exposition's Horticultural Hall ✉ *N. Horticultural Dr., West Fairmount Park,* ☎ *215/685–0096.* ☐ *Free.* ☉ *Visitor center and greenhouses, daily 9–3; grounds, daily 9–6.*

⑫ **Japanese House.** This reconstructed 16th-century samurai's dwelling, built in Japan, was exhibited temporarily at the Museum of Modern Art in New York, then reassembled here in 1958. The architectural setting and the waterfall, gardens, Japanese trees, and pond make a serene contrast to the busy city. The house is called Shofu-So, which means "pine breeze villa." A recent renovation gave the home a roof made of the bark of hinoki, a cypress that grows only in the mountains of Japan. Call ahead to see if a traditional tea ceremony is scheduled. ✉ *Lansdowne Dr. east of Belmont Ave., West Fairmount Park,* ☎ *215/878–5097,* WEB *www.shofuso.org.* ☐ *$2.50.* ☉ *May–Oct., Tues.–Sun. 10–4.*

❼ **Laurel Hill.** Built around 1767, this Georgian house on a laurel-covered hill overlooking the Schuylkill River once belonged to Dr. Philip Syng Physick (also owner of Society Hill's Physick House). On some Sunday evenings during the summer, Women for Greater Philadelphia sponsors candlelight chamber music concerts here. ✉ *E. Edgely Dr., East Fairmount Park,* ☎ *215/235–1776,* WEB *www.philamuseum.org/collections/parkhouse.* ☐ *$2.50.* ☉ *Apr.– Dec., Sat. 10–4, Sun. 12–4.*

OFF THE
BEATEN PATH

LAUREL HILL CEMETERY – John Notman, architect of the Athenaeum and many other noted local buildings, designed Laurel Hill in 1836. The cemetery is an important example of an early rural burial ground and the first cemetery in America designed by an architect. Its rolling hills overlooking the Schuylkill River, its rare trees, and its monuments and mausoleums sculpted by greats such as Notman, Alexander Milne Calder, Alexander Stirling Calder, William Strickland, and Thomas U. Walter made it a popular picnic spot in the 19th century; today it's a great place for a stroll. Those buried in this 99-acre necropolis include prominent Philadelphians and Declaration of Independence signers. Burials still take place here. ✉ *3822 Ridge Ave.,* ☎ *215/228–8200; 215/228–8817 for tours through the Friends of Laurel Hill Cemetery; walking tour brochure available from office for $2.* ☉ *Weekdays 8–4:30, Sat. 9–1:30.*

❺ **Lemon Hill.** An impressive example of a Federal-style country house, Lemon Hill was built in 1800 on a 350-acre farm. Its most distinctive features are oval parlors with concave doors and the entrance hall's checkerboard floor of Valley Forge marble. ✉ *Poplar Dr., East Fairmount Park,* ☎ *215/232–4337,* WEB *www.philamuseum.org/collections/parkhouse.* ☐ *$2.50.* ☉ *Apr.–mid-Dec., Wed.–Sun. 10–4.*

⑬ **Memorial Hall.** Architect Hermann J. Schwarzmann's grand stone building with a glass dome and Palladian windows served as an art museum during the Philadelphia Centennial Exposition, a celebration of the nation's 100th birthday. Close to 10 million people attended the exposition to see the novel exhibits of machinery, produce, and art sent by foreign countries. The hall, a notable example of beaux arts architecture, influenced the design of many American and European museums and government buildings. It is the only major building remaining from the event; you can walk in and look around. ⊠ *N. Concourse Dr., West Fairmount Park,* ☎ *215/685–0000.* ☉ *Weekdays 9–4.*

❻ **Mt. Pleasant.** Built in 1761 by John Macpherson, a Scottish sea captain, Mt. Pleasant is one of the finest examples of Georgian architecture in the country. The historically accurate furnishings are culled from the Philadelphia Museum of Art's collection of Philadelphia Chippendale furniture. According to legend, Revolutionary War traitor Benedict Arnold once purchased this house as an engagement gift for Peggy Shippen, but he was banished before the deal was signed. ⊠ *Mt. Pleasant Dr., East Fairmount Park,* ☎ *215/235–7469,* WEB *www.philamuseum.org/ collections/parkhouse.* ☑ *$2.50.* ☉ *Tues.–Sun. 10–5.*

★ ☺ ⑰ **Philadelphia Zoo.** Chartered in 1859 and opened in 1874, America's first zoo is home to more than 2,000 animals representing six continents. It's small and well-landscaped enough to feel pleasantly intimate, and the naturalistic habitats allow you to get close enough to hear the animals breathe. At each exhibit an old-fashioned Talking Storybook provides narration when activated by an elephant-shape key. The Amphibian and Reptile House houses 87 species, from 15-ft-long snakes to frogs the size of a dime. The state-of-the-art 2½-acre Primate Reserve is home to 11 primate species from around the world. Notable attractions include the zoo's rare white lions; Carnivore Kingdom, where meat eaters prowl just inches away; a terrific Bird House; and the African Plains, stomping ground of giraffes and zebras. The recently renovated Rare Animal Conservation Center houses a collection of rare and endangered species, including Matschie's tree-kangaroos and blue-eyed lemurs, along with seriously ugly naked mole rats. Children can climb inside a four-story tree, hatch from an egg, and ride a dinosaur in the Treehouse. The Children's Zoo has pony rides and a barnyard animal petting and feeding area. Set in a lovely 42-acre Victorian garden, the zoo has trees dating from the 18th century. ⊠ *34th St. and Girard Ave., West Fairmount Park,* ☎ *215/243–1100,* WEB *www.phillyzoo.org.* ☑ *$10.95; Treehouse $1 additional.* ☉ *Feb.–Nov., weekdays 9:30–5, weekends 9:30–6; Dec.–Feb., daily 10–4.*

⑭ **Smith Civil War Memorial.** Built from 1897 to 1912 with funds donated by wealthy foundry owner Richard Smith, the memorial honors Pennsylvania heroes of the Civil War. Among those immortalized in bronze are Generals Meade and Hancock—and Smith himself. At the base of each tower is a curved wall with a bench. If you sit at one end and listen to a person whispering at the other end, you'll understand why they're called the Whispering Benches. Unfortunately, the litter around the site reflects its location near an economically struggling neighborhood. ⊠ *N. Concourse Dr., West Fairmount Park.*

❾ **Strawberry Mansion.** The largest mansion in Fairmount Park has furniture from the three main phases of its history: Federal, Regency, and Empire. In the parlor is a collection of rare Tucker porcelain; the attic holds fine antique dolls. ⊠ *Near 33rd and Dauphin Sts., East Fairmount Park,* ☎ *215/228–8364,* WEB *www.philamuseum.org/collections/ parkhouse.* ☑ *$2.50.* ☉ *Tues.–Sun. 10–4.*

⑯ **Sweetbriar.** This three-story Federal mansion dating from 1797 was the first year-round residence in what is now Fairmount Park. It was built by Samuel and Jean Breck to escape the yellow fever epidemic that ravaged the city. ✉ *Lansdowne Dr. off N. Concourse Dr., West Fairmount Park,* ☎ *215/222–1333,* WEB *www.philamuseum.org/ collections/parkhouse.* ⊡ *$2.50.* ⊙ *Apr.–June, by appointment; July– Dec., Wed.–Sun. 10–4.*

OFF THE
BEATEN PATH

THE WISSAHICKON – Of the Philadelphia areas that William Penn encountered, the Wissahickon has changed the least. In the northwestern section of Fairmount Park, this gorge was carved out by the Wissahickon Creek—5½ mi of towering trees, cliffs, trails, and animals. You can easily visualize the Leni-Lenape who lived here and gave the creek its name. Many inns once stood along the banks of the Wissahickon; only two remain. One is now a police station; the other is the **Valley Green Inn** (✉ Springfield Ave. and Wissahickon Creek, ☎ 215/247– 1730), built in 1850. It is in one of the loveliest parts of the Wissahickon gorge. You can sit on a bench alongside the creek, look at the stone bridge reflected in the water, and savor the tranquillity of this spot.

Forbidden Drive, a dirt-and-gravel pathway along the west side of the creek, is a haunt of joggers, bikers, horseback riders, fishermen, and nature lovers. There are foot trails along both sides of the creek and interesting statues along the route. Walking less than a half mile south of the Valley Green Inn brings you to Devil's Pool; Shakespeare Rock, with a quotation carved on its face; and Hermit's Cave, where German mystic Johannes Kelpius and his followers came in 1694 to await the millennium. A visit to Historic RittenhouseTown, America's first paper mill, requires a 3-mi hike south. To the north of the inn are Indian Rock and a covered bridge that was built around 1855, the last still standing within the boundaries of a major American city.

You'll need a car to get here: to reach Valley Green Inn from downtown, take the Schuylkill Expressway west to the Lincoln Drive–Wissahickon Park exit (Exit 32). Follow Lincoln Drive to Allen's Lane, then turn right. At Germantown Avenue turn left, go about a mile, turn left at Springfield Avenue, and follow it to the end. A map of the Wissahickon showing all the trails and sites can be purchased for $5 at the Valley Green Inn's snack-booth window, open daily in warmer months from 9 to 5, weekends only the rest of the year.

❽ **Woodford.** The Naomi Wood collection of antique household goods, including Colonial furniture, unusual clocks, and English delftware, can be seen in this fine Georgian mansion built about 1756. ✉ *Near 33rd and Dauphin Sts., East Fairmount Park,* ☎ *215/229–6115,* WEB *www.philamuseum.org/collections/parkhouse.* ⊡ *$2.50.* ⊙ *Tues.– Sun. 10–4.*

SOUTHWARK AND SOUTH PHILADELPHIA

Strutting South of South

Two of the city's most interesting neighborhoods lie south of South Street—Southwark and South Philadelphia. Southwark, stretching from Front to 6th Street and from South Street to Washington Avenue, was the center of the commercial and ship-building activity that made Philadelphia the biggest port in the Colonies and in the young United States. One of the oldest sections of the city, Southwark was already settled by the Swedes when the English arrived; the Swedish influence shows in street names such as Swanson, Christian, and Queen.

Directly south of Society Hill, Southwark is neither as glamorous nor as historically renowned as its neighbor. Chiseled in stone on one facade are these words: ON THIS SITE IN 1879, NOTHING HAPPENED! But like Society Hill, Southwark's Queen Village neighborhood has been gentrified by young professionals; the restoration attracted chic restaurants and interesting shops.

Through the years South Philadelphia has absorbed boatloads of immigrants—European Jews, Italians, and most recently, Asians. The city's Little Italy, it is a huge area of identical row houses, many with gleaming white marble steps, stretching south and west of Southwark. At the heart of the neighborhood, along 9th Street, is the outdoor Italian Market, packed with vendors hawking crabs and octopus, eggplants and tomatoes. From butcher shop windows hang skinned animals; cheese shops are crammed with barrels of olives. Sylvester Stallone walked along 9th Street in the films *Rocky* and *Rocky II,* and almost every campaigning president has visited the market on his swing through Philadelphia. It's a great photo op for them—and for you.

Although there are chic eateries in South Philadelphia, the majority of the neighborhood restaurants are not fancy (decor such as red-checked vinyl tablecloths and plastic grapes hanging from plastic vines is not uncommon), but the food can be terrific and—more important—authentic. You'll wonder if Mama is in the kitchen preparing a southern Italian specialty just for you. This is the neighborhood that gave the world Mario Lanza, Bobby Rydell, Frankie Avalon, and Fabian, and some area restaurants proudly display gold records earned by these neighborhood celebrities. Plenty of locals and visitors alike head for South Philly's competing culinary shrines, Pat's King of Steaks and Geno's, both at the corner of 9th Street and Passyunk Avenue. One of their cheese steaks makes a perfect prelude to an evening spent at the city's sports complexes, at the southern end of South Philadelphia.

A Good Walk

A leisurely stroll through Southwark and South Philadelphia is a fun day's outing. From Bainbridge Street, proceed south (right turn) on 2nd Street, which old-timers call Two Street. The homes along these streets are the oldest in the city, dating from the mid-1700s. Even when their construction dates are not chiseled on the facades, the settling bricks above the overhangs, the crooked windows, and the shutters that don't hang straight all attest to their vintage. Turn east (left) on Catharine Street and then south (right) on Hancock Street, one of the most charming streets in the city. The tiny clapboard houses at Numbers 813 and 815 were built by a shipwright and are the last of their type. Detour onto Queen Street to see the old firehouse with gas lamps at Number 117. It has been beautifully converted to a single-family home.

Continue down Hancock to Christian Street; go east (left) about one block (under the I–95 overpass) to Swanson Street. Here is **Gloria Dei,** the oldest church in Pennsylvania. Return to 2nd Street by way of Christian Street and walk south (left turn), past a neighborhood landmark, the Shot Tower, where lead shot was made during the War of 1812. At Washington Avenue is the **Mummers Museum,** where you can get a feeling for this local institution. From the museum walk west on Washington Avenue to 9th Street and then proceed north to the five-block-long open-air **Italian Market.** At Christian Street walk east to 5th Street, half a block north to Queen Street, and then east again to the **Mario Lanza Museum,** with memorabilia and photos of the singer.

Following 4th Street north will bring you back to South Street. Dry-goods merchants line 4th Street south of South Street in an area called Fabric Row; you'll find an amazing variety of designer and ethnic textiles, upholstery, and draperies.

TIMING

It's best to visit this neighborhood Tuesday through Saturday, because the Italian Market is closed Sunday afternoon and Monday and the Mummers Museum is closed Sundays in July and August and every Monday. Start early—the Italian Market winds down by mid-afternoon—and allow three–four hours.

Sights to See

Gloria Dei. One of the few remnants of the Swedes who settled Pennsylvania before William Penn, Gloria Dei (Old Swedes') Church was organized in 1642. Built in 1698, the church has numerous intriguing religious artifacts, such as a 1608 Bible once owned by Sweden's Queen Christina. The carvings on the lectern and balcony were salvaged from the congregation's first church, which was destroyed by fire. Models of two of the ships that transported the first Swedish settlers hang from the ceiling—right in the center of the church. Grouped around the church are the parish hall, the caretaker's house, the rectory, and the guild house. The church sits in the center of its graveyard; it forms a picture that is pleasing in its simplicity and tranquillity. ⊠ *916 Swanson St., near Christian St. and Columbus Blvd.,* ☎ *215/389–1513,* WEB *www.nps.gov/glde.* ⊡ *Free.* ☉ *Daily 9–5, but call first.*

Italian Market. It's more Naples than Philadelphia: Vendors crowd the sidewalks and spill out onto the streets; live crabs and caged chickens wait for the kill; picture-perfect produce is piled high. The market dates back to the turn of the century, when it was founded by Italian immigrants. You'll find imported and domestic products, kitchenware, fresh pastas, cheeses, spices, meats, fruits and vegetables, and dry goods. These days the market has lost some of its charm; food stalls share the already crowded street with vendors selling bootleg CDs, logo T-shirts, and dollar-store bargains, but it's still enjoyable to stroll and to duck into a cheese or spice shop. ⊠ *9th St. between Washington Ave. and Christian St.,* WEB *www.phillyitalianmarket.com.* ☉ *Tues.–Sat., 9–late afternoon; Sun. 9–12:30.*

Mario Lanza Museum. In this museum devoted to the famous tenor and Hollywood star (1921–59), you'll find thousands of photos, memorabilia, videocassette showings of Lanza's films, and souvenirs for sale. Lanza was supposedly moving a piano into the Academy of Music when he seized the opportunity to sing from its stage—and was first discovered. Arturo Toscanini said that Lanza had perhaps the greatest natural voice of the century. Lanza's birthplace, at 634 Christian Street, is a few blocks away. ⊠ *In the Settlement Music School, 416 Queen St.,* ☎ *215/468–3623.* ⊡ *Free.* ☉ *Sept.–June, Mon.–Sat. 10–3:30; July–Aug., weekdays 10–3.*

NEED A BREAK?

When your walking tour is over, reward yourself with a dessert that doubles as a work of art at the **Pink Rose Pastry Shop** (⊠ 630 S. 4th St., ☎ 215/592–0565). Check out the white chocolate raspberry mousse cake.

☼ **Mummers Museum.** Even if you aren't in Philadelphia on New Year's Day, you can still experience this unique local institution and phenomenon. Famous for extravagant sequin-and-feather costumes and string bands, the Mummers spend the year preparing for an all-day parade up Market Street on January 1. The museum has costumes, photos of parades, and audiovisual displays of Mummerabilia. You can push buttons to compose your own Mummers medley, with banjos, saxophones, and xylophones, and you can dance the Mummers strut to the strains of "Oh, Dem Golden Slippers." A 45-inch screen shows filmed highlights of past parades.

Early English settlers brought to the Colonies their Christmastime custom of dressing in costume and performing pantomimes—the name Mummers derives from the German *mumme,* meaning "mask or disguise." In Philadelphia, families would host costume parties on New Year's Day; on January 1, 1876, the first individual groups paraded informally through the city. The parade caught on, and by 1901 the city officially sanctioned the parade and 42 Mummers clubs strutted for cash prizes.

In recent years the Mummers have staged a summer Mummers Parade around July 4 (during the city's Welcome America! celebration); in late February they present the "Show of Shows" at the Spectrum. The latter is a chance to hear the original 16 string bands perform indoors. The museum presents free outdoor concerts (weather permitting) on most Tuesday evenings 8–10 from May to September. ✉ *1100 S. 2nd St., at Washington Ave.,* ☎ *215/336–3050,* WEB *www.riverfrontmummers. com/museum.html.* ☎ *$2.50.* ◷ *Sept.–June, Tues.–Sat. 9:30–5, Sun. noon–5; July–Aug., Tues.–Sat. 9:30–5.*

UNIVERSITY CITY

University City is the portion of West Philadelphia that includes the campuses of the University of Pennsylvania, Drexel University, and the Philadelphia College of Pharmacy and Science. It also has the University City Science Center (a leading think tank), the Annenberg Center performing arts complex (part of the University of Pennsylvania), an impressive collection of Victorian houses, and a variety of moderately priced restaurants, movie theaters, stores, and lively bars catering to more than 32,000 students and other residents. The neighborhood stretches from the Schuylkill River west to 44th Street and from the river north to Powelton Avenue.

This area was once the city's flourishing western suburbs, where wealthy Philadelphians built grand estates and established summer villages. It officially became part of the city in 1854. Twenty years later the University of Pennsylvania moved its campus here from the center of the city. The university moved into many of the historic homes, while others were adopted by fraternities. There are still many privately owned, architecturally exciting properties, particularly on Locust, Spruce, and Pine streets. Other areas of West Philadelphia beyond University City are, however, less prosperous today.

Penn has spruced up its campus with the Sansom Common development (between Walnut and Sansom streets, and 36th and 37th streets), which includes shops, a bookstore, and a hotel, the Inn at Penn. To promote University City's visual and performing arts and its international restaurants, the University City District has created a monthly event, Go West! Go International! Third Thursdays (www.gowest.org), modeled after Old City's First Fridays. Museums and galleries host special events the third Thursday of the month (4 PM–8 PM) and stay open late, and restaurants offer special discounts and activities. Metered parking is free after 5 PM and a shuttle bus makes a continuous loop around the neighborhood. **Penn's Information Center** (☎ 215/898–4636) is at 34th and Walnut streets.

A Good Walk

This walk through University City takes in the Ivy League campus of the University of Pennsylvania, where ivy really does cling to many buildings. Begin at the University's **Institute of Contemporary Art,** at 36th and Sansom streets. Walk east (down the hill) on Sansom Street to 34th Street and turn right (south). At 220 South 34th Street is the historic Furness Building, which houses the **Arthur Ross Gallery** and the **Fisher Fine Arts Library.** When you exit the building, you're in the heart of the University of Pennsylvania campus at the edge of College Green (Blanche Levy Park). You'll see a statue of Benjamin Franklin, who founded the university in 1740, in the middle of the green. To your right, the huge Van Pelt Library stretches from 34th Street to 36th Street. In front of it is Claes Oldenburg's *Broken Button.* To your left is College Hall, an administration building said to be the inspiration for the scary Addams House in cartoonist Charles Addams's work. Where the walk splits, stay right. Just west of 36th Street, the Annenberg School of Communications and the Annenberg Center are to the right; the famed Wharton School of Economics, to the left. As you pass the intersection of 37th Street, say hello to the statue of Ben Franklin sitting on a bench. A footbridge takes you over 38th Street (turn around for a good view of Center City) to Superblock, three high-rise student dormitories. Locust Walk ends at 40th Street with the dental school and a row of stores and restaurants.

Follow Locust Walk back to 37th Street and walk south (right) to Spruce Street. The Gothic sprawl ahead of you is the Quad, the university's first dorm buildings. Designed by Cope and Stewardson in 1895, the Quad became the prototype of the collegiate Gothic style prevalent in campuses coast to coast. These dormitory buildings—awash with gargoyles and gables—easily conjure up the England of everyone's dreams. South of the Quad on Hamilton Walk, you're smack back in the 20th century, thanks to Louis Kahn's Alfred Newton Richards Medical Research Laboratories building, a masterpiece by this important architect. Kahn, a brilliant teacher and architectural theorist, did not leave many completed buildings.

Head back to Spruce Street and turn right (east) to 33rd Street to explore the **University Museum of Archaeology and Anthropology,** which holds everything from mummies to Mayan artifacts. Just across the street you see Franklin Field, the university's football stadium. Following 33rd Street north back to Walnut Street brings you to the Moore School of Engineering, home of the post–World War II era **ENIAC,** the world's first all-electronic general-purpose digital computer.

TIMING

University City is at its best when college is in session; the students rushing to classes give this area its flavor. Allow half an hour each in the Arthur Ross Gallery and the Institute of Contemporary Art, two hours in the University Museum, and an hour exploring the campus. If your time is limited, skip all but the University Museum, a don't-miss for the archaeologically inclined.

Sights to See

Arthur Ross Gallery. Penn's official art gallery showcases treasures from the university's collections and traveling exhibitions. The gallery shares its historic landmark building, designed by Frank Furness, with the **Fisher Fine Arts Library.** ⊠ *220 S. 34th St.,* ☎ *215/898–2083.* ▨ *Free.* ☉ *Tues.–Fri. 10–5, weekends noon–5.*

ENIAC. Here's a chance for computer aficionados to see the place where the computer age dawned. During World War II engineers at the Moore School of Engineering at the University of Pennsylvania undertook a secret project to develop the world's first all-electronic, large-scale general-purpose digital computer. They called it ENIAC, an acronym for electronic numerical integrator and calculator. The largest electronic machine in the world, it weighed 30 tons and contained 18,000 vacuum tubes—one of which burned out every few seconds when ENIAC was first built. Although most of ENIAC is now in the Smithsonian Institution, a small portion is still on view at the Moore School. Photos and informative signs tell ENIAC's story. ⊠ *Moore School of Electrical Engineering, 200 S. 33rd St., enter on 33rd St. just below Walnut St.,* ☎ *215/898–2492.* ▨ *Free.* ☉ *By appointment only.*

Fisher Fine Arts Library. One of the finest examples remaining of the work of Philadelphia architect Frank Furness, this was the most innovative library building in the country when it was completed in 1890. It was the first library to separate the reading room and the stacks. Peek into the catalog room, dominated by a huge fireplace, and the reading room, with study alcoves lit from the lead-glass windows above. The unusual exterior stirred controversy when it was built: note the terra-cotta panels, short heavy columns, and gargoyles on the north end. ⊠ *220 S. 34th St.,* ☎ *215/898–8325,* WEB *www.library.upenn.edu/ finearts.* ▨ *Free.* ☉ *Sept.–mid-May, Mon.–Thurs. 8:30 AM–midnight, Fri. 8:30–8, Sat. noon–8, Sun. noon–midnight; mid-May–late Aug., Mon.–Fri. 9–7, Closed Sat.–Sun.*

NEED A
BREAK?

From 10 AM to 10 PM, you can refuel at **Moravian Cafes at Sansom Commons** (⊠ 3409 Walnut St.), a food court with the requisite pizza, ice cream, steak sandwich, salad, and coffee counters.

Institute of Contemporary Art. This museum, part of the University of Pennsylvania, has established a reputation for identifying promising artists and exhibiting them at a critical point in their careers. Among the artists who have had shows at ICA and later gone on to international prominence are Andy Warhol, Robert Mapplethorpe, and Laurie Anderson. ⊠ *118 S. 36th St., at Sansom St.,* ☎ *215/898–7108,* WEB *www.icaphila.org.* ▨ *$3.* ☉ *Wed.–Fri. noon–8, weekends 11–5.*

★ ☼ **University Museum of Archaeology and Anthropology.** Indiana Jones, look out! Rare treasures from the deepest jungles and ancient tombs make this one of the finest archaeological/anthropological museums in the world. The collection of more than a million objects, gathered largely during worldwide expeditions by University of Pennsylvania scholars, includes a 12-ton sphinx from Egypt, a crystal ball once owned by China's Dowager Empress, the world's oldest writing—Sumerian cuneiform clay tablets—and the 4,500-year-old golden jewels from the royal tombs of the kingdom of Ur. The museum has a superb collection of Chinese monumental (large-scale) art and more than 400 artifacts in its Ancient Greek World section. *Canaan and Ancient Israel* showcases ancient pottery, statuary, jewelry, weapons and more, with some artifacts dating from as early as 3000 BC, and includes a full-scale reconstruction of a house of the biblical period. Children run to *The Egyptian Mummy: Secrets and Science* and to *Living in Balance: The Universe of the Hopi, Zuni, Navajo, and Apache.* The museum has two gift shops and a café. ⊠ *33rd and Spruce Sts.,* ☎ *215/ 898–4001,* WEB *www.upenn.edu/museum.* ▨ *$5, free Sun..* ☉ *Labor Day–Memorial Day, Tues.–Sat. 10–4:30, Sun. 1–5; Memorial Day–Labor Day, Tues.–Sat. 10–4:30.*

MANAYUNK: FROM MILL TOWN TO HOT SPOT

FOR MANY PEOPLE, Manayunk's Main Street has replaced South Street as the "hippest street in town." In this former mill town along the banks of the Schuylkill River, 7 mi northwest of Center City, more than 30 restaurants compete for attention with alfresco dining, creative menus, and valet parking. Most of the 80-plus stores are one-of-a-kind; among them are art galleries, antiques shops, and clothing boutiques. On the weekends you'll be strolling with hundreds of visitors—and fighting with them for parking spaces.

In the mid-1800s, when Philadelphia was one of the nation's leading industrial cities, Manayunk was a prosperous town. It was home to a number of the city's 185 cotton mills, which provided raw material for the region's thriving paper and textile industries. The European millworkers who settled here built row houses in the steep hills overlooking the river. During the Civil War the mills switched to wool textiles to produce blankets for the troops. When they eventually closed because of competition with cheaper labor in southern mills, the town's fortunes declined.

Originally called Flat Rock, for the rock formations in this section of the Schuylkill River, the town was rechristened Manayunk, a Leni-Lenape word that translates as "where we go to drink." Today those words seem prophetic. In the mid-1980s the neighborhood was designated a historic district, and business owners saw a golden opportunity. Good fortune struck again in 1986, when the U.S. Pro Cycling championship picked Philadelphia as its home and included Manayunk's steep hills (now dubbed the "Wall") on its route.

The blocks between 3700 and 4400 are lined with shops and restaurants. As you walk east, you'll pass some reminders of the town's former calling: **Ma Jolie** (⊠ 4340 Main St.), a designer boutique, is housed in a historic 1912 bank building; both **Chemistry** nightclub (⊠ 4100 Main St.) and the **Manayunk Brewery and Restaurant** (⊠ 4120 Main St.) occupy old textile mills. Behind the building is the towpath of the Manayunk Canal, built between 1817 and 1823. Along here barges once transported goods to and from the textile mills. You can hike from here—Locks 69 and 70, where the canal flows into the Schuylkill River—two miles west to the Flat Rock Dam.

Bikeline of Manayunk (⊠ 4151 Main St., ☎ 215/487-7433) rents bicycles for $25 a day. Near the store you can pick up the Schuylkill River Trail, a flat, paved path that stretches 12 mi from the outskirts of Center City Philadelphia to Valley Forge National Historical Park.

The **Manayunk Development Corporation** (⊠ 111 Grape St., ☎ 215/482-9565, WEB www.manayunk.com) can send you a visitors guide; its Web site lists special events, restaurants, and shops.

Many stores stay open until 9 or 10 on Friday and Saturday nights. If you do come on a weekday, note that most stores don't open until noon.

If you're driving from Center City, follow I-76 west (the Schuylkill Expressway) to the Belmont Avenue exit. Turn right across the bridge and right again onto Main Street and park. You can also take the SEPTA R6 (Norristown) train from Market East, Suburban Station, or 30th Street Station to the Manayunk station (on Cresson Street) and walk downhill to Main Street.

GERMANTOWN AND CHESTNUT HILL

Germantown, about 6 mi northwest of Center City, has been an integrated, progressive community since 13 German Quaker and Mennonite families moved here in 1683 and soon welcomed English, French, and other European settlers seeking religious freedom. The area has a tradition of free thinking—the first written protest against slavery came from its residents. Today it houses a wealth of still-occupied and exceptionally well-preserved architectural masterpieces.

The Germantown area is rich in history. It was the site of Philadelphia's first gristmill (1683) and America's first paper mill (1690). The American Colonies' first English-language Bible was printed here (1743). By the time of the Revolution, Germantown had become an industrial town. In 1777 Colonial troops under George Washington attacked part of the British force here and fought the Battle of Germantown in various skirmishes. After the Revolutionary War Germantown became a rural retreat for wealthy city residents who wanted to escape summer heat and disease. The Deshler-Morris House was the summer White House where President Washington and his family resided in 1793 and 1794, when the yellow fever epidemic drove them from the city. For information on Germantown's historic attractions, visit www.ushistory.org/germantown.

Farther northwest is Chestnut Hill. Although it's part of the city, Chestnut Hill is more like the classy suburbs of the Main Line. When Germantown's second railroad, the Chestnut Hill Line, began operation west of Germantown Avenue in 1884, it spurred the development of Chestnut Hill. Beyond cobblestone Germantown Avenue, lined with restaurants, galleries, and boutiques, you'll find lovely examples of Colonial Revival and Queen Anne houses. The Woodmere Art Museum is in this neighborhood. For tours and information, contact the **Chestnut Hill Business Association** (⊠ 8426 Germantown Ave., ☎ 215/247–6696, WEB www.chestnuthillpa.com).

The best way to tour the area is by car. From Center City follow Kelly Drive to Midvale Avenue and turn right. Follow Midvale up the hill to Conrad Street and turn right, then make a left on Queen Lane, which ends at Grumblethorpe. You can also reach Germantown from Center City via SEPTA Bus 23; pick it up at 11th and Market streets and get off at Queen Lane.

A Good Drive

You can follow Germantown Avenue from lower Germantown north to Chestnut Hill. Many homes you'll see were built when Germantown Avenue was a dirt road; today it's lined with cobblestones. At Queen Lane is John Wister's **Grumblethorpe,** built from stones quarried on the property. A few blocks north on Germantown Avenue is Market Square, a park that was once the site of a prison and its stocks and a focal point for trade. Facing Market Square on your left is the **Deshler-Morris House,** with fine antiques and lovely gardens; diagonally across the square in a row of restored redbrick buildings is the **Germantown Historical Society,** which provides a good introduction to the houses in the area. Drive north a half mile farther to the Quaker-style **Wyck** house, at the corner of Germantown Avenue and Walnut Lane.

Just before Pastorius Street is the tiny, historic Germantown Mennonite Church. On this site in 1708 the Mennonites established their first church in the New World. The little log church was replaced in 1770 by the current building. Turn left on Tulpehocken Street; at Number 200

West is the Victorian Gothic **Ebenezer Maxwell Mansion.** Continue north on Germantown Avenue past the Johnson House (✉ 6306 Germantown Ave.), once a tannery, later a station on the Underground Railway. At Number 6401 is **Cliveden,** an elaborate house set at the end of a long, graceful driveway. Across the street is **Upsala,** a Federal-style home of the Johnson family (who also owned the Johnson House).

Adjacent to Germantown is the residential community of Mount Airy, and farther north, at the "top" of Germantown Avenue, is Chestnut Hill. The town's tony shopping district runs from Number 7900 to 8700. Half a mile north at Number 9201 is the **Woodmere Art Museum,** with works from the 19th and 20th centuries. From here, if it's a nice day, you could detour to the gardens of the Morris Arboretum or the natural setting of the Schuylkill Center for Environmental Education.

TIMING

Each historic house has its own schedule, so it's difficult to coordinate your visit to include all the sights. However, you could catch five homes open on a Thursday afternoon and four on Saturday or Sunday afternoon. You could then head to Chestnut Hill for dinner. Avoid this trip in winter, when most of the homes are closed.

Sights to See

★ **Cliveden.** Its unique history and fine architecture combine to make Cliveden, built in 1763 by Benjamin Chew (1722–1810), one of Germantown's treasures. The area's most elaborate country house is a shining example of Georgian style, with Palladian windows and an elegant entrance hall with pedimented door frames. The home was occupied by the British during the Revolution. On October 4, 1777, Washington's unsuccessful attempt to dislodge the British resulted in his defeat at the Battle of Germantown. You can still see bullet marks on the outside walls. Today a museum, Cliveden occupies a 6-acre plot, with outbuildings and a barn converted into offices and a gift shop. It remained in the Chew family until 1972, when it was donated to the National Trust for Historic Preservation. ✉ *6401 Germantown Ave.,* ☎ *215/848–1777,* WEB *www.cliveden.org.* ▣ *$6.* ☉ *Apr.–Dec., Thurs.–Sun. noon–4.*

Deshler-Morris House. This is where President Washington lived during the yellow fever epidemic of 1793–94, making it the seat of government of the new republic for a short time. In October 1777, during the Battle of Germantown, the house was the headquarters for British General Sir William Howe. Antiques accent the rooms, and, as one of the many Germantown houses built flush with the road, it has enchanting side and back gardens. ✉ *5442 Germantown Ave.,* ☎ *215/596–1748,* WEB *www.nps.gov/edal/dmhouse.htm.* ▣ *$2.* ☉ *Apr.–mid-Dec., Wed., Fri.–Sun. 12–4; other times by appointment.*

Ebenezer Maxwell Mansion. Philadelphia's only mid-19th-century house-museum is a Victorian Gothic extravaganza of elongated windows and arches. This gorgeous 1859 suburban villa has Philadelphia-made furniture and extensive period gardens. Its three-story tower is the incarnation of an old haunted house. ✉ *200 W. Tulpehocken St.,* ☎ *215/438–1861,* WEB *www.ushistory.org/germantown.* ▣ *$4.* ☉ *Apr.–mid-Dec., Fri.–Sun. 1–4; mid-Dec.–Mar. by appointment.*

Germantown Historical Society. The headquarters of the society has a historical and genealogical library and a museum showcasing noteworthy furniture, textile and costume collections, from Colonial highboys and Peale paintings to Quaker samplers and mourning clothes. It is also an orientation point for anyone visiting the Germantown houses.

⊠ *5501 Germantown Ave.,* ☎ *215/844–0514,* WEB *www.libertynet.org/ghs.* 🖾 *Museum, $4; library, $7.50.* ☉ *Tues. and Thurs. 9–5, Sun. 1–5.*

Grumblethorpe. Built by Philadelphia merchant and wine importer John Wister in 1744, this Georgian house is one of Germantown's leading examples of early 18th-century architecture. The Wister family lived here for 160 years; the Courting Door in the parlor and the blood stains of Gen. James Agnew, who was killed here during the Battle of Germantown, are evidence of its former life. ⊠ *5267 Germantown Ave.,* ☎ *215/843–4820,* WEB *www.ushistory.org/germantown.* 🖾 *$3.* ☉ *Apr.–mid-Dec., Tues., Thurs., and Sun. 1–4.*

OFF THE BEATEN PATH

MORRIS ARBORETUM – Begun in 1887 by siblings John and Lydia Morris and bequeathed to the University of Pennsylvania in 1932, this 166-acre arboretum typifies Victorian-era garden and landscape design with its romantic winding paths, a hidden grotto, tropical ferns in a fernery, and natural woodland. An eclectic retreat, the Morris also holds a rose garden, English garden, Japanese garden, and meadows. It has 3,500 trees and shrubs from around the world, including one of the finest collections of Asian plants outside Asia. The arboretum is in the far northwest corner of the city, near the Woodmere Art Museum in Chestnut Hill. ⊠ *Hillcrest Ave. between Germantown and Stenton Aves.,* ☎ *215/ 247–5777,* WEB *www.upenn.edu/morris/. Chestnut Hill East or West commuter trains stop ½ mi away; Bus L stops at the corner of Hillcrest and Germantown Aves.* 🖾 *$6.* ☉ *Apr.–Oct., weekdays 10–4, weekends 10–5; Nov.–Mar., daily 10–4; guided tours weekends at 2.*

SCHUYLKILL CENTER FOR ENVIRONMENTAL EDUCATION – This sanctuary consists of more than 500 acres of wildflowers, ferns, and thickets; ponds, streams, and woodlands; 6 mi of winding trails; and the 8-acre Pine Plantation. You may spot deer, hawks, Canada geese, red foxes, and other animals. Hands-on exhibits in the Discovery Museum explain the flora and fauna, and there are nature programs on weekends. The bookstore and gift shop follow the nature theme. ⊠ *8480 Hagy's Mill Rd., Roxborough,* ☎ *215/482–7300,* WEB *www.schuylkillcenter.org. Bus 27 stops at Henry and Port Royal Aves., 1 mi away.* 🖾 *$3.* ☉ *Sept.–July, Mon.–Sat. 8:30–5, Sun. 1–5; Aug., Mon.–Sat. 8:30–5.*

Upsala. One of Germantown's best examples of Federal-style architecture and interior design, Upsala was built about 1755. The Johnsons, who owned the house, were a well-to-do family of tanners. Continental troops set up their cannons on Upsala's front lawn and shelled the British at Cliveden. ⊠ *6430 Germantown Ave.,* ☎ *215/842–1798,* WEB *www. upsala-phl.com.* 🖾 *$4.* ☉ *Apr.–Nov., Thurs. and Sat. 1–4.*

Woodmere Art Museum. The art and artists of Philadelphia are showcased here, along with American and European art from the 19th and 20th centuries, in a fine collection of paintings and prints. Benjamin West, Frederick Church, and Pennsylvania Impressionists such as Edward Redfield and Daniel Garber are represented. The museum also has a lovely collection of decorative arts, including tapestries, sculptures, porcelains, ivories, and Japanese rugs. ⊠ *9201 Germantown Ave.,* ☎ *215/247–0476,* WEB *www.woodmereartmuseum.org.* 🖾 *$5.* ☉ *Tues.–Sat. 10–5, Sun. 1–5.*

NEED A BREAK?

The British presence can still be felt in this area at **Best of British** (⊠ 8513 Germantown Ave., ☎ 215/242–8848), a cute Chestnut Hill tearoom where you can have lunch or enjoy tea with clotted cream. And since this is America, you can have your afternoon tea beginning at 9:30 AM.

Wyck. One of the most charming of Quaker-style houses, Wyck has an old pump, barn, carriage house, and idyllic gardens. The house remained the property of the same Quaker family from 1736 to 1973; their accumulated original furnishings are on display. Known as the oldest house in Germantown, Wyck was used as a British field hospital after the Battle of Germantown. ⊠ *6026 Germantown Ave.,* ☎ *215/ 848–1690,* WEB *www.wyck.org.* ⊡ *$5.* ☉ *Apr.–mid-Dec., Tues., Thurs., and Sat. 1–4; other times by appointment.*

2 DINING

Once known mainly for multi-meat stuffed sandwiches called hoagies and turtle (a.k.a. snapper) soup, in recent years Philadelphia has expanded its culinary range to embrace the flavors of the world. Distinctive ethnic restaurants and excellent seafood and steak houses now round out the dining scene. Although revamped banks and brokerage houses hold a number of pricey dazzlers, simpler treasures can be found, including some in storefronts and in the celebrated Reading Terminal Market.

By Barbara
Ann Rosenberg

WHETHER YOU'RE IN THE MOOD TO DINE at a fancy restaurant, sample innovative cuisine in one of several creative new spots, or just grab a quick bite, Philadelphia has an abundance of intriguing choices. A startling restaurant renaissance that put the city on the national culinary map began nearly 30 years ago and has been escalating ever since—both in the number and variety of places to eat. As each year passes the tally of restaurants and the range of their cuisines have continued to mushroom until Philadelphia dining options are now truly international in scope.

Over the years the city's restaurants have become more sophisticated in every way. Some have incorporated striking architectural details to augment the excitement of the food. In 1994, a new all-fish restaurant, Striped Bass, put a daring spin on the concept of what dining interiors should look like by moving into a handsomely renovated brokerage house. Other restaurants followed, metamorphosing turn-of-the-last-century banks into trendy dining locations or building contemporary spaces designed for smashing visual impact.

Modest ethnic restaurants of nearly every persuasion, from Vietnamese and Malaysian to Jamaican and Cuban, also enhanced the dining scene. And, despite people's mounting awareness of their cholesterol levels, steak houses have multiplied, both chain-affiliated and individually controlled. In keeping with a nationwide trend, hotel dining has improved significantly. Philadelphia hotels now claim some of the best chefs in the business, including some with national reputations. Italian food in Philadelphia has its own connotations, ranging from South Philadelphia home-style to restaurants that rate among the city's most elegant.

And then there are the somewhat unusual Philadelphia specialties for which locals feel a quirky but bona fide passion. Some of these provincial favorites have produced a number of long-standing rivalries for the title "the best of the best." Hoagies, a Philadelphia spin on Italian sandwiches (called heroes or subs in other cities), have been embraced by nearly everyone who tastes them. Soft pretzels—with mustard, to be authentic—are tolerated by many visitors, but the merits of Philadelphia cheese steaks (as served up at South Philly joints such as Pat's and Geno's, both at 9th Street and Passyunk Avenue) often elude anyone not to the city born. Philadelphia's former mayor, Ed Rendell, enhanced the city's reputation as "the junk food capital of the country" by frequently appearing while stuffing his mouth with a hoagie or cheese steak. When *Men's Fitness Magazine* named Philadelphia "America's fattest city," the current mayor, John Street, made it his mission to help Philadelphians get fit. He announced his initiative while chowing down on a veggie hoagie. Nevertheless, lovers of Philly food may be happy to know that gift packages of everything *but* cheese steaks can be shipped by calling **Philadelphia Favorites to Go** (☎ 800/808–8646) or **A Taste of Philadelphia** (☎ 800/846–2443).

In Philadelphia, as elsewhere, many restaurants have latched on to the habit of serving copious brunches as a high point of the weekend for work-weary patrons. Several top-notch hotels have outstanding (and expensive) brunches that are virtual extravaganzas. Along with those mentioned in the restaurant listings, consider **Founders** at the Park Hyatt Philadelphia at the Bellevue, which has a chef-attended brunch on Saturday, when guests can chat with him about the various dishes. **The Grill** at the Westin has both an à la carte menu and a Personal Service Buffet, where the appetizers and desserts are wheeled to your table on a cart. Other laid-back, casual places are also great for socializing with a not-so-early Sunday coffee—or drink—in hand; **Bridget Foy's Second Street Grill** (✉ 200 South St., ☎ 215/922–1813) has a make-your-own-Bloody-Mary station as part of the fun.

Bear in mind that Philadelphia is becoming a well-attended convention city, and so it's always wise to make reservations and to reconfirm when you get to town. (Le Bec-Fin and Buddakan are generally booked a month ahead for Saturday night.) In general, you should tip 15% of the check (20% in the fanciest places), depending on the service.

In the listings, reservations are noted only when they're essential or not accepted. Many restaurants that don't take reservations for small parties do so for larger groups. Unless otherwise indicated, restaurants are open daily for lunch and dinner. Most of Philadelphia's restaurants can be classified as casual, but not, with the exception of inexpensive spots or the University City area, of the jeans and sneakers variety. Smart casual wear usually works except in the top hotel dining rooms and the most expensive places where trendy chic is the norm. Dress is mentioned in reviews only when men are required to wear a jacket or a jacket and tie. For approximate costs, *see* the dining price chart *in* Smart Travel Tips A to Z.

DISTRICT BY DISTRICT

To make finding restaurants easier, we've divided them geographically into 11 areas. Center City is used to describe the midtown area bounded roughly by the Schuylkill River to the west, 6th Street to the east, South Street to the south, and Vine Street to the north. The majority of Center City's restaurants are clustered along Walnut Street west of Broad Street and in the area surrounding Rittenhouse Square. The latter is where you'll find the best sidewalk cafés. Within Center City is Chinatown, which lies between 9th and 11th streets and Vine and Arch streets. The neighborhood identified as the Historic Area/Old City takes in the area south of Independence National Historical Park to the Delaware River, and between Sansom and Arch streets. Society Hill is the area south of this, bordered on the north and south by Walnut and Bainbridge streets. Also included are two restaurants in Northern Liberties, just north of Old City.

Several restaurants are clustered on or near the Benjamin Franklin Parkway, which leads diagonally from John F. Kennedy Plaza to the Philadelphia Museum of Art. University City, the area west of the Schuylkill River around the campuses of the University of Pennsylvania and Drexel University, has a number of interesting ethnic restaurants. South Philadelphia, south of Bainbridge Street, is the city's "Little Italy." Farther out from Center City is one noteworthy restaurant in the City Line area and several in Manayunk, a former working-class neighborhood northwest of Center City that has been transformed into a trendy shopping and dining destination. Some fine chefs have gone west to open terrific restaurants on the Main Line, that much vaunted western suburban stretch of mansions and high society. These are worth the trip.

A good source for reasonably up-to-the-minute dining information is *Philadelphia*, a monthly magazine with restaurant listings. A couple of free weekly local papers such as the *City Paper* and *Philadelphia Weekly* also have restaurant reviews and numerous listings. These "freebies" are available in metal sidewalk dispensers on nearly every Center City street corner.

KEY

- Market-Frankford Subway
- Broad St. Subway
- Subway-Surface Subway
- Airport Train

0 ————— 440 yards
0 ————— 400 meters

Historic Area/Old City

Afghan

$$ ✕ **Ariana.** This cozy restaurant and its staff introduce patrons to their culture with typical wall hangings: handsome rugs and exotic clothing from the remote country of Afghanistan. The menu, too, is inviting, with straightforward descriptions of subtle, intriguingly seasoned dishes. Appetizers and side plates are delicious, and the rice-based offerings, often with tender lamb and chicken, are extraordinary. Check out the ultra-smooth rosewater-flavor *firney* (a milk-based pudding) for dessert. ⊠ *134 Chestnut St.,* ☏ *215/922–1535. AE, D, MC, V. BYOB. No lunch Sun.*

American

$$$$ ✕ **City Tavern.** You can time-travel to the 18th century at this authentic re-creation of historic City Tavern, where the atmosphere suggests that founding fathers such as John Adams, George Washington, Thomas Jefferson, and the rest of the gang *might* have supped here (they didn't). It was in 1994, under the supervision of the National Park Service, that international consultant/restaurateur Walter Staib refurbished this spot to the specifications of the original 1773 tavern. The food— West Indies pepper pot soup, Martha Washington's turkey stew, honey pecan roast duckling—is prepared from enhanced period recipes and served on Colonial-patterned china. ⊠ *138 S. 2nd St.,* ☏ *215/413– 1443. AE, D, DC, MC, V.*

Contemporary

$$$–$$$$ ✕ **Novelty.** In his first venture outside Manayunk, Bruce Cooper, owner of Jake's in Manayunk, has opened a large restaurant in a storefront that actually sold novelties (thus the name). Novelty serves novel menu choices, such as Chinese short ribs with sweet potato mash and roasted duck breast with cheese grits and red onion chutney. Moreover, Cooper has introduced an excellent modestly priced wine list— a novelty, indeed! ⊠ *15 S. 3rd St.,* ☏ *215/627–7885. AE, MC, V. No lunch Sat. and Sun.*

$$–$$$ ✕ **Fork.** Happy sounds emanate from the diners here—if you can hear them over the noise of the always lively bar patrons. A limited menu of tasty food is attractively served, such as the moderately priced rack of lamb that arrives with potatoes and a green vegetable, or roast pork with multiple vegetables. Fork counts many locals among its regulars. There's usually a wait for a table but not always a place to wait comfortably. Sit as far back in the restaurant as possible to watch the folks at work in the open kitchen. ⊠ *306 Market St.,* ☏ *215/625–9425. AE, D, DC, MC, V. No lunch Sat.*

$–$$ ✕ **Continental Restaurant & Martini Bar.** Light fixtures fashioned like ★ olives pierced with toothpicks are a tip-off to the theme at this cool watering hole and small-plate eatery installed in a classic diner shell in the center of Old City's action. This is the first of Stephen Starr's trendy restaurants, where he serves up lively (but not outré) food to people who know how to enjoy. Don't miss the addictive Szechuan french-fried potatoes with hot mustard sauce. ⊠ *138 Market St.,* ☏ *215/923–6069. AE, DC, MC, V.*

Eclectic

$$–$$$$ ✕ **Buddakan.** Softened by miles of fabric, this former post office has been transformed into a stylish restaurant. A 10-ft-tall gilded Buddha presides over the otherwise all-white, soaring space, seemingly approving of the mostly fusion food that pairs Asian ingredients with various cooking styles. Such relatively familiar dishes as chicken with cashews and tempura lump crab are superb. A long "community" table provides an opportunity to dine with anyone else fortunate enough to

snag this center-stage space. Be prepared for major din as the evening wears on. ⊠ *325 Chestnut St.,* ☎ *215/574–9440. Reservations essential. AE, DC, MC, V. No lunch Sat. and Sun.*

Irish

$$–$$$ **Plough and the Stars.** The cheery first floor of this renovated bank feels like a genuine Irish pub. A long bar with a dozen spigots is invariably spouting several imported and a few local brews, all served at the correct temperature—not really cold, but cooler than room temperature. In winter, people crowd up to a blazing fireplace on stools set around smallish tables. It's possible to munch on good Irish smoked salmon on grainy bread while imbibing; you can also head to the upstairs dining room for some respite from the crush and choose from a panoply of worldly appetizers, salads, and main courses. There's a mid-afternoon menu that features a few Irish specialties such as fish and chips and goat cheese tart. ⊠ *123 Chestnut St., enter on 2nd St.,* ☎ *215/ 733–0300. AE, DC, MC, V.*

Italian

$$–$$$ ✕ **DiPalma.** Rosewood walls and sophisticated appointments set the tone for the service and food. Lobster cannelloni, carefully wrapped in delicate leaves of squid ink pasta, is a favorite starter, and such main courses as grilled langoustines and rack of tiny lamb chops in a wine sauce follow with a flourish. It's no wonder that serious business discussions seem to dominate the tables during the week; on weekends, friends gather here to enjoy the decor and heady food. ⊠ *114 Market St.,* ☎ *215/733–0545. AE, D, DC, MC, V. No lunch Sun.*

$$–$$$ ✕ **Pizzicato.** Although people often mistake the first few letters of the name of this restaurant to mean that pizza is the specialty, as the song says, "It ain't necessarily so." In fact this pleasant restaurant serves a full range of contemporary takes on traditional dishes. All pasta is made in-house and specialties include mushroom tagliatelli and Portobello and red pepper-stuffed veal chops. There's outdoor dining in season. ⊠ *248 Market St.,* ☎ *215/629–5527. AE, D, DC, MC, V.*

$$–$$$ ✕ **Ristorante Panorama.** The name refers to a lovely inside mural rather than a window view from this lively Old City restaurant with the largest wine cruvinet (a wine storage system) in the world. Besides 120 wines available by the glass, there is a huge selection of well-chosen bottles. You can sip them in Il Bar or in the main dining room. The food is authentic Italian, simple and hearty. The ambience is either noisy or animated, depending on your tolerance level. ⊠ *Penn View Hotel, 14 N. Front St.,* ☎ *215/922–7800. Reservations essential. AE, DC, MC, V.*

Latin

$$–$$$ ✕ **Cuba Libre.** People who have been in pre-Castro Havana swear this place is a dead ringer. In any event, it is lovely, with balconies and fancy street lights and even a leaded glass window—on the interior. An entire menu is devoted to rum from everywhere in the Caribbean and Central and South America that it's produced. There's some that's smooth enough to be mistaken for fine brandy and served in snifters. The appetizers, like lobster empanadas and crab cakes, taste fairly authentic; rice and black beans are served with just about every preparation, of course. It's lively and everyone seems to be having a good time. ⊠ *10 S. 2nd St.,* ☎ *215/627–0666. AE, D, DC, MC, V. No lunch.*

Moroccan

$$$–$$$$ ✕ **Tangerine.** Although neither the decor nor the food are totally au-
★ thentic Moroccan, there is enough of the genuine to make people feel as though they are squarely located in that beautiful, exotic country. Take the hundreds of candles twinkling in hundreds of niches. Take the *tagines* (cone-topped clay pots) that hold some of the oven-cooked

dishes, and take the flavors of many of the richly spiced dishes and, some-how, the whole experience adds up to a trip to North Africa, in spirit, at least. Dishes are served family style—meaning in the center of the table, rather than in front of a particular person—so, in theory at least, everyone should be able to have a taste. Preserved duck with couscous and fruit is a good candidate; "midnight kiss" with one ounce of ose-tra caviar won't make it very far for sharing. ⊠ *232 Market St.,* ☎ *215/627–5116. Reservations essential. AE, DC, MC, V. No lunch.*

Seafood

$$$–$$$$ ✕ **Old Original Bookbinder's.** Today the city's most famous restaurant has become more of a landmark (the original opened in 1865) than an essential stop for serious diners, except for oyster lovers who keep the man behind the bar busy opening prime specimens. On the walls hang photos of Elizabeth Taylor and other celebrities and politicians, all pos-ing with past and current owners in the Taxin family. The restaurant is often criticized for being overpriced (entrées range from $22 to $30), and you'll spring for the top end and then some if you're in the mood for lobster. Still, Bookbinder's seems to be a "must" stop for tourists who feel a need to say they've been there. ⊠ *125 Walnut St.,* ☎ *215/925–7027. AE, D, DC, MC, V.*

$$$–$$$$ ✕ **Philadelphia Fish & Company.** A new chef, Anthony Marini, is in com-mand of the adventurous, imaginative menu at this oasis for seafood lovers. Shrimp in three ways is a popular starter; farm-raised black bass is also a favorite. The daily changing raw bar is outstanding. Outdoor dining and drinking take place in season on a deck that overlooks busy Chestnut Street and is good for people-watching—and traffic noise. ⊠ *207 Chestnut St.,* ☎ *215/625–8605. AE, D, DC, MC, V.*

Soul Food

$$–$$$ ✕ **Bluezette.** Looking very much like a work in progress with the steel structure climbing up the front, this ultra-modern converted storefront houses a true exponent of soul food, Caribbean and Latin American style. No matter what taste of home people are looking for, it's all here, along with a top drawer bar. Fried chicken is always a winner; shrimp and grouper creole are special, as is the curried goat. ⊠ *246 Market St.,* ☎ *215/627–3866. AE, DC, MC, V. Closed Mon.*

$$–$$$ ✕ **Warmdaddy's.** This "blues" and "rhythm and blues" club also houses a creditable restaurant serving up a full menu of sincere "down home" cooking: ribs and fried catfish are outstanding. ⊠ *4 S. Front St.,* ☎ *215/627–8400. AE, D, DC, MC, V. No lunch.*

Society Hill

Diners and Philly Food

$ ✕ **Jim's Steaks.** You become sharply aware of the fact that you're com-ing up on Jim's from at least a block away, as the odor of mountains of frying onions overwhelms your senses. Big, juicy, drippy sandwiches of "Philly steaks"—shaved beef piled high on long crusty rolls—come off the grill with amazing speed when the counter workers hit their stride, but be aware that no matter how hard you beg, they will not toast the rolls. Take extra napkins so you won't be wearing your sand-wich as well as eating it. Jim's is mostly takeout, but there are some tables and chairs upstairs. ⊠ *400 South St.,* ☎ *215/928–1911. Reser-vations not accepted. No credit cards.*

French

$$–$$$$ ✕ **Overtures.** A bit of Paris exists just off funky South Street. Not the
★   food, exactly, since Overtures does not cook pure French but rather the inspired interpretations of the owner-chef, Peter Lamlein, a genial man with definite ideas about how to operate his surprisingly moder-

ately priced restaurant. Among the stylish decorative touches are extravagant flower arrangements, trompe l'oeil paintings, and black-and-white floor tiles. Although the menu changes periodically, there's always lavender-scented rack of lamb, a genuine winner. ⊠ *609–611 E. Passyunk Ave., off South St.,* ☎ *215/627–3455. AE, DC, MC, V. BYOB. Closed Mon. No lunch.*

Italian

$$$$ ✕ **Monte Carlo Living Room.** Two mirrored, candlelit dining rooms with
★ crystal chandeliers and sconces create a subtle atmosphere for superb Italian cuisine. Chef Nunzio Patruno and his staff apply a deft touch to foods of the entire country, but fish and shellfish seem to bring out their very best instincts. Homemade pastas, such as black pasta with lobster and a lobster sauce, are ethereal; sautéed diver scallops with a dab of caviar are sublime. If the chef is available to create a special menu, by all means consider the possibility. Dancing in a plush private club upstairs is free to diners. The Wednesday night buffet in the club is first-class and draws a loyal band of people who appreciate it and the overall scene. Although jackets are not required, they are requested and most men wear them. ⊠ *150 South St.,* ☎ *215/925–2220. Reservations essential. AE, MC, V. No lunch.*

$$–$$$ ✕ **Ristorante Primavera.** Get here early: this popular Italian bistro, owned by the same people as the Monte Carlo Living Room, seats only 36. Cozy touches include soft track lighting, exposed brick walls, and pink table linens. Pastas and the veal chop with mozzarella and prosciutto are the high points of the menu. The wine list is small but thoughtfully chosen. There's a full bar but you may bring your own. ⊠ *148 South St.,* ☎ *215/925–7832. AE, MC, V. No lunch.*

Latin

$$–$$$ ✕ **Azafran.** No question that there's an artist at work here, indicated by the big, colorful paintings (sort of weird) and the food that comes out of the kitchen (not at all weird, but different for sure). Pan-Latin is perhaps the best way to describe the food that keeps would-be patrons lined up outside this tiny place on weekends. Empanadas, looking vaguely like eggrolls, are tops. Grazing is probably the best way to sample as much as you can. There's alfresco dining in good weather. ⊠ *617 S. 3rd St.,* ☎ *215/928–4019. Reservations not accepted. AE, DC, MC, V. BYOB. Closed Mon. No lunch.*

Moroccan

$$ ✕ **Fez.** If you want your dining experience to be a bit exotic, Fez—with its Moroccan decor and its menu of Moroccan food, cooked by a Middle Eastern chef—may fill the bill. The restaurant is cramped, but don't take it all too seriously and just enter into the spirit of eating with your hands (after having them washed by a waiter with water from an ornate kettle). The best main-course choices are the lamb with honey and almonds or chicken with olives, both available on the $20 eight-course fixed-price banquet. Sometimes a belly dancer performs; call ahead for information. The à la carte menu is not available on weekends. ⊠ *620 S. 2nd St.,* ☎ *215/925–5367. AE, D, DC, MC, V. No lunch.*

Spanish

$$–$$$$ **Mallorca.** *Sopa de ajo* (garlic soup), gazpacho, and the popular *Paella Valencia* (seafood with seasoned rice), along with everybody's favorite flan, are authentically prepared by an "old country" chef. The majority of the dishes in this charming restaurant hail from Spain, with a few from Portugal. The multi-room restaurant is appropriately colorful with interesting murals. There are numerous ports and sherries and a full bar. ⊠ *119 South St.,* ☎ *215/351–6652. AE, MC, V.*

ity

Belgian

$$–$$$ ✕ **Monk's Cafe.** Mussels are practically the national dish of Belgium. Whether cooked in classic style with wine and shallots or with cream, they are a high point at this casual, lively bar and restaurant, and the fries that accompany them draw raves from the regulars who crowd the place. Burgers, too, are menu favorites. Add to these an outstanding assortment of Belgian beers and you get the picture. ✉ 264 S. 16th St., ☎ 215/545–7005. Reservations not accepted. MC, V. Closed Sun.

Chinese

$$$–$$$$ ✕ **Susanna Foo.** The displays of unusual orchids and contemporary
★ Chinese artwork in this elegant restaurant provide a worthy setting for nationally known food. The chef has achieved many awards for her cuisine, which incorporates Western ingredients into essentially Chinese food. Such favorites as Hundred-Corner Crab Cakes, lobster dumplings with coconut-lobster sauce, and five-spice venison with Mongolian sauce are on the regular menu, while specials (such as foie gras), are offered from time to time. There is a full bar and a pricey wine list as well as imported beers. ✉ 1512 Walnut St., ☎ 215/545–2666. Reservations essential. AE, DC, MC, V. No lunch weekends.

Contemporary

$$$–$$$$ ✕ **Opus 251.** Under the stewardship of owner Brian Marton there is a whole new standard of excellence for the meals served in the two different (but both pleasant) rooms on the first floor of the elegant Philadelphia Art Alliance. Accomplished chefs turn out innovative menus constructed of fine ingredients. Venison loin poivrade and crispy striped bass with lobster and scallop gallette, snow pea shoots salad, and beurre rouge (red butter) are standouts on the regular menu. There are daily specials and vegetarian entrées on request. Good weather brings access to a delightful garden for outdoor dining. ✉ Philadelphia Art Alliance, 251 S. 18th St., ☎ 215/735–6787. AE, DC, MC, V. No lunch Sat.

$$–$$$$ ✕ **Circa.** This restaurant, now firmly entrenched on the dining scene, was the first of the lapsed banks with soaring arched ceilings to be transformed into dining space. The menu, as diverse as the patrons, includes venison and Oriental rubbed duck. You walk into an atmosphere punctuated by flickering blue votive candles; the greeter's station is a church pulpit, and pews do duty as benches in the bar, making for an impressive entrance. The lower floor, open only for dinner, includes the original bank vault. ✉ 1518 Walnut St., ☎ 215/545–6800. AE, DC, MC, V. No lunch Sat.–Mon.

$$–$$$$ ✕ **Rouge.** A jewel box of a restaurant, Rouge opens out onto Rittenhouse Square and is very much a "meet and greet" kind of place, with subtle, smart decor that includes blown-glass fixtures. Ladies who lunch love it—ditto gentlemen whose offices are in the neighborhood—both for a midday repast and a chance to hook up with "everybody" after work at the busy bar or one of the numerous sidewalk or window tables. Martinis are large but food portions can sometimes be small. The tuna tartare is excellent, as are the steak frites and herb-roasted chicken with potato puree. Many regulars opt for the outstanding hamburger. If you can't get in here, try Bleu, its "sister" restaurant, down the street. ✉ 205 S. 18th St., ☎ 215/732–6622. Reservations not accepted. AE, MC, V.

$$–$$$$ ✕ **Treetops.** It's possible to eat three meals a day in this appealing restaurant on the second floor of the Rittenhouse Hotel. The enormous windows overlooking the treetops on handsome Rittenhouse Square give the restaurant its name. The warm pastel shades on the walls give it

its lovely ambience. Celebrity chef Jim Coleman (of radio and TV fame) turns out "big, bold, and beautiful" American flavors. Lobster spring rolls are a favored menu item; roasted onion and garlic-crusted sea bass is another. Reservations are essential on weekends. ⊠ *Rittenhouse Hotel, 210 W. Rittenhouse Sq.,* ☎ *215/790–2533. AE, D, DC, MC, V.*

$$$ ✕ **Zanzibar Blue.** Known primarily as an upscale jazz spot showcasing name performers, this low-lit boîte is reminiscent of the jazz venues of Paris. The eclectic food is prepared by longstanding star chef Al Paris; there's delicious mango barbecued king shrimp scampi and cider-glazed double-cut pork chop. The short ribs are extraordinary. The Sunday brunch features top-notch jazz along with eggs and other brunch specialties. ⊠ *Park Hyatt at the Bellevue, 200 S. Broad St.,* ☎ *215/ 732–5200. AE, D, DC, MC, V. No lunch.*

$$–$$$ ✕ **Art Institute of Philadelphia–Petite Passion.** This simply furnished, intimate 50-seat restaurant is operated by the Culinary Arts students, supervised by talented Chef Joseph Shilling and other well-trained instructors from the school. It provides an opportunity to eat like a king at paupers' prices on Wednesdays and Thursdays: the four-course lunch is $10; the six-course dinner, $20. The menu changes weekly, depending on what's fresh in the market and the inspiration of the students and instructors. ⊠ *2300 Market St.,* ☎ *215/405–6766. Reservations essential. No credit cards. BYOB. Closed Fri.–Tues.*

$$–$$$ ✕ **Bleu.** Another product of high-flying restaurateur-par-excellence Neil Stein, this lively café with its hand-painted French-inspired murals is the "sister" restaurant to Rouge, at the other end of a dynamite block facing Rittenhouse Square. The menu features gorgeous salads of exotic ingredients and a blockbuster hamburger and french fries combo. In pleasant weather you can take advantage of the moving panorama of people walking and cycling by the square and sit at the open windows or snag an increasingly difficult-to-obtain sidewalk table. ⊠ *Sheraton Rittenhouse Square, 227 S. 18th St.,* ☎ *215/545– 0342. Reservations not accepted. AE, DC, MC, V.*

Delicatessens

$ ✕ **Rachael's Nosheri.** All the standard Jewish deli fare appear here, both on the menu and as decoration, such as jars of cucumbers in various stages of pickling. The menu, in typical deli style, is comprehensive with lists of smoked fish and smoked meats, too, for stuffed sandwiches and platters. The take-out business caters to apartments and businesses in the area, but a neat cluster of tables anticipates those people who prefer to polish off their food on the premises. Only breakfast and lunch are served. ⊠ *120 S. 19th St.,* ☎ *215/568–9565. AE, D, DC, MC, V. Closed Sun. No dinner.*

Diners and Philly Food

$ ✕ **Reading Terminal Market.** A Philadelphia treasure, the Reading
★   Terminal Market contains a profusion of more than 80 stalls, shops, lunch counters, and food emporiums in a huge, exciting indoor market. You can choose from numerous raw ingredients and prepared foods—Chinese, Greek, Mexican, Japanese, Thai, Middle Eastern, Italian, soul food, vegetarian, and Pennsylvania Dutch. Food options also include an extensive salad bar, seafood spots, a deli, baked goods, specialty hoagie and cheese steak shops, a sushi bar, and the outstanding Bassetts ice cream counter. Get here early to beat the daily lunch rush. The **Down Home Diner** inside the market has farm-style breakfasts and lunches (and dinner until 8, except Sunday). The market is open Monday to Saturday 8 to 6. ⊠ *12th and Arch Sts.,* ☎ *215/ 922–2317. Closed Sun.*

$ ✕ **Rocco's.** Fortunately for the hungry, one of Philadelphia's prime purveyors of overstuffed hoagies has a convenient location at Reading Terminal Market. (They have another at the basement food court in the Park Hyatt at the Bellevue.) The sandwiches can be made with a variety of fillings, but the classic Italian hoagies earn the most fans. Freshly sliced meats, such as Genoa salami and *capicolla* (spiced ham), join aged provolone and other cheeses in an overstuffed crisp roll specially baked to hold the assortment without spilling over. The simple dressing is the finishing touch. Note: Rocco's closes at 6. ✉ *Reading Terminal Market, 12th and Arch Sts.,* ☎ *215/238–1223. No credit cards. Closed Sun.*

$ ✕ **Salumeria.** A local favorite, Salumeria specializes in hoagies that have
★   taken the basic sandwich one step up to a new level of consciousness. This hoagie includes such ingredients as roasted pimientos and a house dressing among its standard ingredients and offers house-marinated artichoke hearts as an embellishment. Nobody can complain about gilding the lily, however, because these additions are somehow incorporated into a delicious whole. Salumeria closes at 6. ✉ *Reading Terminal Market, 12th and Arch Sts.,* ☎ *215/592–8150. No credit cards. Closed Sun.*

Eclectic

$$–$$$ ✕ **Glöbar.** The 20-ft glowing bar of translucent amber resin underlit with white lights (hence the name) is the centerpiece of this 90-seat restaurant that serves global cuisine until 1 AM. Located on the first floor of the Inn on Locust Street, this new dining spot features international entrées such as mahogany clams with green curry sauce and a runaway favorite, barbecued duck confit pizza. ✉ *1234 Locust St.,* ☎ *215/545–8878. Reservations not accepted. AE, DC, MC, V. Closed Mon.*

$$–$$$ ✕ **Oasis.** The decor at Oasis is sleek and Asian with no single country predominant; the food falls into the same genre—running the gamut from Korean and Japanese delicacies to Chinese and even a few Thai entrées. The Korean seafood "omelette," an unusual and tasty way to start a meal, is plenty for two to share. Each dish is discrete; there's never a hint of "fusion." And, for people who are confused about what beverage goes best with Asian food, there's no contest here: sake is king; served either straight (warm or chilled) or in assorted delicious cocktails that appeal even to those people who profess not to like sake. ✉ *1709 Walnut St.,* ☎ *215/751–0888. AE, D, DC, MC, V.*

French

$$$$ ✕ **Deux Cheminées.** This unique restaurant occupies two 19th-century mansions filled with Oriental rugs, paintings, and objets d'art that create a supremely romantic setting for dining. The French food on the $80 prix-fixe menu is rather classic in style, with touches that owner-chef Fritz Blank feels are appropriate. Some signature dishes are rack of lamb with truffle sauce, and a rich crab bisque with Scotch. A $60 pre-theater dinner is also offered. The service here is truly solicitous. ✉ *1221 Locust St.,* ☎ *215/790–0200. AE, DC, MC, V. Closed Sun. and Mon. No lunch.*

$$$$ ✕ **Le Bec-Fin.** For many years this outpost of cuisine from Lyonnais,
★   with inspired influences from owner Georges Perrier, set a stratospherically high standard for Philadelphia. Despite some recent grumbling, there is still sufficient acclaim (especially with a stellar new chef) to require an advance reservation of a month or more to garner a Saturday-night seat for the $120 per person prix-fixe dinner. Expect to find this haute cuisine served in a luxurious setting of apricot silk walls and gleaming crystal chandeliers that resemble those at Versailles. *Galette de crab* (a sublime crab cake) is a popular signature appetizer. Save room for a magnificent dessert cart. It's possible to indulge in an amazing three-course lunch for a fairly modest $38. Le Bar Ly-

onnais, downstairs from the main dining room, has sm
of some specialty dishes for relatively affordable prices
nut St., ☎ 215/567–1000. *Reservations essential. Jacke.*
D, DC, MC, V. Closed Sun.

$$$–$$$$ ✕ **Brasserie Perrier.** Another work by Georges Perrier, celebrity owner of Le Bec-Fin, this is an exuberant, Americanized version of a brasserie with modern-deco ambience, plush banquettes, and silver leaf ceilings. The cuisine is modern French, with Italian and Asian influences. The menu lists contemporary food such as wild striped bass with ginger sauce, and some traditional brasserie dishes: coq au vin and osso bucco. At lunch, a $26 prix-fixe three-course meal is served. ⊠ *1619 Walnut St.,* ☎ 215/568–3000. *AE, DC, MC, V. No lunch Sun.*

$$–$$$$ ✕ **Caribou Cafe.** All the trappings of a classic Parisian café/bistro are
★ here: warm ambience enhanced by saffron-colored walls, original posters of various French alcoholic beverages, and exquisite photos of the Seine by night. True to tradition, the food also smacks of Paris; the beautifully prepared dishes include steak frites, cassoulet with duck confit, coq au vin, and foie gras, although there are still standards such as salmon and burgers. Several flavors of imported beer are available, along with a full bar. There is an interesting $5 bar menu. ⊠ *1126 Walnut St.,* ☎ 215/625–9535. *AE, MC, V.*

$$–$$$ ✕ **The Blue Angel (L'Ange Bleu).** Step off commercial Chestnut Street
★ through a glass door with a tiny painted blue angel into Paris of 100 years ago. Among the restaurant's authentic retro features are black and white faceted tiled floors and a stained milk-glass ceiling, not to mention yards of polished brass coat and hat racks. The menu is quintessentially French bistro-style: salade lyonnaise (with small chunks of bacon called *lardons*), onion soup served in clay casseroles to melt the stretchy Gruyère cheese topping, garlicky escargot, french fried potatoes that remain shatteringly crisp on the plate, and other Paris-evocative delectables. The rest rooms provide abbreviated recorded French lessons while patrons use the facilities. ⊠ *706 Chestnut St.,* ☎ *215/ 925–6889. AE, DC, MC, V. No lunch weekends.*

Indian

$–$$ ✕ **Samosa.** This Indian vegetarian lunch and dinner buffet is a find for even the strictest of vegetarians. Authentic renditions of various vegetables are served on a daily basis by a Sikh (turbaned) family that seems to enjoy its loyal clientele of "palefaces" who return to the table again and again to fill their tummies with tasty but never too spicy dishes. There are always tasty samosas (triangle-shaped pastry filled with potatoes and peas), perfectly cooked basmati rice, and whatever other veggies the cooks feel are best in the market. Brightly seasoned *dal* (a sauce made from lentils and spices), is combined with rice to form an alliance that substitutes for a complete protein food. Desserts are super, super sweet. No liquor is allowed on the premises. ⊠ *1214 Walnut St.,* ☎ *215/545–7776. MC, V.*

Irish

$$–$$$ ✕ **The Bards.** Although the front section of the restaurant resembles an Irish cottage, the mood changes as you enter the main action. The cottage fades to accommodate the "bards," those celebrated Irish writers for whom the restaurant is named: drawings and photos of Oscar Wilde, George Bernard Shaw, William Synge, and James Joyce grace the walls. The food also supports the authenticity of this pub-restaurant, which features Irish specialties and full-bodied beers to accompany them. The stand-up bar is lively at all hours, and the dining room also hums with contented people chowing down on such pub grub as shepherd's pie (at lunch), potato cakes, Irish smoked salmon, and liver with Irish bacon. ⊠ *2013 Walnut St.,* ☎ *215/569–9585. AE, DC, MC, V.*

$$–$$$ ✕ **Black Sheep.** Recently converted from a private club with blacked-out windows, this Dublin-style lively pub has been packing 'em in for rivers of Irish draft and some of the specialties turned out by the kitchen. Fish and chips could have been produced on the "auld sod" and the malt vinegar to sprinkle over it all does little to dampen the crisp crust. The first-floor bar is noisy and spirited, but the mood gets a bit quieter as you climb the steps to the dining room. ✉ 247 S. 17 St., ☎ 215/545–9473. *Reservations not accepted. AE, D, DC, MC, V.*

$$ ✕ **Fadó.** Noisy, smoky, happening! This restaurant previously bounced around a bit until it finally made up its mind what it wanted to be "when it grew up." Since the right combination came together, the place has been full of eager eaters and drinkers of the seemingly unending river of Guinness that pours from the tap. There are often "would-bes" eagerly waiting on the street to get inside to join the revelry and munch on *boxty* (Irish potato cakes) with a variety of fillings. Oddly enough, the origin of this thoroughly Irish pub chain is not in Ireland at all, but rather Atlanta, Georgia, where they have fashioned such authenticity that someone from Dublin would feel right at home. ✉ *1500 Locust St.,* ☎ *215/893–9700. Reservations not accepted. AE, D, DC, MC, V.*

Italian

$$$–$$$$ ✕ **Avenue B.** This handsome restaurant in the shadow of the brand-new Kimmel Center for the Performing Arts (if one can describe anything being in the shadow of a glass-roofed building) is evocative of Milan. Sleek woodwork and furniture grace the dining area. The food is vaguely Italian in its crisp simplicity, too—Caesar salad with warm polenta croutons and shellfish risotto with saffron. Service needs honing, but knowing owner Neil Stein's style, he won't be content until "all's right with the world." There's alfresco dining on the Spruce Street sidewalk. ✉ 260 S. Broad St., ☎ 215/790–0705. AE, D, DC, MC, V. *No lunch weekends.*

$$$–$$$$ ✕ **Toto.** This elegant space is directly across from the side door of the Academy of Music; the bar area, brightened with white leather upholstery and a marble-top community table, is a favorite meeting place before and after concerts. Tasty, thoroughly Italian small-plate specialties include *rissollini* (Gorgonzola-flavored rice croquettes) with baby spinach and pear salad and *spezzatino* (chicken, sausage, and green peppers gratiné). Toto was formerly home to another, more formal restaurant. With a change of management, the fare has been somewhat simplified though it retains the essential elegance of dishes such as boneless roast rack of lamb with herbed Parmigianno crust, roasted vegetables, and minted barley. When the Academy of Music and Kimmel Center have afternoon concerts, Toto's serves lunch. ✉ 1407 Locust St., ☎ 215/546–2000. AE, MC, V. *Closed Sun.*

$$$–$$$$ ✕ **Vetri.** Owner-chef Mark Vetri blew into town from New York, where his former restaurant had garnered all sorts of kudos. The auspicious, although tiny, space in which he chose to settle was formerly home to such stellar restaurants as Le Bec-Fin. The magic of the location seems to be working again as Vetri's sensitive palate and deft hands turn out feather-light green gnocchi. Shellfish soup and a strange-sounding but exquisite dessert known as chocolate polenta soufflé continue to delight patrons who vie for the limited number of tables. ✉ 1312 Spruce St., ☎ 215/732–3478. *Reservations essential. AE, DC, MC, V. Closed Sun. No lunch.*

Jamaican

$$ ✕ **Jamaican Jerk Hut.** The scintillating flavors of the beautiful island of Jamaica are served here, tasting at least as good as on their original turf. The tiny storefront, overseen by the chef-owner Nicola Shirley, who applied her culinary school training to the tastes of her homeland, is primarily takeout. There are a couple of doll-size tables where people sit to wait for their orders, but you can eat in a charming back garden when the weather permits. Pork or chicken jerk is lovingly tended over an authentic pit; the curries and *roti* (pancakes with fillings such as curried chickpeas or chicken) are exemplary. And it all costs, as they say, a "fish cake." ✉ *1436 South St.,* ☎ *215/545–8644. No credit cards. Closed Sun.*

Japanese

$$–$$$ ✗ **Genji.** When it opened in University City, this restaurant was an early forerunner of the craze for Japanese food. A change of circumstances led it to its minimalist newer Center City location where it continues to cater to the cult of fine raw (and cooked) fish lovers. A sushi specialist, this place even furnishes its beautiful specimens to a fancy foods takeout location in an upscale supermarket. Spare and utterly Japanese, it has a loyal following. ✉ *1720 Sansom St.,* ☎ *215/564–1720. AE, D, DC, MC, V. No lunch weekends.*

Latin

$$$–$$$$ ✗ **Alma de Cuba.** A bit of somewhat-Spanish-looking scrolled ironwork greets diners who have to traipse up one or two flights of stairs to hit the main eating action. The first-story bar that pulsates with Cuban music sets the theme, and lets everyone know this is a "happening" place. But the decor is evocative of—what? Bare brick walls and a lot of black paint don't say much about Cuba being a happy place to be these days. The food contains a few genuine dishes, such as *lechon asado* (crisp-skinned roasted baby pig) and shrimp seviche, prepared by New York celebrity chef Douglas Rodriguez. While oysters are not generally considered Cuban, they are a knockout signature dish of the chef. A trio of house specialties makes an interesting appetizer. Bring a flashlight if you want a shot at reading the menu. ✉ *1623 Walnut St.,* ☎ *215/988–1799. AE, DC, MC, V. No lunch weekends.*

$$$–$$$$ ✗ **¡Pasion!** The rich red entryway sets the tone for the culinary passion inside this smallish restaurant, and a tented ceiling floats over warm-hued flowered walls. Argentine chef Guillermo Pernot's food draws on his intimacy with several South American and Caribbean food styles. He certainly doesn't hold back on the intensity of any of the seasonings. Chilean sea bass is cooked with wild mushrooms and tamarind sauce; the sampler plate of ceviche (fish and shellfish "cooked" in lime or lemon juice) is a specialty. ✉ *211 S. 15th St.,* ☎ *215/875–9895. AE, D, DC, MC, V. No lunch.*

$$–$$$ ✗ **Cibucan.** Another Latin fusion restaurant brought its good taste to town in a simple place that attracts a mix of people enjoying the unusual, lively flavors of the pan-Latino menu. Various protein entrées (tuna with plantain; chicken breast with guava glaze) share table space with tapas (small plates), making it possible to partake in a varied meal at friendly prices. Cibucan is good for a quick meal or snack before or after a show at the alternative theater across the street. ✉ *2025 Sansom St.,* ☎ *215/231–9895. MC, V. No lunch weekends.*

Mexican

$$–$$$ ✗ **Los Catrines Restaurant, Tequila's Bar.** Chef Carlos Molina makes
★ this a prime Center City choice for Mexican food: authentic south-of-the-border dishes such as *chilies rellenos* (moderately spicy poblano peppers stuffed with cheese or ground meat and baked in a tomato sauce or fried in a light batter), or *pozole* (pork and hominy stew). The decor is clearly south of the border, featuring Mexican glassware and ceramics. You can choose from a dozen different Mexican beers and 52 brands of tequila. ✉ *1602 Locust St.,* ☎ *215/546–0181. AE, DC, MC, V. Closed Sun. No lunch Sat.*

Seafood

$$$$
★ ✕ **Striped Bass Restaurant and Bar.** The opening of this all-seafood restaurant in 1994 caused the biggest splash on Philadelphia's dining scene in more than a decade. Capitalizing on the grandeur of a former brokerage house with soaring marble pillars, restaurateur-trendsetter Neil Stein created a visually stunning room with striking appointments that accent the 28-ft ceilings and muslin-draped windows. A spectacular 16-ft sculpture of a leaping striped bass overhangs the exhibition kitchen. There is an extensive raw bar of pristine shellfish. Roasted Maine halibut with foie gras and ginger-orange confit is a winner. There is a five-course chef's tasting menu every night but Saturday. ⊠ *1500 Walnut St.,* ☎ *215/732–4444. Reservations essential. AE, DC, MC, V. No lunch Sat.*

$$$–$$$$ ✕ **Bookbinder's Seafood House.** This Bookbinder's restaurant is the one that causes all the confusion: it is actually owned by a member of the original family, who sold the larger Old Original Bookbinder's, in the Historic Area, to new owners in the 1940s. The typical seafood restaurant decor includes stuffed swordfish on the walls and fishing nets dangling from the ceiling. The fare is equally predictable, with a few daily specials that deviate from the standard dishes. The famous snapper soup is always good; broiled local fish are a dependable choice. ⊠ *215 S. 15th St.,* ☎ *215/545–1137. AE, D, DC, MC, V. No lunch Sat.–Mon.*

$$–$$$$ ✕ **Devon Seafood Grill.** Once you get past the super-hopping bar (it's so popular with young singles that it's practically impossible to get in on Fridays after work), you enter an environment that is quintessential fish house with all the classic dishes of that genre and then some. Lobster in several sizes is always on the menu and generally available in all of them, beautifully cooked to order. Hot biscuits delivered to the table are runaway favorites. ⊠ *225 S. 18th St.,* ☎ *215/546–5940. AE, DC, MC, V.*

$$–$$$$ ✕ **McCormick & Schmick's Seafood Restaurant.** "Big, bold, and beautiful" might be the best way to describe everything about this super-fish-house: the height of the ceiling with its remarkable art deco chandeliers, the dining room, and the second-floor "snuggeries" with tables for six and curtained nooks, just right for private meetings. There are oysters galore and more than 40 daily selections of various fish and seafood from all points, starting with Maine (lobsters) to Valparaiso (Chilean sea bass) to more exotic ports of call. The food is prepared by a knowledgeable kitchen crew and served by a well-trained staff. ⊠ *1 S. Broad St.,* ☎ *215/568–6888. AE, D, DC, MC, V. No lunch weekends.*

$$–$$$$ ✕ **Sansom Street Oyster House.** This is the restaurant that conveys the most authentic "fish house" feeling in the city, almost like "old timey" no-nonsense places in Boston. Cary Neff, the new chef-owner, took over from the Mink family, who set the tone and honchoed the place almost since time immemorial, and left as their legacy a huge collection of antique oyster plates that decorate the walls. Neff follows in the tradition of searching out the freshest and the best and then preparing it simply and well. There's always a whole fish on the varied daily changing menu, cooked just right for its type. If crispy bronzino, a farm-raised Mediterranean fish, is being served, be sure to give it a try. An active raw bar at the front of the restaurant serves whichever top-notch oysters and clams are in the market. ⊠ *1516 Sansom St.,* ☎ *215/567–7683. AE, D, DC, MC, V. Closed Sun.*

Steak

$$$–$$$$ ✕ **Capital Grille.** It's only fair to question whether this is a restaurant or an art gallery. When you first enter the stunning dining room, you'll find the walls covered with exquisitely framed paintings of some famed Philadelphians such as Marian Anderson and John Wanamaker and bronze statues on pedestals. Never fear—check out the plates in front of the satisfied-looking, well-dressed customers and be assured that you're in the right place for the meal you've been anticipating. You'll find steaks and chops in just about every permutation: large and larger. A baby lobster (about a pound) makes an excellent appetizer along with the requisite shrimp cocktail, or salads. The wine cellar is ample and fairly priced for a selection of excellent bottles. ⊠ *1338 Chestnut St., at Broad St.,* ☎ *215/545–9588. AE, D, MC, V. No lunch weekends.*

$$$–$$$$ ✕ **Morton's of Chicago.** This classy steak house, now at a second-floor location a few steps from Broad Street, attracts many visitors familiar with Morton's other outposts of top-quality red meat and humongous lobsters as well as a devoted coterie of local businesspeople. Etched glass and wood dividers provide a semblance of privacy in the large dining room, and there is an intimate stand-up bar. The house specialty, a juicy, tasty, 24-ounce porterhouse, puts the most determined carnivore to the test. Other fine cuts of meat are available, too, presented for selection from a cart that is wheeled to the table. Pristine whole fish and lobsters are priced by the pound. The excellent vegetable portions are large—really enough for two—and are ordered à la carte. ⊠ *1411 Walnut St.,* ☎ *215/557–0724. AE, DC, MC, V. No lunch.*

$$$–$$$$ ✕ **Prime Rib.** The glamorous atmosphere of black-leather steak-house
★ posh, combined with the clubby feel of a longstanding classic restaurant, immediately make you aware you're in for some serious eating. Habitués (of whom there are many) admire the gigantic portions of dry-aged prime beef, glistening fresh seafood (also served in more than generous quantity), addictive baked potato skins, and other sit-up-and-take-notice dishes that keep this handsome restaurant hopping. ⊠ *Warwick Hotel, 1701 Locust St.,* ☎ *215/772–1701. Reservations essential. Jacket required. D, MC, V. No lunch weekends.*

$$$–$$$$ ✕ **Shula's.** There's absolutely no mistaking the orientation of this restaurant: football is the overriding theme, as evidenced by the meat-oriented menu printed on an official NFL game football, signed by Coach Don Shula, for whom the restaurant is named. Before you can say "Hike!" you'll have a menu printed on regular paper and the actual raw ingredients wheeled to your table on a cart. This allows you to behold the 48-ounce steak that, if you consume it all, will get your name emblazoned in a special honor roll, and the other custom-cut certified Angus beef. There's also fresh seafood, giant lobsters, and lamb. All forms of protein are treated with utmost respect, as are the vegetables. The rather formal dark paneled restaurant is enlivened by elaborate gold-framed pictures of the coach in various moods, from benign to ballistic. Shula's Hall of Fame Lounge features martinis, cordials, and fine cigars in a comfortable elegance. ⊠ *Wyndham Franklin Plaza, 17th and Race Sts.,* ☎ *215/448–2700. AE, D, DC, MC, V. No lunch weekends.*

$$$–$$$$ ✕ **Smith & Wollensky.** Adjacent to the Rittenhouse Hotel, an elegant hotel/condominium complex, but with its own outside entrance, this lively outpost of a New York classic steak house is on two levels—a café-type casual bar on the first floor and the whimsical but traditional dining room upstairs. The restaurant serves a typical steak house menu with some unique variances: a roasted pork shank is a permanent menu "special" and a 28-ounce Cajun rib eye that is the runaway patrons' choice. A baby lobster is a delightful appetizer, and the Wollensky salad with potato croutons gives people their vitamins with a "twist." ⊠ *210 Rittenhouse Sq.,* ☎ *215/545–1700. AE, D, DC, MC, V.*

$$–$$$$ ✕ **Davio's.** Billing itself as a "Northern Italian steak house," Davio's is unique in several ways: it is open for a "power" breakfast, as well as lunch and dinner; it features luscious pasta (like asparagus–shiitake

mushroom ravioli and spaghetti Bolognese with veal, beef, and pork); and it serves a variety of scintillating table sauces (try them on the homemade crusty bread). The sautéed chicken liver appetizer is a winner. In spite of many menu choices, the rib eyes, chops and strip steaks are certainly among the reasons that people flock to this upstairs space in the historic Provident Bank Building. ☒ *111 S. 17 St.,* ☎ *215/563–4810. AE, D, DC, MC, V.*

$$–$$$$ ✕ **Palm.** The city's branch of the celebrated Palm group holds forth in a light, bright, busy space off the lobby of the Park Hyatt at the Bellevue. The pure steak house ambience comes complete with bare floors, harried waiters, and huge steaks, chops, and salads whizzing by. Nearly in the shadow of City Hall and the surrounding courts, this is dealmaking territory, and local movers and shakers are frequently seen chatting it up at lunch and dinner. Caricatures of nearly everyone who is anyone in the city are on the walls, and it's fun to match up the people with their likenesses. The flavorful New York strip steak is fine at dinner, and the stupendous steak sandwich (*no* relation to a Philly cheese steak) is a lunchtime value. ☒ *Park Hyatt at the Bellevue, 200 S. Broad St.,* ☎ *215/546–7256. AE, D, DC, MC, V. No lunch weekends.*

Chinatown

Chinese

$$–$$$$ ✕ **Joseph Poon.** Named for its owner-chef, who created Chinese-Italian fusion, this contemporary restaurant decorated with jars of pasta is often the scene of special events, such as free weekly cooking classes. Peking duck pizza, Arch Street cioppino (fish in a black bean, bourbon, and ginger sauce), and fried spinach with five-spice powder and Parmesan are typical creations. Poon is also a celebrity master carver of fruits and vegetables, and his handiwork frequently decorates his plates. ☒ *1002 Arch St.,* ☎ *215/928–9333. AE, D, DC, MC, V. Closed Mon. No lunch weekends.*

$–$$$ ✕ **Ocean Harbor.** At lunchtime this restaurant resembles a Hong Kong–
★   style teahouse with multiple carts flying through the dining room full of dizzying selections of dim sum. Besides the usual pork and shrimp dumplings, the chefs often incorporate specifically Chinese ingredients. You point at what you want and it is transferred to your table and charged to your bill. The bill is in Chinese and prices vary, but no matter how much it takes to stuff your party, it ends up as a pretty reasonable meal. If you don't know what's in the dim sum, ask for a description—sometimes you get it. The clientele at lunch is mainly Chinese and the restaurant is crowded. Evenings are quieter, and the menu features Cantonese, Mandarin, and Szechuan dishes, with plenty of vegetarian options. ☒ *1023 Race St.,* ☎ *215/574–1398. DC, MC, V.*

$–$$ ✕ **Ocean City.** Lacquered ducks and roast pork cuts hang in the window of this restaurant on the eastern periphery of Chinatown, a large, bright place that covers all bases on its huge menu, although it leans heavily toward Cantonese. Fish tanks of creatures, including eels, meant for cooking line the entryway. Banquets for 10 or more people (reserve ahead) are an outstanding specialty. Order one of these, and course after course of well-known—and several lesser known but well-prepared—dishes comes flying to the table. A private ground-floor dining room holds 20, and the vast upstairs accommodates up to 500 people. ☒ *234 N. 9th St.,* ☎ *215/829–0688. AE, MC, V.*

$–$$ ✕ **Sang Kee Peking Duck House.** Although the decor is getting a bit tired, Sang Kee continues to dish up the most delicious noodle soups in town. Egg or rice noodles come in different widths with duck, pork, or beef brisket. If you wish, you can have your soup with both noodles *and* overstuffed, tender wontons. Other traditional foods, besides the house specialty duck, are carried from the kitchen with more speed than style. Beer is available. ✉ *238 N. 9th St.,* ☎ *215/925–7532. Reservations not accepted. No credit cards.*

Malaysian

$–$$$ ✕ **Penang.** The Asian and high-tech decor—bamboo and exposed pipes—of this one-of-a-kind in Philadelphia (although there are New York locations) is indicative of the surprising mix of flavors in this perennially busy restaurant. A taste of India creeps into a scintillating appetizer of a handkerchief-thin crepe with a small dipping dish of spicy chicken curry. Other preparations are redolent of flavors from several other Asian countries. Soups with various types of noodles are unusual, tasty, and filling. ✉ *117 N. 10th St.,* ☎ *215/413–2531. Reservations not accepted. No credit cards.*

Vietnamese

$–$$ ✕ **Vietnam.** This popular restaurant next to a busy police station serves up an extensive selection of Vietnamese food. Restaurateurs from many much fancier eateries often find one another here, comparing notes on which dishes are particularly tasty that day. The crisp spring rolls, squid with black bean sauce, and soups with rice noodles are good picks. Occasionally, however, it seems as if the chef himself is "out to lunch." It's cheap enough, however, to forgive an occasional lapse without damaging the budget. If the first couple of courses don't measure up to expectations on a particular day, it's possible to leave and head to another, similar place across the street to finish your meal. ✉ *221 N. 11th St.,* ☎ *215/592–1163. No credit cards.*

Ben Franklin Parkway/Art Museum Area

Belgian

$$–$$$ ✕ **Cuvée Notredame.** Michel Notredame, the jovial native Flemish chef-owner, is delighted to discuss the menu and the French/Flemish overtones of the dishes served in a very relaxed neighborhood bistro. Mussels, a Belgian favorite, are prepared curried, with leeks or cream, or in several other ways; duck and other traditional foods of the country are available, along with a wide variety of Belgian beers. The owner is the Philadelphia originator of the $5 bar menu—with entrées like "tough steak" with salad and fries or a small order of mussels with fries served at lunch in the dining room and at the bar until 1 AM. ✉ *1701 Green St.,* ☎ *215/765–2777. AE, DC, MC, V.*

Contemporary

$$$$ ✕ **Fountain Restaurant.** Dining at the Fountain is a cosmopolitan ex-
★ perience, blending pleasant, polished service with elegance of appointments. The peak of the experience, however, is unquestionably the food. Chef Martin Hamann and his staff are constantly experimenting to create culinary excitement that changes with the seasons. Among the favorites are lobster in a black truffle envelope and venison chop with an exotic mushroom tower and spinach. "Healthy menu" choices are equally delicious. The restaurant is tucked away off the lavish but understated lobby of the Four Seasons hotel—a culinary oasis for travelers and a favorite dining location for well-heeled locals. Especially popular is the Sunday brunch, a knockout in bounty, elegance—and price. In the Fountain, the latter is determined by the cost of the served-at-the-table entrée, although the rest of the meal is an all-you-can-stuff buffet of delicacies. The adjacent Swann Lounge includes the brunch entrées on a succession of varied buffets at a fixed price. A group plays nonstop classical jazz during the feast. ✉ *Four Seasons Hotel, 1 Logan Sq., Benjamin Franklin Pkwy.,* ☎ *215/963–1500. Reservations essential. Jackets required at dinner. AE, D, DC, MC, V.*

$$$ ✕ **London Grill.** Serving resolutely "today" food, such as sea scallops poached in lobster oil with potato blinis, this longstanding favorite of the locals keeps them interested with its seasonally changing menus that are imaginative and consistently good. So, too, is the bar food; mussels, wings, and quesadillas are popular. ⊠ *2301 Fairmont Ave.,* ☎ *215/978–4545. AE, D, DC, MC, V. No lunch Sat.*

$$$ ✕ **Museum Restaurant.** The venerable Philadelphia Museum of Art gives visitors an opportunity to feed their bodies while nourishing their souls at lunch as well as Wednesday night dinner and Sunday brunch. Run by nationally renowned Restaurant Associates, the restaurant is bright, white, and hung with a rotating display of paintings. The Chef's Table, a buffet with unlimited returns, artfully arranges foodstuffs such as ham, salmon, green beans, Parmesan toasts, crisp salad, and a fine cheese board. The chef is from the Eastern Shore of Chesapeake Bay and has a special way with crab. When the weather is amenable, a cold buffet is presented under a large tent on a terrace with a glorious view of the city. ⊠ *Philadelphia Museum of Art, 26th St. and Benjamin Franklin Pkwy.,* ☎ *215/684–7990. AE, DC, MC, V. Closed Mon. No dinner Thurs.–Tues.*

South Philadelphia

Diners and Philly Food

$–$$ ✕ **Morning Glory Diner.** Although the Morning Glory bills itself as a diner and offers many diner touches such as big mugs of steaming coffee (although the mugs are pewter), the place was transformed from a couple of storefronts and departs from tradition in other ways as well: big breakfasts come with mammoth homemade biscuits, but if you want toast, you pay extra. Tasty turkey meat loaf is a specialty—frequently topped off with nippy, homemade catsup—that gives obeisance to the sparky contemporary style of the owners. The accompanying home-fried potatoes, however, are underseasoned, dreary, and dull. ⊠ *735 S. 10th St.,* ☎ *215/413–3999. No credit cards. Closed Mon.*

$ ✕ **Tony Luke's.** The location—at Front Street and Oregon Avenue, nearly under I–95—earned such a reputation from truckers who stopped for huge beef or pork sandwiches with Italian greens and cheese that locals finally caught on and adopted the diner-like restaurant for their own. The lines are long, though they move quickly, and seating (outside only, under cover) is relatively scarce; still, people flock here from early morning to closing time for generous breakfasts and tasty sandwiches. For large orders, it's possible to call ahead and take food home. To service Center City patrons, **Tony Luke Jr's** was recently opened at 118 S. 18th Street; it's the same menu but not the same ambience. ⊠ *39 E. Oregon Ave.,* ☎ *215/551–5725. Reservations not accepted. No credit cards. Closed Sun.*

Italian

$$–$$$$ ✕ **Pastaria at Franco and Luigi's.** Arias from classic operas, sung mostly by fresh-faced young people who are in training or have done professional stints around Philadelphia and other cities, accompany somewhat unusual, but unquestionably Italian, dishes, such as veal, shrimp and scallops sautéed in scampi sauce over a bed of shredded radicchio. Reserve well in advance to ensure seating on weekends. ⊠ *1547–49 S. 13th St.,* ☎ *215/755–8903. AE. BYOB. Closed Mon. No lunch.*

$$–$$$ ✕ **Tre Scalini.** "Three little steps" are exactly what it takes to enter this restaurant in South Philadelphia, a locus of down-home Italian ambience. The food, too, is more home style than professional kitchen, yet it is unmistakably carefully prepared, including such unusual (for South Philadelphia) appetizers as a tangle of wild mushrooms, beautifully sautéed with garlic and served on their own. Otherwise, pasta

preparations such as black pasta with prawns and crabmeat are best; main courses suffer by comparison. ⊠ *1533 S. 11th St.,* ☏ *215/551–3870. AE, MC, V. BYOB. Closed Mon.*

Steak

$$$–$$$$ ✕ **The Saloon.** For many years this classic paneled restaurant has been
★ a favorite among Philadelphia's most discerning diners and sports figures, who enjoyed steaks and chops in more-than-generous portions and the always-true-to-their-roots Italian specialties. There were no surprises: just fine quality meats and seafood prepared and served simply in a clubby atmosphere where everyone felt familiar and the super-efficient waitstaff kept it that way. The superior quality of ingredients still shines, but with the help of an inspired chef, Gene Betz, a few more innovative twists sneak into the outstanding preparations, although not to the extent that they intrude on the sensibilities of the "regulars." ⊠ *750 S. 7th St.,* ☏ *215/627–1811. AE. Closed Sun. No lunch Sat. and Mon.*

Northern Liberties

Mediterranean

$$ ✕ **Aden.** This charming, funky restaurant in Northern Liberties, north of the Old City action, turns out astonishing food from an open kitchen. The owners are a self-taught chef, Hadaar Nisimi, and his sister, Nurit, a solicitous hostess, who apparently care deeply about pleasing their guests. A grilled vegetable salad cum appetizer is a standout, and osso bucco with barley risotto is a cornerstone of the menu. There is usually a selection of nicely prepared fish. A pleasant garden is open in good weather. ⊠ *614 N. 2nd St.,* ☏ *215/627–9844. AE, D, MC, V. BYOB. No lunch weekends.*

Mexican

$$ ✕ **Las Cazuelas.** This authentically Mexican family-run place is an anomaly in the rather dreary neighborhood. The colors, both inside and out, are warm and typically Mexican. The food is simple and rather gently spiced, apropos of the Puebla origins of the family. The food gives diners the taste of Mexico without being overbearing—perfect for people who want to experience this type of food without being immersed in too rich or too spicy dishes. Reservations are essential for groups larger than four. ⊠ *426–28 W. Girard Ave.,* ☏ *215/351–9144. MC, V.*

University City

Contemporary

$$–$$$$ ✕ **La Terrasse.** This is one of the original dining venues in the University City area—and one that has kept up with the times, renovating its interior decor and retooling the menu to keep pace with changing styles. It is a "stamping ground" for local college faculty and a destination for suburban and Center City types attending cultural events nearby. La Terrasse has gone through several incarnations but has settled down with a talented chef, David Grear, who wields a firm hand over the dining room, where you can sample duck confit with red cabbage or lobster and corn risotto. He's also concocted a first-rate selection of dishes to be devoured at the bar. Huge chicken fingers (tenders, actually) crusted with pretzel crumbs are everyone's favorite. Popcorn shrimp are not far behind. ⊠ *3432 Sansom St.,* ☏ *215/386–5000. AE, D, DC, MC, V. No lunch Sat.*

$$–$$$ ✕ **White Dog Cafe.** The name of this funkily decorated, eclectic restaurant in a brownstone near the University of Pennsylvania campus derives from the story of the 19th-century mystic Madame Blavatsky, who

claimed that while she was living in the house, a white dog lay across her ailing leg and cured it. Innovative restaurateur Judy Wicks took her inspiration from the tale and sponsors all manner of events that would make Madame Blavatsky proud—table talks, story telling, community service days, and more. The restaurant specializes in locally grown and humanely grown products, such as Pocono trout with a hazelnut crust and grass-fed beef; seasonings can be overly ambitious, so choose carefully. Vegetarians can find plenty to please them here. The small, lively bar has a number of American beers on tap and in bottles; the wine list, too, is all-American. The bar and grill menu offers lighter, less expensive fares, like organic chicken wings and a Mexican hoagie. ✉ *3420 Sansom St.,* ☎ *215/386–9224. AE, D, DC, MC, V.*

Eclectic

$$–$$$ ✕ **Nan.** Long before fusion was ever thought of as a way to describe
★   food, the inspired chef here began a wholly different approach to his native Thai food, pairing it with French ingredients and techniques. Others followed his lead, and to reflect on his future he took some time off. Now Kamul Phutlek is back in the swing, bewitching people with an intoxicating mix of flavors that keeps University folk, Center City types, and suburbanites clamoring for dishes such as crisp half-chicken with plum and tamarind sauce and escargots on puff pastry with duxelles and garlic butter. The simple three-course lunch is a downright bargain. Fruit tart is an ethereal dessert. ✉ *4000 Chestnut St.,* ☎ *215/ 382–0818. AE, MC, V. BYOB. Closed Sun and Mon.*

$$–$$$ ✕ **Pod.** The futuristic atmosphere of this restaurant (all-white retro-modern tables and chairs and large enveloping booths called "pods" whose lighting changes color with the touch of a button) is a fitting stage setting for food with strong Asian overtones that ultimately defies precise description. A sushi conveyor belt implies Japanese; Pad Thai, is, of course, evocative of Thai, or at least Thai-influenced since the original contains shrimp and this one crab. A dish that almost everybody orders, the Pod Pu-Pu platter, is a mixture of shrimp siu mai (Chinese), panko crab cake (sort of Japanese), wasabi potato wontons (anybody's guess), and Arctic char satay (ditto). It's all tasty, though, and served in an atmosphere as exciting as this, nobody seems to care much about authenticity. There's an extensive sake bar for aficionados of that alcoholic beverage, and it's served both warm and cold. Reservations are essential on the weekends. ✉ *3636 Sansom St.,* ☎ *215/387–1803. AE, DC, MC, V. No lunch weekends.*

Indian

$–$$$ ✕ **Tandoor India.** Although the ambiance is not particularly elegant in this primarily student, faculty, and Indian-oriented restaurant (you'll see lots of women in *saris* and *cameesh churidar* [baggy pants with overdresses]), there's a full range of delicious foods cooked in the *tandoor* (super-hot clay oven) as well as other dishes prepared in conventional pots and ovens. There is a bargain-price buffet both at lunch and dinner and a full range of other authentic North and South Indian specialities served à la carte. ✉ *106 S. 40th St.,* ☎ *215/222–7122. AE, D, DC, MC, V. BYOB.*

Japanese

$$–$$$$ ✕ **Nara.** This simple, classic looking Japanese place is new, but in a downstairs space formerly occupied by the original Genji, which was probably the earliest of its genre in University City; the majority of its following comes from the nearby college crowd, both students and faculty, but is by no means limited to this group. Now nearly everybody who is addicted to the cult of raw fish in its many guises favors this place

for its pleasant, helpful management, and lovely renditions. ✉ *4002 Spruce St.*, ☎ *215/387–1583. AE, DC, MC, V. No lunch weekends.*

Thai

$–$$ ✕ **Thai Singa House.** Simple and unprepossessing, this pleasant family-run Thai outpost in University City cooks all the usual American- and authentic Thai dishes plus an array of more unusual (for this country, at least) ones, such as venison and wild boar. Pad Thai, a noodle-dish staple that's a good choice if you're not certain you love Thai food, is particularly well prepared, with an authenticity of texture and a fine meld of flavors. The family is fun to talk to, and the proprietor and his wife are helpful both to novices and to experts exploring unfamiliar dishes on the menu. ✉ *3939 Chestnut St.*, ☎ *215/382–8001. AE, D, DC, MC, V.*

City Avenue

Contemporary

$$$–$$$$ ✕ **The Marker.** This restaurant in the Adam's Mark hotel has become increasingly popular as its menu has developed a more adventurous style under the tutelage of creative chef Vincent Alberici. Popular items include asparagus, morel and lobster risotto; pan-roasted day boat scallops; lavender honey-glazed Eberly Farms Cornish hens; and a coconut key lime Alaska. The Library, a cozy room with a fireplace and built-in bookshelves, is a favorite seating choice, but there are two other larger, somewhat more formal areas as well. This is a popular spot for its lavish Sunday brunch, which has two seatings. ✉ *Adam's Mark Hotel, City Line Ave. and Monument Rd.*, ☎ *215/581–5010. AE, D, DC, MC, V.*

Manayunk

American/Casual

$$ **Le Bus.** The American classics, such as meat loaf and great pasta, as well as hearty soups, tasty salads, and vegetarian entrées are all complemented by the wonderful homemade breads this super-casual, friendly place is known for. The children's menu and reasonable prices make Le Bus comfortable for families. On weekends, it's a popular spot for a brunch of omelets, frittatas, and pancakes. It's a mob scene, so go early. In nice weather, you can eat outdoors. ✉ *4266 Main St.*, ☎ *215/487–2663. Reservations not accepted. AE, DC, MC, V.*

Contemporary

$$$–$$$$ ✕ **Jake's.** Owner-chef Bruce Cooper (his wife is Jake) has garnered a ★ reputation for food that is innovative but somehow classic. The place displays the hottest in contemporary crafts, many from local art galleries that punctuate trendy Manayunk. Cooper has a particular affinity for scallops and transforms them into exquisite appetizers. His crab cakes are also outstanding. This is one of the places that helped Manayunk achieve its reputation as a dining mecca. ✉ *4365 Main St.*, ☎ *215/483–0444. AE, DC, MC, V.*

$$–$$$ ✕ **Sonoma.** The first of Chef Derek Davis's ventures as an entrepreneur became the cornerstone of his mini-empire in trendy Manayunk. The contemporary, airy design sets the stage for California-influenced food with Italian touches. The sandwiches on focaccia are standouts, as is the glazed chicken. Sonoma immediately earned a reputation as a hangout for those who are hip; the bar, which regularly stocks 220 varieties of vodka, cemented that reputation. There's sidewalk dining in season. ✉ *4411 Main St.*, ☎ *215/483–9400. Reservations not accepted. AE, D, DC, MC, V.*

Southwestern

$$-$$$ ✕ **Arroyo Grill.** This multilevel restaurant on a tiny island in the middle of the Schuylkill River serves Derek Davis's interpretation of southwestern food, such as Texas barbecue and fried oysters on tortillas with salsa. The ambience is funky and charming; the second-floor deck is the favored location for eating (in decent weather), and the crush of people who know it keeps the servers hopping. Tequila is king at the busy bar. ⊠ *Main and Levering Sts.,* ☎ *215/487–1400. AE, D, DC, MC, V.*

Steak

$$-$$$$ ✕ **Kansas City Prime.** Part of Derek Davis's Main Street Restaurant group, this is the only place in the city that features ultra-tender, ultra-pricy Kobe beef on its menu. In a sleek, elegant, muted-color decor, you'll find all the other steak house accoutrements, including humongous lobsters. The wine list is award-winning. ⊠ *4417 Main St.,* ☎ *215/482–3700. AE, D, DC, MC, V. No lunch.*

Main Line

Contemporary

$$-$$$$ ✕ **Tango.** Neither the attractive facade—nor the interior—of this restaurant gives a clue to its origins as the busy train station through which filtered generations of Bryn Mawr and surrounding preparatory school students. Steaks and pasta share menu space with fish that is picked up daily in New York by a restaurant employee. Sharing a warm spinach and artichoke dip is a good way to start a meal, and steak is an adequate way to continue: the steaks are tasty but don't live up to the tenderness of upscale national steak house standards set by the several newcomers to the Philadelphia scene. But, then, this is the "burbs" with standards of their own. The ambience is pleasant and lively with a good-looking crowd. ⊠ *39 Morris Ave., Bryn Mawr,* ☎ *610/526–9500. AE, D, DC, MC, V. No lunch Sun.*

$$-$$$ ✕ **333 Belrose Bar & Grill.** Once a full-service greenhouse, and maintained as such while opening as a restaurant, this now is home to an atmosphere as contemporary as the fusion cuisine. Chef/Owner Carlo DeMarco's fish and shellfish dishes, such as suger-cane skewered bigeye tuna or diver scallops with saffron risotto, seem to be the entrees of choice for the Main Line locals who are the backbone patrons. For heartier appetites there's pancetta-topped filet mignon and a pork tenderloin in black-bean sauce. ⊠ *333 Belrose St., Radnor,* ☎ *610/293–1000. AE, DC, MC, V. No lunch weekends.*

French

$$$-$$$$ ✕ **Le Mas Perrier.** In Provence a "mas" is an old farm, and true to its roots, this restaurant looks for all the world as if it were transported in its entirety from that charming part of France—updated, of course, to encompass all the best that is "today." The table settings feature plates that reflect the warm colors of Southern France, boasting, in addition, a large stylized "P" in the center—for Perrier (the owner, most assuredly) or Pascal (the chef who comes from Provence?). Never mind, it's what goes on the plates that's most important. A *soup de poisson* (fish soup) is true to its origin and a bouillabaisse (a fancier fish and shellfish soup) is even more so. The ultimate representative of the region is the Salade Niçoise, made with fresh tuna rather than canned, and those tiny, tasty olives. Gravlax, mysteriously called here *fondant de saumon,* is thickly cut in chunks rather than slices, lightly cured and sumptuous, along with celery root sparked with mustard. The wine list includes a number of reasonable bottles, including some from Provence. ⊠ *Spread*

Eagle Village, 503 W. Lancaster Ave., Wayne, ☎ *610/964–2588. AE, D, DC, MC, V. No lunch weekends.*

Italian

$$$–$$$$ ✕ **Toscana Cucina Rustica.** Every inch of this restaurant suggests Tuscany, including some antique amphorae (wine casks) that were used to store the precious wine of that region. The food, too, is reminiscent of that lovely part of Italy, lightly but pleasantly seasoned. Chicken cooked under a brick is a specialty: it's herb-infused and roasted under a special weight. Fried artichokes and pastas are winners. ⊠ *24 N. Merion Ave., Bryn Mawr,* ☎ *610/527–7700. AE, MC, V. No lunch.*

Mediterranean

$$$–$$$$ ✕ **Savona.** Strikingly attractive, thoroughly refined in taste and am-
★ bience, this restaurant with its outstanding Riviera-influenced cuisine is a destination for many people from the surrounding suburbs, corporate types and, yes, Center City Philadelphia folks, too. Every appointment for enjoying the cuisine is in place: gorgeous tableware and other lavish touches of various sorts. Chef Dominique Filoni has won lavish praise for his cuisine. Lobster risotto is exquisite; roast squab is, too. The wine list is extensive and creative, and the service is thoughtful and professional. ⊠ *100 Old Gulph Rd., Gulph Mills,* ☎ *610/520–1200. AE, DC, MC, V. No lunch.*

3 LODGING

From historic digs with four-poster beds
to hotels that favor such grand gestures
as room-service foie gras, Philadelphia has
lodgings for every style of travel. Thanks to
the Pennsylvania Convention Center and a
hotel-building boom, some midprice chains
have moved into town or have spruced up
their accommodations. If you have greater
expectations, you need look no further than
the city's handful of swank hotels, each with
its own gracious character.

By Barbara
Ann Rosenberg

PHILADELPHIA HOTELS RUN THE GAMUT from world class to commonplace, from a plush 1,400-room hotel with every amenity to an intimate seven-room inn in an 1836 Federal period house. There are posh new hotels in historic bank buildings, all-suites hotels in remodeled apartment houses, and boutique business hotels in the heart of the city.

According to the Philadelphia Convention and Visitors Bureau, some 4,000 new rooms have been added to the roster in the past few years; this dramatic growth is credited to the demand created by the Pennsylvania Convention Center. Although there are utilitarian hotels and national chains, both in town and in the area close to the airport, this big city still has a relatively small pool of moderately priced hotels in its downtown area.

Hotels in this chapter are listed geographically. The Historic Area, on the east side of downtown, centers on Independence Hall and extends to the Delaware River. Old City and Society Hill lodgings are included here, and so is a new Hyatt Hotel at Penn's Landing, on the Delaware River waterfront. Center City encompasses the heart of the downtown business district, centered around Broad and Market streets; Rittenhouse Square hotels are in this section. The Benjamin Franklin Parkway/Museum Area runs along the parkway from 16th Street to the Philadelphia Museum of Art. A couple of hotels are in University City, near the West Philadelphia campuses of the University of Pennsylvania and Drexel University. Additional hotels are clustered near Philadelphia International Airport, about 8 mi south (a 20-minute drive) of Center City. Three are in the City Line Avenue area, west of downtown. Other options can be found in outlying areas, including Valley Forge, Lancaster and Bucks counties.

Even with the large number of hotel rooms, it is still occasionally difficult to find a place to stay. Advance reservations are advised. Philadelphia has no off-season rates, but many hotels offer discount packages for weekends, when demand from businesspeople and groups subsides. Besides substantially reduced rates, these packages often include an assortment of freebies, such as breakfast, parking, cocktails or champagne, and the use of exercise facilities. Tickets to popular museum shows have become part of many special packages, too. Always ask about special packages and rates when making a reservation; inquire if you can get a discount for your AARP, AAA, or hotel frequent traveler membership. Most downtown hotels charge an average of $15 a day for parking when it is not included as a package feature. Accommodations are ranked according to the categories described in the lodging price chart for Philadelphia *in* Smart Travel Tips A to Z.

B&B Reservation Services

Bed-and-breakfast establishments in Philadelphia can be appealing for a number of reasons, such as a warm welcome reflecting the personal touch of the owner, or antiques-filled rooms. These sometimes (but not always) less expensive alternatives to hotels offer considerable diversity depending on amenities. Breakfasts range from simple to hearty to elegant. Be aware that some B&Bs welcome children and pets, but others do not. A number of B&Bs are listed in this chapter, and reservation services can help you find others in or near the center of the city or in a variety of other neighborhoods from urban to rural.

$–$$$$ **Bed and Breakfast Connections–Philadelphia** (✉ Box 21, Devon 19333, ☎ 610/687–3565 or 800/448–3619, WEB www.bnbphiladelphia.com) is a reservation service representing more than 100 inspected host

Lodging

homes and inns including a Colonial town house, a converted barn, and a farmhouse on the Main Line. It includes properties in Philadelphia, Valley Forge, Brandywine Valley, Bucks, and Lancaster counties.

Historic Area

$$$ ☒ **Omni Hotel at Independence Park.** With attractive accommodations in the historic district, the Omni has the feel of a much smaller hotel. An ornate fireplace dominates the lobby; you can have cocktails in the adjoining lounge in front of floor-to-ceiling windows overlooking a meticulously groomed park and city streets. The spacious rooms are decorated in pretty floral prints but are otherwise undistinguished; many have park views. The health club includes a lap pool, exercise pool, sauna, and whirlpool. This is a pleasant location for visiting the art galleries and cafés of Old City as well as the Liberty Bell, Independence Hall, and other historic attractions. ☒ *4th and Chestnut Sts., 19106,* ☎ *215/925–0000 or 800/843–6664,* ᖴᴬˣ *215/925–1263,* ᴡᴱᴮ *www.omnihotels.com. 147 rooms, 3 suites. Restaurant, lobby lounge, in-room data ports, no-smoking floors, room service, indoor pool, health club, concierge, business services, parking (fee). AE, D, DC, MC, V.*

$$$ ☒ **Sheraton Society Hill.** Convenient to the historic area, this redbrick neo-Colonial building is two blocks from Penn's Landing, three blocks from Head House Square, and four blocks from Independence Hall. The hotel's pleasant atrium lobby, filled with trees and plants, is framed by archways and balconies and lighted by wrought-iron lanterns. Rooms are furnished traditionally in shades of blue or green and have modern conveniences such as voice mail and coffeemakers. The fourth-floor rooms facing east toward the Delaware River have the best view. ☒ *1 Dock St., 19106,* ☎ *215/238–6000 or 800/325–3535,* ᖴᴬˣ *215/922–2709,* ᴡᴱᴮ *www.sheraton.com. 365 rooms, 14 suites. Restaurant, bar, in-room data ports, minibars, room service, indoor pool, health club, laundry service, concierge, parking (fee). AE, D, DC, MC, V.*

$$–$$$ ☒ **Best Western Independence Park Hotel.** From the rooms facing busy Chestnut Street you'll hear the clop-clop of carriage horses as well as the roar of city buses. Things tend to quiet down during normal sleeping hours, though. The five-story building was built in 1856, opened in 1988 as a hotel and renovated in 2000. The high-ceiling guest rooms are modern but have period touches and come in standard and deluxe. The latter includes a king-size bed and a parlor. VCRs and videos can be rented for a small charge. Complimentary European breakfast and afternoon tea with snacks are served in a courtyard with a glass ceiling. ☒ *235 Chestnut St., 19106,* ☎ *215/922–4443 or 800/624–2988,* ᖴᴬˣ *215/922–4487,* ᴡᴱᴮ *www.independenceparkinn.com. 36 rooms. In-room data ports, parking (fee). AE, D, DC, MC, V. CP.*

$$–$$$ ☒ **Holiday Inn Independence Mall.** The "Independence Mall" in the name is no exaggeration; the hotel lies in America's "most historic square mile," within a block or two of the Liberty Bell and Independence Hall. The eight-story hotel with a rooftop pool was recently refurbished and is looking considerably fresher. Multicolor coverlets, tall lamps, and work desks help create a generally pleasant ambience. ☒ *4th and Arch Sts., 19106,* ☎ *215/923–8660 or 800/843–2355,* ᖴᴬˣ *215/923–4633,* ᴡᴱᴮ *www.holiday-inn.com. 364 rooms, 7 suites. Restaurant, lounge, in-room data ports, pool, shops, coin laundry, business services, parking (fee). AE, D, DC, MC, V.*

$$–$$$ ☒ **Hyatt Regency at Penn's Landing.** The theme here is "room with a view." The first hotel to open on the banks of the Delaware River offers dramatic river views from both back and front rooms of the 22-story tower. The fourth-floor fitness center has views of the city and the waterfront; after you swim in the indoor pool, you can lounge on the outdoor terrace. Likewise, Keating Restaurant has both indoor seating and alfresco dining on a deck overlooking the river. The guest rooms are contemporary and well sized; Business Plan rooms include laptop computers and fax machines. ⊠ *201 S. Columbus Blvd. 19106,* ☎ *215/928–1234 or 800/233–1234,* FAX *215/521–6600,* WEB *www.hyatt.com. 337 rooms, 13 suites. Restaurant, bar, café, in-room data ports, in-room safes, room service, indoor pool, sauna, health club, business services, car rental, free parking. AE, D, DC, MC, V.*

$$–$$$ ☒ **Penn's View Inn.** This cosmopolitan little hotel on the fringe of Old
★ City, an enclave of artists' galleries and studios, has its own brand of urban charm. Housed in a refurbished 19th-century commercial building, Penn's View Inn is owned by a well-regarded Italian-born restaurateur. The owner also runs Panorama, the downstairs eatery and extensive wine bar. Guest rooms are done in subdued tapestry; four deluxe rooms have a whirlpool bath and fireplace with windows overlooking the Delaware River. Accommodations are comfortable and rather European, with Chippendale-style furniture, floral wallpaper, and queen beds. Street noise can be a concern in some of the rooms. A complimentary Continental breakfast buffet is served. ⊠ *14 N. Front St., 19106,* ☎ *215/922–7600 or 800/331–7634,* FAX *215/922–7642.* WEB *www.pennsviewhotel.com. 28 rooms. Restaurant, bar, no-smoking rooms, room service, concierge, parking (fee). AE, DC, MC, V. CP.*

$–$$ ☒ **Comfort Inn at Penn's Landing.** The reasonable price is the most noteworthy draw here, with complimentary Continental breakfast as an additional lure at this 10-story hotel. Decor is contemporary, with oak furniture and a mauve color scheme. A bar helps enliven the small, nondescript lobby. Tucked between the Benjamin Franklin Bridge, Columbus Boulevard, and I–95, the location has more noise than charm—but if you have a room on an upper floor facing the river, you'll enjoy a good view of the Benjamin Franklin Bridge lighted up at night. A nice plus is the courtesy van service to Center City; foot power brings you to the nearby Betsy Ross House, historic Elfreth's Alley, or to the RiverLink Ferry to the New Jersey State Aquarium in Camden. ⊠ *100 N. Columbus Blvd., 19106,* ☎ *215/627–7900 or 800/228–5150,* FAX *215/238–0809,* WEB *www.comfortinn.com. 185 rooms. Lobby lounge, no-smoking rooms, laundry service, meeting rooms, parking (fee). AE, D, DC, MC, V. CP.*

$–$$ ☒ **Thomas Bond House.** It doesn't get much more Colonial than this: you can spend the night in the heart of Old City the way Philadelphians did in the 18th century. Built in 1769 by a prominent local physician, this four-story Georgian house, now a B&B, has undergone a faithful, meticulous restoration of everything from its molding and wall sconces to the millwork and flooring. Rooms have reproduction period furnishings (there are also a few antiques) including four-poster beds, and two have marble fireplaces. Some rooms are cold in winter. A full breakfast is served on weekends. ⊠ *129 S. 2nd St., 19106,* ☎ *215/923–8523 or 800/845–2663,* FAX *215/923–8504,* WEB *www.bnbinns. com/thomasbondhouse.inn. 10 rooms, 2 suites. Breakfast room, parking (fee). AE, MC, V. CP.*

Center City

$$$$ ☒ **Hotel Sofitel Philadelphia.** Opened early in 2000, this link in the French chain is a luxurious 14-story hotel with a facade of limestone and tinted glass. The simplicity of Shaker quilts inspired the lobby floor, done in seven kinds of granite and marble that introduce the hotel's interior color palate of blues, black, and neutral tones; the reception desk is made of blue Brazilian granite. A striking lighting fixture of steel and Murano glass hangs over the main staircase. Guest rooms are sleekly modern yet comfortable. Chez Colette, a contemporary brasserie that is a trademark of Sofitel, pays homage to the famous French writer and has recently acquired an impressive French chef from Alsace. Cherry walls trimmed with satin chrome hold artwork, letters, and other Colette memorabilia. ⊠ *122 S. 17 St., 19103,* ☎ *215/569–8300 or 800/ SOFITEL,* ℻ *215/564–7453,* 𝚆𝙴𝙱 *www.accor.com. 235 rooms, 65 suites. Brasserie, lobby lounge, in-room data ports, minibars, no-smoking rooms, room service, gym, concierge, meeting rooms, parking (fee). AE, D, DC, MC, V.*

$$$$ ★   🏨 **The Rittenhouse.** This small luxury hotel, in a building with condominium residences on several floors, takes full advantage of its Rittenhouse Square location: many of the rooms and the restaurant overlook the city's prettiest park. The expansive white-marble lobby leads to the Mary Cassatt Tearoom and Lounge and a cloistered garden. The 33-story building's sawtooth design gives the guest rooms unusual shapes, with nooks and alcoves. Each room has a very large, luxurious bathroom done in golden brown marble, with a TV and a scale; many have whirlpool tubs. Posh amenities include three telephones, an entertainment center in an armoire, a fully stocked minibar, and a king-size bed. Ninth-floor rooms facing the square have the best views. ⊠ *210 W. Rittenhouse Sq., 19103,* ☎ *215/546–9000 or 800/635–1042,* ℻ *215/732–3364,* 𝚆𝙴𝙱 *www.rittenhousehotel.com. 87 rooms, 11 suites. 2 restaurants, bar, in-room data ports, in-room fax, minibars, no-smoking floor, room service, indoor pool, sauna, spa, health club, concierge, business services, parking (fee). AE, D, DC, MC, V.*

$$$$ ★   🏨 **Ritz-Carlton Philadelphia.** The new 30-story hotel occupies the neoclassical former Mellon Bank building catercorner to City Hall in the heart of Center City. The bank's spectacular rotunda houses public spaces including two popular restaurants; an adjoining tower holds the guest rooms. This new Ritz lives up to the standards of the chain with special Ritz toiletries, complimentary shoe shines, twice-a-day housekeeping, and more. You'll know you're in the lap of luxury if you order a butler-drawn bath from the "bath menu"—the Bubbly Bath comes with rose petals strewn about, votive candles encircling the tub, and champagne and chocolate truffles to eat; the Gentleman's Bath features cedar and sandalwood, and a cigar and Cognac served tub-side. Guest rooms offer spectacular city views, marble baths, and 24-hour in-room dining. The Club rooms, on the top four floors, feature upgraded amenities, a dedicated concierge, and complimentary food in the hand-carved, walnut-panel Ritz-Carlton Club, which occupies the executive boardroom of the former Girard Trust Company. ⊠ *10 Avenue of the Arts (S. Broad St.), 19107,* ☎ *215/735–7700 or 800/241– 3333,* ℻ *215/735–7710,* 𝚆𝙴𝙱 *www.ritzcarlton.com. 299 rooms, 31 suites. 2 restaurants, bar, in-room data ports, minibars, no-smoking floor, room service, gym, laundry service, concierge, business services, parking (fee). AE, D, DC, MC, V.*

$$$$ 🏨 **Sheraton Rittenhouse Square.** A "green" haven, this innovative hotel on the city's prettiest square is billing itself as the "first environmentally smart hotel in America." Built inside a former apartment house, the Sheraton has been creative in many ways. A huge bamboo stand in the lobby helps oxygenate the air, and filtered fresh air circulates in the guest rooms at all times. Furniture in the rooms was made from recycled wooden pallets, and all carpeting comes from 100% recycled surplus synthetic fiber; sheets and bedspreads are organic cotton. In keeping with the organic theme, the hotel's color scheme is soothing beige, sand, tan, and peach. If you hadn't guessed already, no smoking is permitted anywhere in the hotel. In the lobby are Potcheen, an Irish-oriented sports pub, and Bleu, a popular cafe. ⊠ *227 S. 18th St., 19103,* ☎ *215/546–9400 or 800/325–3535,* ℻ *215/*

893–0955, WEB *www.sheratonphiladelphia.com. 193 rooms, 7 suites. 2 restaurants, in-room data ports, gym, meeting rooms, parking (fee). AE, D, DC, MC, V.*

$$$$
★
🏨 **Westin Philadelphia.** Without skipping a beat, Westin took over a location that was formerly occupied by the St. Regis. The 15-story structure is nestled between the twin blue towers of tall, tall Liberty Place (and adjacent to the Shops at Liberty Place—more than 70 stores, boutiques, and restaurants). Rooms are decorated in what can be called luxury Colonial. Breakfronts full of gorgeous china and fine paintings set the tone in the public areas. Guest rooms all have specially designed "Heavenly" beds with all-cotton sheets, two or more king-size down pillows (or non-allergenic fillings), new 27-inch TVs and "hands-free" phones at desks equipped with a fax/copier/printer. ⊠ *17th and Chestnut Sts. at Liberty Place, 19103,* ☎ *215/563–1600 or 800/WESTIN1,* FAX *215/567–2822,* WEB *www.westin.com. 275 rooms, 15 suites. Restaurant, bar, lobby lounge, in-room data ports, no-smoking rooms, room service, health club, baby-sitting, laundry service, concierge, parking (fee). AE, D, DC, MC, V.*

$$$–$$$$ 🏨 **The Inn on Locust.** Small, unique, and charming: these are unusual words, perhaps, to describe a state-of-the-art boutique business hotel. With just 24 rooms, this oasis in a restored Georgian Revival building has unusual features, such as in-room safes, each with an interior plug for recharging your laptop—allowing for security and practicality at the same time—and DVD players, along with a library of new releases. The queen-size bedding is all white, which gives a crisp, fresh look to the rooms; the furniture is smartly designed but spare. Rooms have small kitchenettes and a desk with ergonomic desk chairs. Guests have access to a nearby fitness club. ⊠ *1234 Locust St., 19107,* ☎ *215/985–1905 or 866/956–2878,* FAX *215/985–0945,* WEB *www.innonlocust.com. 24 rooms. Restaurant, bar, in-room data ports, in-room fax, in-room safes, kitchenettes, room service, laundry service, parking (fee). AE, D, DC, MC, V. CP.*

$$$–$$$$ 🏨 **Park Hyatt Philadelphia at the Bellevue.** A Philadelphia institution for more than 90 years, the elegant Bellevue hotel is now managed by Hyatt, with its lower floors transformed into the upscale Shops at the Bellevue (including Tiffany's and Polo/Ralph Lauren), offices, and a food court with a wide range of choices. The Barrymore Room, topped by a 30-ft stained-glass dome, is great for tea and cocktails; Founders, the hotel's posh restaurant, has views of the city from its 19th-floor location. Both these spaces rank among the most visually impressive in town. From the champagne toast or bottled water available at registration to the telephones in the bathrooms, a stay at the Park Hyatt promises luxury. The large, recently refurbished rooms are done in light, bright prints and possess the high ceilings and moldings typical of older hotels; each has an entertainment center with color TV, stereo, and VCR. Guests have free use of the Sporting Club, the poshest health club in town. ⊠ *Broad and Walnut Sts., 19102,* ☎ *215/893–1776 or 800/233–1234,* FAX *215/732–8518,* WEB *www.hyatt.com. 146 rooms, 26 suites. Restaurant, bar, in-room data ports, in-room fax, in-room safes, minibars, no-smoking rooms, room service, hair salon, spa, shops, concierge, baby-sitting, laundry service, parking (fee). AE, D, DC, MC, V.*

$$$–$$$$ 🏨 **Philadelphia Marriott.** If you like big, bustling hotels, this is the place for you. Opened in 1995 and expanded in 1999, this convention hotel—the biggest in Pennsylvania—takes up an entire city block and has so many corridors that sometimes even the staff gets lost. For an intrinsically impersonal type of place, the Marriott tries to meet special needs (iron and ironing board in each room, 24-hour workout room, children's menu from room service); it also offers some of the lowest rates in its price category. The five-story lobby atrium has a water sculpture, piano music

(live and taped), and greenery (real and fake). The more than 1,400 guest rooms are big, beige, and bland; half come with two queen beds, the rest with kings; all have extra counter space in the bathrooms. You can request, at no additional cost, one of the 250 "rooms that work," with an adjustable work table and extra lighting and outlets. ⊠ *1201 Market St., 19107,* ☎ *215/625–2900 or 800/320–5744,* 𝖥𝖠𝖷 *215/625–6000,* 𝖶𝖤𝖡 *www.marriott.com. 1,408 rooms, 76 suites. 2 restaurants, 2 lobby lounges, sports bar, room service, indoor pool, hair salon, spa, health club, coin laundry, laundry service, concierge, business services, meeting rooms, parking (fee). AE, D, DC, MC, V.*

$$$ ⌸ **Courtyard Philadelphia Downtown.** Marriott's largest Courtyard, this new hotel is housed in the historic City Hall Annex, and original brass, copper, and bronze details on the elevators and staircases have been refurbished. The hotel is just across the street from its sister property, the Philadelphia Marriott; both help service the Pennsylvania Convention Center. The hotels share some facilities such as meeting rooms. Each pleasantly comfortable room (smaller than those in the Marriott), decorated in muted shades of red, green, and gold, has a full-size work desk, and two telephones among its amenities. ⊠ *21 N. Juniper St., 19107,* ☎ *215/496–3200 or 800/321–2211,* 𝖥𝖠𝖷 *215/496–3696,* 𝖶𝖤𝖡 *www.marriott.com. 500 rooms, 16 suites. Restaurant, lobby lounge, in-room data ports, room service, indoor pool, gym, coin laundry, laundry service, concierge, business services, meeting rooms, parking (fee). AE, D, DC, MC, V.*

$$$ ⌸ **Rittenhouse Square Bed and Breakfast.** A stay here is like staying in an outlying manor house—but you're actually in the heart of Center City, close to the best shopping, dining, and elegant Rittenhouse Square. This B&B in a renovated 1900s carriage house is loaded with pampering touches, such as concierge service, marble baths, turndown service, oversize towels, robes, and 25-inch TVs with VCR. Some rooms have whirlpool baths, balconies, and data ports. Continental breakfast includes specialty breads from the best bakeries in town, with a choice of beverages; each evening there's a complimentay snack and wine. ⊠ *1715 Rittenhouse Sq., 19103,* ☎ *215/546–6500 or 877/791–6500,* 𝖥𝖠𝖷 *215/546–8787,* 𝖶𝖤𝖡 *www.rittenhousebb.com. 8 rooms, 2 suites. Breakfast room, concierge, parking (fee). AE, DC, MC, V. CP.*

$$–$$$ ⌸ **Latham.** When this hotel opened early in the 20th century, it was reportedly the finest hostelry in America for business travelers. It remains a small, elegant boutique hotel with a European accent; doormen clad in vests and riding boots welcome you to the small lobby. The rooms, which were renovated in 1997, are done in hunter green or more contemporary black and tan; they have marble-top bureaus and Louis XV–style writing desks, full-wall mirrors, and terry robes; bathrooms have marble showers and floors. The hotel, one block from Rittenhouse Square, recently acquired a full-service restaurant, Jolly's, that serves breakfast, lunch and dinner. ⊠ *135 S. 17th St., 19103,* ☎ *215/563–7474 or 877/LATHAM1,* 𝖥𝖠𝖷 *215/568–0110,* 𝖶𝖤𝖡 *www.lathamhotel.com. 138 rooms, 1 suite. Restaurant, room service, gym, business services, meeting rooms, parking (fee). AE, D, DC, MC, V. BP.*

$$–$$$ ✕ **Loews Philadelphia Hotel.** Topped by the red neon letters PSFS, this 1930s building was America's first skyscraper in the International modernist style; it was headquarters to the Pennsylvania Savings Fund Society. Now this National Historic Landmark is home to the dramatic Loews Hotel. Resolutely modern, the hotel guest rooms are all equipped with cordless phones and modems. There are three levels of concierge rooms with a private library and lounge. The lobby lounge and restaurant, which serves regional American cuisine, are both art deco in style. A 15,000-square-ft state-of-the-art fitness center includes a sauna, steam room, spa, and indoor lap pool. ⊠ *1200 Market St., 19107,*

☎ *215/627–1200 or 800/235–6397,* FAX *215/231–7305.* WEB *www.loewshotels.com. 546 rooms, 37 suites. Restaurant, lounge, in-room data ports, in-room safes, minibars, room service, indoor pool, sauna, spa, gym, laundry service, concierge floors, business services, parking (fee). AE, D, MC, V.*

$$–$$$ ☷ **Warwick Hotel & Towers.** The spacious guest rooms in this landmark 1929 English Renaissance style hotel come in three distinct categories—standard, deluxe, and the large Towers rooms. The freshly renovated guest rooms are pleasant and bright, with a floral motif. Bathrooms are marble or tile, and all rooms have voice messaging, a large desk, and free newspaper delivery. The hotel's lobby is large and open, with a balcony; the Towers area has an 18th-floor lounge. ⌧ *1701 Locust St., 19103,* ☎ *215/735–6000 or 800/523–4210,* FAX *215/790–7766,* WEB *www.warwickphilly.com. 523 rooms, 46 suites. 2 restaurants, bar, coffee shop, in-room data ports, room service, gym, sauna, concierge floors, business services, meeting room, parking (fee). AE, DC, MC, V.*

$–$$$ ☷ **Crowne Plaza Philadelphia City Center.** This 25-floor hotel is between Benjamin Franklin Parkway, Rittenhouse Square, and City Hall. The good-size guest rooms have a green-and-beige color scheme and contemporary decor. Rooms designated Executive Edition have extra amenities, including voice mail, irons and ironing boards, coffeemakers, cable TV, hair dryers, and *USA Today.* The Elephant and Castle serves indifferent British food but is a convenient place for a drink. ⌧ *1800 Market St., 19103,* ☎ *215/561–7500 or 800/2CROWNE,* FAX *215/561–4484,* WEB *www.crowneplaza.com. 445 rooms, 2 suites. Restaurant, bar, in-room data ports, no-smoking floor, room service, pool, gym, shop, coin laundry, laundry service, concierge, business services, parking (fee). AE, D, DC, MC, V.*

$–$$$ ☷ **Doubletree Philadelphia.** The hotel's sawtooth design gives each room a peaked bay window with a whopping 180° view. East-side rooms get a panoramic view of the city, the Delaware River, and New Jersey. You can also sit in the four-story atrium lobby lounge and observe one of the busiest corners of Philly's theater district, directly across the street from the handsome Academy of Music. Guest rooms are decorated in earth tones and have modern furnishings. Cafe Academy has all the attributes of an independent dining room, with unusually good contemporary food, particularly the pretheater value and pleasant service. ⌧ *Broad St. at Locust St., 19107,* ☎ *215/893–1600 or 800/222–8733,* FAX *215/893–1664,* WEB *www.doubletree.com. 419 rooms, 8 suites. 2 restaurants, lobby lounge, in-room data ports, room service, indoor pool, sauna, health club, racquetball, laundry service, concierge, concierge floor, business services, meeting rooms, parking (fee). AE, D, DC, MC, V.*

$$ ☷ **Hawthorn Suites.** A recently remodeled factory building, this utilitarian hotel has many of the basics for short or extended stays. The undistinguished pale green suites have a full-size kitchen, dining area, and two televisions. On the edge of Chinatown, the hotel overlooks the Schuylkill Expressway and is convenient to the Pennsylvania Convention Center. The hotel is just a few steps from Reading Terminal Market and Independence Mall. It's also near many Vietnamese, Thai, and Chinese eateries, some of which stay open late for dinner. Rates are variable, depending on availability. A daily hot breakfast buffet is included in the room rate; there's also a complimentary dinner buffet Monday through Thursday evenings. ⌧ *1100 Vine St., 19107,* ☎ *215/829–8300 or 800/527–1133,* FAX *215/829–8104,* WEB *www.hawthorn.com. 225 suites. Bar, café, kitchenettes, gym, shop, coin laundry, meeting rooms, parking (fee). AE, D, DC, MC, V. BP.*

$$ ⊞ **Holiday Inn Express Midtown.** Rooms are more spacious than average here—perhaps because they're older (this Holiday Inn opened in 1964 but has recently been renovated). All have contemporary furnishings and a light, floral motif; the room rate includes a Continental breakfast buffet. The location is excellent: one block from the Broad Street subway, near the theater and shopping district, and three blocks from the Pennsylvania Convention Center. Guests have free access to a nearby health club. ⊠ *1305 Walnut St., 19107,* ☎ *215/735–9300 or 800/564–3869,* FAX *215/732–2682.* WEB *www.holiday-inn.com. 166 rooms. No-smoking rooms, pool, laundry service, parking (fee). AE, D, DC, MC, V. CP.*

$–$$ ⊞ **Alexander Inn.** The nicely rehabbed rooms at this bed and breakfast inn, which occupies a turn-of-the-last-century redbrick hotel, are close to the Pennsylvania Convention Center, the Avenue of the Arts, and most Center City attractions. The rooms and furnishings have an art deco feeling; all rooms have color TVs. The Continental breakfast buffet includes fresh baked muffins and a variety of fruits and juices. ⊠ *12th and Spruce Sts., 19107,* ☎ *215/923–3535 or 877/ALEX–INN,* FAX *215/923–1004,* WEB *www.alexanderinn.com. 48 rooms. Breakfast room, in-room data ports, gym, business services, parking (fee). AE, D, DC, MC, V. CP.*

Benjamin Franklin Parkway/Museum Area

$$$$ ⊞ **Four Seasons.** With its exemplary service, impeccable maintenance, ★   and high-quality food, this luxurious member of the worldwide chain ranks consistently among the best hotels in the United States. The big, square, granite hotel is somewhat forbidding from the outside until you reach the front, embellished with highly polished brass and a portico, as well as solicitous doormen. It shares with other Four Seasons the long, long walk from the elevators to some of the guest rooms; guest room furniture is rather formal Federal style, just right for Philadelphia. The staff indulges you (with in-room exercise equipment and nonallergenic pillows); your children (with bedtime milk and cookies and in-room video games) and your up-to-15-pound pet (with fresh-baked dog biscuits and Evian water served in a silver bowl). Other Four Seasons amenities include a multilingual concierge and limousine service. The Fountain Restaurant is one of the best in town and the Swann Lounge one of the liveliest at cocktail time and late evening. ⊠ *1 Logan Sq., 19103,* ☎ *215/963–1500 or 800/332–3442,* FAX *215/963–9506,* WEB *www.fourseasons.com. 262 rooms; 102 suites. 2 restaurants, outdoor café, in-room data ports, in-room safes, minibar, no-smoking floors, room service, indoor pool, sauna, spa, health club, shops, babysitting, laundry service, concierge, business services, meeting rooms, parking (fee). AE, D, DC, MC, V.*

$$$ ⊞ **Wyndham Franklin Plaza.** This was Philadelphia's biggest and most active meetings location until the Philadelphia Marriott opened adjacent to the Pennsylvania Convention Center in 1995, but people who are willing to travel a few blocks farther still enjoy this facility. All public areas and guest rooms have been renovated and brightened up; rooms are done in soft green. Although it is still primarily a convention hotel, the Wyndham now caters to individual travelers with a variety of added amenities and services. Rooms have full-length mirrors, cable TV, voice mail, coffeemakers, and hair dryers. The 70-ft atrium lobby includes two restaurants (a steak house and an all-purpose place to grab a bite) and numerous sitting areas. ⊠ *17th and Race Sts., 19103,* ☎ *215/448–2000 or 800/822–4200,* FAX *215/448–2864,* WEB *www.wyndham.com/ franklinplaza. 720 rooms, 38 suites. 2 restaurants, bar, in-room data ports, no-smoking rooms, room service, indoor pool, barbershop, hair salon,* *tennis courts, basketball, health club, racquetball, coin laundry, laundry service, concierge, parking (fee). AE, D, DC, MC, V.*

$$–$$$ ☎ **Hotel Windsor.** This round 24-story building was converted from apartments to an all-suites hotel that caters to corporate business as well as to families. It's within easy walking distance of downtown shopping and the four museums on the parkway. The 160 studios and 48 one-bedroom apartments are furnished with fully equipped kitchens; most have balconies. There are two independently managed restaurants on the ground floor: the international, family-owned Peacock on the Parkway, and Joseph's Restaurant, which serves food from the Tuscany region of Italy. A complimentary Continental breakfast is included in the rate. ✉ *1700 Benjamin Franklin Pkwy., 19103,* ☎ *215/981–5678 or 877/784–8379,* FAX *215/981–5687,* WEB *www.windsorhotel.com. 308 suites. 2 restaurants, kitchenettes, in-room data ports, no-smoking rooms, pool, hair salon, health club, coin laundry, laundry service, concierge, parking (fee). AE, D, DC, MC, V. CP.*

$$–$$$ ☎ **Korman Suites Hotel.** The abstract neon sculpture on the roof of this comfortable hotel and corporate apartment complex serves as a colorful landmark in the Philadelphia skyline. Just a few blocks off the Benjamin Franklin Parkway, the business- and family-oriented all-suites facility (with studio, one- and two-bedrooms) offers striking city views from the picture windows in most of the spacious rooms. About half of the accommodations have washer-dryers; otherwise there's one on each floor. Larger suites have fully equipped kitchens with a table and chairs, dishes, and a stove and refrigerator; smaller ones have coffeemakers and microwaves. The hotel restaurant, Tuscan Twenty, offers a well-executed, innovative menu and specializes in Italian food; their single-malt scotch selection is impressive. A complimentary shuttle bus takes guests to Center City six days a week. ✉ *2001 Hamilton St., 19130,* ☎ *215/569–7000 or 888/4KORMAN,* FAX *215/469–0138,* WEB *www.kormansuites.com. 100 suites. Restaurant, lounge, kitchenettes, room service, pool, hair salon, spa, paddle tennis, health club, coin laundry, concierge, business services, meeting rooms, free parking, AE, D, MC, V.*

$ ☎ **Best Western Center City.** A bit far from the heart of Center City but within an easy walk of the Philadelphia Museum of Art and the Rodin Museum, this old-timer (in relative terms) of a motel was renovated a few years ago but is still a bit tired, with rooms done in navy blue. The best views from the guest rooms face south toward the flag-draped Benjamin Franklin Parkway and the downtown skyline. This is still a relative bargain in a city where prices have been rising quickly. ✉ *501 N. 22nd St., 19130,* ☎ *215/568–8300 or 800/528–1234,* FAX *215/557–0259,* WEB *www.bestwestern.com. 179 rooms, 4 suites. Restaurant, sports bar, in-room data ports, no-smoking rooms, pool, gym, laundry service, meeting rooms, free parking. AE, D, DC, MC, V.*

University City

This area just across the Schuylkill River in West Philadelphia is a 5- to 10-minute drive or taxi ride from Center City. The hotels are somewhat less posh (but also less expensive) than those downtown, but they compensate to a degree by being close to the University of Pennsylvania and Drexel University.

$$ ☎ **Inn at Penn.** Part of the Sansom Common redevelopment on the University of Pennsylvania campus, this new hotel opened in fall 1999 and is managed by Hilton Hotels. The inn aims for a residential ambience and is a welcome addition for anyone seeking to stay in University City. Nice elements include tiles from the Moravian Tile Works, a grand stair-

case, a book-lined living room, and a green, burgundy, and yellow color scheme throughout. The amenities are totally 21st century: two phone lines in each room, data ports offering Internet and PennNet access, and pampering touches such as plush terry robes and daily newspapers. You can use the small fitness room for free or the University exercise roomnasium for a fee. The full-service Ivy Grill restaurant is convenient. Note that room rates rise on special event weekends, like graduations. ⊠ *3600 Sansom St.,* ☎ *215/222–0200 or 800/222–8733,* ℻ *215/222–4600,* ⓌⒺⒷ *www.innatpenn.com. 238 rooms, 26 suites. Restaurant, lounge, in-room data ports, no-smoking rooms, room service, gym, baby-sitting, laundry service, concierge, business services, meeting rooms, parking (fee). AE, D, DC, MC, V.*

$$ 🏨 **Penn Tower Hotel.** The University of Pennsylvania purchased and improved this 21-floor former Hilton in 1987, converting half the space to medical offices and improving the rooms in 1992. It is on the eastern edge of the campus, close to the University Museum, Franklin Field, 30th Street Station, Drexel University, and University Hospital. Guest rooms, with traditional mahogany furnishings and cable TV, have excellent views east to Center City and west across campus. The exercise facility on the concierge level is available free to guests on those floors, and to others at a nominal charge. ⊠ *34th St. and Civic Center Blvd., 19104,* ☎ *215/387–8333 or 800/356–7366,* ℻ *215/386–8306. 85 rooms, 2 suites. Restaurant, bar, in-room data ports, room service, gym, concierge floor, parking (fee). AE, D, DC, MC, V.*

Airport District

A 20-minute drive or taxi ride from most sightseeing and entertainment, these hotels about 8 mi south of Center City are somewhat less expensive than those downtown. Although some are within sight of industrial parks, they all have a convenient location near the airport—a plus for business travelers.

$$$ 🏨 **Four Points by Sheraton.** Even though this hotel is surrounded by highways and is across the street from the airport, special construction makes it a quiet place. The five-story L-shape building has pleasant, spacious rooms with two double beds or one king-size bed and a chaise; the neutral decor is inviting. ⊠ *4101 Island Ave., 19153,* ☎ *215/492–0400 or 800/325–3535,* ℻ *215/365–6035,* ⓌⒺⒷ *www.sheraton. com. 176 rooms, 1 suite. Restaurant, lounge, no-smoking rooms, room service, pool, coin laundry, laundry service, business services, meeting rooms, airport shuttle, free parking. AE, D, DC, MC, V.*

$$$ 🏨 **Hilton Philadelphia Airport.** You can take a swim in the lobby pool of this Hilton before jumping on a free shuttle bus for the ride to your airport terminal. During the week this is mostly a business travelers' hotel, but weekends bring honeymooners and vacationing couples—and substantially lower rates. Rooms have wood and wicker dressing tables and bureaus, as well as cable TV. This was one of the earliest of the airport hotels, and it has remained pleasant and not noisy. ⊠ *4509 Island Ave., 19153,* ☎ *215/365–4150 or 800/445–8667,* ℻ *215/937–6382,* ⓌⒺⒷ *www.hilton.com. 328 rooms, 3 suites. Restaurant, sports bar, room service, indoor pool, sauna, health club, laundry service, meeting rooms, airport shuttle, free parking. AE, D, DC, MC, V.*

$$$ 🏨 **Philadelphia Airport Marriott.** Opened in 1995, this sprawling hotel in the Marriott style has a skybridge connecting directly to Terminal B at Philadelphia International Airport. Rooms have dark wood and blue and green color schemes. Three-quarters of the guests rooms are designated as "The Room That Works"; business travelers are accommodated with voice mail, data ports, and a speakerphone. Weekend packages are a good value here. ✉ *1 Arrivals Rd., 19153,* ☎ *215/ 492–9000 or 800/228–9290,* FAX *215/492–6799,* WEB *www.marriott.com. 419 rooms, 5 suites. Restaurant, lounge, room service, indoor pool, health club, shop, coin laundry, laundry service, concierge, business services, meeting rooms, free parking. AE, D, DC, MC, V.*

$$$ 🏨 **Sheraton Suites, Philadelphia Airport.** A glass-wall elevator whisks
★ you to your floor at this all-suites hotel, where front balconies overlook the light-flooded atrium lobby and restaurant. Suites are standard or deluxe; deluxe have a larger living room and a better view. Most accommodations have a king-size bed in the bedroom and a queen-size foldout in the living room, three telephones, two remote-control TV/clock radios, and coffeemakers, plus complimentary daily newspapers. Some rooms have extra aids for business travelers, including speakerphones with data ports. ✉ *4101 Island Ave., 19153,* ☎ *215/365–6600 or 800/ 937–8461,* FAX *215/492–8471,* WEB *www.sheraton.com. 251 suites. Restaurant, lobby lounge, no-smoking rooms, 2 pools (1 indoor), basketball, health club, volleyball, business services, meeting room, airport shuttle, car rental, free parking. AE, D, DC, MC, V.*

$$ 🏨 **Holiday Inn Philadelphia International Airport.** The lobby sets a traditional tone, with green marble, gold-trimmed dark colors, and fireplaces. The slightly oversize guest rooms have pastel color schemes with dark cherry wood furniture. There are good weekend rates here, depending on availability. The hotel is 3 mi south of the airport. ✉ *45 Industrial Hwy., Rte. 291, Essington 19029,* ☎ *610/521–2400 or 800/843–2355,* FAX *610/521–1605,* WEB *www.holiday-inn.com. 307 rooms. Restaurant, lounge, pool, gym, shop, coin laundry, concierge, business services, airport shuttle, free parking. AE, D, DC, MC, V.*

City Line Avenue

If you prefer to stay outside the bustle of downtown and park for less or free, three hotels here may be a good choice. City Line Avenue is only a 10-minute ride on the Schuylkill Expressway to Center City under favorable conditions; however, the expressway is frequently heavily congested at rush hour.

$$–$$$ 🏨 **Radisson Twelve Caesars Hotel.** The Twelve Caesars banquet hall, one of the city's top spots for weddings and bar mitzvahs, expanded upward in January 2000 and opened a Radisson Hotel. The property has an elegant marble lobby with grand chandeliers; guest rooms have one king- or two queen-size beds, telephones with data port, hair dryers, and Nintendo 64 units. Business class rooms, which require a slight extra charge, feature a concierge lounge, complimentary cocktails and hors d'oeuvres, and a free nightly movie. Delmonico's restaurant specializes in western beef; the Polo Lounge also serves food. The rates include a complimentary buffet breakfast. ✉ *4200 City Line, 19131,* ☎ *215/879–4000 or 800/333–3333,* FAX *215/879–9020,* WEB *www. radisson.com. 200 rooms, 10 suites. Restaurant, lounge, in-room data ports, in-room safes, room service, indoor pool, gym, dry cleaning, concierge, concierge floor, business services, meeting rooms, free parking. AE, D, DC, MC, V. BP.*

$–$$$ 🏨 **Adam's Mark.** At 23 stories, the Adam's Mark is one of the tallest hotels in Philadelphia: request a room on the upper floors facing south toward Fairmount Park and the downtown skyline for the best views. The ample rooms are geared primarily to the business traveler, with tailored striped fabrics that are serviceable but without particular charm. The big attraction here is the nighttime activity plus two restaurants (one, rather formal, serving excellent, eclectic food, and the other resembling a bright coffee shop) and Players, a sports bar. ✉ *City Ave. and Monument Rd., 19131,* ☎ *215/581–5000 or 800/444–2326,*

FAX *215/581–5089,* WEB *www.adamsmark.com. 515 rooms, 59 suites. 2 restaurants, sports bar, in-room data ports, no-smoking rooms, room service, indoor/outdoor pool, barbershop, hair salon, sauna, health club, racquetball, shops, laundry service, business services, meeting rooms, car rental, parking (fee). AE, D, DC, MC, V.*

$$ ☎ **Holiday Inn City Line.** This eight-story Holiday Inn is perfectly ordinary, but it's a good value in a choice location. You could stay here to save money and just walk across the parking lot to all the eateries of the Adam's Mark hotel. A five-minute walk takes you to five other restaurants. In the lobby you can sink into an overstuffed easy chair and watch swimmers in the glass-enclosed pool which, with the canopy removed, becomes an outdoor pool in summer. ✉ *4100 Presidential Blvd., 19131,* ☎ *215/477–0200 or 800/642–8982,* FAX *215/473–5510,* WEB *www. holiday-inn.com. 338 rooms, 3 suites. Restaurant, lounge, indoor/outdoor pool, gym, coin laundry, laundry service, concierge, business services, meeting room, car rental, free parking. AE, D, DC, MC, V.*

Hostels

Hostels provide dormitory-style accommodations for less than you'd pay to park your car at a downtown hotel. They also offer a sense of adventure and a chance to share living, eating, and sleeping quarters with travelers from all over the world. The **American Youth Hostel Regional Office and Travel Center** is at 624 South 3rd Street (☎ 215/925–6004).

$ ☎ **Bank Street Hostel.** A member of Hostel International, Bank Street opened in 1992 and, at $18 (members) to $21 (nonmembers) a night, is a downtown-Philly lodging bargain. Independently owned by David Herskowitz, it is on the cusp of Old City in a 140-year-old manufacturing building that has been combined with two neighboring buildings. Rooms are dormitory-style and have shared baths for 70 people. Guests gather around the pool table and the nightly videos. ✉ *32 S. Bank St., 19106,* ☎ *215/922–0222 or 800/392–4678,* FAX *215/922–4082.* WEB *www.bankstreethostel.com. Kitchen, billiards. No credit cards.*

$ ☎ **Chamounix Mansion.** Here's the cheapest place to stay in Philadelphia—$13 a night for American Youth Hostel members, and $16 for nonmembers. Set on a wooded bluff overlooking the Schuylkill River—and, unfortunately, the Schuylkill Expressway—the hostel feels like it's out in the country, though it's in Fairmount Park. The restored 1802 Quaker country estate is loaded with character. Flags line the entrance hall; period rooms have antiques; walls display old maps, sketches, and paintings. There's a self-service kitchen; no smoking is allowed. Chamounix Mansion is hard to find and a way from the bus stop; call for directions. ✉ *Chamounix Dr., 19131,* ☎ *215/878–3676 or 800/ 379–0017,* FAX *215/871–4313,* WEB *www.philahostel.org. 10 rooms for 80 people, with shared baths. Lounge, Ping-Pong, recreation room, bicycles, coin laundry. MC, V. Closed Dec. 15–Jan. 15.*

4 NIGHTLIFE AND THE ARTS

Philadelphia seems to have a rhythm of its own. Whether you're listening to the Philadelphia Orchestra while picnicking on the lawn at the Mann Center for the Performing Arts, or having a jazz brunch at Zanzibar Blue, music adds depth to the experience. This is a city of neighborhoods, and you can find entertainment in all of them. From Broadway shows at the Forrest Theater to performance art and poetry readings at the Painted Bride, there's always something new to explore.

T **HEATER, DANCE, AND MUSIC** from rock to opera: Philadelphia has plenty going on after dark. The city's Avenue of the Arts cultural district on North and South Broad Street is one significant sign of the new energy in town. Of the arts facilities on the avenue, some are long-standing, such as the Academy of Music and the Merriam Theater; others, including the Wilma Theater and the Prince Music Theater, are more recent additions. Adding further excitement to the Avenue of the Arts was the long-awaited opening (in December 2001) of the $255 million Kimmel Center for the Performing Arts, which features a new hall for the Philadelphia Orchestra and a smaller space for chamber music recitals and dance performances.

Updated by
Robert
DiGiacomo

The Avenue of the Arts spaces are providing forums for an ever wider range of talents, both traditional and innovative, from local artists to international stars. On a lighter note, you can relax by partying at clubs along the Delaware River or checking out some of the city's fine jazz.

NIGHTLIFE

In today's Philadelphia you can listen to a chanteuse in a chic basement nightclub, dance 'til 2 AM in a smoky bistro, and sip cocktails in any number of swank lounges. South Street between Front and 9th streets is still hip, with one-of-a-kind shops, bookstores, galleries, restaurants, and bars that attract the young and the restless in droves. Today, however, those in the know head to the trendy bars and clubs of Old City, where the crowd is chic and upscale. Over the past few years Main Street in Manayunk, in the northwest section of the city, has also arrived as a fashionable nightlife destination. More than a dozen clubs line the Delaware River waterfront, most near the Benjamin Franklin Bridge. Besides its club scene, Philadelphia also has larger venues—and draws big names—for rock, pop, and jazz concerts.

Bars and clubs can change hands or go out of business faster than a soft pretzel goes stale. Many places are open until 2 AM; cover charges vary from free to $12. Some may not be open every night, so call ahead. A few places do not accept credit cards, so carry some cash. For current information check the entertainment pages of the *Philadelphia Inquirer*, the *City Paper* and *Philadelphia* magazine. For **Penn's Landing** events, call ☎ 215/923–4992.

Bars and Brew Pubs

The Bards. A lively and authentic Irish pub, the Bards has an Irish crowd, Irish food, full-bodied beers, and great Irish music sessions on Sunday from 5 to 9. ✉ *2013 Walnut St.*, ☎ *215/569–9585.*

Black Sheep. This handsome pub is just off Rittenhouse Square in a refurbished townhouse with a Mission-style fireplace on the main floor and a quiet smoke-free dining room on the upper level. Beer lovers can choose from nearly a dozen local and imported brews on tap, and many more by the bottle. Bring an appetite, too: the impressive kitchen cooks up delicious comfort food like fish and chips and more ambitious fare like grilled duck breast. ✉ *247 S. 17th St.*, ☎ *215/454–9473.*

Copabanana. Need a break from the bustle of South Street? This popular hangout serves up some of the city's best margaritas, along with satisfying bar food such as hamburgers and veggie burgers topped with guacamole or salsa, and spicy Spanish fries with jalapeño peppers and fried onions. Floor-to-ceiling windows in the first floor bar give you great views of the parade of characters outside. ⊠ *344 South St.,* ☎ *215/923–6180.*

Copa, Too. The younger sibling of the popular South Street Copabanana attracts a slightly older crowd in their early thirties and is quite crowded for its after-work happy hour. Besides margaritas and bar food, Copa, Too offers a vast selection of beers—some 100 varieties are available on tap and by the bottle. ⊠ *263 S. 15th St.,* ☎ *215/735–0848.*

Dirty Frank's. Frank is long gone, but this place is still dirty, cheap, and a Philadelphia classic. An incongruous mixture of students, artists, journalists, and resident characters crowd around the horseshoe-shape bar and engage in friendly mayhem. It's open Monday–Saturday. ⊠ *347 S. 13th St.,* ☎ *215/732–5010.*

Dock Street Brasserie. This brewery occupies a large, lively space. You can choose hearty Alsatian dishes with your beer or standards such as steaks and burgers. Several flavors of the house-specialty boutique beer are available on a daily basis. ⊠ *2 Logan Sq.,* ☎ *215/496–0413.*

Fergie's Pub. This cozy taproom is a comfortable spot for a burger and a draught brew. Downstairs there's a fun jukebox with samplings from Sinatra to U2; upstairs, on Tuesday and Thursday, there is always an action-packed round of Quizzo, a team trivia game. Beware the often smoky atmosphere, especially on weekend nights. ⊠ *1214 Sansom St.,* ☎ *215/928–8118.*

New Wave Cafe. To its devoted Queen Village clientele, the New Wave is more than just the place to wait for a table at the always crowded seafood restaurant, Dmitri's, across the street. The regulars come to this long, narrow bar a few blocks off South Street to unwind with a local Yuengling beer, play a game of darts and enjoy a surprisingly innovative menu, including risotto crabcakes and homemade gnocchi. ⊠ *784 S. 3rd St.,* ☎ *215/922–8484.*

Plough and the Stars. An upscale Irish pub-restaurant in the historic Corn Exchange Building seemingly transports you from New World Philadelphia to Old Country Dublin with a mere lifting of a glass of Guinness. Dozens of brews are on tap or sold by the bottle, and the restaurant serves up Irish-style nouvelle comfort food. Shepherd's pie is a winner, but you won't find corned beef and cabbage here. ⊠ *123 Chestnut St., entrance on 2nd St.,* ☎ *215/733–0300.*

SoMa. The clever name—referring to the Old City location south of Market Street—sets the tone at this below street level hip bar–cum–dance club. SoMa has a small bar at the back, upholstered couches along the walls, and lighting best described as intimate, i.e., dark if you're over 40. ⊠ *33 S. 3rd St.,* ☎ *215/413–1433.*

Woody's. Philadelphia's most popular gay bar is spread over two levels, offering several bars—with monitors playing music videos and campy moments from TV shows and movies—and a large disco on the second floor. On Tuesday and Sunday, two-steppers take over the dance floor for country dancing; on other nights the music is a mix of techno and dance tracks. ⊠ *202 S. 13th St.,* ☎ *215/545–1893.*

Comedy Clubs

Comedy Sportz. Anything goes during this once-a-week night of improvisational comedy. There are two shows every Saturday at The Playground at The Adrienne Theater, and the audience is always welcome to participate. ⊠ *2030 Sansom St.,* ☎ *877/985–2844.*

Laugh House. This 250-seat club offers an open-mike night on Wednesday and showcases local and national acts Thursday through Sunday. ⊠ *221 South St.,* ☎ *215/440–4242.*

Dance Clubs

Dave & Buster's. Call this a big amusement park for the somewhat grown-up. A short list of what's going on—besides music and dancing—includes two restaurants, five bars, pool tables, pinball and video games, just-for-fun blackjack and poker, and a virtual reality shooting game. An outdoor deck overlooks the Delaware River. ⊠ *Pier 19 N, 325 N. Columbus Blvd.,* ☎ *215/413–1951.*

Chemistry. Finished that Manayunk shopping spree? Stick around for a meal, have a cigar in the lounge, relax on the outdoor deck, and dance to today's tunes, spun by a DJ. The restaurant and nightclub are open Tuesday–Sunday. ⊠ *4100 Main St., Manayunk,* ☎ *215/483–4100.*

Five Spot. This sleek throwback to the era of the supper club is frequented by a stylish, retro crowd that enjoys a stiff martini and knows how to swing its way around a dance floor. There's live music (big band, Latin, and swing) Tuesday–Sunday. Latin dance lessons are given on Thursday at 9; Sunday at 8 is the time for beginners to learn how to swing. ⊠ *1 S. Bank St.,* ☎ *215/574–0070.*

Fluid. This small dance club atop The Latest Dish restaurant is nearly hidden behind an unmarked door on an alley just off 4th Street, near South. Once inside, follow the funky stairwell to the second floor, where you'll hear a mix of hip-hop, rap, and techno spun by some of the city's best DJs. ⊠ *613 S. 4th St.,* ☎ *215/629–0565.*

KatManDu. Large and usually crowded, this Delaware River waterfront spot is an indoor/outdoor Caribbean restaurant and bar that has live music nightly—world, reggae, rock—and a "Wild Island" dance party on Saturday night. It's open from May to mid-October. ⊠ *Pier 25, 417 N. Columbus Blvd. south of Spring Garden St.,* ☎ *215/629–7400.*

Maui Entertainment Complex. If your idea of heaven is ersatz tropical ambience, beach volleyball, and waitresses in cutoffs and bikini tops hawking drinks to a crowd in their twenties, this place is for you. On the city's biggest dance floor you can dance both indoors and out to live bands (rock, alternative, progressive) and to radio DJ dance-party broadcasts. Maui is open Thursday–Sunday. ⊠ *Pier 53 N, 1143 N. Columbus Blvd.,* ☎ *215/423–8116.*

Monte Carlo Living Room. The DJ at this sophisticated watering hole, on the second floor of a fine Italian restaurant, plays Top 40 hits, European sounds, and South American music for a mostly thirties–fifties crowd. A jacket and tie are required. All the furnishings, from the tapestries to the paintings, are European. It's open Wednesday–Saturday. ⊠ *150 South St.,* ☎ *215/925–2220.*

Polly Esther's and Culture Club. The music and decor of the '70s and '80s take center stage at this hot spot, part of a national chain. The bar is painted to look like the Partridge family's bus, *Charlie's Angels* photographs adorn one wall, and there's a *Saturday Night Fever*–style disco floor. It's open Thursday through Saturday. ⊠ *1201 Race St., next to the Pennsylvania Convention Center,* ☎ *215/851–0776.*

Rock Lobster. From May to September you can join the party at this riverfront tent that resembles a yacht club. The over-thirty set comes for reasonably priced meals and plenty of live music and dancing. ⊠ *Pier 13–14, 221 N. Columbus Blvd.,* ☎ *215/627–7625.*

Shampoo. The look of this trendy club—retro furniture and Pop Art—reflects the origins of its name: the 1975 Warren Beatty movie about a hairdresser with a complicated love life. A former warehouse has been transformed into a mega-club with eight bars and three dance floors. On Wednesday, Thursday, Saturday, and Sunday, the crowd is a fashionable mix of gays and straights; "Shaft" Fridays are predominantly gay and often feature guest DJs and performers from New York, including Lady Bunny of "Wigstock" fame. ⊠ *417 N. 8th St. (entrance on Willow St.),* ☎ *215/922–7500.*

Jazz, Blues, and Cabaret

Philadelphia has a rich jazz and blues heritage that includes such greats as the late, legendary jazz saxophonist John Coltrane and current players like Grover Washington, Jr. That legacy continues today in clubs around town. The Mellon Jazz Festival in June is a popular event. You can contact the **Philadelphia Clef Club of Jazz & Performing Arts** (☎ 215/893–9912) to find out about upcoming events.

Chris' Jazz Cafe. This intimate hangout off the Avenue of the Arts showcases top local talent Monday through Saturday in a cigar- and pipe-friendly environment. ⊠ *1421 Sansom St.,* ☎ *215/568–3131.*

Liberties. This handsomely restored Victorian pub has jazz Friday and Saturday. ⊠ *705 N. 2nd St.,* ☎ *215/238–0660.*

Ortlieb's Jazz Haus. You'll hear good jazz in this 100-year-old bar. Celebrated jazz organist Shirley Scott and her quartet occasionally perform. There's music nightly from Monday through Saturday; Tuesday night includes a jam session for local musicians. ⊠ *847 N. 3rd St.,* ☎ *215/922–1035.*

Philadelphia Clef Club of Jazz & Performing Arts. Dedicated solely to jazz, including its history and instruction, the organization also has a 250-seat cabaret-style theater for concert performances. ⊠ *736–738 S. Broad St.,* ☎ *215/893–9912.*

Warmdaddy's. This rustic, down-home blues club and restaurant, owned by the people who run Zanzibar Blue, serves up live blues and southern cuisine every night except Monday. The Sunday gospel brunch from noon to 3 costs $20 per person. ⊠ *4–6 S. Front St., at Front and Market Sts.,* ☎ *215/627–8400 for reservations; 215/627–2500 for hours and upcoming performances.*

Zanzibar Blue. A hip restaurant and bar adjoins the hottest jazz room in town. The best local talent plays on weeknights; nationally known names take the stage on weekends. There's a jazz brunch on Sunday from 11 to 2 for $20 per person. ⊠ *Downstairs at the Bellevue, Broad and Walnut Sts.,* ☎ *215/732–4500 for reservations; 215/732–5200 for hours and upcoming performances.*

Lounges

Brasserie Perrier. The bar and banquette at this modern deco bistro, owned by Georges Perrier of Le Bec-Fin fame, attract a sophisticated, after-work crowd. ⊠ *1619 Walnut St.,* ☎ *215/568–3000.*

Continental Restaurant & Martini Bar. This retro former diner draws a hip, twentysomething crowd to its swank setting for cocktails and a tapas-style dinner menu. The design, including lots of stainless steel and lighting fixtures resembling olives stabbed with toothpicks, is worth checking out. ⊠ *138 Market St.,* ☎ *215/923–6069.*

Happy Rooster. The boys once ruled this venerable, upscale roost—house rules prohibited unescorted women from sitting at the bar. Today, under owner Rose Parrotta, anyone is free to relax at the handsome rosewood bar accented by brass lanterns. Those seeking more privacy may wish to enjoy a cocktail at one of the cozy booths. In either case, be sure to sample a well-prepared dish from the ever-changing blackboard menu—choices might include a classic Caesar salad, a deluxe burger with fries, or mahimahi fillet in a gingery butter sauce. It's open Monday–Saturday. ⊠ *118 S. 16th St.,* ☎ *215/563–1481.*

Il Bar. The wine bar at Panorama, a northern Italian restaurant in the Penn's View Inn, stands out for its 120-bottle selection, curved bar, and romantic atmosphere. It's open seven nights a week, with a separate entrance from the restaurant. ⊠ *14 N. Front St.,* ☎ *215/922–7800.*

Inn Philadelphia. This meticulously restored Colonial-style restaurant on a quaint side street is best appreciated for its warm, convivial bar-lounge. It's a good place to stop for a cocktail before dinner or a nightcap on your way home. Live piano music is a plus on weekends, and there's seating in the "Secret Garden" in warm months. ⊠ *251– 253 S. Camac St.,* ☎ *215/732–8630.*

Library Lounge. Handsome and wood-paneled, this space on the 19th floor of the venerable Bellevue hotel (now a Park Hyatt) harkens to the days when gentlemen left the ladies behind to retire to the library; today all are welcome here. So, too, are cigars. Oriental carpets, shelves lined with leather-bound volumes, and a roaring fire complete the scene. ⊠ *Broad and Walnut Sts.,* ☎ *215/893–1776.*

The Rotunda and the Vault. Under the soaring, 140-ft-high rotunda of this former bank building, re-fashioned as the Ritz-Carlton Philadelphia, is an elegant lobby bar with marble floors and overstuffed couches—a gracious spot to have a before- or after-dinner cocktail or indulge in a fattening dessert. Just off the lobby is the handsome Vault, a smaller bar specializing in champagnes and fine brandies; here, cigar smoking is more than welcome, it's expected. ⊠ *10 Avenue of the Arts (Broad and Chestnut Sts.),* ☎ *215/735–7700.*

Rouge. With lovely Rittenhouse Square as its backdrop, this French-style bistro from celebrity restaurateur Neil Stein is the place to see and be seen, especially for the city's over-35 set. Noisy and crowded on weekend nights, it's best enjoyed in the warmer weather when the wall of French windows is thrown open and the party spills out into the street. ⊠ *205 S. 18th St.,* ☎ *215/732–6622.*

Swann Lounge. Melodious jazz and luscious desserts are served up on Friday and Saturday nights in this extremely elegant lounge in the Four Seasons Hotel. You can dance to the trio's music in between sampling confections from the Viennese-style dessert buffet. A Sunday brunch with Dixieland music is also offered. ⊠ *18th St. and Benjamin Franklin Pkwy.,* ☎ *215/963–1500.*

Tank Bar. The Tank Bar is tucked away on the second floor of Friday, Saturday, Sunday, a longtime Rittenhouse Square neighborhood restaurant. Tiny white lights, strategically placed mirrors, and a tank full of exotic tropical fish add just the right touches of comfort and sophistication. ⊠ *261 S. 21st St.,* ☎ *215/546–4232.*

Twenty Manning. The intimate lounge area and sleek bar at this chic Rittenhouse Square restaurant/bar make for great people watching. You'll see a mix of Center City professionals, artistic types, and couples on first dates. Wear something black to feel most at home. ⊠ *261 S. 20th St.,* ☎ *215/731–0900.*

Rock and Pop Clubs

Electric Factory. Named in honor of the original Electric Factory, which opened in 1968 and hosted acts ranging from Jimi Hendrix to the Grateful Dead, the new venue is in a cavernous former warehouse just north of Center City and presents mainly alternative rock bands. It has a capacity of about 2,500, but that number mostly refers to standing room; the main concert area doesn't have seats, although you can sit down at a balcony bar and watch the proceedings from there. ⊠ *421 N. 7th St.,* ☎ *215/568–3222.*

The Khyber. Small and loud, this Old City spot has lots of action. The music is all live, including alternative and rock performed by national and local talent. With more than 100 brands of beer, it has one of the best selections in town. The Khyber is open Monday–Saturday. ⊠ *56 S. 2nd St.,* ☎ *215/238–5888.*

Theatre of Living Arts. The TLA, a former independent movie house, is a South Street institution that helped launch John Waters's film career; it was the longtime home of *The Rocky Horror Picture Show.* Today the TLA presents concerts by a range of rock, blues, and adult alternative acts, including Lucinda Williams and John Hammond. ⊠ *334 South St.,* ☎ *215/922–1011.*

Tin Angel Acoustic Cafe. Local and national musicians hold forth at a 105-seat acoustic cabaret above the Serrano restaurant (patrons get preferred seating). You can sit at candlelit tables or at the bar and hear music from blues to folk. Tickets are required except for Wednesday's open-mike evenings. ⊠ *20 S. 2nd St.,* ☎ *215/928–0978.*

Trocadero. This spacious rock-and-roll club in Chinatown occupies a former burlesque house where W. C. Fields and Mae West performed. A lot of the old decor remains: mirrors, pillars, and balconies surround the dance floor. Most every up-and-coming band that's passing through Philly plays here to an under-thirty crowd. On other nights local DJs host dance parties. ⊠ *1003 Arch St.,* ☎ *215/922–5483.*

THE ARTS

Of all the performing arts, it is music for which Philadelphia is most renowned and the Philadelphia Orchestra of which its residents are most proud. Considered one of the world's best symphony orchestras, it rose to fame under the batons of former conductors Leopold Stokowski, Eugene Ormandy, and Riccardo Muti. The orchestra has moved into its new home, the cello-shape Verizon Hall at the Kimmel Center for the Performing Arts. The 2,500-seat hall is the centerpiece of the new performing arts center at Broad and Spruce streets—a dynamic complex housed under a glass-vaulted roof. Orchestra concerts during the September–May season are still among the city's premier social events. If you can get tickets, go. You'll see some of the city's finest performers in an opulent setting, with many Philadelphians dressed to match the occasion. The Opera Company of Philadelphia and the Pennsylvania Ballet perform at the orchestra's former home, the venerable Academy of Music, built in 1857 and modeled after Milan's La Scala opera house.

There is no shortage of live entertainment, ranging from the Philly Pops to the Mellon Jazz Festival. There are also summer concerts of popular and classical music at the Robin Hood Dell East and at Fairmount Park's Mann Center for the Performing Arts. Many rock groups stop in Philadelphia on their national tours, playing at the First Union Center and First Union Spectrum; the Keswick Theatre, in suburban Glenside; or the Tweeter Center in Camden.

Of course, Philly holds a special place in pop music history. *American Bandstand,* hosted by Dick Clark, began here as a local dance show. When it went national in 1957, it gave a boost to many hometown boys, including Fabian, Bobby Rydell, Frankie Avalon, and Chubby Checker. The city's rock-and-roll tradition began in 1955 with Bill Haley and the Comets. In the 1970s the Philadelphia Sound—a polished blend of disco, pop, and rhythm and blues—came alive through Kenny Gamble and Leon Huff; its lush sound has been kept alive by chart toppers such as Hall and Oates, Patti LaBelle, Boyz II Men, and rapper/actor Will Smith, as well as newer acts, notably Jill Scott and Pink.

Until the early 1980s Philadelphia was considered an important tryout town for theatrical productions headed to New York. (Today, due to high production costs, few Broadway shows even have out-of-town tryouts on that scale.) But the rich theatrical tradition continues here. The city serves as a major stop for touring productions of shows from *Les Misérables* to *Rent,* and the local theater scene, which supports more than two dozen regional and local companies, is thriving.

Information and Tickets

For current performances and listings, the best guides to Philly's performing arts are the "Guide to the Lively Arts" in the daily *Philadelphia Inquirer,* the "Weekend" section of the Friday *Inquirer,* and the "Friday" section of the *Philadelphia Daily News.* Two free weekly papers, the *City Paper* and the *Philadelphia Weekly,* have extensive listings of concerts and clubs; they are available free in news boxes all over downtown.

The **Independence Visitor Center** (✉ 6th St., between Market and Arch, (☎ 215/965–7676) has information about performances. The **Philadelphia Dance Alliance** (☎ 215/564–5270) is a good source of information on dance concerts and local companies.

UpStages (✉ 1412 Chestnut St., ☎ 215/569–9700) has tickets for many cultural events. Discount tickets, often reduced up to 50%, are offered on the day of the performance. **TicketMaster** (☎ 215/336–2000) sells tickets to rock concerts and other performing arts events.

Prices for performing arts events vary widely. Tickets for rock or pop concerts range from $10 or $15 for a small venue such as the Tin Angel or lawn seats at the Mann Center, to $75 and up for good seats at the First Union Center to see the Rolling Stones; theater tickets can go from $15 for local productions to $70 for touring productions of Broadway shows; Philadelphia Orchestra tickets range from $18 for the amphitheater to $95 for the best box seats.

Classical Music

Chamber Orchestra of Philadelphia. Directed by Marc Mostovoy, this prestigious group—formerly known as Concerto Soloists of Philadelphia—performs chamber music from October to May at the Perelman Theater at the Kimmel Center for the Performing Arts. ✉ *Broad and Spruce Sts.,* ☎ *215/790–5800; 215/545–5451 for concert information.*

Curtis Institute of Music. The gifted students at this world-renowned music conservatory give free recitals three times a week from October through May at 8 PM. All of its students are on full scholarships; its alumni include such luminaries as Leonard Bernstein, Samuel Barber, and Anna Moffo. The recital hot line lists events. The school also has an opera, alumni recital, and symphony orchestra series. ✉ *1726 Locust St.,* ☎ *215/893–5261 for hot line; 215/893–7902 for Curtis ticket office.*

Peter Nero and the Philly Pops. Grammy-winning pianist and conductor Peter Nero leads an orchestra of local musicians in programs that swing from Broadway to Big Band, or from ragtime to rock and roll, with ease. The six-concert series is presented at the Kimmel Center for the Performing Arts from October to May. ✉ *Broad and Spruce Sts.,* ☎ *215/546–6400.*

Philadelphia Chamber Music Society. From October to May, the society presents more than 50 concerts featuring nationally and internationally known musicians. The schedule is packed with a piano, vocal, and chamber music series, a special events and jazz series, and string recitals. Performances are held in the Perelman Theater at the Kimmel Center for the Performing Arts, at the Pennsylvania Convention Center, and at other locations in the city. ☎ *215/569–8587 or 215/569–8080.*

Philadelphia Orchestra. The world-renown ensemble performs at Verizon Hall at the Kimmel Center for the Performing Arts from September to May. In summer the orchestra stages a concert series at the Mann Center for the Performing Arts. Wolfgang Sawallisch, the current principal conductor and music director, ends his decade-long stint in September 2003, when he will be succeeded by Christoph Eschenbach, a concert pianist and chief conductor of the NDR Symphony in Hamburg. Eschenbach is also music director of the Orchestre de Paris and the summer Ravinia Festival; he will be the orchestra's seventh music director. ⊠ *Broad and Spruce Sts., ☎ 215/893–1999.*

Concert Halls

Academy of Music. Modeled after Milan's La Scala opera house and completed in 1857, the Academy of Music was the Philadelphia Orchestra's home for its first century. In late 2001, the orchestra moved down the street to the Kimmel Center for the Performing Arts. The Academy is now home to the Opera Company of Philadelphia and the Pennsylvania Ballet; the schedule is filled out with performances by major orchestras, theatrical and dance touring companies, and solo artists. It's worth the price of admission to experience the Academy's lavish, neo-baroque interior, with its red velvet seats, gilt, carvings, murals on the ceiling, and huge Victorian crystal chandelier. ⊠ *Broad and Locust Sts., ☎ 215/893–1999.*

Annenberg Center. The performing arts complex on the University of Pennsylvania campus has four stages, from the 120-seat Studio to the 970-seat Zellerbach Theater. Something is going on almost all the time—including productions of musical comedy, drama, dance, and children's theater. ⊠ *3680 Walnut St., ☎ 215/898–3900.*

First Union Spectrum and First Union Center. Rock concerts are often staged in these enormous sports facilities on the south side of the city, each of which holds more than 16,000 fans. Recent headliners have included 'NSYNC, U2, and Eric Clapton; monster truck events, World Wrestling Federation matches, and the Ringley Bros. and Barnum & Bailey Circus are also on the calendar. ⊠ *S. Broad St. and Pattison Ave., off I–95, ☎ 215/336–3600.*

Keswick Theatre. A 1,900-seat former vaudeville house with fine acoustics hosts rock, jazz, and country music concerts as well as musicals; call for directions. ⊠ *Easton Rd. and Keswick Ave., Glenside, ☎ 215/572–7650.*

Kimmel Center for the Performing Arts. This striking new complex evokes Philadelphia's traditional redbrick structures, while making a contemporary design statement. The 450,000-square-ft facility by architect Rafael Viñoly includes the 2,500-seat cello-shape Verizon Hall, the more intimate 650-seat Perelman Theater, a cafe and restaurant, a gift shop, rooftop terrace, and public plaza—all topped by a dramatic vaulted glass roof. Along with its resident companies, such as the Philadelphia Orchestra, the Chamber Orchestra, and the American Theater Arts for Youth, the center will present touring orchestras, and jazz and dance productions. ⊠ *Broad and Spruce Sts., ☎ 215/790–5810 or 215/893–1999, www.kimmelcenter.org.*

Mann Center for the Performing Arts. Pops, jazz, contemporary music, Broadway theatre, opera, dance, and Shakespeare are presented in this open-air amphitheater in Fairmount Park from May through September. From late June through July, the Philadelphia Orchestra is in residence, along with noted soloists and guest conductors. International food booths and a tented buffet restaurant offer dinner before the show. ⊠ *West Fairmount Park, George's Hill near 52nd St. and Parkside Ave., ☎ 215/878–7707 for box office.*

Painted Bride Art Center. By day it's a contemporary art gallery showing bold, challenging works. By night it's a multidisciplinary, multicultural performance center, with performance art, prose and poetry readings, folk and new music, jazz, dance, and avant-garde theater. The gallery is open Tuesday–Friday 10–6, Saturday noon–6; call for the performance schedule. ⊠ *230 Vine St.,* ☏ *215/925–9914.*

Robin Hood Dell East. The Dell is the site for rhythm-and-blues and soul music concerts on Monday and Wednesday evenings in July and August. ⊠ *Strawberry Mansion Dr., East Fairmount Park,* ☏ *215/685–9560.*

Tweeter Center. Formerly known by locals as the E-Centre, the Tweeter Center, across the Delaware River in Camden, programs everything from symphonies to rock and roll in an adaptable space. The indoor section ranges from 1,600 to 7,000 seats; the lawn seats 18,000. Shows include major rock and pop acts, including the Backstreet Boys, Paul Simon, and Jimmy Buffet, as well as touring Broadway shows and children's theater. ⊠ *1 Harbor Blvd., on the waterfront, Camden,* ☏ *856/365–1300 for ticket information and directions.*

Music Festivals

Mellon Jazz Festival. A series of 40 concerts and events (most free or with low ticket prices) are presented in June at locations around town. Look for top names in jazz, such as Pat Martino, Wynton Marsalis, and Chick Corea. ☏ *610/667–3559.*

Philadelphia Folk Festival. First held in 1962, the oldest continuously running folk festival in the country takes place each year for three days during the last week in August. Doc Watson, Taj Mahal, Joan Baez, and Judy Collins are just a few of the artists who have performed here. ⊠ *Old Pool Farm, near Schwenksville,* ☏ *215/242–0150 or 800/556–3655.*

Dance

Dance Celebration/Next Move Series. Modern dance takes the stage at this Annenberg Center series, which presents works by local, national, and internationally known companies. Recent seasons have featured Momix, Dance Theatre of Harlem, and Paul Taylor Dance Company, among others. ⊠ *3680 Walnut St.,* ☏ *215/636–9000.*

Pennsylvania Ballet. Artistic Director Roy Kaiser leads the company through a season of classic favorites and new works; they dance on the stage of the Academy of Music. Their *Nutcracker* production at Christmastime is a city favorite. ⊠ *Broad and Locust Sts.,* ☏ *215/551–7000.*

Philadelphia Dance Company. This modern dance troupe, also known as Philadanco, is recognized for its innovative performances that forge contemporary and classical forms with the traditions of other cultures. Their new performance home is the Kimmel Center for the Performing Arts. ⊠ *Broad and Spruce Sts.,* ☏ *215/387–8200.*

Film

Your best bet for first-run theaters are those listed below, particularly the trio of Ritz Theaters. Avoid what's left of the first-run theaters on Chestnut Street west of Broad Street—they're often frequented by rowdy urban youths.

International Gay and Lesbian Film Festival. Organized by Theatre of Living Arts Video founder Raymond Murray, who has written several books on film, this festival is held annually in early July in venues around the city. ☏ *215/733–0608.*

International House. I-House on the University of Pennsylvania campus presents an international film series throughout the year and also sponsors the popular Philadelphia Festival of World Cinema. ⊠ *3701 Chestnut St.,* ☏ *215/387–5125.*

Philadelphia Festival of World Cinema. Sponsored by International House, this 12-day event in May is filled with screenings, seminars, and events attended by critics, scholars, filmmakers, and cinema buffs. It's held at various venues around the city. ☎ 800/969–7392.

Ritz Five, Ritz at the Bourse and Ritz East. These are the finest movie theaters in town for independent and foreign films. All three have comfortable seats, clean surroundings, first-rate sound systems, and courteous audiences and staff. ⊠ *Ritz Five, 214 Walnut St.;* ⊠ *Ritz at the Bourse, 4th St. north of Chestnut St.;* ⊠ *Ritz East, 2nd St., between Chestnut and Walnut Sts.,* ☎ *215/925–7900 for all three.*

The Roxy. Philly's classic film repertory house offers a unique mix of new and classic films. ⊠ *2023 Sansom St.,* ☎ *215/923–6699.*

Sharon Pinkenson Film Project. Based at the Prince Music Theater—and named after the energetic head of the city's film office who is credited with raising the city's Hollywood profile through films like *Philadelphia* and *The Sixth Sense*—this film series offers a mix of classic and contemporary films and documentaries, with an emphasis on works by local filmmakers. ⊠ *1412 Chestnut St.,* ☎ *215/972–1000 or 215/569–9700.*

United Artists Main Street 6 Theatre. Manayunk has a multiplex to complement its shopping and dining options. ⊠ *3720 Main St., Manayunk,* ☎ *215/482–6230.*

United Artist Riverview Plaza. Showing first-run commercial releases, this renovated cinema is a modern, 19-screen multiplex. ⊠ *1400 S. Columbus Blvd.,* ☎ *215/755–2219.*

Opera

AVA Opera Theatre. The resident artists at the Academy of Vocal Arts, a four-year, tuition-free vocal training program, present four or five fully staged opera productions during their October to May season. They are accompanied by the Chamber Orchestra of Philadelphia and perform at various venues in the city and suburbs. ⊠ *1920 Spruce St.,* ☎ *215/735–1685.*

Opera Company of Philadelphia. The company stages four productions a year, between October and April, at the Academy of Music; some operas have international stars. All performances are in the original language, with computerized English "supertitles" above the stage. ⊠ *Broad and Locust Sts.,* ☎ *215/928–2110.*

Savoy Company. The oldest Gilbert and Sullivan company in the country stages one G&S operetta each May or June at the Academy of Music and at Longwood Gardens in Kennett Square. ☎ *215/735–7161.*

Theater

The Adrienne. The main stage, once home to the prestigious Wilma Theater, now houses two up-and-coming theatrical groups, 1812 Productions (☎ 215/592–9560) and InterAct Theatre (☎ 215/568–8077). The Second Stage offers improv comedy and hosts productions from visiting theater companies. ⊠ *2030 Sansom St.,* ☎ *215/569–9700.*

Arden Theatre Company. The Arden, formed in 1988, is known for premiering new works and offering a mix of classic drama, comedy and musicals, with a special affinity for the works of Stephen Sondheim; the company has won many local Barrymore Awards. Recent productions have included *Picasso at the Lapin Agile, Cat on a Hot Tin Roof,* and *Into the Woods.* Its home is in Old City. ⊠ *400 N. 2nd St.,* ☎ *215/ 922–8900.*

Brick Playhouse. This small theater group, with a space above the Jambalaya Restaurant that seats 70, develops and produces new works by local playwrights and performance artists. ✉ *623 South St.,* ☎ *215/ 592–1183.*

Forrest Theater. The Forrest is the place to catch Broadway blockbusters in Philadelphia. About eight high-profile shows are presented each season; the 2001–02 season included *Contact, Aida, Kiss Me, Kate,* and *Beauty and the Beast.* ✉ *1114 Walnut St.,* ☎ *215/923–1515.*

Freedom Theatre. The oldest and most active African-American theater in Pennsylvania is nationally renowned. Performances are scheduled from September through June. ✉ *1346 N. Broad St.,* ☎ *215/978–8497.*

Merriam Theater. Built in 1918 as the Shubert, the ornate 1,688-seat theater has showcased many American stage greats, including Al Jolson, Helen Hayes, Katharine Hepburn, Sammy Davis Jr., Angela Lansbury, and Sir Laurence Olivier. Now owned by the University of the Arts and named after a local benefactor, the lavishly decorated Merriam hosts a full schedule of national tours of Broadway shows, modern dance companies, and solo performers, from the magicians Penn & Teller to tap dancer Savion Glover. ✉ *250 S. Broad St.,* ☎ *215/732–5446.*

Philadelphia Theater Company. Philadelphia and world premieres of works by contemporary American playwrights are performed here. The company also produces Stages, a program showcasing new plays by American playwrights. ✉ *1714 Delancey St., at Plays and Players,* ☎ *215/735–0630 for theater; 215/985–1400 for PTC office.*

Prince Music Theater. Formerly known as the American Music Theater Festival, this organization has renovated an old movie theater and named it in honor of legendary Broadway director-producer Harold Prince. The theater presents new, original musicals and a cabaret series with national acts, including Andrea Marcovicci and Patti LuPone. The organization is also home to the Sharon Pinkenson Film Project, a venue for independent film. ✉ *1412 Chestnut St.,* ☎ *215/893–1570.*

Society Hill Playhouse. For more than 40 years, this small off-Broadway–style theater, just off South Street, has been mounting original plays. Their *Lafferty's Wake,* a musical about a rowdy Irish funeral service, played for four years. The main stage is for contemporary works; the Second Space Cabaret Theater has musical comedies. ✉ *507 S. 8th St.,* ☎ *215/923–0210.*

Walnut Street Theatre. Founded in 1809, this is the oldest English-speaking theater in continuous use in the United States. The schedule includes musicals, comedies, and dramas in a lovely 1,052-seat auditorium where almost every seat is a good one. Smaller stages showcase workshop productions of new plays and are rented by other theater companies. ✉ *9th and Walnut Sts.,* ☎ *215/574–3550.*

Wilma Theater. Under artistic director Blanka Zizka, the Wilma has gained favorable critical notices for innovative presentations of American and European drama. Its season runs from September to June. ✉ *Broad and Spruce Sts.,* ☎ *215/546–7824.*

5 OUTDOOR ACTIVITIES AND SPORTS

Philadelphians are well-known sports fanatics. You can barely concentrate on a Phillies game when the fans are shouting at or cheering on the players, which is part of the fun, of course. Recreational athletes take full advantage of the city's natural resources, including its parks and rivers. Kelly and West River drives in Fairmount Park are quite the sight on spring weekends, when all the bikers, in-line skaters, and walkers are out enjoying the cherry blossoms.

Updated by
Robert
DiGiacomo

PHILADELPHIA SPORTS FANS have lots to cheer about. Their professional teams—the Eagles (football), the Phillies (baseball), the Flyers (ice hockey), and the 76ers (basketball)—are all popular and make enough trips to the playoffs to keep the fans ever hopeful. Crowds are the norm at the 700,000-square-ft First Union Center sports complex and at Veterans Stadium: Philadelphians buy more tickets to pro sporting events than do residents of any other U.S. city. At this writing, two new facilities for professional football and baseball are under development near the existing sports complex in South Philadelphia, with projected completion dates in 2003 for the Eagles and 2004 for the Phillies.

There are many other sports attractions in the city, but two activities—and images—come immediately to mind. The first is one immortalized in a canvas by Thomas Eakins, Philadelphia's greatest painter, of an oarsman rowing on the Schuylkill River in an elegant single scull. Today, the scene that Eakins depicted in the 19th century is still enacted every week when scores of sculls are launched from Boathouse Row, a string of Victorian boathouses along Kelly Drive housing the city's many rowing clubs.

The second image, of course, is that of boxer Rocky Balboa, pungently captured by Sylvester Stallone in the film *Rocky* and its sequels. Had Rocky been a real Philadelphia boxer, he would have fought at the Blue Horizon, the legendary fight club. You can also see Rocky himself—immortalized in bronze—in front of the First Union Spectrum at Broad Street and Pattison Avenue.

Participant Sports and Fitness

Philadelphia has a wide variety of places for athletes to test their skills, whether the sport is biking, jogging, or in-line skating. On weekend mornings (7–noon) from April through October, the West River Drive is closed to car traffic, making this a prime spot for sports enthusiasts. In the afternoons, only the section from the Sweetbriar Cutoff to the East Falls Bridge is closed.

Biking

One popular treat for cyclists is to ride the paved path along the east side of the **Schuylkill River**, cross East Falls Bridge, and return on the west side of the river. The path begins behind the Philadelphia Museum of Art and is parallel to Kelly Drive. This 8-mi loop is about an hour of casually paced biking. **Forbidden Drive**, a 5½-mi dirt-and-gravel bridle path along a stream in the Wissahickon, in the northwestern section of Fairmount Park, is a great ride.

The **Bicycle Club of Philadelphia** (WEB www.phillybikeclub.org) organizes bike tours, from afternoon outings to weeklong events. Bike rentals, as well as in-line skates, are available from May through September, Wednesday through Friday 4–8 and weekends 9–6, at **Lloyd Hall** (☎ 215/685–3936), a contemporary addition at the eastern end of Boathouse Row. There's also a café. You can rent bikes for $15–$25 a day from **Bike Line** (✉ 1028 Arch St., ☎ 215/735–1503).

Fishing

On the banks of Wissahickon Creek and Pennypack Creek, you can find good trout fishing in attractive natural settings; call **Fairmount Park** (☎ 215/685–0000) for information. Both creeks are stocked for the mid-April–December season. You'll need a license ($17), available at some local sporting goods stores and at Kmart (⊠ 424 Oregon Ave., ☎ 215/336–1778).

Golf

Philadelphia has six 18-hole courses that are open to the public. Cobb's Creek is the most challenging; Roosevelt is the easiest.

For golfers who love lots of action, **Cobb's Creek and Karakung** (⊠ 7200 Lansdowne Ave., ☎ 215/877–8707) are two adjacent courses. Cobb's Creek plays in and around the creek itself, making for lovely vistas and challenging shots. Karakung has hilly fairways and smaller greens. Both are par 71. Greens fees are $29 weekdays, $35.25 weekends and holidays.

Franklin D. Roosevelt (⊠ 20th St. and Pattison Ave., ☎ 215/462–8997) is a flat, relatively easy par 69; it's particularly recommended for beginners. Greens fees are $18–$22 weekdays, $18–$26 weekends.

J. F. Byrne (⊠ 9500 Leon St., ☎ 215/632–8666), a short but semichallenging course with small greens and water on six holes, is rated par 67. Greens fees are $20–$23 weekdays, $23.75–$27.25 weekends.

With lots of hills, trees, and the Frankford Creek running through it, **Juniata** (⊠ L and Cayuga Sts., ☎ 215/743–4060) is an impressive par 66. Greens fees are $18.25 weekdays, $22.50 weekends.

Narrow tree-lined fairways make **Walnut Lane** (⊠ 800 Walnut La., ☎ 215/482–3370), a short (4,500 yards) course, into a semichallenging par 62. Greens fees are $17.25–$19.75 weekdays, $21–$24 weekends.

Outside Philadelphia, the privately owned **Valley Forge Golf Club** (⊠ 401 N. Gulph Rd., King of Prussia, ☎ 610/337–1776), near Valley Forge National Historic Park, is open to the public. Trees, doglegs, and small greens make this course (6,266 yards, par 71) a challenging one. Greens fees are $19 weekdays, $23 weekends.

Health Clubs

Some downtown clubs allow nonmembers (with photo I.D.s) to have day or week guest privileges for $10–$25. Three good facilities are **Central YMCA** (⊠ 1425 Arch St., ☎ 215/557–0082); **Rittenhouse Square Fitness Club** (⊠ 2002 Rittenhouse Sq., ☎ 215/985–4095); and **12th Street Gym** (⊠ 204 S. 12th St., ☎ 215/985–4092).

Hiking

There are 25 mi of fine solo walks or hikes in Fairmount Park and 54 mi in the unspoiled Wissahickon, a northern section of the park; call **Fairmount Park** (☎ 215/685–0000) for information. Despite the bucolic quality of these areas, it's important to remember that you are in an urban setting and should take appropriate precautions. If you're alone, keep to the main paths along Kelly Drive and West River Drive, or consider joining a hiking group.

Hiking takes on an added dimension if you opt for some of the organized hikes in the area. You can meet hikers at the **Batona Hiking Club** (☎ 215/659–3921 or 215/482–4397) on Sunday morning at a central Philadelphia location (such as Broad and Arch streets) and carpool to hiking areas within a two-hour drive of the city, including the Appalachian Trail, the Delaware Water Gap, and the New Jersey Pine Barrens. Hikes range from 7 mi to 12 mi and tend to be more strenuous than those of the other clubs.

The Department of Recreation sponsors the **Wanderlust Hiking Club** (☎ 215/424–8510). Relatively easy hikes of 5–8 mi, many through Fairmount Park and Pennypack Park, begin every Saturday afternoon at

1:30. Check the "Weekend" section of the Friday Philadelphia *Inquirer* for locations each week.

Horseback Riding

Of the numerous bridle paths coursing through Philadelphia, the most popular are the trails of the Wissahickon in the northwest, Pennypack Park in the northeast, and Cobb's Creek Park in the southwest. One riding academy that has instruction, trail rides, and rentals is **Circle K Stables** (⊠ 4220 Holmesburg Ave., ☎ 215/335–9975), which charges $30 per hour for lessons, $20 per hour to rent. **Ashford Farms** (⊠ River Rd., Miquon, ☎ 610/825–9838), just over the northwestern border of the city, has trail-ride fees of $30 per hour and lessons for $45–$60 per hour.

Ice-Skating

You can skate outdoors—with the Delaware River and Benjamin Franklin Bridge as a backdrop—daily from November to March at the **Blue Cross RiverRink** (⊠ Festival Pier, Columbus Blvd. at Spring Garden St., north of Penn's Landing, ☎ 215/925–7465). Admission is $5 to $6. You can skate indoors at the **University of Pennsylvania Class of 1923 Ice Rink** (⊠ 3130 Walnut St., ☎ 215/898–1923), which is open to the public from September to March; admission is $5.50.

In-Line Skating

In-line skating enthusiasts can take to the narrow city streets for high-flying, but safe—helmets are mandatory—10–12 mile treks. You can meet skaters of the **Landskaters Inline Skate Club** (☎ 856/988–9898) April through October on the steps of the Philadelphia Museum of Art on Sunday at 10 AM, and Tuesday and Saturday at 7 PM.

Jogging

Joggers can be seen on streets all over the city, but probably no area is favored more than Kelly and West River drives, a scenic 8-mi route along the Schuylkill River. Then, of course, there are the steps of the Art Museum itself, host to Rockylike runners who raise their arms in salute during early morning jaunts. The **Northeast Roadrunners of Philadelphia** (c/o Gerard Nolan, ⊠ 3904 I St., 19124, ☎ 215/535–7335) has more information about jogging and running in the city.

Fairmount Park (☎ 215/685–0000)—especially along the river drives and Wissahickon Creek—is a natural for joggers and runners. Forbidden Drive along the Wissahickon offers more than 5 mi of soft-surface trail along a picturesque creek in a secluded valley. Only runners, walkers, bikers, and horses can use the trail—motor vehicles aren't allowed.

Pennypack Park (⊠ Pine Rd. and Bloomfield Ave., ☎ 215/214–2524 or 215/685–0000), in the northeast section of the city, has an 8-mi macadam trail along Pennypack Creek. Those interested in the ultimate in running—through wide-open spaces on bike trails, horse trails, and grassy hills and dales—have to head outside Philadelphia to **Valley Forge National Park.**

From dawn to dusk the south walkway of the **Benjamin Franklin Bridge** provides a tough but rewarding 3½-mi round-trip run with a terrific view of the Delaware River waterfront.

Tennis

Fairmount Park has more than 100 free public courts, but many players must bring their own nets. Courts are first-come, first-served. Call the **Department of Recreation** (☎ 215/686–3650) for information.

Among the main courts is **Chamounix Tennis Courts** (⊠ Chamounix Dr., off Belmont Mansion Dr., West Fairmount Park). The **West Park**

Tennis Courts (✉ George's Hill, near 52nd and Parkside) are adjacent to the Mann Center, West Fairmount Park.

Spectator Sports

Whether their teams win or lose, Philadelphians remain avid sports fans who support both professional and collegiate teams. The major-league sports teams play their home games in Veterans Stadium, the impressive First Union Center, or the First Union Spectrum. These venues are all around Broad Street and Pattison Avenue, near I–95, at the southern edge of the city. The Broad Street subway stops nearby at Pattison Avenue; Bus C also runs down Broad Street. The Eagles and the Phillies play at Veterans Stadium (separate new stadiums are planned for the teams by 2003 for the Eagles and 2004 for the Phillies); the 76ers and the Flyers call the First Union Center home. Some collegiate games are played in these stadiums, too; others are played on the campuses of the various colleges and universities.

Tickets to professional baseball, basketball, football, and hockey games are available at Veterans Stadium or the First Union Spectrum through **TicketMaster** (☎ 215/336–2000), at ticket agencies, and by mail and phone from the respective teams. You should plan to buy tickets as early as possible.

Baseball

The **Philadelphia Phillies** play from April to October at Veterans Stadium (✉ 3501 S. Broad St., ☎ 215/463–1000). Tickets cost $8–$24.

The minor league **Camden River Sharks,** a member of the independent Atlantic League, play May through September at Campbell's Field in Camden, across the Delaware River from Penn's Landing (✉ 2 Riverside Dr., ☎ 856/963–2600 or 866/742–7579). Tickets are $6–$9.

Basketball

The **Philadelphia 76ers** play at the First Union Center (✉ Broad St. at I–95, ☎ 215/339–7676) from November to April. Tickets are $14–$50.

Collegiate Big Five basketball (✉ Big Five Office, Hutchinson Gym, 220 S. 32nd St., ☎ 215/898–4747) features teams from LaSalle, St. Joseph's, Temple, the University of Pennsylvania, and Villanova. The season runs from December to March.

Bicycling

One of the world's top four bicycling events, the **First Union U.S. Pro Cycling Championship** (WEB www.firstunioncycling.com) is held here each June. The 156-mi race starts and finishes at Benjamin Franklin Parkway, with 10 loops including the infamous Manayunk Wall.

Boxing

The **Blue Horizon** (✉ 1314 N. Broad St., ☎ 215/763–0500) is the city's legendary fight club. It has more than a thousand seats, but every one is close to the action.

Football

The **Philadelphia Eagles** can be seen in action at Veterans Stadium (✉ 3501 S. Broad St., ☎ 215/463–5500) from September through January. At this writing, the team was scheduled to move in 2003 to its new $320 million, state-of-the-art facility at 11th Street and Pattison Avenue with a grass playing field and seating for 66,000–68,000 fans. Many seats go to season-ticket holders; individual tickets are $40.

Hockey

The **Philadelphia Flyers** of the NHL hit the ice at First Union Center (✉ Broad St. at I–95, ☎ 215/755–9700) from October to April. Tickets are $37–$80.

The energetic **Philadelphia Phantoms,** the city's minor-league hockey team, are the Flyers' AHL affiliate. You can see them at the First Union Spectrum (✉ Broad St. and Pattison Ave., ☎ 215/465–4522) from October through April. Seats cost $17.

Horse Racing

Thoroughbred racing takes place at **Philadelphia Park** (✉ Street Rd., Bensalem, ☎ 215/639–9000). Post time is usually 12:10 PM in the winter, 12:35 PM in the summer, Saturday–Tuesday year-round. For off-track betting, the **Turf Club Center City** (✉ 1635 Market St., ☎ 215/246–1556) is open daily from 11:30 through the last race, usually about midnight.

Lacrosse

The **Philadelphia Wings,** an indoor lacrosse team, have won several major indoor Lacrosse League championships in recent years. The team plays at the First Union Center (✉ Broad St. at I–95, ☎ 215/389–9464); the season runs from January through March. Tickets cost $16–$25.

Rowing

The elegant boathouses, the regattas, the placid Schuylkill River, and a climate that allows an average of 360 rowing days a year all make Philadelphia the rowing capital of the world. From February to October you can watch single and team races out on the river, usually from 5 AM to dusk. Dozens of major meets are held here, including the largest rowing event in the country, the **Dad Vail Regatta** (☎ 215/248–2600). This May event includes up to 500 sculls from more than 100 colleges. Free shuttle buses for spectators provide transportation from remote parking areas. The May **Stotesbury Cup Regatta** (☎ 215/332–8531) includes more than 2,500 students from 110 schools. More than a thousand individual and club-member rowers compete in the **Independence Day Regatta** (☎ 215/332–8531), held around July 4.

Soccer

Philadelphia Kixx, the city's first national professional soccer team, draws crowds of exuberant fans to the First Union Spectrum (✉ Broad St. and Pattison Ave., ☎ 888/888–5499). You can catch the team in action from October through April; tickets are $10–$20.

Track and Field

The **Penn Relays** (☎ 215/898–6154), the world's largest and oldest amateur track meet, held the last week of April at the University of Pennsylvania's Franklin Field, stars world-class performers in track and field. The **Philadelphia Distance Run** (☎ 610/526–9188), the nation's top half-marathon, takes place in September. The **Philadelphia Marathon** (☎ 215/685–0054) runs through Center City and along the Schuylkill River and is held the Sunday before Thanksgiving. The **Broad Street Run** (☎ 215/563–6184), a 10-miler down Broad Street, is a May event.

6 SHOPPING

Delight in the discoveries of Philadelphia shopping. In a city rich with history and culture, old meets new on cobblestone streets and city blocks. Soak up the flavor of this city of neighborhoods in just a quick stroll: find cutting-edge fashion on Walnut Street, bohemian chic in Old City, antique displays on Pine Street. Pick up a souvenir in a museum gift shop or hunt for fine cheese and olive oil in the Italian Market.

Updated by
Melissa
Solomon
Rosten

HOMEY MEETS HAUTE IN PHILADELPHIA, where stores hold a vast array of goodies as diverse as the city itself. You'll find it all here—funky artwork and highbrow housewares, fine jewels, and haute couture. Indeed, Philadelphia has spawned some influential fashion retailers. Nationally known clothing designer Paula Hian works out of a studio in Manayunk. The Urban Outfitters chain was borne from a storefront in West Philadelphia. Its sophisticated sister, Anthropologie, also has its roots in Philadelphia. Lagos, the popular high-end jewelry line, was founded here, and all items are still produced locally. High fashion boutiques Joan Shepp, Knit Wit, and Plage Tahiti, all in the Rittenhouse Square area, are well-regarded by locals for designer clothing and accessories.

Some of the most spirited shopping in town is also pleasing to the palate. The indoor Reading Terminal Market and the outdoor Italian Market are bustling with urban dwellers buying groceries and visitors in search of the perfect Philadelphia cheese steak. Equally welcoming is the city's quaint and cobblestone Antiques Row, the three-block stretch of Pine Street crammed with shops selling everything from estate jewelry to stained glass and rare books. Also worth a trip is Jewelers' Row, the oldest and second largest diamond district in the country.

Most stores accept traveler's checks and Visa, MasterCard and American Express; Diners Club and Discover are less widely accepted. Policies on personal checks vary. Pennsylvania has a 6% sales tax, and the city adds another 1%. These taxes do not apply to clothing, medicine, and food bought in stores. For shopping hours, *see* Business Hours *in* Smart Travel Tips A to Z.

Blitz Tours

Philadelphia makes the old new again with its plethora of antiques and art and crafts galleries. Use these themed shopping itineraries as guides for exploration by foot or bus. For further information about these stores, refer to the individual listings.

Antiques

Begin your shopping in the generally expensive shops on Pine Street between 9th and 12th streets, long known as Antiques Row. **M. Finkel and Daughter** (⊠ 936 Pine St.) is best known for furniture and needlework from the late 18th and early 19th centuries. **G. B. Schaffer Antiques** (⊠ 1014 Pine St.) carries stained glass, silver, and a large selection of paintings and prints. Then walk five blocks north to Chestnut Street, which is lined with mostly urban-inspired, inexpensive clothing and variety stores. Continue west to **Freeman's** (⊠ 1808 Chestnut St.), an auction house one block away from the upscale Shops at Liberty Place. Freeman's, the oldest building designed specifically for an auction house, spans six floors. Explore the store's specialty departments, which include fine American and European art and rare books and prints. In this area you'll find plenty of places to stop for a quick bite. Walk a block south on 19th Street to Rittenhouse Square and stroll through the park for a taste of the good life in the city. A number of antiques shops can be found in the elegant area surrounding the park. Visit **Metro Antiques** (⊠ 257 S. 20th St.), between Locust and Spruce streets, for sterling silver, period jewelry, and decorative collectibles. **Niederkorn Silver,** also near Rittenhouse Square (⊠ 2005 Locust St.), specializes in decorative items such as antique silver picture frames.

When you pack your MCI Calling Card, it's like packing your loved ones along too.

Your MCI Calling Card is the easy way to stay in touch when you travel. Use it to call to and from over 125 countries. Plus, every time you call, you can earn frequent flier miles. So wherever your travels take you, call home with your MCI Calling Card. It's even easy to get one. Just visit **www.mci.com/worldphone.**

EASY TO CALL WORLDWIDE

1. Just enter the WorldPhone® access number of the country you're calling from.
2. Enter or give the operator your MCI Calling Card number.
3. Enter or give the number you're calling.

Aruba ✥	800-888-8
Bahamas ✥	1-800-888-8000

Barbados ✥	1-800-888-8000
Bermuda ✥	1-800-888-8000
British Virgin Islands ✥	1-800-888-8000
Canada	1-800-888-8000
Mexico	01-800-021-8000
Puerto Rico	1-800-888-8000
United States	1-800-888-8000
U.S. Virgin Islands	1-800-888-8000

✥ Limited availability.

EARN FREQUENT FLIER MILES

SEE THE WORLD
IN FULL COLOR

Fodor's Exploring Guides bring all the great sights vividly to life with hundreds of photographs, fascinating historical background, and colorful anecdotes. Detailed maps and practical information keep you headed in the right direction.

Pair a **Fodor's** Exploring Guide with your trusted Gold Guide for a complete planning package.

Art and Crafts Galleries

Philadelphia is an excellent hunting ground for arts and crafts, particularly in the heart of Center City and in Old City. Begin downtown, amid Chestnut and Walnut, two major shopping streets. Between 16th and 18th streets you'll find some wonderful galleries specializing in contemporary art, such as **Schmidt/Dean Gallery** (⌧ 1636 Walnut St.), which presents paintings by local artists. **Works on Paper** (⌧ 1611 Walnut St.) is well regarded for its selection of modern prints. You can find contemporary art in trendy Old City as well, by venturing down Chestnut Street by foot or bus to 3rd Street. For a great selection of contemporary prints head to **The Works** (⌧ 303 Cherry St.). **Snyderman Gallery,** on the top floor at the same address, sells beautiful handmade furniture and glass pieces.

Shopping Districts and Malls

Pine Street from 9th Street to 12th Street has long been Philadelphia's **Antiques Row.** The three-block area has dozens of antiques stores and curio shops, many specializing in expensive period furniture and Colonial heirlooms.

Across the street from the Liberty Bell is the **Bourse** (⌧ 21 S. 5th St., between Market and Chestnut Sts., ☎ 215/625–0300), an elegantly restored 1895 commodities exchange building. The six-story skylighted atrium contains a few fun shops catering to tourists, such as Best of Philadelphia, as well as a festive international food court.

The **Chestnut Street Transitway,** which extends from 8th to 18th streets, is somewhat seedy after dark but buzzes with urban vitality during the day. It has stores that sell rare and used books, custom tailors, sporting goods stores, and inexpensive trendy clothing stores.

Franklin Mills Mall (⌧ off I–95 at Exit 24, Rte. 63, Woodhaven Rd., ☎ 215/632–1500) is a bargain-lover's paradise spanning 1.7 million square ft, with 200 stores and two food courts. Discount outlet stores include Ann Taylor Loft, Nordstrom Rack, Off Fifth–Saks Fifth Avenue Outlet, and Last Call Neiman Marcus. The mall, about 20 mi from downtown, is nearly a mile in length, and the parking lot holds almost 9,000 cars. Be sure to pick up a map to help you navigate the mall, which is arranged in color-coded sections. For a break, you can visit one of the 14 theaters in the GCC Franklin Mills multiplex (☎ 215/281–2750).

A block north of Chestnut Street is Philadelphia's landmark effort at urban-renewal-cum-shopping, the **Gallery at Market East** (⌧ Market St. between 8th and 11th Sts., ☎ 215/925–7162), America's first enclosed downtown shopping mall. The four-level glass-roof structure near the Pennsylvania Convention Center contains 150 mid-price retailers. It includes 40 food outlets and two department stores—**JCPenney** (☎ 215/238–9100) and **Strawbridge's** (☎ 215/629–6000), which has somewhat higher-quality merchandise. Strawbridge's, now part of the May Company chain, is home-grown; it was founded by prominent local businessmen Justus C. Strawbridge and Isaac Clothier.

If you want local color, nothing compares with South Philadelphia's **Italian Market.** On both sides of 9th Street from Christian Street to Washington Avenue and spilling out onto the surrounding blocks, hundreds of outdoor stalls and indoor stores sell spices, cheeses, pastas, fruits, vegetables, and freshly slaughtered poultry and beef, not to mention household items, clothing, shoes, and other goods. It's crowded and filled with the aromas of everything from fresh garlic to imported salami. The vendors can be less than hospitable, but the food is fresh and the prices are reasonable. Food shops include the Spice Corner, DiBruno Brothers House of Cheese, Claudio's, and Talluto's Authentic Italian Foods. Fante's is well known for cookware. The market's hours are Tuesday–Saturday 9–5:30; some vendors open earlier, and others close around 3:30. Some shops are open Sunday from 9:30 to 12:30.

Jewelers' Row, centered on Sansom Street between 7th and 8th streets, is one of the world's oldest and largest markets of precious stones: more than 350 retailers, wholesalers, and craftspeople operate here. The 700 block of Sansom Street is a brick-paved enclave occupied almost exclusively by jewelers.

Lord & Taylor (✉ between 13th, Juniper, Market, and Chestnut Sts., ☎ 215/241–9000) displays the chain's classic merchandise in the spacious former John Wanamaker department store, a Philadelphia landmark. Its focal point is the nine-story grand court with its 30,000-pipe organ—the largest ever built—and a 2,500-pound statue of an eagle, both remnants of the 1904 Louisiana Purchase Exposition in St. Louis. The new owners have continued the famous Christmas sound-and-light show and the organ performances.

For browsing, a visit to the historic and hip **Manayunk** neighborhood (☎ 215/482–9565) is worth the 7-mi trip from Center City. (Take the train; parking is next to impossible.) This former mill town along the Schuylkill River is crammed with art galleries and clothing boutiques, and with one-of-a-kind stores selling everything from clocks and crystals to board games and Balinese artifacts. Many stores are on Main Street between 4400 and 3900. Alfresco dining, lively bars, and stay-open-late shops make this a great evening destination.

Market Place East (✉ Market St. between 7th and 8th Sts., ☎ 215/592–8905), across from the Gallery, is in a historic building saved from the wrecker's ball at the 11th hour. The century-old former Lit Brothers department store went through a $75 million renovation to emerge as an office building with a five-level atrium full of moderately priced stores and restaurants.

Once a commercial waterfront district, **Old City** (✉ Front to 5th Sts. and Chestnut to Vine Sts. ☎ 215/440–7000) is home to all things artsy. Lofts, art galleries, furniture stores, and unique home decor shops line the streets; there are also the requisite trendy clothing and shoe stores. After dark, young professionals and students (many live in area warehouses and factories converted into apartment buildings) flock to the area's bars and clubs. Some of Philadelphia's most innovative restaurants can also be found here. One of the best times to explore Old City's gallery scene is during First Friday. As the name implies, on the First Friday of each month, from 5 PM to 9 PM, Old City galleries are open to the public. Many offer refreshments, and the street scene becomes quite festive by dark.

Serious shoppers will want to make a trip to **The Plaza & The Court at King of Prussia** (✉ Rte. 202 at the Schuylkill Expwy. ☎ 610/265–5727 for the Plaza; 610/337–1210 for the Court), the largest retail shopping complex on the East Coast. The two malls are an elegant place to stroll and shop; there are nearly 400 specialty shops and eight department stores including Nordstrom, Neiman Marcus, and Bloomingdale's. Moderately priced home-furniture-giant Crate & Barrel recently opened a store here. The mall is about 20 mi from downtown; SEPTA Bus 124 or 125 runs here from 17th Street and John F. Kennedy Boulevard.

The roots of the **Reading Terminal Market** (✉ 12th and Arch Sts., ☎ 215/922–2317) date back to 1892, when the Reading Railroad commissioned a food bazaar to be built in the train shed, its grand expansion plans. Stroll amidst the bustling see and smell old and new culinary delights. Amish m goods and produce straight from the farm alongside ve the latest gourmet vegetarian dishes, artisan breads, and sushi. dors also sell exotic spices, flowers, crafts, jewelry, clothing, and cookbooks. Eighty-six merchants are represented here, but try not to miss Amish-owned Fisher's Soft Pretzels for piping hot, freshly rolled soft pretzels; Bassetts Ice Cream, America's oldest ice cream makers; Jill's Vorspeise, for an array of interesting and healthy soups, salads, sandwiches, and other prepared foods; and Metropolitan Bakery, for hearty breads and light pastries. The Market is open from Monday through Saturday, from 8 AM to 6 PM. The Amish vendors are open Wednesday through Saturday.

Shop-till-you-droppers, make a beeline for **Rittenhouse Row,** the area between Broad and 21st streets, and Spruce and Market streets. Stroll down Walnut Street between Rittenhouse Square and Broad Street for the greatest concentration of swanky stores and tony boutiques, art galleries, and jewelers. On 18th Street in the block north of Rittenhouse Square, you'll find a sidewalk vendor selling handmade Peruvian shawls, street artist Joe Barker painting watercolors of Philadelphia cityscapes, and a shop—Scoop De Ville—that sells homemade chocolate and custom-blended frozen yogurt.

At 16th and Chestnut streets is the upscale **Shops at Liberty Place** (⊠ 1625 Chestnut St., ☎ 215/851–9055). The complex features a food court and popular stores including Benetton, Barami, the Coach Store, J. Crew, Speedo Authentic Fitness, the Body Shop, and Country Road Australia. More than 60 stores and restaurants are arranged in two circular levels within a strikingly handsome 90-ft glass-roof atrium.

The elegant **Shops at the Bellevue** (⊠ Broad and Walnut Sts.) include Polo/Ralph Lauren, with the designer's classic styles; the chic clothes of Nicole Miller; Tiffany & Co.; Origins bath and body products; and a Williams-Sonoma cookware store. A downstairs food court is bustling at lunchtime; several upscale restaurants in the historic building, which also houses an elegant hotel, are popular in the evening.

For some of the most entertaining people-watching in the city, head to **South Street,** just south of Society Hill. Hot-pink–haired teens vie for space with moms wheeling strollers on this bustling strip from Front Street near the Delaware River to 9th Street. More than 300 unusual stores—high-fashion clothing, New Age books, music and health food, avant-garde art galleries, and 100 restaurants—line the area. Most shops are open in the evening. You'll find a few of the national chains, but 95% of the stores are individually owned, selling things you won't find in the mall back home.

Specialty Stores

Antiques

Many dealers in higher-price wares cluster on Antiques Row—Pine Street between 9th and 12th streets. Some less expensive shops, carrying newer treasures such as '50s and '60s designs, are clustered off South Street, on Bainbridge Street between 4th and 9th streets. Call to check hours, as dealers may open late or be closed a few days a week.

Architectural Antiques Exchange. Victorian embellishments from saloons and apothecary shops, stained and beveled glass, gargoyles, and advertising memorabilia entice the shoppers here. ⊠ 715 N. 2nd St., ☎ 215/922–3669.

Calderwood Gallery. Art nouveau and art deco furniture, glass, bronzes, and rugs tempt discerning collectors at this fine establishment. ⊠ *1427 Walnut St.,* ☎ *215/568–7475.*

Freeman's. This is not only the city's most prominent auction house, but also America's oldest (founded in 1805). An estate sale is held the first Wednesday of each month; free appraisal days (no reservations required) are scheduled for the third Wednesday of each month. Specialty departments include fine paintings, fine American and European furniture and decorative arts, 20th-century design, and rare books and prints. Freeman's auctioned one of the original flyers on which the Declaration of Independence was printed and posted throughout the city. It sold for $404,000 in 1968. ⊠ *1808 Chestnut St.,* ☎ *215/563– 9275.*

G. B. Schaffer Antiques. Fine 18th-, 19th-, and early 20th-century American furnishings, stained glass, silver, porcelain, paintings, and prints are the specialties here. ⊠ *1014 Pine St.,* ☎ *215/923–2263.*

Gargoyles. You can wander through 11,000 square ft of displays of antiques and reproduction decorative and architectural pieces—archways, mantels, entranceways, carousel horses, stained-glass windows, and ornate mirrors. ⊠ *512 S. 3rd St.,* ☎ *215/629–1700.*

M. Finkel and Daughter. Late-18th- and early 19th-century American furniture, quilts, needlework, samplers, and folk art make this an important outpost for Americana buffs. ⊠ *936 Pine St.,* ☎ *215/627–7797.*

Metro Antiques. The store displays a wide variety of objects: sterling silver pieces, art deco jewelry, bar glassware, and African masks and statues. ⊠ *257 S. 20th St.,* ☎ *215/545–3555.*

Niederkorn Silver. A fine selection of silver items, including jewelry, pieces for the desk and dresser, and a nice selection of baby silver, make this a worthwhile stop. ⊠ *2005 Locust St.,* ☎ *215/567–2606.*

Olde City Antiques & Collectibles. Four floors carry consignments of antique and reproduction furniture, rugs, paintings, and glassware. ⊠ *33 S. 2nd St.,* ☎ *215/413–1944.*

South Street Antiques Market. An indoor center about half a block below South Street holds the stalls of 25 dealers who sell everything from furniture, paintings, and stained glass to jewelry and '50s collectibles. It's closed Monday and Tuesday. ⊠ *615 S. 6th St.,* ☎ *215/592–0256.*

Vintage Instruments. Antique strings and woodwinds are displayed; the store specializes in violins and also carries American fretted instruments—banjos, guitars, and mandolins. ⊠ *1529 Pine St.,* ☎ *215/ 545–1100.*

W. Graham Arader. This is the flagship store of a highly respected chain that stocks the world's largest selection of 16th- to 19th-century prints and maps, specializing in botanicals, birds, and the American West. ⊠ *1308 Walnut St.,* ☎ *215/735–8811.*

Art and Crafts Galleries

For current shows in Philadelphia's numerous galleries, see the listings in *Philadelphia* magazine or the Weekend section of the Friday *Philadelphia Inquirer.* Many galleries are near Rittenhouse Square; others are on South Street or scattered about downtown. In recent years Old City has become the hottest gallery area.

American Pie Contemporary Crafts. An eclectic mix of handcrafted jewelry, blown glass, and Judaica is displayed here. Artists from around the country are represented, including the innovative craftsman Sticks, who makes personalized hand-painted wood pieces. Sales staff are especially knowledgeable and helpful. ⊠ *327 South St.,* ☎ *215/922–2226;* ⊠ *4303 Main St., Manayunk,* ☎ *215/487–0226.*

Clay Studio. A nonprofit organization runs the gallery and conducts classes as well as an outreach program to inner city schools. There are clay works and pottery by well-known artists; the gallery has juried shows and group exhibits. ✉ *139 N. 2nd St.,* ☎ *215/925–3453.*

David David Gallery. American and European paintings, drawings, and watercolors from the 16th to the 20th centuries are on display. ✉ *260 S. 18th St.,* ☎ *215/735–2922.*

Fabric Workshop and Museum. A nonprofit arts organization runs this center and store dedicated to creating new work in fabric and other materials, working with emerging and nationally and internationally recognized artists. ✉ *1315 Cherry St.,* ☎ *215/568–1111.*

Fleisher Ollman Gallery. You'll find fine works by 20th-century self-taught American artists here. ✉ *211 S. 17th St.,* ☎ *215/545–7562.*

Helen Drutt. This gallery presents contemporary American and European artists, with a focus on ceramics and jewelry. ✉ *1721 Walnut St.,* ☎ *215/735–1625.*

I. Brewster. The specialty here is contemporary paintings and prints by such artists as Louis Icart, Erté, Andy Warhol, Roy Lichtenstein, and Red Grooms. ✉ *1628 Walnut St.,* ☎ *215/731–9200.*

Gross McCleaf Gallery. This is a good place to see works by both prominent and emerging artists, with an emphasis on Philadelphia painters. ✉ *127 S. 16th St.,* ☎ *215/665–8138.*

Locks Gallery. Shows present works by an impressive assortment of contemporary regional, national, and international painters, sculptors, and mixed-media artists. ✉ *600 Washington Sq. S,* ☎ *215/629–1000.*

Muse Gallery. Established in 1978 by the Muse Foundation for the Visual Arts, Muse Gallery is an artist's cooperative in Old City committed to increasing the visibility of local artwork and presenting experimental work in a variety of media. ✉ *60 N. 2nd St.,* ☎ *215/627–5310.*

Newman Galleries. This gallery carries a range of works from 19th-century paintings to contemporary lithographs and sculpture. It's strong on 20th-century painters from the Bucks County area. ✉ *1625 Walnut St.,* ☎ *215/563–1779.*

Nexus Foundation for Today's Art. A group of artists started this non-profit organization in 1975. The emphasis is on experimental art as well as new directions in traditional media. ✉ *137 N. 2nd St.,* ☎ *215/ 629–1103.*

Schmidt/Dean Gallery. Contemporary paintings, sculpture, prints, and photographs are shown; the specialty is work by Philadelphia artists. ✉ *1636 Walnut St.,* ☎ *215/546–7212;* ✉ *1721 Spruce St.,* ☎ *215/ 546–9577.*

School Gallery of the Pennsylvania Academy of the Fine Arts. Stop here to see rotating exhibits of works by faculty, alumni, and students in the school's attractively renovated building near the Pennsylvania Convention Center. ✉ *1301 Cherry St.,* ☎ *215/972–7600.*

Schwarz Gallery. Eighteenth- to 20th-century American and European paintings are the focus, with an emphasis on Philadelphia artists of the past. ✉ *1806 Chestnut St.,* ☎ *215/563–4887.*

Snyderman Gallery. One-of-a-kind handmade furniture pieces and glass objects are displayed at this Old City gallery. ✉ *303 Cherry St., top floor,* ☎ *215/238–9576.*

The Works. This Old City gallery showcases contemporary American crafts in wood, fiber, ceramics, and metals. ✉ *303 Cherry St., ground floor,* ☎ *215/922–7775.*

Works on Paper. The contemporary prints here have won the gallery a reputation as one of the city's best. ✉ *1611 Walnut St.,* ☎ *215/988– 9999.*

Bookstores

AIA Bookstore & Design Center. Run by the Philadelphia chapter of the American Institute of Architects (AIA), this shop specializes in books on architectural theory, building construction, interior design, and furnishings. It also sells architectural drawings and watercolors, blueprint posters, international magazines, home furnishings, and unusual gifts. ✉ *117 S. 17th St.,* ☎ *215/569–3188.*

Barnes & Noble. A prime location on Rittenhouse Square, a Starbucks café, plus an extensive travel section (featuring lots of regional books and maps) make this a great place to browse, unwind, or people-watch. Author readings and children's programs are regular features. ✉ *1805 Walnut St.,* ☎ *215/665–0716.*

Borders. Some locals find this the friendliest bookstore in Philadelphia. You can sit on a couch, listen to live guitar music, and read for hours. The 110,000 titles and more than half million books are spread over three levels. There's a second-floor espresso bar, and Saturday and Sunday morning children's programs are held at 11:30. ✉ *1727 Walnut St.,* ☎ *215/568–7400.*

Giovanni's Room. Focusing on books dealing with feminist, gay, and lesbian topics, this well-regarded store stocks an extensive inventory and sponsors many author appearances. ✉ *345 S. 12th St.,* ☎ *215/923–2960.*

Joseph Fox. This small bookstore specializes in art, architecture, and design. ✉ *1724 Sansom St.,* ☎ *215/563–4184.*

Penn Bookstore. The 60,000-square-ft store, operated by Barnes & Noble, is the largest academic bookstore in the United States. Highlights include tomes from the University of Pennsylvania faculty, loads of Penn-insignia clothing and memorabilia, a multimedia section, and a children's reading room. You'll also find a Starbucks café and the requisite best-sellers. ✉ *3601 Walnut St.,* ☎ *215/898–7597.*

Robin's Bookstore. Not the biggest bookstore in town and maybe not the best, but it's definitely the sentimental favorite of devotees of literature, poetry, and minority studies. Owner Larry Robin has been promoting literature and fighting literary censorship for more than 30 years. Book fans are drawn to its frequent poetry readings and book signings by local authors. ✉ *108 S. 13th St.,* ☎ *215/735–9600.*

Whodunit. The city's only store specializing in mysteries, spy stories, and adventure books also stocks out-of-print mysteries. Co-owner Art Bourgeau has published six mysteries and a nonfiction book on mystery writing. ✉ *1931 Chestnut St.,* ☎ *215/567–1478.*

RARE AND USED BOOKS

Bauman Rare Books. An antiquarian bookstore with volumes dating as far back as the 15th century, this is a treasure trove for collectors in the fields of law, science, literature, travel, and exploration. Bauman's also has a print and map collection. ✉ *1215 Locust St.,* ☎ *215/546–6466.*

Book Trader. You'll find great browsing on the two floors of this eclectic used-book store, though prices are on the high side. It's open daily 10 AM–midnight. ✉ *501 South St.,* ☎ *215/925–0219.*

Hibberd's. Rare and used books, remainders, and a large selection of unusual art books are the sizable draws for book aficionados. ✉ *1306 Walnut St.,* ☎ *215/546–8811.*

William H. Allen Bookseller. This store carries one of the city's best collections of used and scholarly books; specialties are history, literature, and philosophy. Note the extensive collection of books on ancient Greece and Rome, in English and the original Greek or Latin. ✉ *2031 Walnut St.,* ☎ *215/563–3398.*

Cameras and Photographic Equipment

Mid-City Camera. This major stock house carries a large line of darkroom equipment and all major camera brands in all formats. It also buys and sells used cameras and has a service department and rentals. ⊠ *1316 Walnut St.,* ☎ *215/735–2522.*

Roth Camera Repairs. If you have camera trouble, here's the place to go. The store prides itself on extra-quick service. ⊠ *1015 Chestnut St., Jefferson Bldg. lobby, Room 102,* ☎ *215/922–2498.*

Clothing

CHILDREN'S CLOTHING

Born Yesterday. This shop is filled with unique clothing and toys for haute tots. Specialties include handmade goods, imported fashions, and styles not available elsewhere. ⊠ *1901 Walnut St.,* ☎ *215/568–6556.*

Children's Boutique. The store carries a look between conservative and classic in infant to preteen clothes and shoes. You can buy complete wardrobes, specialty gifts, and handmade items. An extensive toy department is stocked with the latest in kiddie crazes. ⊠ *1702 Walnut St.,* ☎ *215/732–2661.*

Kamikaze Kids. Unique designer fashions for infants to preteens are showcased in a child-friendly atmosphere, with cloud-painted walls and play areas. ⊠ *527 S. 4th St.,* ☎ *215/574–9800.*

MEN'S AND WOMEN'S

Banana Republic. The well-known chain's Philadelphia flagship store is set in a grand building that once housed the Manufacturer's and Banker's Club. Men's and women's clothing, shoes, and accessories are stylish, modern, and versatile. ⊠ *1401 Walnut St.,* ☎ *215/751–0292.*

Burberrys Ltd. Named after Thomas Burberry, who designed the trench coat in the mid-1850s, this British-owned establishment stocks British raincoats, overcoats, sport coats, and cashmere sweaters. The signature neutral-tone plaid is a classic and covers everything from trench coats to bikinis. ⊠ *1705 Walnut St.,* ☎ *215/557–7400.*

Hats in the Belfry. Pass by this bright corner shop and you'll be tempted to try on a hat from the huge window display. Go funky or fancy, casual or classic—you'll find hats to suit each and every whim. ⊠ *245 South St.,* ☎ *215/922–6770.*

Nicole Miller. You'll find loads of this successful designer's thematic, quirky scarves, boxer shorts and ties at eponymous boutiques in Center City and Manayunk. Women's collections include simple and elegant sportswear, evening wear, and handbags in beautiful colors. ⊠ *Shops at the Bellevue, Broad and Walnut Sts.,* ☎ *215/546–5007;* ⊠ *4249 Main St., Manayunk,* ☎ *215/930–0307.*

Polo/Ralph Lauren. The city's entry in the Lauren retail empire of classically styled apparel carries the designer's women's, men's, and home collections. ⊠ *Shops at the Bellevue, Broad and Walnut Sts.,* ☎ *215/985–2800.*

Urban Outfitters. What started out as a storefront selling used jeans to students in West Philadelphia is now a trend-setting chain on campuses across the country. Three floors showcase an eclectic array of hip clothing, unusual books, and funky housewares that can go from the dorm room to the family room. ⊠ *1627 Walnut St.,* ☎ *215/569–3131.*

Zipperhead. For almost 20 years this has been the alternative clothing landmark for the spiked-hair-and-nose-ring set. Offerings here include motorcycle jackets, rock band T-shirts, and hard-to-find body jewelry for those hard-to-pierce places. ⊠ *407 South St.,* ☎ *215/928–1123.*

MEN'S CLOTHING

Allure. Classic and stylish Italian clothing draws a cosmopolitan crowd. Brioni, Pal Zileri, Verri, Donna Karan, and Canali are some of the designers here. ⊠ *4255 Main St., Manayunk,* ☎ *215/482–5299.*

Boyds. The largest single-store men's clothier in the country has nine shops that present the traditional English look, avant-garde Italian imports, and dozens of other styles and designers, from Armani to Zegna. The store has departments for extra tall, large, and short men; formalwear; shoes; an excellent café for lunch; free valet parking; and 60 tailors on the premises. Women will find a small selection of high-quality designer clothes, too. ⊠ *1818 Chestnut St.,* ☎ *215/564–9000.*

Brooks Brothers. This is the oldest men's clothing store in America, founded in New York in 1818. You'll find business attire appropriate for Monday morning through casual Friday. ⊠ *1513 Walnut St.,* ☎ *215/564–4100.*

Wayne Edwards. Stylish without being intimidating, the store carries exclusive lines of classic contemporary clothing from Italy, Japan, France, and the United States. Designers include Barbera, Palzileri, and Armani. ⊠ *1521 Walnut St.,* ☎ *215/563–6801.*

WOMEN'S CLOTHING

Asta De Blue. This funky boutique is set in a brownstone off Rittenhouse Square. Find upbeat contemporary clothing, jewelry, accessories, and gifts. Key collections include Zelda, Harari, Lilith, and Tse. The owners say they have the largest collection of Arche footwear outside Manhattan. ⊠ *265 S. 20th St.,* ☎ *215/732–0550.*

Joan Shepp. Cutting-edge fashion is displayed in a setting reminiscent of a New York loft. Notable designers include Yohji Yamomoto, Dries Van Noten, and Jean-Paul Gaultier, and shoes by Prada and Miu Miu. ⊠ *1616 Walnut St.,* ☎ *215/735–2666.*

Knit Wit. High-fashion clothes and accessories from sportswear to cocktail dresses are the focus here. Alberta Ferretti, Anna Molinari, and Vestimenta are among the designers. ⊠ *1721 Walnut St.,* ☎ *215/564–4760.*

Lele. Body-conscious styles and gorgeous fabrics are local designer Lele Tran's trademarks. The tools of her trade—rolling racks, several dressmaker's forms, and a large table covered with patterns—take up much of Tran's tiny Old City store. Customers select samples from the racks, and if a dress or skirt needs altering, Tran will do it on the spot. You can also choose a different fabric or make adaptations to existing styles for a custom design. ⊠ *30 S. 2nd St.,* ☎ *215/592–8474.*

Paula Hian Designs. This local designer's fashions have been among those presented at the prestigious Mercedes-Benz New York Fashion Week in Bryant Park. Hian's Manayunk showroom features her modern, minimalist, body-conscious fashions, including sportswear, eveningwear, and knitwear. Hian designs some fabrics; others are imported from France and Italy. Appointments are suggested, especially for custom work. ⊠ *106 Gay St., Manayunk,* ☎ *215/487–3067.*

Plage Tahiti. A leading showcase for promising young high-fashion designers carries a wide selection of chic and charming swimwear. ⊠ *128 S. 17th St.,* ☎ *215/569–9139.*

Public Image. Trendy clothing is the focus of this Manayunk boutique. Designers include Anna Sui, Vivienne Tam, and Nanette Lepour. A sister accessories store next door carries accoutrements by Kate Spade, Stella Pace, and many others. ⊠ *4390 Main St., Manayunk,* ☎ *215/482–4008.*

Discount Shopping

Cambridge Clothing Factory Outlet. This is a manufacturers' outlet for men, with 10 national brands starting at 40% off retail. Out-of-town-ers can get immediate alterations. ⊠ *1520 Sansom St., 2nd floor,* ☎ *215/568–8248.*

Daffy's. Housed in an attractive Egyptian deco–style building, Daffy's carries higher-end American and European designs for men, women, and children at 40%–75% off list (sometimes even more with special markdowns). Be forewarned: patience is a virtue here. Carefully rummage through the racks (especially on the fourth floor, which houses women's designer suits and evening wear) and you might score a number by Moschino, Jean-Paul Gaultier, or Les Copines. ⊠ *1700 Chestnut St.,* ☎ *215/963–9996.*

Dan's Shoes. Shrewd shoppers find Ferragamo slingbacks, Prada sneakers, or Fendi sandals for a fraction of their retail price. Racks of shoes in sizes 4 to 14 line this store, where affordability supplants ambiance. ⊠ *1733 Chestnut St.,* ☎ *215/568–5257.*

Thos. David Factory Store. Upstairs they make it; downstairs they sell it. High-quality men's and women's business clothing and sportswear are sold at almost wholesale prices. ⊠ *401 Race St.,* ☎ *215/922–4659.*

Food

The Italian Market is a classic Philly experience and the Reading Terminal Market is a city gem, but you'll also find smaller specialty stores that sell fine cheese, chocolate, caviar, and more.

Caviar Assouline. Looking for that very special food gift? This stylish store carries imported and American caviar, smoked seafood, truffles, foie gras, Valrhona chocolate, and more. If you can't decide, pick up a catalog and order by mail from home. ⊠ *505 Vine St.,* ☎ *215/627–3511.*

Chef's Market. Enter this food emporium and you'll be tempted by luscious displays brimming with Brie, fontina, and Jarlsburg (among the 100 varieties of cheese the store carries); decadent homemade desserts like crème brûlée and tiramisu, and savory entrées and side dishes. Packaged items include 150 varieties of imported jams, 40 olive oils, and 60 flavored vinegars. ⊠ *231 South St.,* ☎ *215/925–8360.*

DiBruno Bros. The original DiBruno Bros. was founded in 1939 in the Italian Market; grandsons Bill and Emilio opened the Rittenhouse Square location in 1997. DiBruno's is a mecca for gourmet cheese lovers—the store carries more than 300 different varieties of cheese from around the world, as well as some homemade kinds. You'll also find barrels of olives, Abbruzze sausage, imported olive oils, and balsamic vinegar that's been aged for 75 years. The staff is very knowledgeable and helpful and will provide friendly advice on storage, preparation, and serving ideas. Ask for recipes and samples. ⊠ *109 S. 18th St.,* ☎ *215/665–9220;* ⊠ *930 S. 9th St.,* ☎ *215/922–2876.*

Maron Fine Chocolates. America's oldest independent retail candy store is tucked inside an unassuming storefront just off Rittenhouse Square. Swiss candymaker Conrad Maron settled in Philadelphia and began selling his handmade chocolates in 1850. Still family run, the confectionery's specialties include chocolate-dipped fruits, truffles, personalized candies, sugar-free items, and molded chocolates. Sweet tooth still not satisfied? Maron also has an ice cream parlor, Scoop de Ville, in the rear of the store. Choose from an extensive list of decadent toppings to create a custom-blended treat. ⊠ *107 S. 18th St.,* ☎ *215/988–9992.*

Gifts and Souvenirs

Best of Philadelphia. Here's a fun place for cheap Philly souvenirs: on display are more than 100 different items, including earrings, flags, jigsaw puzzles, coloring books, Ben Franklin key chains, T-shirts, and, of course, Liberty Bells. ⊠ *Bourse Bldg., 21 S. 5th St.,* ☎ *215/629–0533.*

The Black Cat. This University City gift store with a social conscience is located in connecting brownstone rowhouses next to its sister business, the White Dog Cafe. Most products are made from recycled or other Earth-friendly materials. Look for the beautiful journals, picture frames, and photo albums covered in handmade paper. ⊠ *3426 Sansom St.,* ☎ *215/386–6664.*

Hand of Aries. You'll find everything for the discriminating witch—books, candles, incense, tarot cards, ritual robes, capes, and long dresses (black only). ⊠ *509 S. 6th St.,* ☎ *215/923–5264.*

Holt's Cigar Company. Stogie aficionados make a point to stop by this cigar emporium, whose Philadelphia roots date back over 100 years. The shop features a comfortable smoking lounge and one of the nation's largest walk-in humidors. Find private label Ashton cigars, a wide array of smoking accessories and humidors, and writing instruments from Mont Blanc, Waterman, and Cross. ⊠ *1522 Walnut St.,* ☎ *215/732–8500.*

Scarlett Alley. Owned and operated by Mary Kay Scarlett and her daughter Liz, this treasure trove features an ever-changing assortment of unique jewelry, housewares and stationery, as well as toys, soaps and teas. Items are displayed on furniture that is designed and handcrafted by Richard Scarlett, Liz's father; it's also for sale or custom order. ⊠ *241 Race St.,* ☎ *215/592–7898.*

Touches. Upscale shoppers come to this attractive shop for its handmade shawls, handbags, belts, unusual jewelry, and children's gifts. ⊠ *225 S. 15th St.,* ☎ *215/546–1221.*

Warner Bros. Studio Store. For those who love Bugs, Sylvester, Daffy, and Tweety on their mugs, T-shirts, key chains, puzzles, and golf club covers, this is the place. ⊠ *Shops at Liberty Place, 1625 Chestnut St.,* ☎ *215/981–0680.*

Xenos Candy and Gifts. Asher chocolates and Philly souvenirs from key chains to T-shirts are stocked here, near the sites of the historic district. ⊠ *231 Chestnut St.,* ☎ *215/922–1445.*

Home Decor

Anthropologie. Every nook and cranny in this beautiful, spacious store holds a treasure. Housewares, furniture, and gift items are reproductions; designs are inspired by items found in Europe, India, and the Far East. You'll also find lovely bed, bath, and table linens, and a year-round gardening section. Some of the women's clothing and accessories lines are exclusive to the store. ⊠ *1801 Walnut St.,* ☎ *215/568–2114.*

Flotsam and Jetsam. Run by two interior designers, this colorful, bright store showcases a diverse mix of styles that juxtapose the old and new. Modern metal and glassware is displayed alongside restored antiques and found objects from around the world. Take note of the gorgeous handpainted floors and vibrant walls. About 75% of the store's crafts, art, furniture, and accessories is designed locally. ⊠ *149 North 3rd St.,* ☎ *215/351–9914.*

Usona. Furniture and accessories are what the owner calls "global modern," reflecting a fusion of different styles, periods, and materials. Accent pieces, like picture frames and mirrors, are interesting and affordable. ⊠ *223 Market St.,* ☎ *215/351–9160.*

Housewares and Accessories

Fante's. One of the nation's oldest gourmet supply stores has the largest selection of coffeemakers and cooking equipment in the United

States. Family owned since 1906, Fante's is famous for oddball kitchen gadgets such as truffle shavers and pineapple peelers; restaurants and bakeries all over the country and overseas order from the store. It's in the Italian Market, so you can combine a visit here with other food shopping. ⊠ *1006 S. 9th St.,* ☎ *215/922–5557.*

Foster's Urban Homeware. Quirky and useful home accessories are displayed in this spacious store that has a cool, industrial-hip flavor. A sister operation, a cookware purveyor, is located in the Reading Terminal Market. ⊠ *124 N. 3rd St.,* ☎ *267/671–0588.*

Home Grown. Unique tableware, including ceramic serving pieces from around the United States and Europe, is the focus of an upscale home accessories shop that carries everything from Calvin Klein dinnerware to Mackenzie-Childs pottery. ⊠ *4321 Main St., Manayunk,* ☎ *215/482–1910.*

Kitchen Kapers. From one store in South Jersey, this family business has grown to be one of the largest independent kitchenware stores in the United States. This is a good source for fine cookware, French copper, cutlery, coffees, and teas. ⊠ *213 S. 17th St.,* ☎ *215/546–8059.*

Williams-Sonoma. High quality cookware and dishes and interesting gadgets like ergonomic potato peelers and asparagus shavers bring out the gourmand in anyone. ⊠ *Shops at the Bellevue, Broad and Walnut Sts.,* ☎ *215/545–7392.*

Jewelry

Jewelry shoppers in search of antique and contemporary pieces have many options in Philadelphia. Bauble selection is most concentrated on Jewelers' Row, but also look for unique pieces in galleries, antique shops, and boutiques.

Bailey, Banks & Biddle. This old-line store, in business since 1832, is known for diamond and gold jewelry, objets d'art, silver, and crystal. ⊠ *1530 Chestnut St.,* ☎ *215/564–6200.*

Halloween. If the sheer quantity of baubles crammed into this tiny shop doesn't take your breath away, the gorgeous, one-of-a-kind designs will. Shelves, drawers, displays, and even the second-floor balcony overflow with rings, necklaces, earrings, bracelets, pins, and much more. Owner Henri David (who designs some pieces) is well-known locally for his lavish and outrageous Halloween fetes. He'll do custom work, such as creating mates for single earrings. ⊠ *1329 Pine St.,* ☎ *215/732–7711.*

Harry Sable. Harry "king of the wedding bands" Sable has been selling engagement rings, diamond rings, gold jewelry, and watches for more than 50 years. ⊠ *8th and Sansom Sts.,* ☎ *215/627–4014.*

J. E. Caldwell. A local landmark since 1839, the store is adorned with antique handblown crystal chandeliers by Baccarat, making it as elegant as the jewels it sells. Along with traditional and modern jewelry, Caldwell has one of the city's largest selections of giftware and stationery. ⊠ *1339 Chestnut St.,* ☎ *215/864–7800.*

Jack Kellmer Co. Fine jewelry, watches and gift items are offered (some at below retail prices) in a grand building that once housed a bank. The store's dramatic entranceway, 50-ft vaulted ceiling, travertine marble walls, and Colonial-inspired brass chandeliers are the perfect setting for precious stones. ⊠ *717 Chestnut St.,* ☎ *215/627–8350.*

Lagos–The Store. Here you'll find the largest selection of Lagos jewelry; all pieces are handcrafted and designed in Philadelphia by Ann and Steven Lagos. Lagos is famous for its "golden wheat" collection of 22-karat contemporary gold jewelry, sold in the boutiques of upscale department stores. ⊠ *1735 Walnut St.,* ☎ *215/567–0770.*

Richard Kenneth. On display is jewelry from the late-Georgian, Victorian, art nouveau, art deco, and '40s-retro periods. Kenneth also specializes in repairs and appraisals. ⊠ *202 S. 17th St.,* ☎ *215/545–3355.*

Scriven. Designer Keith Scriven started selling handmade jewelry from a section of his Old City gallery, Dizyners. When First Friday gallery-goers were more interested in the jewelry than the art, Scriven knew it was time to open a separate store. His spare, elegant shop showcases his signature bold designs, formed from precious metals and precious and semi-precious stones. The intricate "Angela" link necklace is exquisite. ⊠ *1602 Spruce St.,* ☎ *215/545–8820.*

Tiffany & Co. This is the local branch of the store, famous for its exquisite gems, fine crystal, and china, and, of course, its signature blue gift box. ⊠ *Shops at the Bellevue, 1414 Walnut St.,* ☎ *215/735–1919.*

Luggage and Leather Goods

Robinson Luggage. The shop carries popular, moderate to expensive brands of luggage, leather, and travel accessories. The selection of briefcases and attaché cases is the largest in the Delaware Valley. ⊠ *201 S. Broad St.,* ☎ *215/735–9859.*

Music

Theodor Presser. The best selection of sheet music in Center City draws musicians from far and wide. The store specializes in classical but also carries pop and will special order anything. ⊠ *1718 Chestnut St.,* ☎ *215/568–0964.*

Tower Records. Open 9 AM to midnight 365 days a year, Tower stocks more than 250,000 CDs and tapes—the largest selection in the city. The Avenue of the Arts location has an extensive classical section. ⊠ *100 S. Broad St.,* ☎ *215/568–8001;* ⊠ *610 South St.,* ☎ *215/574–9888.*

Perfumes and Cosmetics

Body Shop de le Parfumier. This "scent boutique" for men and women imports new fragrances, some not yet available elsewhere in the United States. The shop also carries cosmetics, perfume bottles, discontinued scents, and accessories. ⊠ *Bourse Bldg., 21 S. 5th St.,* ☎ *215/922–7660.*

Parfumerie Douglas Cosmetics. A wide selection of major brands of perfume, cosmetics, and beauty accessories is found here. ⊠ *Shops at Liberty Place, 1625 Chestnut St.,* ☎ *215/569–0770;* ⊠ *3603 Walnut St.,* ☎ *215/222–2366.*

Scarlett. Fragrance and makeup junkies crowd this funky boutique, which carries hard-to-find scents, hair products, bath and body items, and an exclusive make-up collection formulated by owner Scarlett Messina. High-end product lines include Bumble & Bumble, Creed, Delux, Molton Brown, and Parfums D'Nicolai. ⊠ *104 S. 13th St.,* ☎ *215/875–9408.*

Shoes

Beige. You'll find a good selection of women's Italian leather shoes in sizes 4–12, priced toward the high end. ⊠ *1715 Walnut St.,* ☎ *215/564–2395.*

Bottino. Men's shoes and accessories are the stars here, all handmade and imported from Italy. Some very big feet get shod here, including those of regular customers Michael Jordan and Sylvester Stallone. ⊠ *121 S. 18th St.,* ☎ *215/854–0907.*

Danielle Scott, Ltd. A tiny accessories boutique in the heart of Rittenhouse Square stocks high-end stilettos, mules, and sandals straight off the runway. Noteworthy designers include Jimmy Choo, Robert Clergerie, and Richard Tyler. ⊠ *126 S. 19th St.,* ☎ *215/569–1218.*

Sherman Brothers Shoes. This off-price retailer of men's shoes has name-brand merchandise and excellent service. The store carries 28 lines of shoes and stocks extra-wide and extra-narrow widths, as well as sizes up to 16. ⊠ *1520 Sansom St.,* ☎ *215/561–4550.*

Strega. There's a wide range of looks for men here, including some exclusive footwear and many top Italian designers. ⊠ *1521 Walnut St.,* ☎ *215/564–5932.*

Sporting Goods

City Sports. Besides sports equipment from in-line skates to bike helmets, the store carries plenty of brand-name active wear and its own line of clothing. ⊠ *1609 Walnut St.,* ☎ *215/985–5860.*

Eastern Mountain Sports. Outdoorsmen and women will find a large selection of clothing and equipment for activities like running, skiing, camping, and boating. Located on the University of Pennsylvania campus, the shop features an in-store rock-climbing wall. Equipment rentals are available. ⊠ *130 S. 36th St.,* ☎ *215/386–1020.*

Everyone's Racquet. As you might guess, this store's specialty is goods related to racket sports: tennis, racquetball, badminton, squash. Next-day racket-stringing service is available. ⊠ *132 S. 17th St.,* ☎ *215/ 665–1221.*

The Original I. Goldberg. This army-navy-and-everything store is hip and practical, with an emphasis on sporting apparel and camping gear. Goldberg's is crammed with government-surplus, military-style clothing, jeans and work clothes, unusual footwear, and exclusive foreign imports. Rummaging here is a sport in itself. ⊠ *902 Chestnut St.,* ☎ *215/925–9393.*

Rittenhouse Sports. The focus is on shoes and gear for triathlon sports—running, swimming, and cycling—but the store also stocks aerobic and workout shoes and gear. ⊠ *126 S. 18th St.,* ☎ *215/569–9957.*

Wine and Liquor

Pennsylvania liquor stores are state operated. State stores (as they're known) are generally open Monday and Tuesday 11–7, Wednesday–Saturday 9–9. You may find chilled beer at delis and gourmet shops.

Wine and Spirits Shoppe. This shop carries one of the best selections of fine wines and liquors in the city. ⊠ *1913 Chestnut St.,* ☎ *215/560–4215.*

7 SIDE TRIPS FROM PHILADELPHIA

The Brandywine Valley

Valley Forge

Updated by
Anne
Dubuisson
Anderson

IT'S EASY TO expand your view of the Philadelphia area by taking one or more day trips to destinations that are within an hour's drive of the city. Head southwest and in 30 minutes you can be immersed in a whole new world. Or make that worlds: first you can see the verdant hills and ancient barns of the Brandywine Valley, home to three generations of Wyeths and other artists inspired by the rural landscapes outside their windows. Then you can visit the extravagant realm of du Pont country, including Winterthur, an important repository of American decorative furnishings, over the border in Delaware. Or you can visit the Revolutionary War battlefield of Brandywine, at Chadds Ford. These attractions are favorites of Philadelphians, and area B&Bs and inns make the Brandywine appealing as an overnight or weekend trip as well as a day excursion.

The historical park at Valley Forge adds another dimension to the revolutionary story that began in Independence Hall. Not far away, the town called King of Prussia dates to that period, but today it's primarily synonymous with shopping, thanks to two huge upscale malls just a half hour from Philadelphia and easily accessible by public transportation.

Pleasures and Pastimes

Dining
It seems that most restaurants in the Brandywine Valley serve what is called Continental-American cuisine, with creative contemporary touches at the better establishments. Most also present local specialties—fresh seafood from the Chesapeake Bay and dishes made with Kennett Square mushrooms. For approximate costs, *see* the dining price chart *in* Smart Travel Tips A to Z.

Gardens
The Brandywine area is home to some of America's most spectacular botanic sights, including the renowned Longwood Gardens. While touring the Hagley Museum and Library, as well as nearby Winterthur, take time to step outside and appreciate the gorgeous natural backgrounds designed to complement the architecture. The grounds of Rockwood, a rural Gothic manor in Wilmington, Delaware, have splendid landscaping.

Spring is the most obvious time to visit these glorious oases, but other seasons can be rewarding, too: Longwood Gardens, a treat at any time of year, has one of the world's largest conservatories, and Rockwood has a similarly stunning, though smaller, Victorian cast-iron-and-glass garden room. At the Brandywine River Museum, the Brandywine Conservancy's Wildflower and Native Plant Gardens are a riot of fall colors, as are the grounds surrounding the French-inspired parterres of the Hagley Museum and Library. Winterthur's Enchanted Woods is a whimsical children's garden.

Lodging
Many Brandywine Valley accommodations may be considered bed-and-breakfasts because of their intimate atmosphere, but they are far from the typical B&B—which is usually a room in a private home—and are more accurately characterized as inns or small hotels. For approximate costs, *see* the lodging price chart *in* Smart Travel Tips A to Z.

THE BRANDYWINE VALLEY

Chances are that you may experience a strong sense of déjà vu during a journey to the Brandywine Valley. Andrew Wyeth immortalized the special landscape of the valley, creating some of the most beloved works in 20th-century American art and making its vistas instantly recognizable. Using colors quintessentially Brandywine—the earthen brown of its hills, gray slate of its stone farmhouses, and dark green of its spruce trees, the famous American realist artist captured the unique personality of the valley: decidedly private, unostentatiously beautiful. He also inspired many people to flock to this valley and fall in love with its peaceful byways. Today, new housing developments continuously crop up and the main highway, U.S. 1, is lined with strip malls and gas stations. Yet, places off the main paths to make you feel you have discovered a tucked-away treasure.

The Brandywine Valley actually incorporates parts of three counties in two states: Chester and Delaware counties in Pennsylvania and New Castle County in Delaware. Winding through this scenic region (about 25 mi southwest of Philadelphia), the Brandywine River flows lazily from West Chester, Pennsylvania, to Wilmington, Delaware. Although in spots it's more a creek than a river, it has nourished many of the valley's economic and artistic endeavors.

KINGDOM OF THE DU PONTS

Although paintings of the Wyeth family distilled the region's mystery, it was the regal du Pont family that provided more than a bit of its magnificence, recontouring the land with grand gardens, mansions, and mills. Their kingdom was established by the family patriarch, Pierre-Samuel du Pont, who had escaped with his family from post-Revolutionary France and settled in northern Delaware. The Du Pont company was founded in 1802 by his son Éleuthère Irénée (E. I.), who made the family fortune, first in gunpowder and iron and later in chemicals and textiles.

E. I. and five generations of du Ponts lived in Eleutherian Mills, the stately family home on the grounds of a black-powder mill that has been transformed into the Hagley Museum. The home, from which Mrs. Henry du Pont was driven after accidental blasts at the powder works, was closed in 1921. Louise du Pont Crowninshield, a great-granddaughter of E. I., restored the house fully before opening it to the public. Louise's relatives were busy, too. Henry Francis du Pont was filling his country estate, Winterthur, with furniture by Duncan Phyfe, silver by Paul Revere, splendid decorative objects, and entire interior woodwork fittings salvaged from homes built between 1640 and 1860.

Pierre du Pont (cousin of Henry Francis) devoted his life to horticulture. He bought a 1,000-acre 19th-century arboretum and created Longwood Gardens, where he entertained his many friends and relatives. Today 350 acres of the meticulously landscaped gardens are open to the public. Displays range from a tropical rain forest to a desert; acres of heated conservatories, where flowers are in bloom year-round, create eternal summer. Pierre also built the grand Hotel du Pont, adjacent to company headquarters, in downtown Willmington. No expense was spared; more than 18 French and Italian craftspeople labored for two years, carving, gilding, and painting. Alfred I. du Pont's country estate, Nemours, was named after the family's ancestral home in north-central France. It encompasses 300 acres of French gardens and a mansion in Louis XVI style.

WYETH COUNTRY

Although Andrew Wyeth is the most famous local artist, the area's artistic tradition began long before, when artist-illustrator Howard Pyle started a school in Wilmington in 1900. He had more than 100 students, including Andrew's father, N. C. Wyeth; Frank Schoonover;

Jessie Willcox Smith; Maxfield Parrish; and Harvey Dunn. It was this tradition that inspired Andrew and his son Jamie.

In 1967 local residents formed the Brandywine Conservancy to prevent industrialization of the area and pollution of the river; their actions included significant land purchases. In 1971 the organization opened the Brandywine River Museum in a preserved 19th-century gristmill. It celebrates the Brandywine School of artists in a setting much in tune with their world.

OTHER PLEASURES

The valley is also the site of one of the more dramatic turns in the American Revolution, the Battle of Brandywine, and an offbeat museum that celebrates the mushroom. Antiques shops, fine restaurants, and cozy country inns dot the region. Your best bet is to rent a car and explore on your own.

If you start early enough, and limit your time at each stop, you can tour the valley's top three attractions—the Brandywine River Museum, Longwood Gardens, and Winterthur—in one day. If you have more time to spend in the valley, you can visit additional sites in Pennsylvania and then move on to Wilmington.

Numbers in the text correspond to numbers in the margin and on the Brandywine Valley map.

West Chester

30 mi west of Philadelphia.

The county seat of Chester since 1786, this historic mile-square city holds distinctive 18th- and 19th-century architecture, with fine examples of Greek Revival and Victorian styles. A small but vital downtown has shopping possibilities as well as restaurants and bars serving everything from classic American fare to the latest microbrews. Fine examples of classical architecture, including the Chester County Courthouse and Market Street Station, can be found near the intersection of High and Gay streets. The town is also home to one of the area's most visited attractions, the **QVC Studios,** in an industrial park off Route 202.

A good place to begin a visit, the **Chester County Historical Society** (⌧ 225 N. High St., ☎ 610/692–4800) was once an opera house where Buffalo Bill performed; a history center has exhibits about the region.

★ ❶ **QVC Studio Park** is ground zero for the world's largest electronic retailer, which in one year alone answered 110 million phone calls, shipped more than 67.7 million packages, and made more than $3.4 billion in sales. On a one-hour guided tour of the company headquarters, you can catch a glimpse of its round-the-clock live broadcast from five studio views and see how QVC products make the route from testing to sale. The tour is designed for ages 6 and up. If you want to be part of a studio audience for a live broadcast, call to make a reservation; it's free. ⌧ *1200 Wilson Dr.,* ☎ *800/600–9900,* WEB *www. qvctours.com.* ⌧ *Studio tours $7.50.* ◷ *Daily 10–4.*

Ever since Philadelphian Harold Pitcairn made the first rotorcraft flight in 1928, the Southeastern Pennsylvania area has been considered the birthplace of the helicopter industry. In fact, two of the three major U.S. helicopter manufacturers trace their roots to this region. This her
★ ❷ itage is showcased at the **American Helicopter Museum and Education Center,** where you can learn about and climb aboard more than two dozen vintage and modern aircraft that reflect the copter's historic roles in war and rescue missions, in agriculture, and police surveillance. ⌧ *1200 American Blvd.,* ☎ *610/436–9600,* WEB *www.helicoptermuseum. org.* ⌧ *$6.* ◷ *Wed.–Sat. 10–5, Sun. noon–5.*

Dining and Lodging

$$$–$$$$ ✕ **Dilworthtown Inn.** Fresh seafood from the Chesapeake Bay and grilled ostrich tenderloin are among the entrées at this longtime area favorite for romantic dining. The 15 candlelit dining rooms are decorated with Oriental rugs and antiques. The wine cellar stocks more than 860 different vintages. ⌧ *1390 Old Wilmington Pike, Dilworthtown, south of West Chester,* ☎ *610/399–1390. AE, D, DC, MC, V. No lunch.*

$–$$$ ✕ **Iron Hill Brewery.** The old Woolworth's building in the historic city center has been converted into a bustling restaurant and brew pub with tin ceilings and maple floors intact. Jamaican jerked pork porterhouse, grilled lamb meatloaf, and Oktoberfest pizza are a few of creatively prepared entrées. In warm weather, the outdoor tables provide a nice spot for people·watching. ⌧ *3 West Gay St.,* ☎ *610/738–9600. AE, D, DC, MC, V.*

$$–$$$ ⌂ **Whitewing Farm Bed & Breakfast.** Although it has a West Chester address, this 1700s Pennsylvania farmhouse is adjacent to Longwood Gardens and within minutes of other attractions. Despite this, the tranquillity and elegance of these accommodations makes you feel as if you're miles away from the action. Nestled among 43 acres are four houses for guests, including a gatehouse suite, a renovated stable, and a house by a large pond. Bedrooms are formally but comfortably decorated in English country style, and all have marble-floor baths. The main house has a porch, cozy sitting rooms, and a billiard room. In good weather, full country breakfasts (stuffed French toast or pancakes with raspberry sauce) are served on the terrace overlooking the pond. ⌧ *370 Valley Rd., 19382,* ☎ *610/388–2664,* FAX *610/388–3650,* WEB *www.whitewingfarm.com. 7 rooms, 1 suite. Pool, putting green, tennis court, billiards, fishing. No credit cards. BP.*

Shopping

Baldwin's Book Barn (✉ 865 Lenape Rd./Route 100, ☎ 888/901–8822) is a book lover's dream. This off-the-beaten-path bookstore in a converted barn is filled with five floors of used and rare books on almost every subject, maps, and prints. The shop's rural setting, country-store feeling, and friendly service invite hours of browsing.

Chadds Ford

11 mi south of West Chester, 30 mi southwest of Philadelphia.

A Revolutionary War battlefield park and a museum celebrating area artists make this historic town appealing. There are some pretty side roads to explore as well. The **Chaddsford Winery** (✉ U.S. 1, ☎ 610/388–6221), in a restored barn, offers tastings and tours of its winemaking facilities.

❸ **Brandywine Battlefield State Park** is near the site of the Battle of Brandywine, where British general William Howe and his troops defeated George Washington on September 11, 1777. The Continental Army then fled to Chester, leaving Philadelphia vulnerable to British troops. The visitor center has audiovisual materials and displays about the battle that are a good introduction to the area's history. On the site are two restored Quaker farmhouses that once sheltered Washington and Lafayette. The 50-acre park is a fine place for a picnic. ✉ *U.S. 1,* ☎ *610/459–3342,* WEB *www.ushistory.org/brandywine.* 🖼 *Park free; house tours $3.50.* ☯ *Tues.–Sat. 9–5, Sun. noon–5.*

★ ❹ In a converted Civil War–era gristmill, the **Brandywine River Museum** showcases the art of Chadds Ford native Andrew Wyeth, a major American realist painter, and his family: his father, N. C. Wyeth, illustrator of many children's classics; and his son Jamie. The collection also emphasizes still lifes, landscape paintings, and American illustration, with works by such artists as Howard Pyle and Maxfield Parrish. The glass-wall lobby overlooks the river and countryside that inspired the Brandywine School earlier in the century. The museum uses a system of filters, baffles, and blinds to direct natural light. Outside the museum, you can visit a garden with regional wildflowers and follow a 1-mi nature trail along the river.

The N. C. Wyeth Studio, where N. C. painted and raised his children, is open part of the year; this highlight gives an intimate feeling for his artistic process and is worth the extra fee. The 1911 studio, set on a hill, holds many of the props N. C. used in creating his illustrations. A shuttle takes you from the museum to the studio for a 60-minute guided tour. ✉ *U.S. 1 and Rte. 100,* ☎ *610/388–2700.* WEB *www.brandywinemuseum. org.* 🖼 *$5; $3 additional for studio.* ☯ *Museum daily 9:30–4:30; studio Apr.–Oct., Wed.–Sun. 10–3:15.*

Dining and Lodging

$$$–$$$$ ✕ **Chadds Ford Inn.** Washington's officers slept here before the Battle of Brandywine. Later, the inn was a lively rest stop on the Wilmington–Philadelphia–Lancaster commerce route. Today, it's a rest stop for Brandywine Valley visitors, who dine on regional American cuisine in a Colonial-period dining room, complete with candlelight, stone hearths, and Wyeth prints. Entrées such as shrimp fettucine and pan-seared pork loin on a bed of apple–sage bacon are served up in generous portions. It's across the highway from the Brandywine River Museum. ✉ *Rte. 100 and U.S. 1,* ☎ *610/388–7361. AE, DC, MC, V.*

$–$$$ ✕ **Hank's Place.** The locals flock to this very casual outpost for hearty breakfasts, lunches, and early dinners (Hank's closes at 7). ✉ *U.S. 1 and Rte. 100,* ☎ *610/388–7061. No credit cards. No dinner Sun. and Mon.*

$$ 🏨 **Brandywine River Hotel.** The small, modern two-story hotel across the highway from the Brandywine River Museum has tasteful Queen Anne furnishings, classic English chintz, and florals that create a homey feeling. Suites have fireplaces and whirlpool baths. Afternoon tea and an expanded Continental breakfast are included in the rate. In the courtyard are original Colonial homesteads that have been reborn as gift, craft, and candy shops, and an art gallery. Request a room that overlooks the surrounding pasture. The hotel's restaurant, the Chadds Ford Inn, is adjacent. ⊠ *Rte. 100 and U.S. 1, 19317,* ☎ *610/388–1200,* FAX *610/388–1200,* WEB *www.virtualcities.com/pa/brh.htm. 30 rooms, 10 suites. Restaurant, coffee shop, gym, business services, meeting room. AE, D, DC, MC, V. CP.*

Kennett Square

7 mi west of Chadds Ford.

This town has a long history that has left its downtown full of interesting buildings in different styles, but most people come here to visit Longwood Gardens and perhaps to stop at the mushroom museum that celebrates one of the area's most important businesses.

★ ⑤ **Longwood Gardens,** 3 mi northeast of Kennett Square, has established an international reputation for its immaculate, colorful display gardens full of flowers and blossoming shrubs. In 1906 Pierre Samuel du Pont (1870–1945) bought a simple Quaker farm, famous for its trees, and turned it into the ultimate early 20th-century estate garden. Seasonal attractions include magnolias and azaleas in spring; roses and water lilies in summer; fall foliage and chrysanthemums; and winter camellias, orchids, and palms. You can stroll in the Italian water garden or explore a meadow full of wildflowers on the garden's 350 acres. Bad weather is no problem here, as 4 acres of exotic foliage, cacti, ferns, and bonsai are housed in heated conservatories; it's easy to spend an hour or more touring these. Many garden areas and activities are designed for younger visitors, including the Children's Garden with a maze and small splashing fountains and Kid's Corner, with a sunflower house, an A–Z garden, and a weather station. The spectacular illuminated fountain displays on Tuesday, Thursday, and Saturday evenings in summer are very popular; the gardens stay open until almost 10. The cafeteria (open year-round) and dining room (closed January–March) serve varied, reasonably priced meals. ⊠ *U.S. 1,* ☎ *610/388–1000,* WEB *www.longwoodgardens.com.* 🎫 *$12 ($8 Tues.).* ☉ *Apr.–Oct., daily 9–6; Nov.–Mar., daily 9–5; plus some evenings in summer and Thanksgiving–Christmas.*

⑥ The **Mushroom Museum at Phillips Place** is a small museum devoted exclusively to a fungus—the mushroom. Eastern Pennsylvania provides 25% of the nation's mushroom crop, and most are grown in Kennett Square, which labels itself the "mushroom capital of the world." The history, lore, and growing process of mushrooms is explained with dioramas, exhibits, a growing wall, and a 13-minute film. The gift shop sells several varieties of fresh and dried mushrooms from portobellos to black trumpets. The adjacent **Maxwell Creeds** restaurant serves dishes prepared with the day's crop. ⊠ *909 E. Baltimore Pike (U.S. 1),* ☎ *610/388–6082,* WEB *www.phillipsmushroomplace.com.* 🎫 *Free.* ☉ *Daily 10–6.*

Lodging

$$–$$$ 🏨 **Fairville Inn.** Tom and Eleanor Everitt's inn, halfway between Longwood Gardens and Winterthur, has bright, airy rooms furnished with Queen Anne and Hepplewhite reproductions. There's a main house, built in 1826; a springhouse; and a carriage house. Most of the rooms have a private deck. The main house has a striking living room with a large fireplace. The Fairville serves a complimentary breakfast that may include such specialties as caramel pecan–French toast and an afternoon tea with homebaked cookies. ⊠ *506 Rte. 52 (Kennett Pike), Mendenhall 19317,* ☎ *610/388–5900,* FAX *610/388–5902,* WEB *www. fairvilleinn.com. 12 rooms, 3 suites. Dining room. AE, D, MC, V. BP.*

$ 🏠 **Meadow Spring Farm.** Anne Hicks's farmhouse is a gallery for her family's antiques, dolls, teddy bears, and Santas. Rooms have Amish quilts and televisions. A full country breakfast is served daily on the glassed-in porch. Children may particularly enjoy the farm animals. ⊠ *201 E. Street Rd., 19348,* ☎ *610/444–3903. 6 rooms, 4 with bath. Pool, hot tub, fishing, recreation room. No credit cards. BP.*

Wilmington

15 mi southeast of Kennett Square.

Although it's small in comparison to big-city neighbors such as Philadelphia, Wilmington should not be overlooked. Delaware's commercial hub and largest city has handsome architecture—with good examples of styles such as Federal, Greek Revival, Queen Anne, and art deco— and abundant cultural attractions. Wilmington began in 1638 as a Swedish settlement and later was populated by employees of various du Pont family businesses and nearby poultry ranches. The four-block **Market Street Mall** marks the city center and is distinguished by the **Grand Opera House.** The four-story Grand, a working theater, was built by the Masonic Order in 1871 and has a cast-iron facade painted white in French Second Empire style to mimic the old Paris Opera. The adjoining Giacco Building houses a smaller theater and art galleries. Outside Wilmington's compact city center are several outstanding museums, including some that are legacies of the du Ponts.

★ ❼ Henry Francis du Pont (1880–1969) housed his 89,000 objects of American decorative art in a sprawling nine-story mansion called **Winterthur;** today the collection is recognized as one of the nation's finest. The 1640–1860 furniture, silver, paintings, and textiles are displayed in 175 period room settings in the original house. A selection of these can be seen on guided tours. The museum also has galleries with permanent displays and changing exhibitions of decorative arts and crafts that you can study at your own pace. Surrounding the museum are 966 acres of landscaped lawns and gardens, which you can visit on a 30-minute narrated tram ride or on your own. The Enchanted Woods is a fantasy-theme 3-acre children's garden with an 8-ft-wide bird's nest, a faerie cottage with a thatched roof, and a troll bridge. Garden lectures are given on Sunday in the spring when the azaleas, peonies, and magnolias are flowering. A gift shop, cafeteria, and restaurant are also on the grounds. ⊠ *Rte. 52, 5 mi south of U.S. 1,* ☎ *302/888– 4600,* WEB *www.winterthur.org.* 🎫 *$8–$21 (depending on tour selected, but all include garden tram).* ☉ *Mon.–Sat. 9–5, Sun. noon–5; garden open until dusk.*

❽ A restored mid-19th-century mill community on 240 landscaped acres, the **Hagley Museum and Library** provides a glimpse of the du Ponts at work and an enlightening look at the development of early industrial America. This is the site of the first du Pont black-powder mills, built by E. I. du Pont. Live demonstrations and exhibits, including a restored workers' community complete with schoolhouse, depict the dangerous work of the early explosives industry. One building holds dioramas and working models. Admission includes a bus ride with stops at Eleutherian Mills, an 1803 Georgian-style home furnished by five generations of du Ponts, and a French Renaissance–style garden. Allow about two hours for your visit. The coffee shop is open for lunch except in winter. ⊠ *Rte. 141 between Rte. 100 and U.S. 202,* ☎ *302/658–2400,* WEB *www.hagley.org.* 🖭 *$9.75.* ☉ *Mar. 15–Dec., daily 9:30–4:30; Jan.–Mar. 14, weekends 9:30–4:30; winter tours, weekdays at 1:30.*

❾ For a look at how the very wealthy and tasteful lived, visit **Nemours Mansion and Gardens,** a 300-acre country estate built for Alfred I. du Pont in 1910. This modified Louis XVI château showcases 102 rooms of European and American furnishings, rare rugs, tapestries, and art dating to the 15th century. The gardens, reminiscent of those at Versailles, are landscaped with fountains, pools, and statuary. The estate can be seen only on the guided two-hour tours. Visitors must be over 11 years old. ⊠ *1600 Rockland Rd., between Rte. 141 and U.S. 202,* ☎ *302/651–6912,* WEB *www.nemours.org.* 🖭 *$10.* ☉ *May–Nov.; tours Tues.–Sat. at 9, 11, 1, and 3; Sun. at 11, 1, and 3 (reservations required).*

The **Wilmington Public Library,** catercorner to the Hotel du Pont downtown, holds a wonderful bounty among its shelves: 14 of 17 canvases, plus the jacket and endpaper paintings, done by N. C. Wyeth in 1920 to illustrate Daniel Defoe's *Robinson Crusoe.* ⊠ *10th and Market Sts.,* ☎ *302/571–7415.* ☉ *Mon.–Thurs. 9–8, Fri.–Sat. 9–5.*

❿ A medium-size treat for art lovers, the **Delaware Art Museum** has several notable strengths, including a good collection of paintings by Howard Pyle (1853–1911), a Wilmington native known as the "father of American illustration," and his students—N. C. Wyeth, Frank Schoonover, and Maxfield Parrish. Other American artists represented are Benjamin West, Winslow Homer, Edward Glackens, and Edward Hopper. The museum also houses the largest American collection of 19th-century English pre-Raphaelite paintings and decorative arts and a children's interactive gallery. ⊠ *2301 Kentmere Pkwy.,* ☎ *302/571–9590,* WEB *www.delart.org.* 🖭 *$7.* ☉ *Tues., Thurs.–Sat. 9–4, Wed. 9–9, Sun. 10–4.*

⓫ **Rockwood,** a quietly elegant English-style country house and a fine example of rural Gothic architecture, stands in contrast to the opulent, French-inspired du Pont homes in the area. Built in 1851 by Joseph Shipley, a Quaker banker, the house is now a museum filled with 19th-century decorative arts and furnishings. Sixty acres of rambling grounds surround the house. The mansion can be visited by guided tour only. ⊠ *610 Shipley Rd.,* ☎ *302/761–4340.* 🖭 *$5.* ☉ *Jan.–Feb., Tues.–Sat. 11–3; Mar.–Dec., Tues.–Sun. 11–3.*

The **First USA Riverfront Arts Center,** which hosts major touring art exhibitions with an international focus, was constructed as the first step in the ongoing revitalization of Wilmington's waterfront. It has no permanent displays. Tickets for exhibitions must be purchased in advance for a specific date and entry time. ⊠ *800 S. Madison St.,* ☎ *888/862–2787.* 🖭 *Varies with exhibition.* ☉ *Call for exhibit schedule and times.*

Dining and Lodging

$$$$ ✕ **Green Room.** For years Philadelphians and locals have trekked here
★ to celebrate special occasions in the famous Hotel du Pont restaurant. Such delicacies as pomegranate-glazed duck breast and rack of lamb with dried cherries can be savored in Edwardian splendor under a gold-encrusted ceiling with massive Spanish chandeliers and tall French windows. Harp music accompanies formal dinners. You can also try the hotel's dark-panel Brandywine Room; the menu is similar, and paintings by artists including N. C. Wyeth line the walls. ⊠ *Hotel du Pont, 11th and Market Sts.,* ☎ *302/594–3100. Reservations essential. Jacket required. AE, D, DC, MC, V.*

$$$–$$$$ ✕ **Krazy Kat's.** Oil paintings of regal felines watch over diners at this
★ plushly furnished restaurant between Kennett Square and Wilmington. Leopard-print chairs and soft lighting round out the atmosphere of elegance with a grin. The unique setting and creative menu draw regulars from Philadelphia and beyond. Entrées include pan-seared crab cakes and rack of lamb stew. ✉ *Inn at Montchanin Village, Rte. 100 and Kirk Rd.,* ☎ *302/888–4200. AE, D, DC, MC, V. No lunch weekends.*

$$$–$$$$ ✕ **Restaurant 821.** Warm colors, a wood-burning oven, leather banquettes, slate floors, and soft amber lighting contribute to a Mediterranean ambience at this relative newcomer to Wilmington's thriving restaurant scene. The highly inventive, changing menu may include fennel-and-coriander-grilled pork tenderloin served with mascarpone whipped potatoes; braised shortrib with roasted garlic polenta; natural jus and crispy sage; and gnocchi and spinach salad with braised fennel and white-truffle vinaigrette. ✉ *821 Market St.,* ☎ *302/652–8821. AE, D, DC, MC, V. Closed Sun. No lunch Sat.*

$$$ ✕ **Deep Blue.** Ultra-modern, airy, and convivial, this bar and bistro presents a contrast to the formal Hotel du Pont across the street. Oysters, tuna, salmon, and crabs are the stars of imaginatively seasoned and beautifully presented dishes. The bar has a wide selection of microbrews on tap. A jazz band entertains on Thursday and Saturday nights. ✉ *111 W. 11th St.,* ☎ *302/777–2040. AE, D, DC, MC, V.*

$$–$$$$ 🏨 **Hotel du Pont.** Built in 1913 by Pierre-Samuel du Pont, the hotel is an elegant 12-story building with an old-world feel. The lobby has a spectacular decorative ceiling, polished marble walls, and carved paneling. The spacious, formal guest rooms, done in soothing earth tones, have high ceilings, 18th-century reproduction furnishings, and original art. ✉ *11th and Market Sts., 19801,* ☎ *302/594–3100 or 800/441–9019,* FAX *302/594–3108,* WEB *www.dupont.com/hotel/home.htm. 216 rooms, 11 suites. 3 restaurants, lobby lounge, gym, theater. AE, D, DC, MC, V.*

$$–$$$ 🏨 **Inn at Montchanin Village.** This small luxury hotel includes 11 painstakingly restored 19th-century cottages that once housed du Pont powder-mill workers. Each elegant guest unit is decorated with oil paintings, antique reproduction furniture, four-poster or canopy beds, and chain-stitch rugs. Rooms have kitchenettes and luxurious marble baths. The "village," 10 minutes from downtown Wilmington, is a series of peaceful gardens, terraces, and landscaped walkways winding around the buildings. The inn is no-smoking. ✉ *Rte. 100 and Kirk Rd., Montchanin, 19710,* ☎ *302/888–2133 or 800/269–2473,* FAX *302/888–0389,* WEB *www.montchanin.com. 27 rooms, 6 suites. Restaurants, lobby lounge, kitchenettes. AE, D, DC, MC, V.*

Brandywine Valley A to Z

BUS TRAVEL

From Philadelphia, Greyhound Lines operates out of the terminal at 10th and Filbert streets, just north of the Market East commuter rail station. There are about 10 daily departures to the Wilmington terminal at 101 North French Street. The trip takes one hour.

➤ BUS INFORMATION: **Greyhound Lines** (☎ 215/931–4075 or 800/231–2222).

CAR TRAVEL

Take U.S. 1 south from Philadelphia; the Brandywine Valley is about 25 mi from Philadelphia, and many attractions are on U.S. 1. To reach Wilmington, pick up U.S. 202 south just past Concordville or take I-95 south from Philadelphia.

TOURS

Brandywine Tours picks you up at your Philadelphia hotel on Wednesday, Friday, or Saturday morning for full-day excursions in a 15-person van. Colonial Pathways organizes full-day bus tours through the Brandywine Valley. Northbrook Canoe Company has a variety of scenic canoe and tubing trips on the Brandywine River.

➤ TOUR INFORMATION: **Brandywine Tours** (✉ 20 Woodland Dr., Glen Mills 19342, ☎ 610/358–5445). **Colonial Pathways** (✉ Box 879, Chadds Ford 19317, ☎ 610/388–2654, WEB www.colonialpathways.com). **Northbrook Canoe Company** (✉ 1810 Beagle Rd., West Chester, ☎ 610/793–2279).

TRAIN TRAVEL

Amtrak has frequent service from Philadelphia's 30th Street Station to Wilmington's station at Martin Luther King Jr. Boulevard and French Street on the edge of downtown. It's a 25-minute ride.

SEPTA's R2 commuter train has hourly departures to Wilmington from Philadelphia's Suburban, 30th Street, and Market East train stations. The trip takes one hour.

➤ TRAIN INFORMATION: **Amtrak** (☎ 215/824–1600 or 800/872–7245). **SEPTA** (☎ 215/580–7800).

VISITOR INFORMATION

The Brandywine Conference and Visitors Bureau publishes a free seasonal visitors' guide with listings for dining, lodging, and attractions, as well as a calendar of events. It is available at attractions and hotels. You can also phone the bureau's "funline" for upcoming events. The Brandywine Valley Tourist Information Center, in the Longwood Progressive Meeting House at the entrance to Longwood Gardens, is open daily 10–6 from May through September and 10–5 from October through April.

➤ INFORMATION: **Brandywine Conference and Visitors Bureau** (✉ 200 E. State St., Suite 100, Media 19063, ☎ 610/565–3679 or 800/343–3983, WEB www.brandywinecvb.org). **Brandywine Valley Tourist Information Center** (✉ U.S. 1 north of Kennett Square, ☎ 610/388–2900 or 800/228–9933, WEB www.brandywinevalley.com). **Greater Wilmington Convention and Visitors Bureau** (✉ 100 W. 10 St., Wilmington, 19801, ☎ 302/652–4088, WEB www.wilmcvb.org).

VALLEY FORGE

The monuments, markers, huts, and headquarters in Valley Forge National Historical Park illuminate a decisive period in U.S. history. The park, with its quiet beauty that seems to whisper of the past, preserves the area where George Washington's Continental Army endured the bitter winter of 1777–78. The 225th anniversary of this "Philadelphia Campaign" was being marked in 2002 with reenactments and living-history events at several Valley Forge historic sites.

Other nearby attractions are Mill Grove, the home of naturalist John James Audubon; the studio and residence of craftsman Wharton Esherick; and The Plaza & The Court, a vast shopping complex.

Numbers in the text correspond to numbers in the margin and on the Valley Forge map.

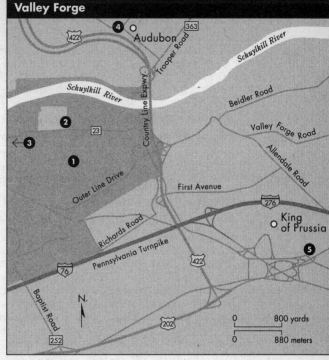

Valley Forge

20 mi northeast of downtown Philadelphia.

A major site of the Revolutionary War is near the suburban village of Valley Forge. The town was named because of an iron forge built in the 1740s.

★ ❶ **Valley Forge National Historical Park,** administered by the National Park Service, is the location of the 1777–78 winter encampment of General George Washington and the Continental Army. Stop first at the visitor center to see the 18-minute orientation film (shown every 30 minutes), view exhibits, and pick up a map for a 10-mi self-guided auto tour of the attractions in the 3,600-acre park. From June through September you can also purchase an auto-tour cassette tape for $8. Stops include reconstructed huts of the Muhlenberg Brigade and the National Memorial Arch, which pays tribute to the soldiers who suffered through the brutal winter. Other sites are the bronze equestrian statue of General Anthony Wayne, in the area where his Pennsylvania troops were encamped; Artillery Park, where the soldiers stored their cannons; and the Isaac Potts House, which served as Washington's headquarters.

The park is quiet today, but in 1777 the army had just lost the nearby battles of Brandywine, White Horse, and Germantown. While the British occupied Philadelphia, Washington's soldiers were forced to endure horrid conditions here—blizzards, inadequate food and clothing, damp quarters, and disease. Many men deserted, and although no battle was fought at Valley Forge, 2,000 American soldiers died.

The troops did win one victory that winter—a war of will. The forces slowly regained strength and confidence under the leadership of Prussian drillmaster Friedrich von Steuben. In June 1778 Washington led his troops away from Valley Forge in search of the British. Fortified, the Continental Army was able to carry on the fight for five years more.

The park contains 6 mi of jogging and bicycling paths and hiking trails, and you can picnic at any of three designated areas. A leisurely visit to the park takes no more than half a day. ⊠ *Rtes. 23 and 363,* ☎ *610/783–1077,* WEB *www.nps.gov/vafo.* ⊠ *Washington's headquarters $2, park free.* ⊙ *Visitor center and Washington's headquarters, daily 9–5; park grounds daily 6 AM–10 PM.*

② The **Valley Forge Historical Society Museum** tells the Valley Forge story through the letters, weapons, and personal effects of the Continental soldiers. A large collection of surveying equipment and other items that belonged to George Washington is also on display. The nearby Chapel Cabin Shop sells homemade goodies such as Martha's 16-Bean Soup. ⊠ *Alongside the Washington Memorial Chapel on Rte. 23,* ☎ *610/783–0535,* WEB *www.ushistory.org/valleyforge/vfhs.* ⊠ *$2.* ⊙ *Apr.–Dec., Mon.– Sat. 10–5, Sun. 1–5; Jan.– Mar., Wed.–Sat. 10–4, Sun. 1–4.*

③ The **Wharton Esherick Museum** preserves the former home and studio of the "Dean of American Craftsmen." Best known for his sculptural furniture, Esherick (1887–1970) shaped a new aesthetic in decorative arts by bridging art with furniture. The museum houses 200 examples of his work—paintings, woodcuts, furniture, and wood sculptures. The studio, in which everything from the light switches to the spiral staircase is hand-carved, is one of his monumental achievements. The museum is 2 mi west of Valley Forge National Historical Park. ⊠ *1520 Horseshoe Trail,* ☎ *610/644–5822,* WEB *www.levins.com/esherick.html.* ⊠ *$9.* ⊙ *Mar.–Dec., Sat. 10–5, Sun. 1–5 for hourly guided tours (reservations required). Group tours (at least 5 people) weekdays.*

Audubon

2 mi north of Valley Forge.

④ Audubon is linked to the renowned American naturalist of the same name. **Mill Grove** was the first American home of Haitian-born artist and naturalist John James Audubon (1785–1851). Built in 1762, the house is now a museum displaying Audubon's major works, including reproductions, original prints, his paintings of birds and wildlife, and a double-elephant folio of his *Birds of America.* The attic has been restored to a studio and taxidermy room. The Audubon Wildlife Sanctuary has 175 acres with 5 mi of hiking trails. ⊠ *Audubon and Pawlings Rds.,* ☎ *610/666–5593.* ⊠ *Free.* ⊙ *Museum Tues.–Sat. 10–4, Sun. 1–4; grounds Tues.–Sun. dawn–dusk.*

King of Prussia

5 mi southeast of Audubon.

⑤ Shopping is a main draw in this busy suburban town. For lunch or an afternoon of browsing, head to **The Plaza & The Court at King of Prussia,** one of the nation's largest shopping complexes. These two adjacent malls contain more than 35 restaurants, 350 shops and boutiques, and nine major department stores, including Bloomingdale's, Nordstrom, and Neiman Marcus. ⊠ *Rte. 202 at the Schuylkill Expressway, 160 N. Gulph Rd.,* ☎ *610/265–5727 for the Plaza; 610/337–1210 for the Court.* ⊙ *Mon.–Sat. 10–9:30, Sun. 11–6.*

Dining and Lodging

$$$–$$$$ ✕ **Kennedy Supplee Restaurant.** French cuisine with an accent on regional specialties is served in an 1852 Italian Renaissance mansion overlooking Valley Forge National Historic Park. Seven elegant rooms bedecked with chandeliers and marble floors provide a fitting backdrop for entrées such as sautéed quail with juniper berries and Madeira wine sauce and seared buffalo tenderloin with morels and medoc sauce. ⊠ *1100 W. Valley Forge Rd.,* ☎ *610/337–3777. Jacket required. AE, MC, V. No lunch weekends.*

$$$–$$$$ ✕ **Lily Langtry's Dinner Theater.** This lavishly appointed Victorian-era restaurant/cabaret serves American and Continental dishes, but the campy Las Vegas–style entertainment—corny comedians, showgirls, and some fine singers and dancers—is the real draw here. ⊠ *Radisson Valley Forge Hotel, 1160 1st Ave.,* ☎ *610/337–5459. Reservations essential. AE, D, DC, MC, V. Closed Mon.*

$$–$$$$ ✕ **Jefferson House.** Bouillabaisse, baked jumbo lump crab, Black Angus filet mignon, and a seasonal game plate of boar and venison are the specialties at this stately Georgian mansion on 11 acres of lush grounds. After dinner, you can stroll around the duck pond and Italian gazebos. ⊠ *2519 DeKalb Pike, Norristown, 4 mi northeast of King of Prussia,* ☎ *610/275–3407. AE, DC, MC, V. No lunch Sat.*

$$–$$$$ 🏨 **Radisson Valley Forge Hotel and Convention Center.** Two bustling high-rises cater to groups and couples escaping to whirlpool bath–equipped fantasy theme suites—a prehistoric cave, a wild-and-woolly jungle, the outer-space-like "Outer Limits." Regular rooms and executive suites are contemporary in style. The hotel offers excellent champagne-and-dinner-theater packages at Lily Langtry's Dinner Theater. ⊠ *1160 1st Ave., 19406,* ☎ *610/337–2000 or 800/325–3535,* FAX *610/768–3222,* WEB *www.radissonvalleyforge.com. 398 rooms, 50 suites, 40 fantasy suites. 4 restaurants, piano bar, pool, health club, comedy club, theater, convention center. AE, D, DC, MC, V.*

Valley Forge A to Z

BUS TRAVEL

On weekdays, SEPTA Bus 125 leaves from 16th Street and John F. Kennedy Boulevard (hourly starting at 5:30 AM) for King of Prussia (including The Plaza & The Court) and continues on to Valley Forge National Historical Park. On Saturday transfer at the plaza to the Royersford Bus 99, which goes through the park. Bus 99 departs hourly. On Sunday Bus 99 does not run; Bus 125 goes as far as the Radisson Valley Forge Hotel, less than a mile from the park but along busy roads.
➤ BUS INFORMATION: **SEPTA** (☎ 215/580–7800).

CAR TRAVEL

Take the Schuylkill Expressway (I–76) west from Philadelphia to Exit 25 (Goddard Boulevard). Take Route 363 to North Gulph Road and follow signs to Valley Forge National Historical Park. Exit 25 also provides easy access to The Plaza & The Court shopping complex.

TOURS

The Valley Forge National Historical Park Bus Tour, a narrated minibus tour, originates from the park's visitor center. Passengers can visit sites and reboard. Tours run from mid-May through September; times vary. The cost is $6.
➤ TOUR INFORMATION: **Valley Forge National Historical Park Bus Tour** (⊠ Rte. 23 and N. Gulph Rd., ☎ 610/783–1077).

TRANSPORTATION AROUND VALLEY FORGE

You can get to several sites, such as Valley Forge National Historical Park and The Plaza & The Court, by bus, but a car is helpful for touring the large park and for traveling between sights.

VISITOR INFORMATION

The Valley Forge Country Funline has information about special events and exhibits.

➤ INFORMATION: **Valley Forge Convention and Visitors Bureau** (✉ 600 W. Germantown Pike, Suite 130, Plymouth Meeting 19462, ☎ 610/834–1550 or 800/441–3549, WEB www.valleyforge.org). **Valley Forge Country Funline** (☎ 610/834–8844).

8 BUCKS COUNTY

It's no wonder so many artists have found glorious inspiration in this Delaware River valley countryside. Despite inevitable pockets of development, the area remains a feast of lyrical landscapes—canal and river vistas, rolling hills, ancient stone barns—with plenty of low-key diversions. Quiet little towns, important historic sites, appealing overnight inns, dozens of antiques shops, and one of the most dramatic drives in the state make Bucks County the classic weekend getaway from Philadelphia.

Updated by
Robert
DiGiacomo

BUCKS COUNTY, about an hour's drive northeast of Philadelphia, could have remained 625 square mi of sleepy countryside full of old stone farmhouses, lush rolling hills, and covered bridges if it hadn't been discovered in the '30s by New York's Beautiful Brainy People. Such luminaries as writers Dorothy Parker and S. J. Perelman and lyricist Oscar Hammerstein II bought country homes here, a short drive from Manhattan. Pulitzer Prize– and Nobel Prize–winning author Pearl S. Buck chose to live in the area because it was "a region where the landscapes were varied, where farm and industry lived side by side, where the sea was near at hand, mountains not far away, and city and countryside were not enemies." Author James A. Michener, who won the 1947 Pulitzer Prize for his *Tales of the South Pacific,* was raised and worked in Doylestown. The region quickly gained a nickname: the Genius Belt.

Over the years Bucks County has become known for art colonies and antiques, summer theater, and country inns. And although parts of the county have fallen prey to urban sprawl and hyperdevelopment, many areas of central and upper Bucks County remain as bucolic as ever. One of Bucks County's agrarian pursuits is a cottage vineyard industry. Five local wineries have opened their doors for tours and tastings.

A BIT OF HISTORY

Named after England's Buckinghamshire, Bucks County was opened to European settlement by William Penn in 1681 under a land grant from Charles II. The county's most celebrated town, New Hope, was settled in the early 1700s as the industrial village of Coryell's Ferry. (One of the original gristmills is now the home of the Bucks County Playhouse.) The town was the Pennsylvania terminal for stagecoach traffic and Delaware River ferry traffic. Barges hauled coal along the 60-mi Delaware Canal until 1931.

Commerce built up New Hope, but art helped sustain it. An art colony took root in the late 19th century and was revitalized first in the 1930s by New York theater folk and more recently with the formation of the New Hope–Lambertville Gallery Association, a cooperative network of gallery owners, artists, and the community. Over the past decade, artists from New York and other parts of the country have been relocating to the region. The James A. Michener Art Museum, showcasing 19th- and 20th-century American art, occupies the renovated former Bucks County jail.

INNS AND ADVENTURES

Although you can see all the major attractions in a day-long whirlwind tour of Bucks County, many people plan overnight stays at some of the prettiest inns in the Mid-Atlantic region. A number of houses and mills, some dating back to a half century before the Revolution, are now bed-and-breakfasts and excellent restaurants. A hearty meal, blissful sleep, and a day spent driving leisurely along River Road (Route 32) are what make visits to Bucks County most enjoyable.

Among the leading destinations is New Hope, a hodgepodge of old stone houses, narrow streets and alleys, pretty courtyards, and busy restaurants. Summer weekends can be frantic here, with traffic jams along Main Street and shoppers thronging the tiny boutiques and galleries. The Delaware Canal threads through town, and you can glide lazily along it in a mule-pulled barge. Or you can stroll across a bridge over the Delaware River to Lambertville, New Jersey, a postcard-perfect small town known for its wealth of antiques shops and galleries.

Doylestown, the county seat, was an important coach stop during the 18th century. Today the town is best known as the home of Henry Chapman Mercer, curator of American and Prehistoric Archaeology at the University of Pennsylvania Museum, master potter, self-taught architect, and writer of Gothic tales. When Mercer died in 1930, he left a legacy of artistic creativity, along with a magnificently bizarre castle named Fonthill, a museum displaying 50,000 implements and tools, and a pottery and tile works that still makes Mercer tiles.

The county is also a repository of Colonial history. Among the most interesting sites is Pennsbury Manor, a careful reconstruction of the brick Georgian-style mansion and estate William Penn built for himself in the late 1600s. On the banks of the Delaware, the 500-acre Washington Crossing Historic Park is situated where George Washington and his troops crossed the icy river on Christmas night 1776 to surprise the Hessian mercenaries at Trenton, New Jersey.

The Delaware River and the canal that follows its path offer opportunities for canoeing, kayaking, and fishing. Thousands float down the river each year in inner tubes or on rubber rafts. Joggers, hikers, bicyclists, cross-country skiers, and horseback riders take full advantage of the 60-mi canal towpath.

The town of Lahaska is the center of shopping in Bucks County. The bargain-price American treasures that made the area an antiques-hunter's paradise are now few and far between, but there is good prowling between New Hope and Doylestown all along U.S. 202. In the 75 shops in Peddler's Village in Lahaska, you can find fine furniture, hand-crafted chandeliers, hand-woven wicker, and homespun fabrics.

A premier family attraction in Langhorne is Sesame Place, a theme park based on the public-television series. There are shows starring Bert and Ernie, water play such as Big Bird's Rambling River raft ride, a computer gallery, and lots of colorful structures on which to climb and jump.

Pleasures and Pastimes

Antiques

Bucks County has long been known for antiques shops full of everything from fine examples of early American craftsmanship to fun kitsch. You'll find formal and country furnishings plus American, European, and Asian antiques. Many shops are along a 4-mi stretch of U.S. 202 between Lahaska and New Hope and on intersecting country roads. You can walk across the bridge from New Hope to Lambertville, New Jersey, for dozens more shops full of treasures that include armoires from Provence, Depression glass, and vintage 20th-century toy rocket ships. Shops are generally open on weekends, with weekday hours by appointment only: it's best to call first.

Covered Bridges

Twelve covered bridges are all that remain of the 36 originally built in Bucks County. Although the romantically inclined call them "kissing bridges" or "wishing bridges," the roofs were actually intended to protect the supporting beams from the ravages of the weather. The bridges are examples of the lattice-type construction of overlapping triangles, without arches or upright beams. They are delightful to stumble upon, but if you're serious about seeing them, contact the Bucks County Conference and Visitors Bureau. Locations of the bridges are listed in the final two pages of the county's Visitors Guide and marked on the Visitors Guide map.

Dining

Bucks County has no regional specialties to call its own, but you can discover some sophisticated restaurants as well as casual country spots. What makes dining here unique are the enchanting settings, ranging from a French-style auberge to Colonial-era manor. Fine meals of French or contemporary American fare are served in restored mills, pre-Revolutionary taverns, stagecoach stops, small cafés, and elegant Victorian mansions. For approximate costs, *see* the dining price chart *in* Smart Travel Tips A to Z.

Lodging

Bucks County has relatively limited lodging options for families; larger inns, hotels and motels, and campgrounds are the best bets. There are numerous choices for couples: accommodations ranging from modest to elegant can be found in historic inns, small hotels, and bed-and-breakfasts. Most hostelries include breakfast in their room rates. Plan and reserve early—as much as three months ahead for summer and fall weekends. You should also ask about minimum stays; many accommodations require a two-night minimum stay on weekends and a three-night minimum on holiday weekends. Many inns prohibit or restrict smoking. Since some inns are historic homes furnished with fine antiques, the owners may not allow children or may have age restrictions. For approximate costs, *see* the lodging price chart *in* Smart Travel Tips A to Z.

Outdoor Activities and Sports

One of the best ways to experience the beauty of Bucks is to stroll along the grassy towpath of the Delaware Canal, one of Pennsylvania's most picturesque byways. Dotted with fieldstone bridge-tender houses and clapboard toll-collector offices—now private studios and homes—and shaded by magnificent trees, the path runs parallel to the Delaware River and River Road (Route 32). Constructed in 1832 to allow access for coal barges, the canal and towpath are known today as the Delaware Canal State Park. You can enjoy the 60-mi towpath for biking, hiking, jogging, and in winter, cross-country skiing. In winter the canal freezes over to form a great ice-skating rink. Tubing or canoeing the Delaware River rates as another popular activity. County parks have plenty of places for hiking, fishing, and boating.

Exploring Bucks County

Many Bucks County sights are contained within the triangle formed by the towns of New Hope, Doylestown, and Newtown. Other interesting places are along River Road (Route 32) from Pennsbury Manor north to pretty river villages such as Erwinna. Lambertville, New Jersey, a five-minute walk across the Delaware River bridge from New Hope, is as an appealing adjunct to Bucks County, replete with inns, restaurants, and antiques shops.

Numbers in the text correspond to numbers in the margin and on the Bucks County map.

Great Itineraries

It's entirely possible to "do" Bucks County as a day trip from Philadelphia, but a few days more allows you to sample many of the area's pleasures. If you have young children along, you may want to spend half a day at Sesame Place in the southern part of the county rather than at some of the nearby historic attractions.

IF YOU HAVE 1 DAY

Start in **Doylestown** ⑦ at Fonthill, the fantastic mansion built by local Renaissance man Henry Chapman Mercer. As lunchtime approaches, wend your way along U.S. 202, stopping at any antiques shops dis-

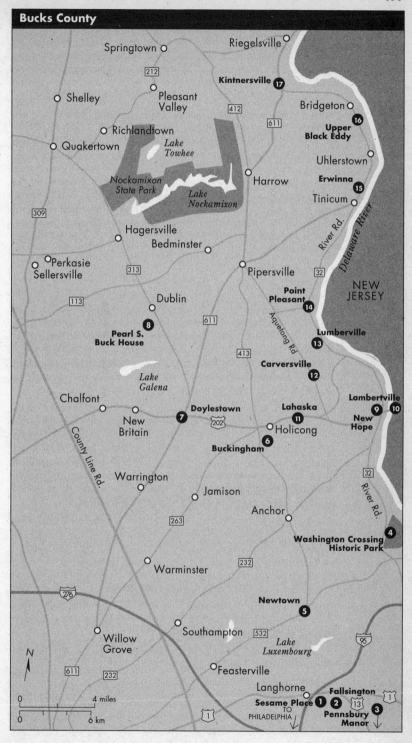

Bucks County

Springtown

Riegelsville

212

Kintnersville 17

Shelley

Pleasant
Valley

412

Bridgeton

Upper
Black Eddy 16

Richlandtown

Lake
Towhee

611

Quakertown

Uhlerstown

Nockamixon
State Park

Lake
Nockamixon

Harrow

Erwinna 15

Tinicum

309

Hagersville

Bedminster

Pipersville

32

NEW
JERSEY

Perkasie
Sellersville

313

Point
Pleasant 14

113

Dublin

8

611

Pearl S.
Buck House

413

Lumberville 13

Carversville

12

Lake
Galena

Chalfont

Doylestown

Lahaska

Lambertville

9 10

New
Britain

7

202

11

Holicong

6

New
Hope

Buckingham

Warrington

Jamison

Anchor

Washington Crossing
Historic Park 4

263

County Line Rd.

River Rd.

32

Warminster

232

276

Newtown

5

Willow
Grove

Southampton

532

Lake
Luxembourg

95

N

611

232

Feasterville

Langhorne

Fallsington

1

0   4 miles

Sesame Place 1 2

13

0   6 km

1

TO
PHILADELPHIA

Pennsbury
Manor 3

playing wares along the roadside, usually indicating they're open for business. Have lunch in **New Hope** ⑨, take a quick stroll through town to check out the eclectic boutiques and gracious historic buildings, and then head north on River Road (Route 32) for a stirring drive along the Delaware River up to **Lumberville** ⑬ or **Erwinna** ⑮. Have dinner at one of the inns in these towns.

IF YOU HAVE 2 DAYS

At your starting point in **Washington Crossing Historic Park** ④, you can see where George Washington set off across the river with his troops on that fateful Christmas night in 1776. Then drive up River Road (Route 32) to ⚡ **New Hope** ⑨ and have lunch, perhaps outside. In the afternoon head west to explore Mercer Mile in **Doylestown** ⑦ and return to New Hope to spend the night at an inn. On Day 2 check out the antiques shops across the river in **Lambertville** ⑩ and then drive upriver in Pennsylvania on River Road for about 17 mi. Stop to stretch your legs along the way with a stroll on the scenic Delaware Canal towpath. Have dinner and spend the night at an inn in ⚡ **Erwinna** ⑮ or ⚡ **Kintnersville** ⑰.

IF YOU HAVE 3 DAYS

Drive up River Road to ⚡ **Erwinna** ⑮. In season—roughly from May to October—even the mildly athletic might enjoy an 11-mi canoe trip south on the Delaware River, beginning at the rental facility Bucks County River Country, in **Point Pleasant** ⑭. It's a terrific way to appreciate the area's natural splendors and get some fresh-air exercise. Afterward you're justified in lounging for a few hours on the veranda of your inn with a good book. As an alternative, rent bikes in **Lumberville** ⑬ and take a ride on the river's bucolic towpath.

On Day 2 drive downriver to ⚡ **New Hope** ⑨ for breakfast at Mother's. Shop and see the town, then head west on U.S. 202. Visit the museums on Mercer Mile in **Doylestown** ⑦. If you enjoy art, linger in Doylestown and spend the afternoon at the James A. Michener Art Museum, where many paintings by the Pennsylvania Impressionists are on permanent display. Another choice is to spend the afternoon at Peddler's Village in **Lahaska** ⑪; check out its boutiques full of delicious nonessentials. Back in New Hope for the evening, consider dinner and window-shopping just across the river in **Lambertville** ⑩.

History buffs can fill their plate on Day 3 by starting out with a tour of the pre-Revolutionary village of **Fallsington** ② and **Pennsbury Manor** ③, William Penn's country retreat, both near Morrisville in the southern part of the county. Have lunch in **Newtown** ⑤, ideal for strolling and browsing. Drive toward the river in the afternoon, and you'll end up at **Washington Crossing Historic Park** ④, where a visitor center, two historic buildings, and a walk through the glorious parkland can easily occupy the rest of the day.

When to Tour Bucks County

Spring, summer, or fall—each time of year has its own pleasures and seasonal festivals. Summer and fall weekends are very busy, so make reservations well ahead and be ready for some crowds; a weekday trip could be more relaxing. Winter has its appeal here, too, especially around the holidays; the snow-covered buildings and fields are lovely.

Langhorne

25 mi northeast of Philadelphia.

For years families have visited this town because of a popular TV-theme attraction. The good times roll, crawl, climb, and jump at **Sesame**

Place, a theme park with 15 water rides and more than 50 play activities designed for children ages 2 to 13. The highlight for most is Sesame Neighborhood, a replica of the beloved street on the public-TV show. Kids can also go wild playing on Cookie Mountain and discovering Ernie's Bed Bounce, or get a thrill on the Vapor Trail, a roller coaster with Super Grover as its mascot. Newer attractions include Elmo's World Live!, an interactive stage show in which Elmo demonstrates different dances and invites audience members to sing and dance with him, and Sesame Playhouse, an arcade area with games of skill and chance. This is the largest water park in the Philadelphia area, with slides and rides for all ages, so don't forget your bathing suit. The most popular water ride is Sky Splash, in which you flow down through five stories in a giant, raft-like tube. ⊠ *100 Sesame Rd., off Oxford Valley Rd. near junction of U.S. 1 and I–95,* ☎ *215/752–7070,* WEB *www.sesameplace.com.* ☞ *$34.95, parking $6.* ☉ *Mid-May–mid-Sept., daily; early May and mid-Sept.–mid-Oct., weekends. Peak season (June–Aug.) 10–8; call for spring and fall hrs.*

Fallsington

➋ *2 mi east of Langhorne.*

Fallsington, the pre-Revolutionary village where William Penn attended Quaker meetings, displays 300 years of American architecture, from a simple 17th-century log cabin to the Victorian excesses of the late 1800s. Ninety period homes are found in the village, which is listed on the National Register of Historic Places. Some private homes are open to the public on the second Saturday in October.

Three historic buildings—a tavern, a log cabin, and a house—have been restored and opened for guided tours by **Historic Fallsington Inc.** ⊠ *4 Yardley Ave., off Tyburn Rd. W (off U.S. 13),* ☎ *215/295–6567,* WEB *www.bucksnet.com/hisfalls.* ☞ *$4.* ☉ *Mid-May–Oct., Mon.–Sat. 10:30–3:30, Sun. 12:30–3:30.*

Morrisville

➌ *3 mi east of Fallsington.*

On a gentle rise 150 yards from the Delaware River, **Pennsbury Manor** is a 1938–39 reconstruction of the Georgian-style mansion and plantation William Penn built in the 1680s as his country estate. Living-history demonstrations on 43 of the estate's original 8,400 acres provide a glimpse of everyday life in 17th-century America. The property, including formal gardens, orchards, an icehouse, a smokehouse, and a bake-and-brew house, helps paint a picture of the life of an English gentleman 300 years ago. The plantation also shows that although history portrays Penn as a dour Quaker, as governor of the colony he enjoyed the good life by importing the finest provisions and keeping a vast retinue of servants. These extravagances led to financial difficulties that resulted in Penn spending nine months in a debtor's prison. The house can be seen only on the tour. ⊠ *400 Pennsbury Memorial Rd., Tyburn Rd. E off U.S. 13, between Morrisville and Bristol,* ☎ *215/946–0400,* WEB *www.pennsburymanor.org.* ☞ *$5.* ☉ *Tues.–Sat. 9–5, Sun. noon–5. Tours Mar.–Nov., weekdays at 10, 11:30, 1:30, 3:30, Sat. at 11, 12:30, 2, 3:30, Sun. at 12:30, 1:30, 2:30, 3:30; Dec.–Feb., weekdays at 11 and 2, weekends at 2.*

Washington Crossing Historic Park

④ *7 mi north of Fallsington.*

It was here, at what is now a lovely Delaware River Park, that on Christmas night in 1776 General Washington and 2,400 of his men crossed the Delaware River, surprised the mercenary Hessian solders, and captured Trenton. A 1917 granite statue of Washington marks the point from which the soldiers embarked that snowy night. Memorials and attractions are divided between the Lower and the Upper Park, which are about 5 mi apart.

In the Lower Park, the fieldstone **Memorial Building and Visitors Center,** on Route 32, 7 mi south of New Hope, displays a reproduction of Emanuel Leutze's famous painting of the crossing (the original hangs in the Metropolitan Museum of Art in New York). Descendants of men who made that crossing sometimes come to gaze upon the painting and point out the resemblance between themselves and the soldiers in the boat. It's a vain exercise: Leutze was in Düsseldorf, Germany, when he painted the figures, and for his models he used either young men from villages along the Rhine River or American artists living abroad. But past and present do merge—magically—during the annual Christmas Day reenactment of the crossing, when locals don Colonial uniforms and brave the elements in small boats (at nearby restaurants later in the day, you may discover troops, still in uniform, enjoying their holiday bird). The **McConkey Ferry Inn** is where Washington and his staff had Christmas dinner while waiting to cross the river. It's near the Memorial Building. You also can tour the **Taylor Mansion,** a completely restored 19th-century residence in the Lower Park.

In the Upper Park, about 5 mi north of the Memorial Building on Route 32, stop at the landmark **Bowman's Hill Tower,** named after a surgeon who sailed with Captain Kidd. Washington used the hill as a lookout point. You can get a much better view of the countryside than he did by riding the elevator up the 110-ft-tall memorial tower. It's open April through November, Tuesday through Sunday 10–4:30.

A half mile north of Bowman's Hill Tower, the 100-acre **Wildflower Preserve** (☎ 215/862–2924) showcases hundreds of species of wildflowers, trees, shrubs, and ferns native to Pennsylvania. Take the guided tour (offered April through October for $3 per person; $5 per family) or follow the short trails, which are clearly marked to bring you back to your starting point. At the same location, the **Platt Bird Collection** displays more than 100 stuffed birds and 600 eggs. The **Thompson-Neely House,** an 18th-century farmhouse, is furnished just as it was when the Colonial leaders planned the attack on Trenton in its kitchen. ✉ *Rtes. 532 and 32,* ☎ *215/493–4076,* WEB *spiritof76. net/wchp.* 🅿 *Parking in picnic areas $1 per car. 45-min. walking tour of 5 historic park buildings plus tower $4, (available at the visitor center, Thompson–Neely House, and Bowman's Hill Tower).* ☉ *Park Tues.–Sat. 9–5, Sun. noon–5. Tours Tues.–Sat. 9, 10, 11, 1, 2, 3; Sun. noon, 1, 2, 3; Apr.–Oct., last tour at 4.*

Newtown

⑤ *6 mi west of Washington Crossing Historic Park.*

Until the 1980s, Newtown was a busy village serving the commercial needs of the surrounding rural community. Today it's the bustling center of sprawling suburban development. Still, the town takes pride in its many 18th- and 19th-century homes and inns; the downtown historic district is on the National Register of Historic Places.

The **Newtown Historic Association,** in a Colonial-era tavern, has regional antiques and a double-sided tavern painting by renowned local artist Edward Hicks. An association brochure provides a walking tour of the town. ✉ *Court St. and Center Ave.,* ☎ *215/968–4004,* WEB *www.twp.newtown.pa.us/historic/nha.html.* 🎫 *Free.* ☉ *June–Aug., Sun. 2–4.*

Dining

$$$–$$$$ ✗ **Jean Pierre's.** Owner–chef Jean Pierre Tardy, formerly executive chef
★ at Philadelphia's distinguished Le Bec-Fin, prepares classic French cuisine in a country-French setting. Roasted monkfish stuffed with lobster and Dijon-encrusted rack of lamb with a rosemary lamb *jus* (sauce) are two of the chef's favorites. ✉ *101 S. State St.,* ☎ *215/968–6201. Reservations essential. AE, D, DC, MC, V. Closed Mon. No lunch Sat.–Wed.*

Buckingham

❻ *8 mi north of Newtown.*

This village, which dates to the Colonial era, remains primarily rural and is the site of many large farms.

The **Buckingham Valley Vineyard & Winery** is a small family-owned operation that produces distinguished estate-bottled varietal wines. It was one of the state's first farm wineries. The vineyards and wine cellars are open to tours and tastings. ✉ *1521 Rte. 413, 2 mi south of U.S. 202,* ☎ *215/794–7188,* WEB *www.pawine.com.* 🎫 *Free self-guided tour.* ☉ *Tues.–Sat. 11–6, Sun. noon–4. Winter hours may vary.*

Shopping

At **Brown Brothers** three or four auctioneers simultaneously conduct auctions in various categories—jewelry, silver, linens, tools, books, frames, furniture, and box lots. ✉ *Rte. 413 south of Rte. 263,* ☎ *215/794–7630.* ☉ *Sept.–May, Sat. 8–3; June–Aug., Thurs. 3–9:30.*

Doylestown

❼ *5 mi west of Buckingham, 12 mi north of Newtown.*

Doylestown, the county seat, is a showcase of American architecture, with stately federal brick buildings on Lawyers' Row and plenty of gracious Queen Anne, Second Empire, and Italianate homes. The historic district, with its nearly 1,200 buildings, is listed on the National Register of Historic Places. A brochure, available at the Central Bucks Chamber of Commerce and at area B&Bs, inns, and bookstores, maps out three walking tours highlighting the architecture and history of Doylestown. The town has interesting shops and restaurants and is also home to the James A. Michener Art Museum.

The most unusual buildings in Doylestown are those created by Henry Chapman Mercer. Bucks County has seen its share of eccentrics, but even in such august company Henry Mercer stands out. Expert in prehistoric archaeology, a homespun architect, and writer of Gothic tales, Mercer is best remembered for the three brilliantly theatrical structures, including his home and the Mercer Museum, found on what is known as Mercer Mile. All are constructed with reinforced concrete, using a technique perfected by Mercer in the early part of this century.

★ You almost expect to see a dragon puffing smoke outside **Fonthill,** Henry Chapman Mercer's storybook home and surely one of the most unique abodes in the country. Mercer, a Harvard-educated millionaire, designed the house in 1910, modeling it after a 13th-century Rhenish castle. Outside, the stone mansion bristles with turrets and balconies. Inside, the multilevel structure is truly mazelike: Mercer built his castle from the inside out—without using blueprints—and Gothic doorways, sudden stairways, dead-ends, and inglenooks follow one after the other, all creating a fairy-tale effect. Fonthill's wealth of books, prints, and Victorian engravings is enhanced by the setting: the ceilings and walls are embedded with tiles from Mercer's own kilns and with ancient tiles from around the world. As a final touch, every chamber has a different shape. ✉ *E. Court St. and Swamp Rd. (Rte. 313),* ☎ *215/348–9461,* WEB *www.fonthillmuseum.org.* ✆ *$7.* ☉ *Mon.–Sat. 10–5, Sun. noon–5. Hr-long guided tours, last tour at 4.*

The **Moravian Pottery and Tile Works,** on the grounds of the Fonthill estate, still produces unique Arts and Crafts–style picture tiles. These "Mercer" tiles adorn such structures as Graumann's Chinese Theater in Hollywood and the Harvard Lampoon Building. As author and Bucks County resident James Michener described them, "Using scenes from the Bible, mythology, and history, Henry Chapman Mercer produced wonderfully archaic tiles about 12 or 14 inches square in powerful earth colors that glowed with intensity and unforgettable imagery." Reproductions of Mercer's tiles can be purchased in the Tile Works Shop. The factory, built in 1912, resembles a Spanish mission. ✉ *130 Swamp Rd. (Rte. 313),* ☎ *215/345–6722.* ✆ *$3.* ☉ *Daily 10–4:45. 45-min. self-guided tours every ½ hr; last tour at 4.*

The **Mercer Museum,** opened in 1916, displays Mercer's collection of tools, representing every craft and including more than 50,000 objects from before the age of steam. An archaeologist, Mercer worried that the rapid advance of progress would wipe out evidence of America's productivity before the industrial revolution. Consequently, from 1895 to 1915 he scoured the back roads of eastern Pennsylvania buying folk art, tools, and articles of everyday life. This must be one of the most incredible attics in the world: the four-story central court is crammed with log sleds, cheese presses, fire engines, boats, and bean hullers, most suspended by wires from the walls and ceiling. The **Spruance Library,** on the third floor, holds 20,000 volumes on Bucks County history. ✉ *84 S. Pine St.,* ☎ *215/345–0210,* WEB *www.mercermuseum.org.* ✆ *$6.* ☉ *Mon. and Wed.–Sat. 10–5, Tues. 10–9, Sun. noon–5.*

The **James A. Michener Art Museum,** across the street from the Mercer Museum, has a permanent collection and changing exhibitions (photography, crafts, textiles, sculpture, and painting) that focus on 19th- and 20th-century American art and Bucks County art. It was endowed by the late best-selling novelist, a native of Doylestown. The Pennsylvania Impressionists, who worked in the area in the early part of the 20th century, are represented by such artists as Edward Redfield and Daniel Garber.

The museum occupies the buildings and grounds of the former Bucks County Jail, which dates from 1884. A 23-ft-high fieldstone wall surrounds seven exhibition galleries, an outdoor sculpture garden, and a Gothic-style warden's house. There is also a re-creation of Michener's Doylestown study. The Mari Sabusawa–designed Michener Wing has a library, archives, and a room with 12 interactive exhibits, each honoring a prominent Bucks County arts figure such as Pearl S. Buck and Oscar Hammerstein II. ✉ *138 S. Pine St.,* ☎ *215/340–9800,* WEB *www.michenermuseum.org.* ✆ *$6.* ☉ *Tues., Thurs., Fri. 10–4:30, Wed. 10–9, weekends 10–5.*

The **National Shrine of Our Lady of Czestochowa,** a Polish spiritual center, has drawn millions of pilgrims, including Pope John Paul II, many U.S. presidents, and Lech Wałesa, since its opening in 1966. The complex includes a modern church with huge panels of stained glass depicting the history of Christianity in Poland and the United States. The gift shop and bookstore sell religious gifts, many imported from Poland, and the cafeteria serves hot Polish and American food on Sunday. ⊠ *Ferry Rd. off Rte. 313,* ☎ *215/345–0600,* WEB *www.polishshrine.com.* 🖼 *Free.* ⊙ *Daily 9–4:30; church opens daily at 7:15 AM for 7:30 and 8 mass.*

Dining and Lodging

$$$–$$$$ ✕ **Cafe Arielle.** This nouvelle French bistro serves delicious grilled seafood dishes (including tuna steak), prime meats, and pistachio-encrusted rack of lamb. The setting is appealing, with country French furnishings and striking artwork. ⊠ *100 S. Main St., in the Doylestown Agricultural Works,* ☎ *215/345–5930. AE, DC, MC, V. Closed Mon. and Tues. No lunch weekends.*

$$–$$$ ✕ **The Black Walnut Cafe.** Lodged in an 1846 townhouse, this restau-
★ rant—with its original plank hardwood floors and its white tablecloths—looks traditional, but the cuisine is a different story: chef Jack Gudin serves up an innovative brand of new American cooking with global touches. Dishes include a galette of goat cheese in puff pastry, and Brazilian lobster tails with shiitake mushroom dumplings. ⊠ *80 W. State St.,* ☎ *215/348–0708. AE, D, DC, MC, V. Closed Mon. and Tues. No lunch.*

$–$$ ✕🖼 **Sign of the Sorrel Horse.** Catering to weary (and hungry) travelers, this inn has one of the finest restaurants in the area. The 1714 gristmill houses the formal Escoffier Room ($$$–$$$$, jacket preferred). Chef Jon Atkin grows his own herbs and does wonders with fresh game dishes. His wife, Monique, oversees the dining rooms and his son, Christian, combs area stores for the best varietal wines. For espresso and desserts, repair to the Waterwheel Lounge. If you plan to stay the night, you'll be put up in a 1714 gristmill that once supplied flour for Washington's army and lodged Lafayette. Today it is decorated in the style of a French auberge. Period antiques fill the guest rooms; one has a fireplace, and one has a whirlpool bath. ⊠ *4424 Old Easton Rd., 18901,* ☎ *215/230–9999,* FAX *215/230–8053,* WEB *www.sorrelhorse.com. 5 rooms. Restaurant. AE, DC, MC, V. Inn and restaurant closed Mon.– Tues. CP.*

$$$ 🖼 **Pine Tree Farm.** This Colonial farmhouse dating to 1730 has been decorated with cheerful country antiques set in the light and airy rooms. Room 1, the largest room and a favorite, has a white twig bed and a dressing table in the bathroom. The glass-enclosed garden room in the rear of the house overlooks 16 acres of pine trees, a pond, and the pool. Breakfast, served poolside in summer, may include Grand Marnier French toast and fresh-baked muffins; lighter fare is also available. This B&B is no-smoking and there is a two-night minimum stay. ⊠ *2155 Lower State Rd., 18901,* ☎ *215/348–0632. 3 rooms. Pool. AE, MC, V. BP.*

$$–$$$ 🖼 **Doylestown Inn.** In the middle of town at the crossroads of Route 611 and U.S. 202, this Victorian hotel dates to 1902. In 2001, it was completely refurbished; the first two levels were converted into office and retail space; with guest rooms on the third floor. Dark woods and traditional furniture set the tone in the guest rooms, some of which have whirlpool tubs and fireplaces. Mercer tiles are found in the lobby. ⊠ *18 W. State St.,* ☎ *215/345–6610,* FAX *215/345–4017,* WEB *www. deauvillegroup.com/doylinn.htm. 11 rooms. Restaurant, in-room data ports, minibars. AE, D, DC, MC, V.*

$$–$$$ 🖼 **Highland Farms.** If only this house could talk . . . or rather, sing. This
★ Bucks County estate was the home of lyricist Oscar Hammerstein II from 1941 to 1960. Not far from the field where the *Oklahoma!* co-creator

could enjoy what he originally called "corn as high as an elephant's eye," this pretty 1840s federal-style country home often hosted the greats of Broadway and even Hollywood. Today antiques and Hammerstein family memorabilia furnish the house elegantly. A four-course country breakfast is served in the formal dining room or on the brick patio overlooking the 60-ft pool; at night you can settle in with a film from the video library stocked with Rodgers and Hammerstein favorites. ⊠ *70 East Rd., 18901,* ☎ *215/340–1354,* WEB *www.web-comm.com/highland. 4 rooms. Dining room, pool, tennis court, library. AE, MC, V. BP.*

$$ ⌂ **Inn at Fordhook Farm.** The Burpee family (of seed-catalog fame) country estate is now a B&B set on 60 lovely acres and loaded with family memorabilia and antiques. Built in 1760 and purchased in 1888 by W. Atlee Burpee, the house has spacious high-ceiling bedrooms (three with Mercer tile fireplaces) brightened with floral prints, a large federal-style living room, and a dining room with another tile fireplace. The country breakfast, with oatmeal–buttermilk pancakes and cream cheese–filled French toast, is served in the Burpee family dining room. The carriage house, with its dark wood paneling and vaulted cathedral ceiling, is a more modern alternative to the main house. ⊠ *105 New Britain Rd., 18901,* ☎ *215/345–1766,* FAX *215/345–1791,* WEB *www.fordhook.com. 7 rooms, 5 with bath. Dining room, badminton, croquet. AE, MC, V. BP.*

Perkasie

6 mi north of Doylestown.

Outside this small town (but closer to Dublin) is the home of writer Pearl S. Buck (1892–1973), a National Historic Landmark. Two of the area's covered bridges are nearby, too.

❽ The **Pearl S. Buck House** is filled with the writer's collection of Asian and American antiques and personal belongings. Green Hills Farm, Buck's country home (built in 1835), is where she wrote nearly 100 novels, children's books, and works of nonfiction while raising seven adopted children and caring for many others. The house still bears the imprint of the girl who grew up in China and became the first American woman to win both the Nobel and Pulitzer prizes. Buck is best known for her novel *The Good Earth.* Pearl S. Buck International, which supports displaced children in Asia, has offices on the 60-acre property. ⊠ *520 Dublin Rd., off Rte. 313,* ☎ *215/249–0100 or 800/220–2825,* WEB *www.pearl-s-buck.org.* ☒ *$6.* ☉ *Mar.–Dec., farmhouse tours Tues.–Sat. 11, 1, and 2; Sun. 1 and 2.*

Outdoor Activities and Sports
Haycock Riding Stables (⊠ 1035 Old Bethlehem Rd., off Rte. 313, ☎ 215/257–6271) escorts riders on one- and two-hour trips through lovely Nockamixon State Park, 4 mi to the north. It's closed Monday, except on holiday weekends; reservations are needed.

New Hope

❾ *18 mi southeast of Perkasie, 40 mi northeast of Philadelphia.*

The cosmopolitan village of New Hope is a mecca for artists, shoppers, and lovers of old homes—and hordes of day-trippers and backpackers on summer weekends. The town, listed on the National Register of Historic Places, is easy to explore on foot; the most interesting sights and stores are clustered along four blocks of Main Street and on the cross streets—Mechanic, Ferry, and Bridge streets—which lead to the river. Unfortunately, lower Main Street has succumbed to tourist blight (do try Gerenser's Exotic Ice Cream, at 22 South Main, though), but if you take a walk on Ferry Street or along the towpath, there's plenty of charm. For a good orientation to New Hope, take the Bucks County Carriages horse-drawn tour, which starts by the cannon alongside the Logan Inn. And if you're eager for more country charm and more antiques, you can take Bridge Street over the Delaware River to Lambertville in New Jersey.

The **Parry Mansion,** a stone house built in 1784, is notable because the furnishings reflect decorative changes from 1775 to the Victorian era—including candles, whitewashed walls, oil lamps, and wallpaper. Wealthy lumber-mill owner Benjamin Parry built the house, which was occupied by five generations of his family. ⊠ *S. Main and Ferry Sts.,* ☎ *215/862–5652,* WEB *www.parrymansion.org.* ⊡ *$5.* ☉ *May–Dec., Fri.–Sun. 1–5.*

Beginning in 1832, coal barges plied the Delaware Canal. Today the canal is a state park, and you can ride a mule-pulled barge from the

☺ **New Hope Canal Boat Company.** The one-hour narrated excursion travels past Revolutionary-era cottages, gardens, and artists' workshops. A barge historian/folk singer is aboard the 60-passenger boat. ⊠ *New and S. Main Sts.,* ☎ *215/862–0758,* WEB *www.canalboats.com.* ⊡ *$7.95.* ☉ *Apr., Fri.–Sun. 12:30, 3; May–Oct., daily noon, 1:30, 3, 4:30.*

☺ The **New Hope & Ivyland Rail Road** makes a 9-mi, 50-minute scenic run from New Hope to Lahaska. The passenger train, pulled by an authentic steam locomotive or vintage diesel, crosses a trestle used in the rescue scenes in the old "Perils of Pauline" movies. The New Hope depot is an 1891 Victorian gem. Theme rides, which require reservations, include Saturday evening dinner trains, Santa trains at Christmas, and Sunday brunch trains. ⊠ *W. Bridge and Stockton Sts.,* ☎ *215/862–2332,* WEB *www.newhoperailroad.com.* ⊡ *$9.50.* ☉ *Mid-June–Oct., daily; Nov., Fri.–Sun.; Dec., Thurs.–Sun.; Jan.–mid-June, weekends and holidays; trains run hourly 11–4 or 12–3.*

Dining and Lodging

$$$$ ✕ **La Bonne Auberge.** Some critics consider this to be Bucks County's
★ most elite and expensive restaurant, thanks to the owners—chef Gerard Caronello, a native of Lyon, France, and his wife, Rozanne, of Great Britain. The consistently classic French cuisine is served in a pre-Revolutionary farmhouse. The Terrace Room, used for dining, has a modern country French ambience. Some specialties are poached Dover sole with a champagne and lobster sauce and rack of lamb. The five-course table d'hôte menu, available Wednesday and Thursday evenings in addition to the regular menu, is a bargain. The restaurant is within a residential development called Village 2; when you call for reservations, travel directions are provided. ⊠ *Village 2 off Mechanic St.,* ☎ *215/862–2462. Reservations essential. Jacket required. AE, MC, V. Closed Mon. and Tues. No lunch.*

$$$–$$$$ ✕ **Moonlight.** This dramatically designed restaurant—almost everything from the tablecloths to the artwork is stark white—presents new American dishes with a French-Asian influence. Standouts from head chef Matthew Levin include seared foie gras with a cherry–clove sauce, Maine lobster "cappuccino" soup, seared wild striped bass with lentils, and a veal chop with tomato–prosciutto ragout. ⊠ *36 Mechanic St.,* ☎ *215/862–3100. Reservations essential for Sat. AE, D, MC, V.*

$$–$$$$ ✕ **Odette's.** In 1961 Parisian actress Odette Myrtil Logan converted a former canal lock house into a restaurant. The atmosphere is French country bistro; the cuisine, updated Continental with a menu that changes seasonally and offers such choices as pine nut–crusted swordfish and roasted rack of veal. Sunday brunch is buffet style. You may want to request a table at one of the dining rooms with a river view.

Entertainment consists of a nightly session around the piano bar, legendary among local show-tune buffs, plus regular appearances by nationally known cabaret performers. ⊠ *S. River Rd., ½ mi south of Bridge St.,* ☎ *215/862–2432. AE, DC, MC, V.*

$$–$$$ ✕ **Havana Bar and Restaurant.** Grilled specialties enhance the American regional and contemporary fare at the Havana. Menu items include sesame onion rings, a grilled eggplant and Brie sandwich, and a nouvelle hamburger with Gorgonzola cheese and spiced walnuts. The bar is enlivened by jazz, blues, and dance bands from Thursday through Sunday nights and by karaoke on Monday night. The view of Main Street is ideal for people-watching, especially from the outdoor patio. ⊠ *105 S. Main St.,* ☎ *215/862–9897. AE, D, DC, MC, V.*

$$–$$$ ✕ **Martine's.** Reminiscent of an English pub with its beam ceiling, plaster-over-stone walls, and fireplace, Martine's has an eclectic menu that includes filet mignon au poivre, pasta, duckling, and steamed seafood mélange. Try the French onion soup. Outdoor dining is on a small patio. ⊠ *7 E. Ferry St.,* ☎ *215/862–2966. AE, MC, V.*

$$–$$$ ✕ **Mother's.** One of New Hope's most popular dining spots, Mother's main claim is still its truly sinful desserts, such as chocolate mousse pie and apple walnut cake. Homemade soups, pastas, and unusual pizzas are offered on the extensive menu, but your best bet for good food is to visit for breakfast. In summer meals are also served in the garden. Expect to wait; it's often crowded here. ⊠ *34 N. Main St.,* ☎ *215/ 862–9354. AE, D, MC, V.*

$$–$$$ ✕⌂ **Logan Inn.** Established in 1727 as an extension of the Ferry Tavern, this inn accommodated passengers who used the Delaware River ferry to Lambertville. George Washington is said to have stayed here at least five times—and one can only imagine what he would think of the crowds of shoppers who stroll right outside the inn, smack dab in the busiest part of town. Rooms have original and reproduction Colonial and Victorian furnishings and canopy beds; some have river views. Full or Continental breakfast on the tented patio is included. As for the friendly restaurant (**$$–$$$$**), the Logan serves three menus: lunch (11–3:30), dinner (4–closing), and a popular all-day tavern menu, with such favorites as nachos, buffalo wings, salads, and burgers. ⊠ *10 W. Ferry St., 18938,* ☎ *215/862–2300,* WEB *www.loganinn.com. 16 rooms. Restaurant. AE, D, DC, MC, V. CP.*

$–$$$ ✕⌂ **Hotel du Village.** Flower-filled grounds surrounding the large, old stone boarding school create the feeling of an English manor house. The guest rooms have country furniture, and a Continental breakfast is served in the parlor. You can feast on country French fare in the restaurant (closed Monday and Tuesday; no lunch), either in a Tudor-style room or on the sunporch. Chef–owner Omar Arbani prepares tournedos Henri IV, a beef fillet with béarnaise sauce; sweetbreads with mushrooms in Madeira sauce; and fillet of sole in curried butter. Desserts are extravagant. ⊠ *2535 N. River Rd. (Rte. 32), 18938,* ☎ *215/862–9911,* FAX *215/862–9788,* WEB *www.hotelduvillage.com. 19 rooms. Pool, 2 tennis courts. AE, DC. CP.*

$$$–$$$$ ⌂ **Mansion Inn.** Romantic luxury and calm surround you inside this
★   elegant 1865 Second Empire–style Victorian inn, although busy Main Street is just steps away from the massive front door. Even the pool and English garden feel pleasantly private. Depression glass, local art, antiques, and comfortable furniture fill the inviting, high-ceiling yellow and beige sitting rooms. Guest rooms (two in a separate building) have antique pieces, plush linens, and modern baths, some with fireplaces and whirlpool tubs. Breakfast includes everything from fresh muffins and fruit to an egg dish or French toast. There's a two-night minimum on weekends, three on holidays; smoking isn't allowed. ⊠ *9 S. Main St., 18938,* ☎ *215/862–1231,* FAX *215/862–0277,* WEB *www.*

themansioninn.com. 7 rooms, 5 suites. Breakfast room, pool. AE, MC, V. BP.

$–$$$ ⊞ **Wedgwood Inn.** The Wedgwood Inn B&B lodgings include three
★ buildings: a blue "painted lady" 1870 Victorian house with a gabled roof, porch, and a porte cochere; a federal-style 1840 stone manor house; and the Aaron Burr House, another 1870 Victorian building. Just steps from Main Street, the inn has landscaped grounds with gazebos and gardens. Wedgwood pottery, antiques, fireplaces, and wood-burning stoves add to the charm. Five rooms have two-person whirlpool tubs. A Continental-plus breakfast is served on the sunporch, gazebo, or in your room. For a fee you can have tennis and pool privileges at a nearby club. The inn is no-smoking. ⊠ *111 W. Bridge St., 18938,* ☎ *215/862–2570,* WEB *www.new-hope-inn.com. 15 rooms, 4 suites. Concierge. AE, MC, V. CP.*

$–$$ ⊞ **Best Western New Hope Inn.** This serviceable motel is a few minutes from New Hope and 30 minutes from Sesame Place. It's handy for single-night accommodations on busy fall weekends, when the country inns are often fully booked. ⊠ *6426 Lower York Rd. (Rte. 202), 18938,* ☎ *215/862–5221 or 800/467–3202,* FAX *215/862–5847,* WEB *www.bwnewhope.com. 159 rooms. Restaurant, lobby lounge, pool, tennis court. AE, D, DC, MC, V.*

Nightlife and the Arts

The **Bucks County Playhouse** (⊠ 70 S. Main St., ☎ 215/862–2041, WEB www.buckscountyplayhouse.com), housed in a historic mill, stages Broadway musical revivals. Shows have included *Footloose* and *Kismet.* The season runs from April through December.

Outdoor Activities and Sports

New Hope Cyclery (⊠ 186 Old York Rd., ☎ 215/862–6888) rents mountain bikes for $31 per day. The staff can direct you to scenic bike routes.

West End Farm (⊠ River Rd. in Phillips Mill, north of New Hope, ☎ 215/862–5883) offers one-hour escorted rides on horseback along the Delaware Canal for $35 a person; call to make a reservation.

Shopping

New Hope's streets are lined with shops selling crafts and handmade accessories, art, antiques, campy vintage items, and contemporary wares.

ANTIQUES

Hobensack & Keller (⊠ Bridge St., ☎ 215/862–2406) stocks antique and authentic reproduction garden ornaments, cast-iron furniture, fencing, and Oriental rugs. **Katy Kane** (⊠ 34 W. Ferry St., ☎ 215/862–5873) is the place for antique, vintage, and designer clothing; accessories; and fine linens. The shop is open by appointment only. **Olde Hope Antiques** (⊠ Creamery Rd., ☎ 215/297–0200) carries hooked rugs, Pennsylvania German textiles, hand-painted furniture, and folk art; the shop is open by appointment only. The **Pink House** (⊠ W. Bridge St., ☎ 215/862–5947) has magnificent European 18th- and 19th-century furnishings and textiles.

ART GALLERIES

Many artists live in Bucks County, and numerous galleries showcase paintings, prints, and sculpture. The New Hope Information Center can tell you about other galleries. The **Golden Door Gallery** (⊠ 52 S. Main St., ☎ 215/862–5529) displays works by Bucks County painters, sculptors, and printmakers, as well as by artists from other parts of the country.

BOOKSTORE

The crowded shelves at **Farley's Bookshop** (⊠ 44 S. Main St., ☎ 215/
862–2452) hold plenty of choices, including books about the area.

Lambertville

❿ *Across the Delaware River from New Hope.*

If you're interested in all that New Hope has to offer but prefer it in
a lower key, this New Jersey village, dating to 1796, is just a walk or
short drive away, over the Delaware River; use the bridge on New Hope's
Bridge Street. You'll find more charm and even better antiques—some
30 dealers in a town less than one square mile—as well as a delight-
fully chic assemblage of shops, galleries, federal and Victorian houses,
and fine restaurants. One of Lambertville's chief pleasures doesn't in-
volve commerce at all: the towpath along the Delaware Canal is a bucolic retreat for strolling, running, or biking. Heading south takes you
to the popular Washington Crossing State Park; the less busy northern route leads past other appealing river hamlets.

Dining and Lodging

$$$ ✕ **Hamilton's Grill Room.** This casually elegant, neighborhood BYOB
★ has justifiably earned a fine reputation for its changing menu of sim-
ply prepared Mediterranean-inspired meat and fish dishes. As the
name suggests, an open grill—the centerpiece of the main dining room
and usually attended by executive chef Mark Miller—figures heavily
in the kitchen's preparations. Starters might include shad roe with ca-
pers, butter and lemon, or chilled asparagus and calamari escabeche;
entrées might be grilled breast and leg of duck with dates and almonds
or grilled tuna with avocado chutney. ⊠ 8½ Coryell St., ☎ 609/397–
4343. Reservations essential. AE, MC, V. No lunch. BYOB.

$$–$$$ ✕ **Full Moon.** This funky, casual eatery surveys a wide range of cuisines—
from Asian to Cajun to Mediterranean. Specialties for breakfast include
omelets and egg dishes, and for lunch there's hearty meatloaf, along
with vegetarian offerings such as Portobello mushrooms topped with
cheese and sautéed with onions and peppers in pesto olive oil. At din-
ner (Fridays and Saturdays only), owner-chef Jacqueline Bowe might
serve seafood bisque, baked artichoke, or grilled pork chops seasoned
with Cajun spices. ⊠ 23 Bridge St., ☎ 609/397–1096. No credit
cards. Closed Tues. No dinner Sun.–Thurs.

$$ ✕ **DeAnna's.** Known for its homemade ravioli and pasta dishes (Gor-
gonzola cream sauce is a specialty), DeAnna's has a cozy ambience with
a bohemian flare. Banquettes in the main dining room have colorful
overstuffed cushions. You can also eat in a second dining room, which
has a more traditional feel, or on a lovely outdoor, covered patio—
perfect for alfresco dining in the warm weather months. There is no
liquor license, but you're welcome to bring your own. ⊠ 18 S. Main
St., at Lilly St., ☎ 609/397–8957. No credit cards. Closed Mon. No
lunch. BYOB.

$$–$$$ ✕🛏 **The Inn at Lambertville Station.** Each guest room at this small hotel
★ overlooks the Delaware River. All rooms are decorated with antiques
and reproduction furnishings in styles ranging from Parisian to New Orleans to Oriental; suites have sitting areas and gas fireplaces. The inn's
restaurant and bar are housed in an 1867 stone building designed by
Thomas Ustick Walter, architect of the dome on the U.S. Capitol, as the
headquarters of the Belvidere Delaware Railroad. The contemporary American menu offers a range of meat, fish, and pasta dishes—including
grilled ostrich in a shallot–brandy cream sauce, and pan-roasted Atlantic
salmon with a lemon–dill pesto aioli. A casual pub serves sandwiches
and snacks. ⊠ Bridge St. and the Delaware, 08530, ☎ 609/397–8300

or 800/524–1091, FAX *215/862–0277,* WEB *www.lambertvillestation.com. 37 rooms, 8 suites. Restaurant, bar. AE, MC, V. BP.*

$$$ ⚑ **Historic Lambertville House.** This former stagecoach stop—dating
★ to 1812—overlooks Lambertville's compact downtown; the hand-
some stone building is steps away from the antique shops of North Union
Street and about a block from the bridge to New Hope. Rooms, most
with whirlpool tubs and some with fireplaces, are furnished with a mix
of antiques and period pieces. On the first floor is Left Bank Libations,
a cozy spot for cocktails with an inviting outdoor porch that's open
seasonally. ⊠ *32 Bridge St., 18938,* ☎ *609/397–0200 or 888/867–8859,*
FAX *609/397–0511,* WEB *www.lambertvillehouse.com. 20 rooms, 6 suites.
Bar. AE, MC, V. BP.*

Shopping

Union Street heading north from Bridge and the intersecting cross
streets are lined with antiques shops, furniture stores, and galleries. This
is where the serious antiques collectors—as well as those seeking con-
temporary crafts and furniture—shop.

A Mano Gallery (⊠ 36 N. Union St., ☎ 609/397–0063) stocks jew-
elry, clay, glass, and wearable art, as well as wood and iron furniture.
Broadmoor Antiques (⊠ 6 N. Union St., ☎ 609/397–8802) packs in
10 galleries of antiques and decorative items. **The Orchard Hill Collec-
tion** (⊠ 22 N. Union St., ☎ 609/397–1188) has a fine collection of
Dutch Colonial antiques and hand-crafted furniture. **The Urban Ar-
chaeologist** (⊠ 63 Bridge St., ☎ 609/397–9588) specializes in home
and garden accessories from Italy and Greece.

There are dozens of vendors—both indoors and out—at the **Golden
Nugget Antique Flea Market** (⊠ 1850 River Rd., ☎ 609/397–0811)
and the **Lambertville Antique Flea Market** (⊠ 1864 River Rd., ☎ 609/
397–0456) on Wed., Sat., and Sun., 8–4.

NEED A Tired from too much antiquing? Stop by **Lambertville Trading Company**
BREAK? (⊠ 43 Bridge St., ☎ 609/397–2232) for some homemade goodies
(the lemon bars are highly recommended) and a smooth cappuccino.
You can browse through the assortment of coffees and teas or hop on
a stool to mull over your next shopping stop and consider the evening's
activities.

Lahaska

⓫ *3.5 mi west of Lambertville.*

Shopping packs in the crowds here, primarily because of the bou-
tiques at Peddler's Village. If bargains are your goal, you can also find
outlets here. Along U.S. 202 between New Hope and Lahaska you'll
see many antiques shops.

Dining and Lodging

$$$–$$$$ ✕ **Jenny's Bistro.** American regional cuisine is served in a Victorian or
a country French room. Balsamic-glazed ahi tuna and filet mignon with
cheddar cheese, bacon, and horseradish sauce are favorites. You can
hear piano music Friday and Saturday nights. ⊠ *U.S. 202, Peddler's
Village,* ☎ *215/794–4000. AE, D, DC, MC, V. No dinner Mon., ex-
cept in Dec.*

$$–$$$ ✕ **Spotted Hog.** This casual country bistro in the Golden Plough Inn
serves American cuisine such as New York strip steak, grilled chicken
with melted Monterey Jack cheese in an oyster–sherry sauce, Philadel-
phia cheese steaks, barbecued ribs, pizza, and pasta. The bar stocks
35 American microbrewery beers. The Spotted Hog is the only restau-

rant in Peddler's Village to serve breakfast. ⊠ *Peddler's Village, Rte. 202 and Street Rd.,* ☏ *215/794–4000. AE, D, DC, MC, V.*

$$–$$$ ⊞ **Barley Sheaf Farm.** If Bucks County was once known as the Ge-
★   nius Belt, this famous estate was probably its buckle. Home to play-
wright George S. Kaufman—author of and collaborator on such jewels
as *Dinner at Eight* and *You Can't Take It with You*—the house was
then called Cherchez la Farm. The inn's 30-acre parklike setting includes the 1740 fieldstone mansion, a duck pond, a pool, and a meadow
full of sheep. You retire to bedrooms decorated with country antiques,
brass, and four-poster beds. A hearty breakfast is served on the glass-
enclosed sunporch. Rooms in the adjacent cottage are smaller but
share the same country decor. Barley Sheaf Farm is in Holicong, a mile
west of Lahaska. ⊠ *5281 York Rd. (U.S. 202), Holicong 18928,* ☏
215/794–5104, 𝔽𝔸𝕏 *215/794–5332,* 𝕎𝔼𝔹 *www.barleysheaf.com. 15
rooms. Pool, badminton, croquet, meeting room. AE, MC, V. BP.*

$$–$$$ ⊞ **Golden Plough Inn.** Nestled within Peddler's Village, the main build-
★   ing of this inn has 22 spacious guest rooms, many with four-poster beds,
rich fabrics, and cozy window seats that beautifully evoke 19th-cen-
tury Bucks County. All rooms come with air-conditioning, remote-con-
trol TV, a small refrigerator, and a complimentary bottle of champagne,
and some have a fireplace or whirlpool bath. The remainder of the guest
rooms are scattered about the village—in an 18th-century farmhouse,
a historic carriage house, and in Merchant's Row. There is a complimentary Continental breakfast or a credit toward breakfast on the
à la carte menu at the Spotted Hog. ⊠ *Peddler's Village, Rte. 202
and Street Rd., 18931,* ☏ *215/794–4004,* 𝔽𝔸𝕏 *215/794–4000,* 𝕎𝔼𝔹 *www.
peddlersvillage.com/lodging.html. 66 rooms. Restaurant. AE, D, DC,
MC, V. CP.*

$$ ⊞ **Ash Mill Farm.** This country B&B is a handsome 18th-century field-
stone manor house set on 10 acres. High ceilings, ornate moldings, and
deep-sill windows add character to the parlor; rooms have family an-
tiques, reproductions, and thoughtful extras such as hair dryers and
down comforters on canopy or four-poster beds. A full country break-
fast is served, and afternoon refreshments are available. The porch has
a view of resident sheep. This B&B is just south of Lahaska. ⊠ *5358
York Rd. (Rte. 202), Holicong 18928,* ☏ *215/794–5373,* 𝕎𝔼𝔹 *www.
ashmillfarm.com. 3 rooms, 2 suites. MC, V. BP.*

Shopping

Peddler's Village (⊠ U.S. 202 and Rte. 263, ☏ 215/794–4000, 𝕎𝔼𝔹
www.peddlersvillage.com) began in the early 1960s, when Earl Jami-
son bought a 6-acre chicken farm, moved local 18th-century houses
to the site, and opened a Carmel, California–inspired collection of spe-
cialty shops and restaurants. Today the 75 shops in the 42-acre village
peddle books, cookware, toys, leather goods, clothes, jewelry, con-
temporary crafts, art prints, candles, and other decorative items. The
Grand Carousel, a restored 1922 Philadelphia Toboggan Company cre-
ation, still operates. Crowd-drawing seasonal events include the Straw-
berry Festival and display, in May; the Teddy Bear's Picnic, in July; and
the Scarecrow Festival, in September. On the grounds is the Golden
Plough Inn.

Penn's Purchase Factory Outlet Stores (⊠ 5881 York Rd., at U.S. 202,
☏ 215/794–0300) include more than 40 stores selling name-brand mer-
chandise at 20%–60% off regular retail prices. You'll find Adidas, Coach,
Easy Spirit, Geoffrey Beene, Izod, Nine West, Orvis, Nautica, and
more, as well as restaurants. All 15 buildings in this complex have been
designed in an Early American country style that harmonizes with the
look of Peddler's Village, right across the road.

Rice's Sale and Country Market (⊠ Green Hill Rd., Solebury, near Peddler's Village, ☎ 215/297–5993) is a mostly open-air market with bargains on canned goods, clothing, linens, shoes, back-issue magazines, and plants; there are a few antiques, too. It opens Tuesday (year-round) and Saturday (March–December) around 7 AM and closes at 1:30 PM. Call for additional holiday openings.

Carversville

⑫ *4 mi northeast of Lahaska.*

One pleasure of traveling in Bucks County is driving on lovely back roads and discovering tiny old mill villages such as Carversville. If you're traveling east from Lahaska, make a left turn onto Aquetong Road and into one of the most beautiful areas of the state.

At the **Carversville General Store** (⊠ Carversville and Aquetong Rds., ☎ 215/297–5353), locals gather for gossip and take-out coffee and pick up picnic supplies.

Dining

$$$ ✕ **Carversville Inn.** Its out-of-the-way location has made this circa-1813
★ inn one of the area's best-kept secrets. Chef Will Mathias's regional American cuisine with a Southern flair is a local favorite. The menu changes seasonally, but you can always count on flavorful dishes such as Gulf shrimp étouffée or roast tenderloin of pork in a rosemary–garlic demiglacé. ⊠ *Carversville and Aquetong Rds.,* ☎ *215/297–0900. AE, MC, V. Closed Mon.*

Lumberville

⑬ *3 mi east of Carversville.*

In tiny Lumberville you can picnic along the Delaware Canal or on Bull's Island, accessible by the footbridge across the Delaware River. Open since 1770, the Lumberville Store is the focus of village life— the place to mail letters, buy groceries (and picnic supplies), and rent a bicycle. Across the street stands the Black Bass Hotel, a famous Colonial-period inn that was once the country retreat of President Grover Cleveland. To get here from Carversville, continue to Fleecy Dale or Old Carversville roads (ignore the ROAD CLOSED sign—it's been there for years). Both of these backcountry roads lead to River Road (Route 32) and Lumberville.

Dining and Lodging

$ ✕🏠 **Black Bass Hotel.** This inn has been a favorite stopover along the Delaware River for more than 240 years. Although it sits snug within a region that witnessed many events of the American Revolution, don't look for any GEORGE WASHINGTON SLEPT HERE plaques: the hotel and its clientele were loyalists to the British Crown, and, coincidentally, its current owner, Herb Ward, is as Anglophile as they come. He's even adorned the inn with a fabulous collection of British royal memorabilia. A wayside inn (and it is truly wayside, since the hotel's facade sits directly on Route 32), the Black Bass also has an excellent restaurant ($$$–$$$$) serving dishes like lobster bouillabaisse and cumin-rubbed grilled pork chop and an outdoor deck overlooking the river—just the place for a picture-perfect summer dinner. ⊠ *Rte. 32,* ☎ 215/297–5770, FAX 215/297–0262, WEB *www.blackbasshotel.com. 9 rooms, 2 with bath. AE, DC, MC, V.*

Outdoor Activities and Sports

A recommended 6-mi route for hikers and bikers starts in Lumberville. Cross the pedestrian bridge to Bull Island State Park; go south on the

New Jersey side along the Delaware and Raritan Canal to Stockton. Cross the river again to Center Bridge, Pennsylvania, and head back up the Delaware Canal towpath to Lumberville.

Lumberville Store Bicycle Rental Co. (✉ River Rd., ☎ 215/297–5388) rents mountain bikes with wide tires from mid-April through November; daily rental is $25. The staff can direct you to scenic bike routes.

Point Pleasant

🅮 *2 mi north of Lumberville.*

This town's location on the Delaware River makes it a focus for recreational activities. It's a lovely area to explore, and two of the county's covered bridges are a few miles northwest of town. Two fine parks, **Tohickon Valley County Park** (Point Pleasant) and **Ralph Stover State Park** (Pipersville), are joined along Tohickon Creek near town.

More than 100,000 people a year—from toddlers to grandparents—negotiate the Delaware on inner tubes or in canoes from **Bucks County River Country Canoe and Tube** (✉ Byron Rd. at River Rd., ☎ 215/297–5000, WEB www.rivercountry.net). The cost is around $15 per person, and the company also rents rafts and kayaks during its April-through-October season. A bus transports people upriver to begin three- or four-hour tube or raft rides down to the base. No food, cans, or bottles are permitted on the tube rides. Wear sneakers you don't mind getting wet and lots of sunscreen; life jackets are available at no charge. Reservations are required.

En Route   Between the villages of Point Pleasant and Erwinna run some of the most Edenic stretches of the **Delaware Canal towpath,** parallel to River Road. This is the section of Bucks County that is reminiscent of the Cotswolds of England, with bridge-keeper lodges and corkscrew bends in the road.

Erwinna

🅯 *7 mi north of Point Pleasant.*

The bucolic river town of Erwinna is a fine place to unwind. There are three covered bridges nearby, and you can visit a park and a local winery. Nearby Tinicum was once home to Dorothy Parker and S. J. Perelman.

One of the most active in the county parks system, 126-acre **Tinicum Park** (✉ River Rd., ☎ 215/757–0571, WEB www.bccvb.org/parks.html) has hiking, picnicking, fishing and more. On weekend afternoons from May through September (or by appointment), you can also tour the **Erwin-Stover House** (☎ 215/489–5133), an 1800 federal house with 1840 and 1860 additions.

Sand Castle Winery opens its doors for tastings and a variety of tours of its vineyard and underground wine cellar. The $3, 20-minute tour doesn't require reservations. You may want to ask about longer 2½-hour VIP tours, too. ✉ *755 River Rd., Rte. 32,* ☎ *610/294–9181 or 800/722–9463,* WEB *www.sandcastlewinery.com.* 🔲 *$3–$15 for tours.* ☉ *Mon.–Sat. 10–6, Sun. 11–6.*

Dining and Lodging

$$–$$$ ✕🏨 **Evermay on-the-Delaware.** The Barrymores used to play croquet
★   on the lawn in front of this cream-color clapboard house, a fine Victorian mansion along the Delaware. Today, Evermay is as popular for its restaurant ($$$$; open Fri.–Sun. for one dinner seating) as for its stylish hostelry; reservations a month in advance are essential. William

Finnegan serves an impressive prix-fixe six-course dinner. His contemporary American menu offers a choice of two entrées, such as pan-seared salmon in beurre blanc and roast loin of lamb in mint demiglacé, and includes champagne, hors d'oeuvres, and a cheese course. Upstairs (try to book a room with a river view) and in the nearby cottage and carriage house, guest rooms have antiques and fresh flowers. A breakfast of fresh fruit compote, croissants, cereal, juice, and coffee is served in the garden room. You can enjoy a predinner sherry or afternoon tea in the stately parlor warmed by its twin fireplaces. ⊠ *River and Headquarters Rds., 18920,* ☎ *610/294–9100,* WEB *www.evermay.com. 18 rooms. Restaurant. MC, V. CP.*

$–$$ ✕🛏 **Golden Pheasant Inn.** One of the prettiest places along the Delaware
★ Canal, this 1857 Bucks County landmark has been restored as a rustic yet elegant French auberge by Michel and Barbara Faure, a husband-and-wife team of chef and hostess. In the solarium of the restaurant ($$$–$$$$; dinner Wednesday through Sunday and Sunday brunch), diners eat beneath potted plants—and the stars. Other diners prefer the tavern room, with its working fireplace, gleaming copper cooking vessels, and pierced tin chandeliers. An ex-chef at Paris's Ritz Hotel, Michel deliciously melds the culinary traditions of the New and Old Worlds. The menu changes by season but might include such entrées as roasted pheasant in an apple–Calvados sauce or shrimp with a spicy tomato Creole sauce. Upstairs are the guest rooms, all with four-poster beds and river or canal views; these are often booked months in advance. Note that some rooms front River Road, at times a heavily trafficked thoroughfare. ⊠ *River Rd., 18920,* ☎ *610/294–9595 or 800/ 830–4474,* FAX *610/294–9882,* WEB *www.goldenpheasant.com. 6 rooms, 1 suite. Restaurant. AE, D, DC, MC, V. CP.*

Upper Black Eddy

⑯ *6 mi north of Erwinna.*

This is another Bucks County river town that's a fine place in which to relax or explore the countryside. You can drive across the river here to Milford and explore the Jersey side of the Delaware. A few miles south of Milford are the antiques shops and restaurants of pretty Frenchtown; then you can recross to Uhlerstown and drive back north to Upper Black Eddy.

Lodging

$$–$$$ 🛏 **Bridgeton House on the Delaware.** Wide, screened porches and a terrace provide close-up views of the Delaware River and the bridge to Milford, New Jersey. This small, 150-year-old, brick inn is decorated in the Arts and Crafts style; guest rooms have folk murals on their walls and ceiling. A two-course country breakfast is served, as are afternoon tea and sherry. Request a river view: although other rooms face the road directly outside the front entrance, riverfront rooms have French doors to private screened porches. In the modern penthouse the marble fireplace and huge windows are delightful. A loft cottage with room for four guests, a whirlpool tub, and river views was to open in 2002. No smoking is allowed; afternoon tea is included. ⊠ *River Rd., 18972,* ☎ *610/982–5856,* FAX *610/982–5080,* WEB *www.bridgetonhouse.com. 7 rooms, 3 suites, 1 cottage. In-room data ports. MC, V. BP.*

Kintnersville

⑰ *5 mi northwest of Upper Black Eddy.*

Well-situated near the pleasures of the river and the towpath, the hamlet of Kintnersville is also just a few minutes' drive from 5,000-acre

Nockamixon State Park, a popular spot for boating, swimming, biking, and hiking. You can explore the scenic back roads and farm country of northern Bucks County, too.

Dining and Lodging

$–$$$ ✕ **Great American Grill.** Bright primary colors, recorded music from the '50s and '60s, and tables stocked with paper and crayons (more than 200 creations by diners hang on the walls) set a casual tone at this cheerful eatery. The menu emphasizes grilled and smoked items such as burgers and ribs, and is known for its 22-ounce smoked prime-rib special, available only on weekends. ⊠ *Rtes. 32 and 611,* ☎ *610/847–2023. AE, D, DC, MC, V. Closed Mon. and Tues. Labor Day–Memorial Day.*

$$ ⌂ **Bucksville House Bed & Breakfast.** This country-style inn was a stagecoach stop for over a century and later served a different mission as a speakeasy during Prohibition. The original 1795 building has fireplaces in some guest rooms; plenty of antique quilts, baskets, and country Colonial furniture add warmth. On the inn's 4½ acres are a large pond and an herb and perennial garden. In summer the full breakfast—dishes might include three-cheese puffy omelets or fresh fruit parfait—is served on a modern octagonal deck; at other times you eat in an enclosed gazebo. ⊠ *4501 Durham Rd., 18930,* ☎ FAX *610/847–8948 or 888/617–6300,* WEB *www.bucksvillehouse.com. 5 rooms. Breakfast room, library. AE, D, MC, V. BP.*

BUCKS COUNTY A TO Z

BUS TRAVEL

Greyhound Lines has four buses a day to Doylestown from Philadelphia. The trip takes 75–90 minutes and costs $4.60 one way, $8.70 round trip.

➤ BUS INFORMATION: **Greyhound Lines** (☎ 800/231–2222, WEB www.greyhound.com).

CAR TRAVEL

From Philadelphia the most direct route to Bucks County is I–95 north, which takes you near sights in the southern part of the county. I–95 crosses Route 32, which runs along the Delaware River past Washington Crossing Historic Park and on to New Hope. New Hope is about 40 mi northeast of Philadelphia.

EMERGENCIES

➤ CONTACTS: **Ambulance, fire, and police** (☎ 911). **Doylestown Hospital** (⊠ 595 W. State St., Doylestown, ☎ 215/345–2200).

LODGING

B&BS

Bed & Breakfast Inns of Bucks and Hunterdon Counties is an association of 11 inns, 9 of which are in Bucks County. Bucks County Bed & Breakfast Association of Pennsylvania represents 32 area inns.

➤ RESERVATION SERVICES: **Bed & Breakfast Inns of Bucks and Hunterdon Counties** (⊠ Box 215, New Hope 18938, ☎ 215/766–9332, WEB www.bucksinns.com). **Bucks County Bed & Breakfast Association of Pennsylvania** (⊠ Box 154, New Hope 18938, ☎ 215/862–2570, WEB www.visitbucks.com).

TOURS

Bucks County Carriages shows off the area on 20-minute horse-drawn carriage tours. Horses are "parked" at the Logan Inn in New Hope, near the bakery in Peddler's Village, and at the Lambertville Station in Lambertville, New Jersey. There are daytime and evening rides depending on the season and departure location. A ride to a catered picnic and customized tours are available by reservation.

Coryell's Ferry Ride and Historic Narrative, which runs mid-April through October, is a half-hour sightseeing ride on the Delaware River in a 27-passenger dual pontoon boat. From June through November, Ghost Tours of New Hope leads a one-hour lantern-led walk that explores the haunting tales of the area. Haunted Hayride, sponsored by the Phoenix Sports Club in Feasterville, conducts a spook-filled evening ride in the woods on certain dates in October.

Marlene Miller of Executive Events Inc. has customized group tours and tour groups for individual travelers in 28-passenger minivans. Some trip themes include covered bridges, historic mansions, arts, wineries, antiques, and shopping.

Wings of Gold pilots 30- and 60-minute hot-air balloon flights over Bucks County. Flights leave from Newtown, Richboro, or Lahaska, and are scheduled within two hours of sunrise or sunset, when the winds are best. Cost is $100–$175 per person.
➤ CONTACTS: **Bucks County Carriages** (☎ 215/862–3582). **Coryell's Ferry Ride and Historic Narrative** (☎ 215/862–2050). **Ghost Tours of New Hope** (☎ 215/957–9988). **Haunted Hayride** (☎ 215/942–9787). **Marlene Miller of Executive Events Inc.** (☎ 215/766–2211). **Wings of Gold** (☎ 215/244–9323).

TRAIN TRAVEL
SEPTA provides frequent service from Philadelphia's Market Street East, Suburban, and 30th Street stations to Doylestown on the R5 line. The trip takes up to 85 minutes, depending on the number of local stops.
➤ TRAIN INFORMATION: **SEPTA** (☎ 215/580–7800, WEB www.septa.org).

TRANSPORTATION AROUND BUCKS COUNTY
Bucks County is a large area—40 mi long and up to 20 mi wide—and is almost impossible to tour without a car. Main roads are River Road (Route 32), U.S. 202, and Rte. 611. One great pleasure of a visit here can be exploring country back roads.

VISITOR INFORMATION
A visitor center operated by the Bucks County Conference and Visitors Bureau, including information specialists, a gift shop, and a theater that shows a film about the county was scheduled to open in early 2002 in the Lower Bucks County town of Bensalem, right off I–95 at the Pennsylvania Turnpike. Call for the hours of operation. The Central Bucks Chamber of Commerce has brochures with walking tours and other information. It's open weekdays 8:30–4:30. The New Hope Information Center has a free lodging referral service. It's open daily, usually 10–5, but hours vary seasonally.
➤ TOURIST INFORMATION: **Bucks County Conference and Visitors Bureau** (✉ 3207 Street Rd., Bensalem 19020, ☎ 800/836–2825, WEB www.bccvb.org). **Central Bucks Chamber of Commerce** (✉ First Union Bank Bldg., 115 W. Court St., Doylestown 18901, ☎ 215/348–3913, WEB www.centralbuckschamber.org). **New Hope Information Center** (✉ 1 W. Mechanic St., at Main St., New Hope 18938, ☎ 215/862–5880 for automated menu; 215/862–5030 for a travel counselor, WEB www.newhopepa.com).

9 LANCASTER COUNTY, HERSHEY, AND GETTYSBURG

In Lancaster County, especially among the Amish, an entirely different culture comes alive for you. Farmers drive horses in the fields, and drivers slow down for buggies on country roads. You can eat hearty Pennsylvania Dutch cooking and shop at farmers and antiques markets, quilt shops, and outlet stores. Beyond Lancaster County are the battlefield and museums at Gettysburg and the amusement park and chocolate-theme pleasures of Hershey.

NEATLY PAINTED FARMSTEADS dot the countryside of Lancaster County, nearly 65 mi west of Philadelphia. Wooden fences outline pastures, and the land looks like a huge quilt of neat rectangles. On country roads horse-drawn buggies jockey with impatient motorists for position. This is Pennsylvania's Amish Country, a place where time seems to stand still.

Updated by
Laura Knowles
Callarian

Here, the plain and fancy live side by side. You can glimpse what rural life was like 100 years ago because whole communities of the "Plain" people—as the Old Order Amish are called—shun telephones, electricity, and the entire world of American gadgetry. Clinging to a centuries-old way of life, the Amish, one of the most conservative of the Pennsylvania Dutch sects, eschew the amenities of modern civilization, using kerosene or gas lamps instead of electric lighting, horse-drawn buggies instead of automobiles. Ironically, in turning their backs on the modern world, the Amish have attracted its attention.

Today the county's main roads are lined with souvenir shops and sometimes crowded with busloads of tourists. The area's proximity to Philadelphia and Harrisburg has brought development as non-Amish farmers sell land. In fact, in 1999 the National Trust for Historic Preservation put Lancaster County on its annual list of the nation's 11 most endangered historic places because of rapid suburbanization. But beyond the commercialism and development, the general stores, one-room schoolhouses, country lanes, and tidy farms remain. You'll find instructive places to learn about the Amish way of life, pretzel factories to tour, quilts to buy, and a host of railroad museums to explore.

THE CULTURE OF THE PENNSYLVANIA DUTCH

The country's largest and oldest settlement of Plain people—about 85,000 people in more than 41 Amish, Mennonite, and Brethren sects—makes Lancaster County it's home. Collectively, the sects are known as the Pennsylvania Dutch. Despite their name, they aren't Dutch at all, but descendants of German and Swiss immigrants who came to the Lancaster area to escape religious persecution. Because of a corruption of the word *Deutsch,* meaning German, they became known as the "Dutch."

The Mennonite movement, named after its leader, Dutch Catholic priest Menno Simons, began in Switzerland in the early 16th century, the time of the Reformation. This radical religious group advocated nonviolence, separation of church and state, adult baptism, and individual freedom in choosing a religion. In 1710 eight families led by Mennonite bishop Hans Herr accepted William Penn's invitation to settle in Lancaster County.

In 1693 Swiss Mennonite bishop Jacob Amman, whose stricter interpretation of church tenets had attracted a following, broke off from the movement and formed his own group to adhere more to the founding beliefs and practices. This group became known as the Amish. Like the Mennonites, the Amish came to live in Lancaster County.

Today approximately 150,000 Amish people live in North America, in 20 states and one Canadian province. Lancaster County has the second-largest community in the country, with 22,000 Old Order Amish (Holmes County, Ohio, is first). That the number of Amish has doubled in the past two decades suggests that theirs is still a viable lifestyle.

The eight Amish, 24 Mennonite, and nine Brethren groups differ in their interpretations of the Bible, their use of technology, the value they place on education, their use of English, and their degrees of interaction with outsiders. Brethren and Mennonite groups use modern conveniences more than Old Order Mennonites and Amish sects do, particularly the Old Order Amish, who shun modern technology.

The Amish religion and way of life stress separation from the world, caring for others of the faith, and self-sufficiency. What may appear as unusual behavior results from religious convictions based on biblical interpretation. The Amish, who reject compulsory school attendance and military registration, do not accept social-security benefits or purchase life or property insurance.

Old Order Amish send their children to one-room schoolhouses with eight grades to a room. They avoid larger public schools to prevent the exposure of their children to the influence of "outsiders." Though Amish students study many of the traditional subjects, they learn less about science and technology than their worldly counterparts. The Supreme Court has ruled that Amish children need not attend school beyond the eighth grade, after which students learn agriculture, building trades, and domestic skills at home.

Farmers work with teams of mules to plow, plant, and harvest their crops. The average farm is small, about 55 acres, but good farming practices make the land extremely productive. Tobacco is one of the crops. When the tobacco leaves mature in September, whole families take to the fields to cut stalks, after which they hang them in rows from floor to ceiling in tobacco sheds.

Lancaster County's most visible sect, the Amish can be recognized by their clothing, which is similar to that worn by their ancestors. Dress and grooming symbolize each person's role in Amish society. Men must begin to grow a beard upon marriage, and they wear several different styles of hats to distinguish their age, status, and their religious district. Amish women wear full-length dresses, capes, and aprons. Those who are baptized wear white organdy caps and don't cut their hair.

Although some changes have been thrust upon them by the government, the Amish do change and update some rules themselves. Some have telephones in their barns or on the edge of their property, for emergency use only; many will accept a ride in an automobile or take public transportation. The Amish live a lively, rich life of discipline and caring. They seek to be at peace with themselves, their neighbors, their surroundings, and their God.

HISTORIC LANCASTER, HERSHEY, AND GETTYSBURG

The Amish are not the only reason to explore Lancaster County. Lancaster, which the English named after Lancashire, is an intriguing place. This appealingly residential city of row houses is one of the nation's oldest inland cities, dating from 1710. Historic sites in the area include Wheatland, the home of U.S. President James Buchanan. Around Lancaster you can visit the Landis Valley Museum, devoted to rural life before 1900. Ephrata Cloister provides a look at a religious communal society of the 1700s. And Main Street in Lititz, founded in 1756, is an architectural treat.

Western Lancaster County, which includes the towns of Marietta, Mount Joy, and Columbia, is a quieter part of the county, where you can bicycle down winding lanes, sample local wines and authentic Mennonite cooking, and explore uncrowded villages. Its history is rooted in the Colonial period. The residents are of Scottish and German descent, and architecture varies from log cabins to Victorian homes.

If you've brought your children as far as Lancaster, you may want to continue northwest to Hershey, the "Chocolate Town" founded in 1903 by Milton S. Hershey. Here the number-one attraction is Hersheypark, a theme park with kiddie and thrill rides, theaters, and live shows. Or you may wish to journey southwest to the Civil War battlefields and museums of Gettysburg, also within driving distance. Here—as in many other area destinations—you can journey back in time.

Pleasures and Pastimes

History and Culture

A visit to Lancaster County and the surrounding area captures a lot of history in a relatively small space. In towns such as Bird-in-Hand and Intercourse, you can see the Amish living their traditional lifestyle. Museums and activities help interpret complex social and religious history; a drive along country roads off the beaten path also gives you a feeling for this way of life. The city of Lancaster has Revolutionary War sites and President James Buchanan's home, Wheatland. Even if you're not a history buff, a trip to Gettysburg, site of the pivotal 1863 Civil War battle, can be a moving experience.

Dining

Like the German cuisine that influenced it, Pennsylvania Dutch cooking is hearty and uses ingredients from local farms. To sample regional fare, eat at one of the bustling restaurants where diners sit with perhaps a dozen other people and the food is passed around in bowls family style. Meals are plentiful and basic, including fried chicken, ham, roast beef, dried corn, buttered noodles, mashed potatoes, chowchow (pickle relish), bread, pepper cabbage, and more. Entrées are accompanied by traditional "sweets and sours," vegetable dishes made with a vinegar-and-sugar dressing. This is the way the Amish, who hate to throw things out, preserve leftover vegetables.

Be sure to indulge your sweet tooth with shoofly pie (made with molasses and brown sugar), *snitz* (dried apple) pie, and other kinds of pies, even for breakfast. Bake shops proudly point out that this region invented the hole in the doughnut by cutting out the center of *fastnacht* cakes; in fact, the English word *dunk* comes from the Pennsylvania Dutch *dunke*.

Lancaster County has numerous smorgasbords and reasonably priced family restaurants, along with a number of Continental and French restaurants in contemporary settings and historic inns. Unless otherwise noted, liquor is served. For approximate costs, *see* the dining price chart *in* Smart Travel Tips A to Z.

Lodging

Lancaster County lodgings are much like the people themselves—plain or fancy. You can rough it in one of the many campgrounds in the area, stay at a historic inn, or indulge yourself at a full-frills resort. A good selection of moderately priced motels caters to families. Though hotels welcome guests year-round, rates are highest in summer and lower at other times. Some inns and bed-and-breakfasts may have minimum stays in high season.

Many working Amish and non-Amish farms throughout Lancaster County welcome guests to stay for a few days to observe and even participate in farm life. Operated as bed-and-breakfast establishments with a twist, the farms invite you to help milk the cows and feed the chickens and afterward share a hearty breakfast with the farmer and his family or help with other farm chores. Reservations must be made weeks in advance as most farms are heavily booked in summer. The Pennsylvania Dutch Convention & Visitors Bureau has a listing of all area B&Bs and farms that welcome guests. For approximate costs, *see* the lodging price chart *in* Smart Travel Tips A to Z.

Shopping

Shoppers in Lancaster County can find everything from farmers markets to several hundred outlet stores. The county's main arteries, U.S. 30 and Route 340, are lined with gift shops and outlets. Some outlets are factory stores, with top-quality goods at good discounts.

On Sunday antiques hunters frequent the huge antiques malls along Route 272 between Adamstown and Denver. As many as 5,000 dealers may turn up on Extravaganza Days, held in late spring, summer, and early fall. You can spend hours browsing among old books and prints and looking at Victorian clothing, pewter, silver, pottery, and lots of furniture. Or you can stop in a store along a country road to shop for the crafts and handmade quilts for which the area is famous. Galleries, boutiques, roadside stands, and farmers markets abound, with a temptingly wide variety of merchandise.

Exploring Lancaster County

The city of Lancaster is close to the heart of Pennsylvania Dutch Country. East of it lie towns such as Intercourse and Bird-in-Hand, with markets, outlet shops, and sights that interpret Amish life. Also nearby is Strasburg, with its railroad museums. Less than half an hour north of Lancaster, the historic towns of Ephrata and Lititz are near farmers markets and antiques malls. The quiet western part of Lancaster County has the Susquehanna River towns of Columbia and Marietta, as well as country towns to the north. If you're on an extended tour of south-central Pennsylvania, you can also explore Gettysburg and Hershey, which are both west of the county.

Great Itineraries

Most people come to Lancaster County to get a glimpse of the Amish and their lifestyle. The territory covered is not that large, and you can see many area sights in a week, though you could spend twice that time. If you have only a couple of days, you'll probably want to concentrate on key Amish towns and Lancaster. With a few more days you can explore the area north of Lancaster or visit Strasburg. If you have up to a week, you can see the western part of the county and continue on to Hershey or Gettysburg.

Numbers in the text correspond to numbers in the margin and on the Lancaster County map.

IF YOU HAVE 2 DAYS

Begin your tour of Amish Country in **Intercourse** ② and visit People's Place, a cultural interpretation center with good introductory films and an exhibit for children. If you'd rather see the area by Amish buggy, follow Route 340 west to **Bird-in-Hand** ③ and take a tour with Aaron & Jessica's Buggy Rides. Also in this area are such attractions as the Amish Farm and House and the Amish Experience. Farmers markets and shops easily fill the day before you head to ⊞ **Lancaster** ① for the night. On Day 2 explore this historic city. The Heritage Center Museum shows the work of Lancaster County artists and craftspeople, past and present. The Historic Lancaster Walking Tour is a 90-minute stroll through the heart of town. On Tuesday, Friday, or Saturday, be sure to visit the Central Market, with its open-air stalls brimming with produce and baked goods. Antiques lovers may want to see Historic Rock Ford Plantation.

IF YOU HAVE 4 DAYS

Follow the two-day itinerary above; spend another night in Lancaster and on Day 3, continue to explore the **Lancaster** ① area. While in the city visit Wheatland and the Hans Herr House. Take an hour or two

Lancaster County

to explore the country roads east of the city. Drive the side roads between Routes 23 and 340 to see Amish farms (the ones with windmills and green blinds) along the way. You can stop at roadside stands and farms with signs advertising quilts and fresh produce. Then head up the Oregon Pike (Route 272) to visit the Landis Valley Museum, an outdoor museum of Pennsylvania German rural life and folk culture before 1900, and drive on to ⚄ **Ephrata** ⑤ or ⚄ **Lititz** ⑦, either of which is good for an overnight. On Day 4 you can visit the Ephrata Cloister, tour a pretzel or chocolate museum in Lititz, or, depending on the day of the week, spend the day shopping for antiques in **Adamstown** ⑥. Another choice for Day 4 is to spend your time in ⚄ **Strasburg** ④, which has the Railroad Museum of Pennsylvania and the don't-miss Strasburg Rail Road ride. Also here is the Amish Village, including a blacksmith shop, one-room schoolhouse, and smokehouse.

IF YOU HAVE 7 DAYS

Follow the four-day itinerary for the beginning of your trip. On Day 5 head west to the sleepy towns of Marietta, Columbia, and Mount Joy; any of these is fine for your overnight. The river town of ⚄ **Columbia** ⑧ has the excellent National Watch and Clock Museum, as well as Wright's Ferry Mansion, the former residence of English Quaker Susanna Wright. The restored town of ⚄ **Marietta** ⑨ is perfect for strolling and browsing. You can tour a historic brewery in ⚄ **Mount Joy** ⑪ or take the wine-tasting tour at the **Nissley Vineyards and Winery Estate** ⑩, near Bainbridge. You can devote Days 6 and 7 to ⚄ **Hershey** ⑬, with its amusement park, zoo, and Chocolate World, or to touring the Civil War battlefields and museums of ⚄ **Gettysburg** ⑭.

When to Tour Lancaster County, Hershey, and Gettysburg

Lancaster County can be hectic, especially on summer weekends and in October, when the fall foliage attracts crowds. Farmers markets and family-style restaurants overflow with people. The trick is to visit the top sights and then get off the beaten path. If possible, plan your trip for early spring, September, or Christmas season, when the area is less crowded. You should note that although many restaurants, shops, and farmers markets close Sunday, commercial attractions remain open.

AROUND LANCASTER

Lancaster, in roughly the center of the county, has plenty to see and also makes a good base for exploring the surrounding countryside. East of the city, between Routes 340 and 23 in towns with names such as Intercourse, Blue Ball, Paradise, and Bird-in-Hand, lives most of Lancaster County's Amish community. Strasburg, to the southeast, has sights for train buffs. No more than 12 mi north of Lancaster, Ephrata and Lititz are lovely, historic towns.

When you are visiting among the Amish, remember to respect their values. They believe that photographs and videos with recognizable reproductions of them violate the biblical commandment against making graven images. You will likely be asked to refrain from photographing or making videos of the Amish, and you should comply.

Lancaster

❶ *75 mi west of Philadelphia.*

Near the heart of Pennsylvania Dutch Country, Lancaster is a colorful small city that combines the Colonial past with the Pennsylvania Dutch present. During the French and Indian War and the American

Revolution, its craftsmen turned out fine guns, building the city's reputation as the arsenal of the Colonies. On September 27, 1777, Lancaster became the national capital for a day, as Congress fled the British in Philadelphia. Today markets and museums preserve the area's history. East of town on U.S. 30 are some of the area's more commercial attractions, such as miniature golf and fast-food eateries.

The **Historic Lancaster Walking Tour,** a 90-minute stroll through the heart of this old city, is conducted by costumed guides who impart anecdotes about 50 points of architectural and historical interest. Tours of the six-square-block area depart from the visitor center downtown. ⊠ *S. Queen and Vine Sts. near Penn Sq.,* ☏ *717/392–1776.* ⬚ *$7.* ☉ *Apr.–Oct., Tues. and Fri.–Sat. at 10 and 1, Sun.– Mon. and Wed.–Thurs. at 1; Nov.–Mar., by reservation only.*

★ **Central Market,** which began with open-air stalls in 1742, is where locals shop for fresh fruit and vegetables, meats (try the Lebanon bologna), flowers, and baked goods such as sticky buns and shoofly pie. The current Romanesque building, in the heart of town, was constructed in 1889 and is one of the oldest covered markets in the country. It's a good place to pick up food for a picnic. ⊠ *Penn Sq.,* ☏ *717/291–4723.* ☉ *Tues. and Fri. 6–4, Sat. 6–2.*

The **Demuth Foundation** includes the restored 18th-century home, studio, and garden of Charles Demuth (1883–1935), one of America's first modernist artists. A watercolorist, Demuth found inspiration in the geometric shapes of machines and modern technology. A few of his works are usually on display. The complex includes a museum shop and the oldest operating tobacco shop (1770) in the country. ⊠ *120 E. King St.,* ☏ *717/299–9940,* WEB *www.demuth.org.* ⬚ *Donation requested.* ☉ *Feb.–Dec., Tues.–Sat. 10–4, Sun. 1–4.*

The Old City Hall, reborn as the **Heritage Center Museum,** documents the Colonial history of the region and the culture of the Pennsylvania German settlers. It's a showcase for the work of Lancaster County artisans and craftspeople—clocks, furniture, homemade toys, Fraktur (documents in a style of calligraphy with folk art decorations), and Pennsylvania long rifles. ⊠ *King and Queen Sts. on Penn Sq.,* ☏ *717/ 299–6440,* WEB *www.lancasterheritage.com.* ⬚ *Donation requested.* ☉ *May–Dec., Tues.–Sat. 10–5.*

Historic Rock Ford Plantation is the restored home of General Edward Hand, Revolutionary War commander, George Washington's adjutant, and member of the Continental Congress. Eighteenth-century antiques and folk art are displayed in a 1794 Georgian-style mansion. The **Kauffman Museum,** in the restored 18th-century barn, holds the Zoe and Henry Kauffman collection of pewter, brass, copper, tin, firearms, and furniture. ⊠ *Lancaster County Park, 881 Rock Ford Rd.,* ☏ *717/392– 7223,* WEB *www.rockfordplantation.org.* ⬚ *$5.* ☉ *Apr.–Oct., Tues.–Fri. 10–4, Sun. noon–4. Yuletide tours Thanksgiving–Christmas, weekends only. The Kauffman Museum can be visited by appointment only.*

★ **Wheatland** was the home of the only president from Pennsylvania, James Buchanan, who served from 1857–1861. The restored 1828 Federal mansion and outbuildings display the 15th president's furniture just as it was during his lifetime. A one-hour tour includes a profile of the only bachelor to occupy the White House. ⊠ *1120 Marietta Ave., Rte. 23, 1½ mi west of Lancaster,* ☏ *717/392–8721,* WEB *www.wheatland. org.* ⬚ *$5.50.* ☉ *Apr.–mid-Dec., daily 10–4.*

★ The **Hans Herr House,** the oldest in Lancaster County, is considered the best example of medieval-style German architecture in North

America. The subject of several paintings by Andrew Wyeth, the house was the Colonial home of the Herr family, to whom the Wyeths are related. Today the house is owned by the Lancaster Mennonite Historical Society, which educates the public about the Mennonite religion through exhibits in its visitor center. The 45-minute tours cover the grounds and the 1719 sandstone house, a former Mennonite meeting place. ⊠ *1849 Hans Herr Dr., 5 mi south of Lancaster off U.S. 222,* ☎ *717/464–4438,* WEB *www.hansherr.org.* ⊡ *$4.* ☉ *Apr.–Nov., Mon.–Sat. 9–4.*

★ The **Landis Valley Museum** is an outdoor museum of Pennsylvania German rural life and folk culture before 1900. Owned by brothers Henry and George Landis, the farm and village are now operated by the Pennsylvania Historical and Museum Commission. You can visit more than 15 historical buildings, from a farmstead to a country store. There are demonstrations of skills such as spinning and weaving, pottery making, and tinsmithing, the products of which are for sale in the Weathervane Shop. ⊠ *2451 Kissel Hill Rd., off Oregon Pike, Rte. 272,* ☎ *717/569–0401,* WEB *www.landisvalleymuseum.org.* ⊡ *$7, $19 family.* ☉ *Mar.–Dec., Mon.–Sat. 9–5, Sun. noon–5.*

☾ The 44 acres of games and rides at **Dutch Wonderland** amusement park are suited for families with younger children. Most rides are tame. Diving shows, an animated bear show, and concerts supplement the rides. ⊠ *2249 U.S. 30, east of Lancaster,* ☎ *717/291–1888,* WEB *www.dutchwonderland.com.* ⊡ *$23.95 for unlimited rides.* ☉ *Memorial Day–Labor Day, daily 10–6 or later; Labor Day–Oct. and Easter– Memorial Day, weekends 10–6.*

Dining and Lodging

$$$–$$$$ ✕ **Carr's Restaurant.** The creation of chef Tim Carr, the setting is refreshingly simple and appealing with the look of a French café. Fresh meats, vegetables, fruit, and fowl are featured; Carr's signature dish is a classic Eberly Farms French-style chicken prepared in a herb-infused marsala jus with chive–potato puree. ⊠ *Market and Grant Sts., across from Central Market,* ☎ *717/299–7090. AE, D, DC, MC, V. Closed Mon.*

$$$–$$$$ ✕ **The Log Cabin.** Consistency is the appeal here: several generations
★ have made this their special-occasion place for classic fare such as veal Milanese (dipped in bread crumbs and Parmesan and fried) and steaks served with local produce. The steaks, as well as lamb chops and seafood, are prepared on a charcoal grill in this 1928 expanded log cabin on a wooded hillside. The atmosphere in the 10 candlelit dining rooms is elegant, and an impressive collection of 18th- and 19th-century American paintings enhances the setting. ⊠ *11 Lehoy Forest Dr., off Rte. 272, 6 mi northeast of Lancaster, Leola,* ☎ *717/626–1181. AE, MC, V. No lunch.*

$$–$$$$ ✕ **The Meritage.** Hidden away in a quiet corner of Lancaster, Meritage is situated in Place Marie. Owners David and Linda Eshleman are highly experienced as chef and manager, respectively. The setting is warm and intimate, with a stone and brick wall in the dining area. In warm weather, the enclosed outdoor dining area is a delight. Selections include gingered sea scallops, coconut-and-pecan striped bass, and mesquite-marinated flank steak. The wine list is extensive. ⊠ *51 North Market St.,* ☎ *717/396–1189. AE, D, DC, MC, V. Closed Sun. and Mon.*

$$–$$$ ✕ **Mazzi Designed Dining.** One of the area's newest restaurants, Mazzi
★ is the unique concept of chef Ralph Mazzocchi, who prepares a blend of Mediterranean, Oriental, and American cuisine in a lush setting with golden stucco walls, heavy oak furnishings, greenery, and original artwork. Among the many flavors of Mazzi are hot lobster and shrimp

salad on spinach greens, baked penne with prosciutto and goat cheese, and Moroccan chicken. ⊠ *46 Deborah Drive, off Rte. 23, 7 mi northeast of Lancaster, Leola,* ☎ *717/656–8983. AE, D, DC, MC, V.*

$–$$$ ✕ **J-M's Bistro.** This favorite among locals is known for its relaxed, convivial setting, with colorful French Provincial accents and an attractive oak and granite bar. You can choose among a wide variety of well-prepared foods, from salads, gourmet pizzas, and mussels to superb steaks, rack of lamb, and crab cakes. ⊠ *377 N. Queen St.,* ☎ *717/392–5656. AE, D, MC, V.* ☉ *No lunch weekends.*

$$ ✕ **Lancaster Dispensing Co.** Fajitas, salads, sandwiches, and nachos are served until midnight in this stylish, boisterous, Victorian pub. The selection of imported beers is extensive. You can hear live music on weekends. ⊠ *33–35 N. Market St.,* ☎ *717/299–4602. AE, D, MC, V.*

$–$$ ✕ **The Pressroom.** The menus look like newspapers, and headline banners hang over the bar in this casual bistro in an old warehouse. The open kitchen has an exposed baking hearth. On the menu are sandwiches (named after newspaper cartoon characters), salads, pizza, and pasta dishes. In summer you can eat in the park outside. ⊠ *26–28 W. King St.,* ☎ *717/399–5400. AE, MC, V.*

$$–$$$ 🏨 **Best Western Eden Resort Inn.** Attractive grounds and spacious rooms with cherry-wood Colonial furnishings make a stay here pleasant. The inn has a tropical indoor pool and whirlpool under a retractable roof; request a poolside room if you have children in tow. The chef at Arthur's is noted for seafood and pasta dishes; casual fun food is presented in Garfield's. If you're spending a few days in the area, consider one of the extended-stay suites. ⊠ *222 Eden Rd., U.S. 30 and Rte. 272, 17601,* ☎ *717/569–6444 or 800/528–1234,* ℻ *717/569–4208,* 🌐 *www.edenresort.com. 275 rooms, 40 suites. 2 restaurants, lounge, in-room data ports, in-room safes, refrigerators, room service, indoor pool, outdoor pool, sauna, tennis court, gym. AE, D, DC, MC, V. CP.*

$$–$$$ 🏨 **King's Cottage.** An elegant 1913 Spanish Mission Revival mansion
★ on the National Register of Historic Places has been transformed into a B&B. The blend of decorative and architectural elements encompasses Chippendale-style-dining room furniture and an art deco fireplace and stained-glass windows. Several rooms have whirlpools and fireplaces. A library and an outdoor goldfish pond are additional pleasures. The price includes full breakfast and afternoon tea; a small kitchen is available to guests. ⊠ *1049 E. King St., 17602,* ☎ *717/397–1017 or 800/ 747–8717,* ℻ *717/397–3447,* 🌐 *www.kingscottagebb.com. 6 rooms, 1 suite, 1 cottage. Library. D, MC, V. BP.*

$$–$$$ 🏨 **Lancaster Host Resort and Conference Center.** This sprawling family resort has a striking marble lobby and comfortable, contemporary rooms with cherry-wood furnishings. You can jog or rent a bike and ride around the beautifully landscaped golf course and grounds. Complimentary buggy rides are also available. ⊠ *2300 Lincoln Hwy. E (U.S. 30), 17602,* ☎ *717/299–5500 or 800/233–0121,* 🌐 *www.holidayhost. com. 330 rooms, 8 suites. 2 restaurants, piano bar, in-room data ports, room service, indoor pool, outdoor pool, driving range, 18-hole golf course, miniature golf, putting green, 6 tennis courts, bicycles, convention center, meeting rooms. AE, DC, MC, V.*

$$ 🏨 **Lancaster Hilton Garden Inn.** An elegant, contemporary hotel popular with business travelers, the Garden Inn has oversize rooms, many with cathedral ceilings and large desks. There's free coffee in the rooms. The hotel is in a corporate center on the edge of town. ⊠ *101 Granite Run Dr., intersection of Rtes. 72 and 283, 17601,* ☎ *717/560–0880,* ℻ *717/560–5400,* 🌐 *www.hiltongardeninn.com. 156 rooms. Restaurant, room service, indoor pool, hot tub, gym, coin laundry, laundry service, business services, meeting room. AE, D, DC, MC, V.*

$$ 🖭 **Willow Valley Family Resort and Conference Center.** Smorgasbord meals, large rooms, a duck pond, and indoor pools make this large, stylish resort a great family place. Rooms are spread out over three buildings; those in the Atrium Building surround a striking skylighted lobby. The extensive Sunday Brunch in the Palm Court is a favored feast. Since the resort is Mennonite owned, liquor isn't permitted on the premises. ✉ 2416 Willow St. Pike, 17602, ☎ 717/464–2711 or 800/444–1714, FAX 717/464–4784, WEB www.willowvalley.com. 346 rooms, 50 suites. 2 restaurants, 2 indoor pools, outdoor pool, hot tub, sauna, steam room, 9-hole golf course, 2 tennis courts, basketball, gym, recreation room, video games, playground, business services, meeting rooms. AE, D, DC, MC, V.

Nightlife and the Arts

The 1,600-seat **American Music Theatre** (✉ 2425 Lincoln Hwy. E, ☎ 717/397–7700 or 800/648–4102, WEB www.americanmusictheatre.com) presents full-scale original musical productions, the 1940s review *Hit Waves,* and the inspirational *One Voice.* There are late-morning, afternoon, and evening shows.

The draws at the 400-seat **Dutch Apple Dinner Theater** (✉ 510 Centerville Rd., at U.S. 30, ☎ 717/898–1900, WEB www.dutchapple.com) are a candlelight buffet plus Broadway musicals and comedies such as *Camelot* and *Singin' in the Rain.* Call for reservations for matinees and dinner shows.

A National Landmark, the 19th-century **Fulton Opera House** (✉ 12 N. Prince St., ☎ 717/397–7425, WEB www.fultontheatre.org) is home to the Fulton Theater Company, the Actors Company of Pennsylvania, the Lancaster Symphony Orchestra, and the Lancaster Opera. Restored to its previous grandeur, the Fulton is the oldest continuously operating theater in the United States.

Outdoor Activities and Sports

The **Lancaster Host Resort and Conference Center** (✉ 2300 Lincoln Hwy. E, ☎ 717/299–5500) has 18 holes of regulation golf. Greens fees are $63 and include the use of a cart. Rental clubs are available.

Shopping

CRAFTS

Although craftspeople in the Lancaster County area produce fine handiwork, folk art, quilts, and needlework, much of the best work is sold to galleries nationwide and never shows up in local shops. Still, there are some good places you can check.

The **Olde Mill House Shoppes** (✉ 105 Strasburg Pike, ☎ 717/299–0678), one of Lancaster's oldest country stores, stocks a fine choice of pottery, folk art, country and Shaker furniture, and custom handcrafted early American reproduction interior and exterior lighting.

Pandora's Antiques (✉ 2014 Old Philadelphia Pike, just east of U.S. 30, ☎ 717/299–5305) sells antique quilts and textiles made in Lancaster County. Call ahead.

Among the few places that carry fine local crafts is the **Weathervane Shop** (✉ 2451 Kissel Hill Rd., ☎ 717/569–9312), at the Landis Valley Museum, where craftspeople sell the wares they make on-site—tin, pottery, leather, braided rugs, weaving, and cane chairs.

OUTLETS

U.S. 30 is lined with outlets of varying quality; be sure to check the retail prices of whatever you want before you leave home. With more than 120 stores, from Sony to Gap to Nike, the **Rockvale Square Outlets** (✉ U.S. 30 and Rte. 896, ☎ 717/293–9595) is the largest outlet center in Lancaster. The **Tanger Outlet Center** (✉ 311 Outlet Dr., Rte. 30 E, ☎ 717/392–7260) is a collection of 65 designer outlets, including Ann Taylor, Ralph Lauren, and Eddie Bauer.

Intercourse

❷ *10 mi east of Lancaster.*

Intercourse is a center of Amish life. Many places that help you better understand this community can be found between here and Bird-in-Hand. The town is at the intersection, or intercourse, of two roads (today's Routes 340 and 772), which is how it got its name in Colonial times.

★ ↻ The **People's Place,** a "people-to-people interpretation center," provides an excellent introduction to the Amish, Mennonite, and Hutterite communities. A 30-minute multiscreen slide show titled *Who Are the Amish?* has close-ups of Amish life and perceptive narration. 20Q (short for 20 Questions), an interactive family museum, highlights the differences between Amish and Mennonite societies. Children can try on bonnets and play in the "feeling box." Don't miss the collection of wood carvings by Aaron Zook. There's a bookstore, too. ✉ *3513 Old Philadelphia Pike/Rte. 340,* ☎ *717/768–7171 or 800/390–8436,* WEB *www.thepeoplesplace.com.* ✆ *$8.* ☉ *Memorial Day–Labor Day, Mon.–Sat. 9:30–8; Labor Day–Memorial Day, Mon.–Sat. 9:30–5.*

Dining and Lodging

$$ ✕ **Stoltzfus Farm Restaurant.** Homemade Pennsylvania Dutch foods are served family style in a small country farmhouse, with most ingredients grown on the farm. Most dishes are so tasty (especially the ham loaf with vinegar and brown sugar) you'll likely want the recipes— and the owners happily supply them. The price is fixed at $13.75 for adults. ✉ *Rte. 772E, ½ mi east of Rte. 340,* ☎ *717/768–8156. Closed Sun. Closed Dec.–Mar.; call for limited hours in Apr. and Nov.*

$–$$ ✕ **Kling House.** The Kling family home has been converted into a pleasant, casual restaurant that serves innovative breakfast and lunch selections. The turkey Reuben and sausage platter are favorites, as are the *knepp* (ham) entrées, which come with a complimentary appetizer of red-pepper jam and cream cheese with crackers. The soups are homemade, and desserts are luscious. A children's menu is available. Dinner is served seasonally. Call first. ✉ *Kitchen Kettle Village, Rtes. 340 and 772,* ☎ *717/768–8261. D, MC, V. Closed Sun.*

$ ⚠ **Spring Gulch Resort Campground.** Glorious farmland and forest are the setting for the campsites (pleasantly shaded) and a limited number of rental cottages at $84 to $127. A full schedule of weekend activities includes country dances and chicken barbecues. ✉ *Rte. 897 between Rtes. 340 and 322, New Holland 17557,* ☎ *717/354–3100 or 800/ 255–5744,* WEB *www.springgulch.com. 500 sites, 4 cottages. 2 pools, lake, spa, miniature golf, tennis court, gym, volleyball, fishing, recreation room.*

Shopping

Amishland Prints (✉ 3504 Old Philadelphia Pike, ☎ 717/768–7273) sells prints depicting the Amish in rural daily life as well as landscapes by artist and folklorist Xtian Newswanger.

The 32 shops of **Kitchen Kettle Village** (✉ Rte. 340, ☎ 717/768–8261 or 800/732–3538) showcase local crafts, including decoy carving; furniture making; leather tooling; relish-, jam-, and jelly-making; and tin punching. The Kling House serves homemade local recipes, and Lapp Family Farms sells great ice cream. The shops are closed Sunday.

The **Old Country Store** (✉ 3510 Old Philadelphia Pike, ☎ 717/768–7101) carries items from more than 450 local craftspeople, including quilts and discounted fabrics. A small Quilt Museum displays antique Amish and Mennonite quilts.

The **Old Road Furniture Company** (✉ 3457 Old Philadelphia Pike, ☎ 717/768–0478 or 800/760–7171) has lovely furniture handcrafted by Amish and Mennonite craftspeople, including harvest and farm tables, chairs, chests, cupboards, and desks. It takes custom orders, too. The store is closed Sunday.

Bird-in-Hand

❸ *3 mi west of Intercourse.*

This village, like many others, took its name from the sign on an early inn and tavern. Today it is a center for the Pennsylvania Dutch farming community.

★ ☼ **Aaron & Jessica's Buggy Rides** offers tours of the countryside in an authentic Amish carriage. The rides depart from Plain & Fancy Farm. ✉ *Rte. 340 between Bird-in-Hand and Intercourse,* ☎ *717/768–8828.* 🖃 *$10.* ☾ *Mon.–Sat., 8 AM–dusk.*

On **Abe's Buggy Rides,** a 2-mi spin down country roads in an Amish carriage, Abe chats about the customs of the Pennsylvania Dutch. ✉ *2596 Old Philadelphia Pike,* ☎ *717/392–1794.* 🖃 *$10.* ☾ *Mon.–Sat. 9 AM–dusk.*

The **Amish Experience** is a multimedia theatrical presentation about the history of the Amish, using 3-D sets, multiple screens, and special effects. In *Jacob's Choice,* the teenage main character struggles between traditional ways and the temptations of the present. A $25.95 package includes the show, the Amish Country Homestead and Amish Country Tours, a bus tour of the farmlands. ✉ *Rte. 340 between Bird-in-Hand and Intercourse at Plain & Fancy Farm,* ☎ *717/768–8400,* WEB *www.amishexperience.com.* 🖃 *$6.95, $10.50 for combination ticket with Amish Country Homestead.* ☾ *Apr.–June, Mon.–Sat. 8:30–5, Sun. 10–5; July–Oct., Mon.–Sat. 8:30–8, Sun. 10:30–5; Nov.–Mar., daily 10–5; shows on the hour.*

The **Amish Country Homestead,** a re-creation of a nine-room Old Order Amish house, is the fictional home of the characters in the Amish Experience film *Jacob's Choice.* On a guided tour of nine furnished rooms, you can learn about the culture and clothing of the Amish and how they live without electricity. ✉ *Rte. 340 between Bird-in-Hand and Intercourse at Plain & Fancy Farm,* ☎ *717/768–3600.* 🖃 *$5.95, $10.50 for combination ticket with Amish Experience.* ☾ *July–Oct., Mon.–Sat. 9:45–6:45; Apr.–June and Nov., Mon.–Sat. 9:45–4:15; Dec.–Mar., weekends 9:45–4:15.*

The **Amish Farm and House** has 40-minute tours through a 10-room circa-1805 house furnished in the Old Order Amish style. A map guides you to the animals, waterwheel, lime kiln, and barns on the 25-acre farmstead. ✉ *2395 Lincoln Hwy. E, Smoketown,* ☎ *717/394–6185,* WEB *www.amishfarmandhouse.com.* 🖃 *$6.50.* ☾ *Apr.–May and Sept.–Oct., daily 8:30–5; June–Aug., daily 8:30–6; Nov.–Mar., daily 8:30–4.*

The **Folk Craft Center** includes a museum, shops, and a bed-and-breakfast, housed in 18th- and 19th-century buildings. The museum presents an authentic overview of the lifestyles and culture of the Pennsylvania Germans, with displays of pottery, household implements, toys, glassware and quilts, and a gallery of photographs by Mel Horst. An antique loom is on exhibit in a log cabin built in 1762. Woodworking and print-shop demonstrations show early techniques. In spring and summer the ornamental and herb gardens come alive with color. Amish quilts and pillows, hooked rugs, punch tinware, and other crafts are for sale in the shops. The B&B, in an 1845 farmhouse, has four suites. ⊠ *441 Mt. Sidney Rd., ½ mi west of town, north of Rte. 340, Witmer,* ☏ *717/397–3609,* WEB *www.folkcraftcenter.com.* ⊠ *Donation requested.* ☉ *Apr.– Nov., Mon.–Sat. 10—5, Dec., Feb.–Mar., Sat. 10–5.*

Dining and Lodging

$$ ✕ **Plain & Fancy Farm.** You'll get heaping helpings of stick-to-your-ribs Pennsylvania Dutch food at this family-style restaurant. Also on the grounds are specialty shops selling art, quilts, and baked goods, and other attractions including Aaron & Jessica's Buggy Rides, the Amish Experience presentation, and Amish Country Tours. ⊠ *Rte. 340 between Bird-in-Hand and Intercourse,* ☏ *717/768–4400. AE, MC, V.*

$–$$ ✕ **Amish Barn Restaurant.** Pennsylvania Dutch cuisine is served family style, which means generous helpings of meat and produce, breads, and pies are brought to your table in big bowls or platters. You can also choose from an à la carte menu. Apple dumplings and shoofly pie are specialties. Breakfast is available, too. No liquor is served. ⊠ *3029 Old Philadelphia Pike/Rte. 340, between Bird-in-Hand and Intercourse,* ☏ *717/768–8886. AE, D, MC, V.*

$–$$ ✕ **Bird-in-Hand Family Restaurant.** This family-owned diner-style
★ restaurant has a good reputation for hearty Pennsylvania Dutch home cooking. The menu is à la carte, but there's a lunch buffet weekdays. It's an excellent place to sample local specialties such as apple dumplings and chicken potpie. No liquor is served. ⊠ *2760 Old Philadelphia Pike/Rte. 340,* ☏ *717/768–8266. MC, V. Closed Sun.*

$–$$ ✕ **Good 'N Plenty.** You share a table with about a dozen other cus-
★ tomers and are treated to huge servings of hearty regional fare, including traditional sweet and sours. More than 650 can be served at this bustling family-style restaurant, set within a remodeled Amish farmhouse. ⊠ *Rte. 896, ½ mi north of U.S. 30,* ☏ *717/394–7111. MC, V. Closed Sun. and Jan.*

$–$$ ✕ **Miller's Smorgasbord.** The spread here is lavish, with a good selection
★ of Pennsylvania Dutch foods. The breakfast buffet (served daily June through October and on weekends November through May) is sensational, with omelets, pancakes, and eggs cooked to order, fresh fruits, pastries, bacon, sausage, potatoes, and much more. ⊠ *2811 Lincoln Hwy. E/U.S. 30, Ronks,* ☏ *717/687–6621. AE, D, MC, V.*

$–$$ 🏨 **Bird-in-Hand Family Inn.** The rooms are simple, clean, and comfortable, and the staff is friendly at this family-run motel.The property offers a host of recreational opportunities. ⊠ *2740 Old Philadelphia Pike/Rte. 340, 17505,* ☏ *717/768–8271 or 800/537–2535,* FAX *717/768–1768,* WEB *www.bird-in-hand.com/familyinn. 125 rooms, 4 suites. Restaurant, refrigerators, 2 indoor pools, outdoor pool, hot tub, miniature golf, tennis court, basketball, gym, lake, bicycles, video games, playground. AE, D, DC, MC, V.*

$–$$ 🏨 **Village Inn of Bird-in-Hand.** The Victorian flavor of this three-story country-style inn, built in 1734 to serve travelers along the Old Philadelphia Pike, is tempered by the modern comforts of cable TV and whirlpools in some rooms. Continental breakfast, an evening snack, and a two-hour tour of the area are complimentary. Guests have pool and tennis privileges at the nearby Bird-in-Hand Family Inn. ⊠ *2695 Old Philadelphia Pike/Rte. 340, 17505,* ☏ *717/293–8369 or 800/914–2473,* WEB *www.bird-in-hand.com/villageinn. 5 rooms, 6 suites. Breakfast room, no-smoking rooms. AE, D, MC, V. CP.*

$ ⚠ **Historic Mill Bridge Village and Campresort.** This campground is attached to a restored 18th-century village that was home to Herr's Grist Mill. Campers are given free admission to the village, with its ice cream parlor, craftsman and Amish schoolhouse, and a complimentary buggy ride. There's a general store on the grounds. ✉ *S. Ronks Rd., ½ mi south of U.S. 30, Ronks 17579,* ☎ *717/687–8181 or 800/645–2744,* WEB *www.millbridge.com. 101 sites. Snack bar, fishing.*

Shopping

Bird-in-Hand Farmers Market (✉ Rte. 340, ☎ 717/393–9674) is an indoor market with produce stands, baked goods, gift shops, outlets, and a snack counter. It's open Wednesday through Saturday July through October; Wednesday, Friday, and Saturday November and April through June; and Friday and Saturday December through March.

Strasburg

❹ *5 mi south of Bird-in-Hand.*

Although settled by French Huguenots, the village of Strasburg is today a community of Pennsylvania Dutch. It's best known as the railroad center of eastern Pennsylvania; railroad buffs can easily spend a day here. You can also visit the Amish Village, which has buildings typical of the area.

☺ The **Strasburg Rail Road** makes a scenic 45-minute round-trip excursion through Amish farm country from Strasburg to Paradise on a rolling antique chartered in 1832 to carry milk, mail, and coal. Called America's oldest short line, the Strasburg run has wooden coaches pulled by an iron steam locomotive. You can lunch in the dining car or buy a box lunch in the restaurant at the station and have a picnic at Groff's Grove along the line. There are seasonal Santa, Pumpkin, and Easter Bunny train rides. ✉ *Rte. 741,* ☎ *717/687–7522,* WEB *www.strasburgrailroad.com.* ☜ *$8.75–$12.75.* ☉ *Mid-Feb.–mid-Apr. and Nov.–mid-Dec., weekends 12–2; mid-Apr.–Oct., weekdays 11–4, weekends 11–5 or later, dinner train boards at 6:30. Trains depart every hour, depending on season; call for schedule.*

★ ☺ The **Railroad Museum of Pennsylvania,** across the road from the Strasburg Rail Road, holds 75 pieces of train history, including 13 colossal engines built between 1888 and 1930; 12 railroad cars, among them a Pullman sleeper; sleighs; and railroad memorabilia documenting the history of Pennsylvania railroading. More than 50 of the pieces of equipment are kept indoors in the Rolling Stock Hall. ✉ *Rte. 741,* ☎ *717/687–8628,* WEB *www.rrmuseumpa.org.* ☜ *$6.* ☉ *May–Oct., Mon.–Sat. 9–5, Sun. noon–5; Nov.–Apr., Tues.–Sat. 9–5, Sun. noon–5.*

★ ☺ The **National Toy Train Museum,** the showplace of the Train Collectors Association, displays antique and 20th-century model trains. The museum has five huge operating layouts, with toy trains from the 1800s to the present, plus nostalgia films and hundreds of locomotives and cars in display cases. Take the children to see the special hands-on layouts every Friday from June through August. ✉ *Paradise La. just north of Rte. 741,* ☎ *717/687–8976,* WEB *www.traincollectors.org.* ☜ *$3.* ☉ *May–Oct. and Christmas wk, daily 10–5; Apr. and Nov.–mid-Dec., weekends 10–5.*

What started as a family hobby in 1945 with a single train chugging
☺ around the Groff family Christmas tree is now the **Choo-Choo Barn, Traintown, USA.** This 1,700-square-ft display of Lancaster County in miniature has 18 trains in O-gauge and 130 animated scenes, including an authentic Amish barn raising, a huge three-ring circus with an-

imals and acrobats, and a blazing house fire with fire engines rushing to the disaster. Periodically, the overhead lights dim, and it becomes night, when streetlights and locomotive headlights glow in the darkness. ⊠ *Rte. 741,* ☎ *717/687–7911,* WEB *www.choochoobarn.com.* 🎟 *$5.* ☉ *Apr.–Dec., daily 10–5.*

The **Amish Village** offers guided tours through an authentically furnished Amish house. Afterward you can wander around the village, which includes a one-room schoolhouse, a blacksmith shop, village store, and an operating smokehouse built by Amish craftsmen. ⊠ *Rte. 896 between U.S. 30 and Rte. 741,* ☎ *717/687–8511.* 🎟 *$6.50.* ☉ *Mar.–mid-May and Sept.–Oct., daily 9–5; mid-May–Aug., daily 9–6; Nov.–Feb., house tours weekends 10–4.*

Dining and Lodging

$$$–$$$$ ✕ **Iron Horse Inn.** A rustic pub and fine restaurant with candlelight is housed in the original 1780s Hotel Strasburg. Best bets are the catch of the day, the homemade breads, and, for dessert, the great warm apple pie. The wine list is extensive. There's live entertainment on weekends. ⊠ *135 E. Main St.,* ☎ *717/687–6362. AE, D, DC, MC, V. Closed Mon. Dec.–May.*

$–$$ ✕🏨 **Historic Strasburg Inn.** The five buildings of this Colonial-style inn are set on 58 peaceful acres overlooking farmland. The rooms, simply and comfortably furnished, have rocking chairs. The Washington House Restaurant ($$–$$$$) offers elegant candlelight dining in two dining rooms. The updated American menu lists steaks, jumbo lump crab cakes, and wild game. The lunch buffet is bountiful. A Continental-plus breakfast, served in the restaurant, is included in the room rate. ⊠ *Rte. 896, Historic Dr., 17579,* ☎ *717/687–7691 or 800/872–0201,* FAX *717/687–6098,* WEB *www.historicstrasburginn.com. 102 rooms, 9 suites. 2 restaurants, pool, hot tub, gym, bike rentals, buggy rides. AE, D, DC, MC, V.*

$$ 🏨 **Hershey Farm Restaurant and Motor Inn.** This motel just south of Bird-in-Hand overlooks flower and vegetable gardens, a picture-perfect pond, and a farm. Ask for one of the large rooms in the newer building. The handy restaurant serves a complimentary breakfast smorgasbord and reasonably priced buffet and à la carte meals, featuring home-grown produce. Walking trails lace the grounds. ⊠ *Rte. 896, Ronks 17572,* ☎ *717/687–8635 or 800/827–8635,* FAX *717/687–8638,* WEB *www.hersheyfarm.com/motorinn.htm. 57 rooms, 2 suites. Restaurant, no-smoking rooms, pool, playground. AE, D, MC, V. BP.*

$–$$ 🏨 **Fulton Steamboat Inn.** Named after Lancaster native Robert Fulton, who built the first passenger steamer in 1807, this inn is at one of Lancaster County's busiest intersections, across from Rockvale Square Outlets. Designed to look just like a steamboat, the upper deck has whirlpool baths and private outdoor decks; the no-smoking middle deck has staterooms with two queen-size beds; and the lower deck has nautical-theme cabins with bunk beds. ⊠ *Rtes. 30 and 896, Box 333, 17579,* ☎ *717/299–9999; 800/922–2229 outside PA,* FAX *717/299–9992,* WEB *www.fultonsteamboatinn.com. 96 rooms, 5 suites. Restaurant, refrigerators, indoor pool, hot tub, gym. AE, MC, V.*

$–$$ 🏨 **Limestone Inn Bed and Breakfast.** Richard and Denise Waller are the gracious hosts in their 1786 Georgian home, listed on the National Register of Historic Places. A formal living room, a library, and a sitting room with a fireplace serve as common areas; you may also relax outside by the fish pool in the small garden. The bedrooms are decorated in traditional Colonial colors with Amish quilts and four-poster beds; if there's no private bath, you can reserve one down the hall. The hearty breakfast might include raisin French toast or egg strata with country sausage. The B&B is in the center of the village, within walking distance of many Strasburg attractions. ⊠ *33 E. Main St., 17579,* ☎ *717/687–8392 or 800/278–8392,* FAX *717/687–8366,* WEB *www. thelimestoneinn.com. 6 rooms, 2 with private baths. Dining room, library. No credit cards. BP.*

$ 🍴 **Mill Stream Country Inn and Restaurant.** Long a popular choice, this freshly renovated motel overlooks a picturesque stream. Breakfast is available in the restaurant, but alcohol is not served. Guests have exercise privileges at the Willow Valley Family Resort in Lancaster. ⊠ *Rte. 896, 17576,* ☎ *717/299–0931,* FAX *717/295–9326,* WEB *www. willowvalley.com/millstrhome.htm. 52 rooms, 3 suites. Restaurant, no-smoking rooms, pool. AE, D, MC, V. BP.*

$ 🍴 **Strasburg Village Inn.** This circa-1788 house in the heart of town has rooms elegantly appointed in the Williamsburg style. Most have a canopy or four-poster bed; three have a whirlpool bath. A sitting/reading room is on the second floor; an old-fashioned porch overlooks Main Street. ⊠ *1 W. Main St., 17579,* ☎ *717/687–0900 or 800/541–1055,* WEB *www. strasburg.com. 5 rooms, 5 suites. AE, D, MC, V. BP.*

Ephrata

⑤ *22 mi north of Strasburg, 12 mi northeast of Lancaster.*

Ephrata is a classic American town, with an old-fashioned Main Street, a variety of shops and dining experiences, and a truly fun farmers market just north of town. There is little to remind you of the town's austere beginning as a religious commune, except for the Ephrata Cloister.

★ The **Ephrata Cloister** preserves the remains of a religious communal society founded in 1728 by German immigrant Conrad Beissel. The monastic society of brothers and sisters lived an ascetic life of work, study, and prayer. They ate one meal a day of grains, fruits, and vegetables and encouraged celibacy. The society was best known for its a cappella singing and its Fraktur, as well as for its publishing center and the medieval German architecture of the buildings. The last sister died in 1813. Guides lead 45-minute tours of three restored buildings, after which you can browse through the stable, print shop, and craft shop. There is also on-site archaeological research. ⊠ *Rtes. 272 and 322,* ☎ *717/733–6600,* WEB *www.cob-net.org/cloister.htm.* 🎫 *$6.* ☉ *Mon.–Sat. 9–5, Sun. noon–5.*

Fridays are bustling at the **Green Dragon Farmers Market and Auction,** a traditional agricultural market with a country-carnival atmosphere. In the morning livestock and agricultural commodities are auctioned. Throughout the day, local Amish and Mennonite farmers tend many of the 400 indoor and outdoor stalls selling meats, fruits, vegetables, fresh-baked pies, and dry goods. One of the state's largest farmers markets (occupying 30 acres), it also has a flea market and an evening auction of small animals. ⊠ *955 N. State St., off Rte. 272,* ☎ *717/738–1117,* WEB *www.greendragonmarket.com.* ☉ *Fri. 9 AM–9 PM.*

Dining and Lodging

$$–$$$ ✕ **Lily's on Main.** Drummer Steve Brown changed careers to open ★ Lily's in 1998. His contemporary fare, which draws on regional American cuisine, is artistically presented in a stylish art deco–café. Tables are draped with crisp white linens and topped with a single lily. Favorite dishes include pan-roasted duck breast with crispy Chinese dumplings and horseradish-crusted Atlantic salmon. You can also dine on light fare, such as a black bean–veggie burger, or pizza. The gorgeous view overlooking the town of Ephrata is another reason to dine here. ⊠ *124 E. Main St., in the Brossman Business Complex,* ☎ *717/ 738–2711. AE, D, DC, MC, V.*

$–$$ ✕ **Nav Jiwan Tea Room.** This quiet café in the Ten Thousand Villages
★ store provides a palate-pleasing experience in international dining.
Each week the tea room serves cuisine from a different country, such
as India, Mexico, Laos, Haiti, Ethiopia, Nepal, Philippines, Tanzania,
and Thailand. The lunch entrées are prepared in an authentic style and
served by volunteers. A bountiful Friday evening buffet offers a sampling of foods from the featured country. ⊠ *240 N. Reading Rd.,* ☎
717/721–8400. D, MC, V. Closed Sun. Dinner Fri. only.

$–$$$ ✕🏨 **The Inns at Doneckers.** Four properties dating from the 1770s to
the 1920s have been tastefully furnished with French country antiques
and decorated by hand stenciling. Rooms are light and airy; suites have
fireplaces and whirlpool baths. At the inn's Restaurant at Doneckers
($$$–$$$$; closed Wed. and Sun.), classic and country French cuisine
is served downstairs amid Colonial antiques and upstairs in a coun-
try-garden setting. It's best known for its chateaubriand for two, but
other good Doneckers entrées include stuffed Maine lobster tail with
vegetables in a cognac–citrus sauce and fillet of beef with jumbo lump
crabmeat. The service is attentive and the wine cellar extensive. ⊠ *318–
333 N. State St., 17522,* ☎ *717/738–9502 or 800/377–2206,* 🌐
*www.doneckers.com. 27 rooms, 13 suites. Restaurant, shops. AE, D,
DC, MC, V. CP.*

$–$$$ 🏨 **Smithton Inn.** This B&B, a historic former stagecoach inn built in
★ 1763, has been lovingly and authentically restored and includes hand-
tooled furniture, woodwork, and architectural details true to the period. The rooms have fireplaces and canopy beds; the third-floor suite
has a skylight, cathedral ceiling, and Franklin stove fireplace. Nice touches
abound: oversize pillows, nightshirts, and flowers. Feather beds are available upon request when you book a room. Outside are a lily pond, a
fountain, English lawn furniture, and a huge dahlia garden. Full breakfast is included, as is complimentary coffee and tea. ⊠ *900 W. Main
St., at Academy Dr., 17522,* ☎ *717/733–6094,* 🌐 *www.historic-
smithtoninn.com. 7 rooms, 1 suite. Breakfast room. AE, MC, V. BP.*

Shopping

CRAFTS

The Mennonite Central Committee operates **Ten Thousand Villages** (⊠
Rte. 272 just north of Ephrata Cloister, ☎ 717/721–8400, 🌐 www.ten-
thousandvillages.com), where you can shop with a social conscience.
Ten Thousand Villages is an alternative trading organization (ATO),
designed to benefit artisans in low-income countries rather than to max-
imize profits. The vast store stocks more than 3,000 items—including
jewelry, Indian brass, onyx, needlework, baskets, toys, handwoven rugs,
and clothing—from more than 30 countries. The Oriental Rug Room
has handknotted Persians, Bokharas, Kilims, Dhurries, and Afghani
tribal rugs crafted by fairly paid adult labor. Sales in January and July
offer excellent bargains. You can sample a different country's cuisine
each week in the Nav Jiwan Tea Room.

Adamstown

❻ *21 mi northeast of Lancaster on Rte. 222 and Rte. 272.*

There's a good reason the Adamstown area is known as "Antiques Capital USA." In just a few miles of roadway near Exit 21 of the Pennsylvania Turnpike, there are dozens of antiques shops, antiques markets,
and antiques galleries. The big markets, such as Renninger's Antique
Market and Stoudt's Black Angus Antiques Mall, have aisles and aisles
of collectible treasures, including furniture, toys, estate jewelry, lighting, crystal, linens, china, glassware, and coins. For outdoor antiquing,
there's nothing like Shupp's Grove, with acres of shady woods filled

with an array of antiques and collectibles. There are many other smaller markets and galleries. For more information on Adamstown, check out its Web site at www.antiquescapital.com.

Dining and Lodging

$$–$$$$ ✕ **Stoudt's Black Angus.** Prime rib cut from certified Angus beef is the specialty of this Victorian-style restaurant, adjacent to the Black Angus Antiques Mall. Also notable are its raw oyster and seafood bar and German dishes such as Wiener schnitzel. Stoudt's beer, brewed right next door, is on tap. On weekends from August through October, a Bavarian Beer Fest with German bands and a pig roast takes over Brewery Hall. There are brewery tours Saturday at 3 and Sunday at 1. ⊠ *Rte. 272,* ☎ *717/484–4385. AE, DC, MC, V. No lunch Mon.–Thurs.*

$–$$ ✕ **Zinn's Diner.** You can't miss this classic Adamstown landmark, where the massive Pennsylvania Dutch figure of Amos stands outside to welcome guests. Long known for local fare such as chicken rivel soup and knockwurst with sauerkraut, Zinn's has been around for more than 50 years. These days, the diner has expanded its menu to include lighter fare and more-contemporary choices. Breakfast is a favorite among the locals. In warm-weather months, the outdoor park provides family fun with miniature golf, Water Wars, batting cages, an arcade, and an ice cream stand. ⊠ *Rte. 272, one block north of PA Turnpike Exit 21,* ☎ *717/336–2210. D, MC, V.*

$–$$$ 🏨 **Inns at Adamstown.** These two elegant Victorian inns are less than
★ a half block from each other. Both the Adamstown Inn and the Amethyst Inn have spacious rooms with private baths, handmade quilts, fresh flowers, and lace curtains. A number of the rooms have whirlpools, fireplaces, and Euro-style steam showers. Set high on a hill, the Amethyst Inn is a true Painted Lady, with an exterior of deep eggplant, green, and five other colors. There's even an Old English Sheepdog to greet you. A hearty Continental breakfast is served each morning in the Adamstown Inn's dining room. ⊠ *62 West Main St., 17522,* ☎ *717/484–0800 or 800/ 594–4808,* ⓦⒺⒷ *www.adamstown.com. 8 rooms. AE, MC, V.*

Shopping

ANTIQUES

The huge **Renninger's Antique and Collector's Market** (⊠ Rte. 272, ½ mi north of Pennsylvania Turnpike Exit 21, ☎ 717/336–2177) draws thousands of collectors and dealers on Sundays from 7:30 to 5. Nearly 400 indoor stalls, open year-round, overflow with every conceivable type of antique; on good-weather days, the outdoor flea market adds to the selection.

★ **Shupp's Grove** (⊠ just off Rte. 897, south of Adamstown, ☎ 717/484–4115, ⓦⒺⒷ www.shuppsgrove.com), the oldest of the Adamstown antiques markets, has acres of dealers in an outdoor tree-shaded grove. Tables are piled with antiques, art, and collectibles. The market is open weekends from April through October, 7–5.

At **Stoudt's Black Angus Antiques Mall** (⊠ Rte. 272, ☎ 717/484–4385) more than 500 dealers display old books and prints, estate jewelry, linens, china and glassware, coins, and plenty of furniture, inside and outside. There's also a restaurant. The mall is open Sundays, 7:30–5.

Lititz

➐ *10 mi southwest of Ephrata.*

Lititz was founded in 1756 by Moravians who settled in Pennsylvania to do missionary work among the Native Americans. Its tree-shaded main street, lined with 18th-century cottages and shops selling antiques, crafts, clothing, and gifts, is a fine place for a walk. Around the main square are the Moravian communal residences, a church dating from 1787, and a hospital that treated the wounded during the Revolutionary War. You can pick up a Historical Foundation walking tour brochure at the General Sutter Inn (⊠ 14 E. Main St.) or the Johannes Mueller House (⊠ 137–139 E. Main St.).

At the **Julius Sturgis Pretzel House,** the oldest pretzel bakery in the United States, pretzels are twisted by hand and baked in brick ovens the same way Julius Sturgis did it in 1861. At the end of the 20-minute guided tour, you can try your hand at the almost extinct art of pretzel twisting. ⊠ 219 E. Main St., ☎ 717/626–4354. ☞ $2. ☉ Mon.–Sat. 9:30–4:30.

The first thing you notice in Lititz is the smell of chocolate emanating from the **Wilbur Chocolate Company's Candy Americana Museum and Factory Candy Outlet,** which has a small museum of candy-related memorabilia and a large retail store. ⊠ 48 N. Broad St., ☎ 717/626–3249. ☞ Free. ☉ Mon.–Sat. 10–5.

Dining and Lodging

$–$$ ✕▭ **General Sutter Inn.** Built in 1764, the oldest continuously run inn
★ in Pennsylvania was named after the man who founded Sacramento in 1839, 10 years before the discovery of gold on his California property started the gold rush. Sutter retired in Lititz and the inn named after him is a Victorian delight with furnishings such a Louis XIV sofas and marble-top tables. The inn stands at the crossroads of town, within easy walking distance of the buildings of the historic district. The 1764 Restaurant ($$–$$$$) offers fine dining with an artistic flourish; favorite selections include a veal and lobster ratonnet and daily presentation of Pennsylvania trout. There's also a casual café. In warm weather, you can dine on the brick patio. ⊠ 14 E. Main St., corner of Rtes. 501 and 772, 17543, ☎ 717/626–2115, ᶠᴬˣ 717/626–0992, ᵂᴱᴮ www.generalsutterinn.com. 16 rooms, 3 suites. Restaurants, café, bar, no-smoking rooms. AE, D, MC, V.

$$–$$$ ▭ **Swiss Woods.** Innkeepers Werner and Debrah Mosimann designed
★ this chalet while they were still living in Werner's native Switzerland. They planted it on 30 acres, creating an open and airy, European-style B&B with light pine furnishings, contemporary country decor, and goose down comforters. Nestled on the edge of the woods overlooking Speedwell Forge Lake, the chalet is surrounded by extensive flower gardens. Each room has its own patio or balcony. ⊠ 500 Blantz Rd., 17543, ☎ 717/627–3358 or 800/594–8018, ᶠᴬˣ 717/627–3483, ᵂᴱᴮ www.swisswoods.com. 6 rooms, 1 suite. Hiking, boating, fishing. AE, D, MC, V. BP.

WESTERN LANCASTER COUNTY

You can avoid the crowds and commercialism of parts of eastern Lancaster County by staying in the peaceful towns along or near the Susquehanna River, including Columbia, Marietta, and Mount Joy. There's plenty of scenery and Colonial history to explore, and you can sample good Mennonite food here.

Columbia

❽ 10 mi west of Lancaster.

They're quiet towns now, but Columbia and other river communities were bustling and important in the days when rivers were one of the easiest methods of transportation. Eighteenth-century Quaker missionary John Wright worked in this area, and two of his sons set up a ferry that became an important transportation point for settlers moving west. Today there are several museums and the tranquil countryside to explore.

★ A visit to the **National Watch and Clock Museum** provides an entertaining trip through the history and future of timekeeping. The Time Tunnel takes you from exhibits of water clocks through a turn-of-the-last-century watch and clock shop and a 20th-century watch factory. More than 10,000 timepieces and time-related items are on view, including early sundials; a 19th-century Tiffany globe clock; a German Black Forest organ clock with 94 pipes; moon-phase wristwatches; and the showstopper, the Engle Clock, an 1877 timepiece intended to resemble the famous astronomical cathedral clock of Strasbourg, France. ✉ *514 Poplar St.,* ☎ *717/684–8261,* WEB *www.nawcc.org.* ✑ *$6.* ☉ *Tues.–Sat. 10–5, Sun. noon–4.*

The **Market House and Dungeon,** built in 1869, is one of the oldest farmers market sites in the state. The basement used to be a dungeon; you can still see the ground-level windows through which prisoners were shoved down a chute into the darkness. ✉ *308 Locust St., off Rte. 441,* ☉ *Dungeon by appointment only; contact* ✉ *Susquehanna Heritage Visitors Center, 3rd and Linden Sts.,* ☎ *717/684–5249.*

Wright's Ferry Mansion was the residence of English Quaker Susanna Wright, a silkworm breeder whose family helped open Colonial Pennsylvania west of the Susquehanna. The 1738 stone house showcases period furniture in the Philadelphia William & Mary and Queen Anne styles and a great collection of English needlework, ceramics, and glass, all predating 1750. ✉ *38 S. 2nd St.,* ☎ *717/684–4325.* ✑ *$5.* ☉ *May–Oct., Tues.–Wed. and Fri.–Sat. 10–3.*

Dining and Lodging

$$–$$$ ✕ **Prudhomme's Lost Cajun Kitchen.** Owned by David and Sharon Prudhomme, relatives of the famous Paul Prudhomme of New Orleans, this Cajun style restaurant attracts visitors from as far as Philadelphia and Baltimore. Here, you can dine on authentic Louisiana fare, such as crawfish étouffée, blackened catfish, gumbo, jambalaya, and fried alligator. The dishes are prepared as hot as you like, or more mild mannered with reduced spices. ✉ *Rte. 462 and Cherry St.,* ☎ *717/684–1706. AE, D, MC, V. No dinner Sun. No lunch Mon.*

$–$$ ⌂ **The Columbian.** In this Victorian mansion in the heart of the village, a tiered staircase leads to rooms filled with antiques. Several rooms have fireplaces. The rate includes an ample country breakfast, often prepared with herbs from the garden. ✉ *360 Chestnut St., 17512,* ☎ *717/684–5869 or 800/422–5869,* WEB *www.columbianinn.com. 6 rooms, 2 suites. Playground. MC, V. BP.*

Marietta

❾ *8 mi northwest of Columbia.*

Almost half of the buildings in Marietta are listed on the National Historic Register; the architecture ranges from log cabins to more-recent Federal and Victorian homes. This restored river town, now seeing new life as an artists' community, is perfect for a stroll past the well-preserved facades of art galleries and antiques shops.

❿ At the 52-acre **Nissley Vineyards and Winery Estate,** you can review the grape-growing process on a self-guided tour. This scenic winery, which produces award-winning vintage wines, also has tastings, and bottles are for sale. You can picnic on the grounds. In summer there is a musical concert series with a cost for admission. ✉ *140 Vintage Dr., north-*

west of Marietta near Bainbridge, 1½ mi off Rte. 441, ☎ *717/426–3514,* WEB *www.nissleywine.com.* ☒ *Free.* ☉ *Mon.–Sat. 10–5, Sun. 1–4.*

Lodging

$ ⊡ **Olde Fogie Farm Bed and Breakfast.** You can milk the goats and bottle-feed the calves on this farm, and then go swimming in a water garden pond with waterfalls and giant Japanese koi. Hosts Tom and Biz Fogie have been organically farming this land for more than 30 years, and they have a good sense of humor; they boast that they "maintain a four-pig rating by using good old horse sense." The old frame home has an Amish cookstove; the property has a petting farm, a creek, a playhouse, and a stable for pony rides. A hearty breakfast is included with the two bed-and-breakfast rooms; folks in the efficiency apartments are given ingredients to make their own. From after Thanksgiving through March, the Fogies welcome adults only with romantic packages and an on-site massage therapist. ☒ *106 Stackstown Rd., 17547,* ☎ *717/426–3992 or 877/653–3644,* WEB *www.oldefogiefarm.com. 2 rooms, 2 efficiency apartments. Pond, hot tub. BP. MC, V.*

Shopping

George's Woodcrafts (☒ 9 Reichs Church Rd., ☎ 717/426–1004 or 800/799–1685) sells handcrafted furniture in walnut, oak, and cherry for every room in the house. You can watch items being made and then put in an order. The store is closed Sunday.

Mount Joy

⓫ *5 mi northeast of Marietta.*

This small town is highlighted by a historic brewery and some good restaurants. Dating from before the Civil War, **Bube's Brewery** is the only brewery in the United States that has remained intact since the mid-19th century. A guided tour takes you 43 ft below the street into the brewery's vaults and passages, which were built in a cave; these passages also served as part of the Underground Railroad. It's a pleasant way to learn about beer-making in Victorian times. ☒ *102 N. Market St.,* ☎ *717/653–2056,* WEB *www.bubesbrewery.com.* ☒ *Free.* ☉ *Tours Memorial Day–Labor Day, daily 10–5.*

Dining and Lodging

$$–$$$$ ✕ **Bube's Brewery.** The only intact pre-Prohibition brewery in the country contains four unique restaurants. The Bottling Works, in the original bottling plant of the brewery, serves steaks, light dinners, salads, burgers, and subs at lunch and dinner. Alois's presents prix-fixe six-course international dinners (reservations required; closed Monday) in a Victorian hotel attached to the brewery. The dinner-only Catacombs serves traditional steak and seafood dishes in the brewery's aging cellars below street level. A feast master presides over a medieval-, pirate-, or Roman-theme dinner (reservations required) every Sunday night. Wine and ale flow, musicians entertain, and diners participate in the festivities. The shady outdoor Biergarten Restaurant is open in the summer. ☒ *102 N. Market St.,* ☎ *717/653–2056. AE, D, MC, V.*

$$–$$$ ✕ **Groff's Farm.** Abe and Betty Groff's 1756 farmhouse restaurant is known for its hearty Mennonite fare. Candlelight, fresh flowers, and original Groff Farm country fabrics and wall coverings contribute to the homey ambience. House specialties include chicken Stoltzfus, farm relishes, and cracker pudding. Dinner begins with seven sweets and sours. Lunch is à la carte, dinner à la carte or family style but served at your own table. Groff's Farm also has an 18-hole golf course, pro shop, and sports bar. ☒ *650 Pinkerton Rd.,* ☎ *717/653–2048. Dinner reservations essential. AE, D, DC, MC, V. Closed Sun. and Mon.*

$ 🏠 **Rocky Acre Farm.** Here you can sleep in a 200-year-old stone farm-house that was once a stop on the Underground Railroad. This is a dairy farm with calves to feed, cows to milk, and dogs, kittens, roosters, and sheep—in the meadow, of course—to enjoy. There's fishing and boating in the creek, and there are free pony, train, and tractor rides. ✉ *1020 Pinkerton Rd., 17552,* ☎ *717/653–4449,* WEB *www.rockyacre.com. 8 rooms, 2 efficiency units. Boating, fishing. No credit cards. BP.*

Manheim

7 mi northeast of Mount Joy.

Baron Henry William Stiegel founded the small town of Manheim and manufactured Stiegel flint glassware here in the 18th century. Today a major draw is a winery a few miles north of town.

⓬ The **Mount Hope Estate and Winery** is an elegant 19th-century mansion with a vineyard on the grounds. The mansion and surrounding gardens have been placed on the National Register of Historic Places. Originally built in 1800 in the Federal style, the house was renovated in 1895 with Victorian touches and enlarged to its current 32 rooms. Turrets, hand-painted 18-ft ceilings, Egyptian marble fireplaces, gold-leaf wallpaper, and crystal gas chandeliers are just some of the decorative elements. The winery bottles about 30 different wines; complimentary tastings are held in the wine shop. ✉ *5 mi north of Manheim on Rte. 72, ½ mi from Exit 20 of the Pennsylvania Turnpike,* ☎ *717/665–7021 Ext. 125.* ☉ *Mon.–Sat. 10–5, Sun. 11–5; house tours by special arrangement.*

Lodging

$ 🏠 **Jonde Lane Farm.** Breakfast with your Mennonite host family is served every day but Sunday at this 100-acre working dairy and poultry farm. You can savor farm living, surrounded by ponies, chickens, and cats. The four guest rooms include a family room that can sleep seven people. There is also a fishing pond. ✉ *1103 Auction Rd., 17545,* ☎ *717/665–4231. 4 rooms, 2 with bath. Fishing. MC, V. Closed Thanksgiving–Easter. BP.*

Nightlife and the Arts

The seasonal **Pennsylvania Renaissance Faire,** on the grounds of the Mount Hope Estate and Winery, transforms the winery into a 16th-century English village ruled by Her Majesty Queen Elizabeth I. You can enjoy human chess matches, jousting and fencing tournaments, knighthood ceremonies, street performances, craft demonstrations, jesters, medieval food, and Shakespearean plays performed on outdoor stages. ✉ *5 mi north of Manheim on Rte. 72, ½ mi from Exit 20 of Pennsylvania Turnpike,* ☎ *717/665–7021,* WEB *www.parenfaire.com.* 🎟 *$18.95.* ☉ *Mid-Aug.–mid-Oct., weekends 10–6:30.*

HERSHEY AND GETTYSBURG

It's easy to combine a trip to Lancaster County with two popular sights not more than an hour's drive from Lancaster. Hershey, to the northwest, has an amusement park and some chocolate-theme attractions. Gettysburg, to the southwest, is the county seat of Adams County and the site of Gettysburg National Military Park and museums that examine the significance of the Civil War battle.

Hershey

⓭ *30 mi northwest of Lancaster.*

Hershey is Chocolate Town, a community built around a chocolate factory and now home to a theme park, the Hershey Museum, and other diversions for children and adults. Founded in 1903 by confectioner Milton S. Hershey, a Mennonite descendant, it celebrates chocolate without guilt, from streetlights shaped like foil-wrapped kisses to avenues named Chocolate and Cocoa. Hershey is also known as a fine golf center. You can call ☎ 800/437–7439 for brochures and room reservations.

☺ At **Hersheypark** they take seriously the saying "You are what you eat." Where else can you find walking Hershey Bars and dancing Reese's Peanut Butter Cups? On 100 landscaped acres are 50 rides, games of chance, five theaters, and ZooAmerica, with animals from North America. Begun in 1907, Hersheypark has been called America's cleanest and greenest theme park. Among its historical rides are the Comet, a 1946-vintage wooden roller coaster, and a carousel built in 1919 with 66 hand-carved wooden horses. Newer rides include the exciting Lightning Racer, a double track wood racing coaster; Great Bear, a steel inverted roller coaster; and six water rides. ⊠ *Hersheypark Dr., Rte. 743 and U.S. 422,* ☎ *717/534–3090,* WEB *www.hersheypa.com.* 🎫 *$33.95, includes ZooAmerica.* ☉ *Memorial Day–Labor Day, daily 10–10 (some earlier closings); May and Sept., weekends only, call for hrs.*

☺ **ZooAmerica,** on the grounds of Hersheypark, is an 11-acre wildlife park with more than 250 animals from throughout North America in recreations of their natural habitats. ⊠ *Rte. 743 and U.S. 422,* ☎ *717/ 534–3860.* 🎫 *$6.25 (or included in Hersheypark admission price).* ☉ *Mid-June–Aug., daily 10–8; Sept.–mid-June, daily 10–5.*

★ ☺ At **Hershey's Chocolate World,** a 10-minute automated ride takes you through the steps of producing chocolate (the crowds are now too large for actual factory tours) from picking the cocoa beans to making candy bars in Hershey's candy kitchens. It also serves as the town's official visitor center. Afterward you may taste-test your favorite Hershey confection and buy gifts in a spacious conservatory filled with tropical plants. ⊠ *Park Blvd.,* ☎ *717/534–4900.* 🎫 *Free.* ☉ *Spring and fall, daily 9–5; summer, daily 9–8.*

★ The **Hershey Museum** preserves the story of Milton S. Hershey, who founded the town bearing his name and just about everything in it. The main exhibition, *Built on Chocolate,* displays Hershey artifacts and memorabilia. Displays of chocolate-bar wrappers and cocoa tins show their evolution through the years, and black-and-white photos of the town from the '30s, '40s, and '50s are hung side by side with color photos of the same sites today. *Adam Danner's World* documents the daily lives of Pennsylvania Germans, and the Native American Collection has art and artifacts from Hershey's personal collection. A children's area provides a hands-on experience. ⊠ *170 W. Hersheypark Dr.,* ☎ *717/534–3439.* 🎫 *$6.* ☉ *Daily 10–5.*

Hershey Gardens began with a single 3½-acre plot of 8,000 rose bushes and has grown to include 10 theme gardens on 23 landscaped acres, along with 1,200 varieties of roses and 22,000 tulips. The gardens come to life in spring as thousands of bulbs burst into bloom. Flowering displays last until fall, when late roses open. Kid-theme areas include a butterfly house and a children's garden. ⊠ *Hotel Rd. near Hotel Hershey,* ☎ *717/534–3492,* WEB *www.hersheygardens.org.* 🎫 *$6.* ☉ *Apr.–Sept. 9–6, Oct. 9–5.*

Chocolatetown Square is a 1-acre park downtown where free concerts are held in summer. ☒ *Intersection of Cocoa and E. Chocolate Aves., near wooden gazebo,* ☎ *717/534–3439 for upcoming events.*

OFF THE
BEATEN PATH
INDIAN ECHO CAVERNS – One of the largest caves in the northeastern United States has a 45-minute guided walking tour of its underground wonderland. Bring a sweater; strollers are not allowed. The children can enjoy panning for gold at Gem Hill Junction. There is a gift shop with souvenirs, and a picnic area. The caverns are about 3 mi west of Hershey. ☒ *Off U.S. 322, Hummelstown,* ☎ *717/566–8131.* ☜ *$8.* ☉ *Memorial Day–Labor Day, daily 9–6; Labor Day–Memorial Day, daily 10–4.*

Dining and Lodging

$–$$ ✕ **Hershey Pantry.** This lace-curtained, family-friendly restaurant serves generous portions of simple food made with fresh ingredients. The menu includes pastas, sandwiches, salads, and homemade desserts; the hearty breakfasts are notable. ☒ *801 E. Chocolate Ave.,* ☎ *717/ 533–7505. No credit cards. Closed Sun.*

$$$$ ✕▥ **Hotel Hershey.** The grande dame of Hershey, this gracious Mediterranean villa-style hotel is a quiet, sophisticated resort with plenty of options for recreation, starting with the golf course that surrounds the hotel. Inspired by the fine European hotels Milton S. Hershey encountered in his travels, it was part of his building program to lift his town out of the Great Depression. Elegant touches abound, from the mosaic-tile lobby to rooms with iron beds, maple armoires, paintings from local artists, and tile baths. Dining options include the Iberian Lounge, Fountain Café, the casual Clubhouse Café, and the formal Circular Dining Room, which overlooks the gardens, fountains, and reflecting pools. Recreational activities include carriage rides, a ropes course, and nature trails. ☒ *Hotel Rd.,* ☎ *717/533–2171 or 800/ 533–3131,* ᴡᴇʙ *www.800hershey.com/accommodations/hotel. 235 rooms, 20 suites. 3 restaurants, coffee shop, lounge, room service, indoor pool, outdoor pool, sauna, spa, 9-hole golf course, 3 tennis courts, basketball, bicycles, gym, baby-sitting, laundry service, concierge, business services, meeting rooms. AE, D, DC, MC, V.*

$$$ ▥ **Hershey Lodge & Convention Center.** This bustling, expansive modern resort caters to both families and business travelers and has two casual restaurants suitable for children, plus a somewhat more formal room for adult dining. The hotel hosts groups of up to 1,300 in its Chocolate Ballroom, and it can be hectic during conventions. Ask for a room in the Guest Tower. ☒ *W. Chocolate Ave. and University Dr., 17033,* ☎ *717/533–3311 or 800/533–3131,* ᴡᴇʙ *www.800hershey.com/ accommodations/lodge. 637 rooms, 28 suites. 3 restaurants, coffee shop, 2 lounge, room service, indoor pool, 2 outdoor pools, miniature golf, 2 tennis courts, basketball, gym, recreation room, baby-sitting, laundry service, concierge, convention center. AE, D, DC, MC, V.*

Outdoor Activities and Sports

The **Country Club of Hershey** (☒ 1000 E. Derry Rd., ☎ 717/533–2464) maintains two private 18-hole courses, which are available to guests of the Hotel Hershey. Greens fees are around $100. The **Hotel Hershey** (☒ Hotel Rd., ☎ 717/533–2171) has nine holes on the hotel grounds. Greens fees are around $16. A public 18-hole course known as the **South Course** (☒ 600 W. Derry Rd., ☎ 717/534–3450) is short but demanding. Greens fees are $55 weekdays, $65 weekends. **Spring Creek Golf** (☒ 450 E. Chocolate Ave., ☎ 717/533–2847), a 9-hole course, was originally built by Milton Hershey for youngsters to hone their strokes. Greens fees are around $11.

Shopping

Ziegler's Antiques Mall (⊠ Intersection Rtes. 322 and 743, ☎ 717/533–7990) has more than 75 dealers and an assortment of antiques and collectibles. It is housed in Hershey's largest parabolic (bowl-shape) barn, which formerly belonged to the Milton Hershey School. The mall is open Thursday to Monday, 10–5:30.

Ziegler's in the Country (⊠ Rte. 743, ☎ 717/533–1662) is on a restored 1850s homestead, with several buildings from that era. An air-conditioned barn has space for 92 dealers and an herb and spice shop (open on weekends). Hours are Thursday to Monday, 9–5.

Gettysburg

⑭ *53 mi west of Lancaster on U.S. 30.*

"The world will little note, nor long remember, what we say here, but it can never forget what they did here." These words from Abraham Lincoln's famous address were delivered in Gettysburg to mark the dedication of its national cemetery in November 1863. Four months earlier, from July 1 to 3, 51,000 Americans were killed, wounded, or counted as missing in the bloodiest battle of the Civil War. The events that took place in Gettysburg during those few days marked the turning point in the war. Although the struggle raged on for almost two more years, the Confederate forces never recovered from their losses.

At the national military park and 20 museums in Gettysburg, you can recapture the power of those momentous days. Plans are under way for a $39 million, 15-acre visitor center and museum to be built at Gettysburg National Military Park on the outskirts of the battlefield, about a half mile away from the existing facility. There has been some local controversy about the center's location and the plans for a private company to build the center. With an anticipated opening in 2004 to 2006, the new building will allow the park to preserve and display its extensive collection of Civil War artifacts. Also planned is a 20-year, $63 million restoration of the battlefield to its 1863 condition.

The **Gettysburg Tour Center** is the departure point for two-hour narrated tours of the battlefield. Open-air double-decker buses depart every 15–45 minutes. ⊠ *778 Baltimore St.,* ☎ *717/334–6296.* ☞ *$16.95.* ☉ *Jan.–June and Sept.–Dec., daily 9–5; July–Aug., daily 9–9.*

★ At what is now **Gettysburg National Military Park,** General Robert E. Lee and his Confederate troops encountered the Union forces of General George Meade. The 5,700 acres are adorned with more than 1,000 markers and monuments honoring the casualties of the battle. More than 30 mi of marked roads lead through the park, highlighting key battle sites. It's best to begin your exploration at the visitor center. ⊠ *97 Taneytown Rd.,* ☎ *717/334–1124,* WEB *www.nps.gov/gett.* ☞ *Free.* ☉ *Park roads 6 AM–10 PM.*

The **Gettysburg National Military Park Visitor Center** distributes a free map with an 18-mi driving tour through the battlefield, as well as an orientation program, Civil War exhibits, and current schedules of ranger-conducted programs and talks. The park service also provides free walking-tour maps, which have short 1-mi loops that include the sites of some of the battle's most pivotal engagements; 3½- and 9-mi trails are also marked. Private, licensed guides may also be hired at the center. To best understand the battle, begin by viewing the **Electric Map,** which uses colored lights to illustrate deployments and clashes during the three days of fighting. Sit on the south side for the best view.

⊠ 97 Taneytown Rd., ☎ 717/334–1124. 🖭 Free; Electric Map $3.
☉ Daily 8–5, later summer hrs; map shows every 45 min.

The **Cyclorama Center** contains a 19th-century in-the-round painting
that puts you in the center of Pickett's Charge, the South's ill-fated frontal
assault during the last day of the battle. ⊠ Taneytown Rd., adjacent
to the visitor center, ☎ 717/334–1124. 🖭 $3. ☉ Showings daily, every
30 min., 9–4:30.

★ The **Gettysburg National Cemetery,** dedicated by President Abraham
Lincoln in his Gettysburg Address, is now the final resting place of more
than 7,000 honorably discharged servicemen and their dependents. ⊠
Off Baltimore Pike, across the street from the visitor center. 🖭 Free.
☉ Daily dawn–dusk.

The **National Civil War Wax Museum** presents the story of the Civil
War era and the Battle of Gettysburg through more than 200 life-size
figures in 30 scenes, including a reenactment of the Battle of Gettysburg and an animated Abraham Lincoln delivering his Gettysburg Address. The battleroom was revamped in 2001 to accommodate a
high-quality DVD format. ⊠ 297 Steinwehr Ave., ☎ 717/334–6245.
🖭 $5. ☉ Daily 9–5 with extended seasonal hours.

The **Hall of Presidents and First Ladies** re-creates in wax the nation's
chief executives from Washington to Clinton, as well as their wives (with
reproductions of their inaugural gowns). The museum also contains a
room displaying paintings by President Dwight D. Eisenhower. ⊠ 789
Baltimore St., ☎ 717/334–5717. 🖭 $5.95. ☉ June–Aug., daily 9–9;
Mar.–May and Sept.–Nov., daily 9–5.

Soldier's National Museum depicts 10 major battles of the Civil War
in miniature dioramas and a life-size encampment scene from the night
of July 2, 1863. ⊠ 777 Baltimore St., ☎ 717/334–4890. 🖭 $5.95. ☉
June–Aug., daily 9–9; Mar.–May and Sept.–Nov., daily 9–5.

The **Lincoln Train Museum** aims to recapture Lincoln's journey from
Washington to Gettysburg in November 1863 to dedicate the national
cemetery. A 12-minute ride simulates the sights, sounds, and most of
all the feel of traveling on a period railcar. The museum also houses
the Alexander Model Train and Military Rail Collection. ⊠ 425 Steinwehr Ave., ☎ 717/334–5678. 🖭 $5.95. ☉ May–June, daily 9–9; July–
Aug., daily 9 AM–10 PM; Sept.–Nov., daily 9–5.

The **Lincoln Room Museum** houses the bedroom where President Lincoln finished writing the Gettysburg Address; the furnishings are copies.
Through a tape featuring a re-creation of Lincoln speaking his thoughts,
doubts, and dreams on November 18, 1963, you can learn the story
behind his words and understand what motivated them. ⊠ 12 Lincoln
Sq., ☎ 717/334–8188. 🖭 $3.50. ☉ Summer, daily 9–7:30; reduced
hrs off-season.

General Lee's headquarters, one of the few historic houses in Gettysburg open to the public. Here, on July 1, 1863, Lee planned his
strategy for the now-famous battle. The old stone building houses a
fine collection of Civil War relics and a souvenir shop. ⊠ Rte. 30 W,
8 blocks west of Lincoln Sq., ☎ 717/334–3141. 🖭 $3. ☉ Mar.–Nov.,
daily 9–9.

The **Schriver House** was the home of George and Henrietta Schriver
and their two children. After George joined the Union troops and his
family fled to safety, the home was taken over by Confederate sharp-
shooters, two of whom were killed in its garret during the battle. The
restored home is a recipient of the PA State Historic Preservation

Award. ⊠ *309 Baltimore St.,* ☎ *717/337–2800.* 🖃 *$5.75.* ☉ *Mon.–Sat. 10–5, Sun. noon–5.*

★ The **Eisenhower National Historic Site** was the farm-turned-country-estate residence of President and Mrs. Dwight D. Eisenhower, who bought it in 1950. The couple used it as a weekend retreat, a sanctuary during illness, and a meeting place for world leaders. From 1961 until the 34th president's death in 1969, it was the Eisenhower's full-time residence. The brick-and-stone farmhouse is preserved in 1950s style, with a number of outbuildings. The farm adjoins the battlefield and is administered by the Park Service, which sells daily ticketed tours only on a first-come, first-served basis at the Gettysburg National Military Park Visitor Center. ⊠ *Off Millerstown Rd.,* ☎ *717/334–1124,* WEB *www.nps.gov/eise.* 🖃 *$5.25.* ☉ *Apr.–Oct., daily 9–5; Nov.–Mar., Wed.–Sun. 9–5.*

Dining and Lodging

$$–$$$ ✕ **Blue Parrot Bistro.** This bustling bar and restaurant is within walking distance of many hotels and attractions. The Blue Parrot serves up creatively prepared light entrées including salads and Portobello and smoked Gouda quesadillas, as well as hearty fare such as meat loaf stuffed with andouille sausage. ⊠ *35 Chambersburg St.,* ☎ *717/337–3739. MC, V. Closed Mon.*

$–$$$ ✕🏠 **Historic Farnsworth House Restaurant & Inn.** The restaurant ($$)
★ at this B&B serves up Civil War–era dishes such as game pie, peanut soup, pumpkin fritters, and spoon bread in an 1810 building that still shows bullet holes from the battle. The tranquil outdoor garden has sculptures and fountains. Each Victorian guest room is lushly and individually decorated with period sewing machines, Victrolas, and antique clothing. The inn conducts ghost tours of Gettysburg (open to guests and the public for $6) that begin with dramatizations and stories in the basement's ghoulish Mourning Theater. Also on the grounds are an art and book gallery and Civil War memorabilia shop. ⊠ *401 Baltimore St.,* ☎ *717/334–8838,* WEB *www.farnsworthhousedining.com. 9 rooms. Restaurant. AE, D, MC, V. BP.*

$–$$ ✕🏠 **Gettystown Inn.** This historical property, which overlooks the spot where Lincoln gave his Gettysburg Address, includes a bed-and-breakfast, two restaurants, and a shop. In an 1860s home, the inn has period furnishings, four-poster beds, and Civil War–era artifacts. There are also guest rooms in two adjacent buildings. The **Dobbin House Tavern** ($$$) was built in 1776, making it the oldest building in town. Fine Colonial and Continental cuisine, such as prime rib and Mandarin orange duck, are served in the tavern's six restored rooms with hand-carved woodwork, fireplaces, candlelight, and antiques. You can dine in wing chairs in the parlor, take your meal in the spinning room, or have dinner in bed in the bedroom. Hotel rates include tea and coffee served in the parlor of the 1860s home. Also on the property is the Springhouse Tavern, an aptly named Colonial alehouse; there are springs coming out of its walls. ⊠ *89 Steinwehr Ave., 17325,* ☎ *717/334–2100,* WEB *www.dobbinhouse.com. 4 rooms, 4 suites. 2 restaurants, shop, business services. AE, MC, V. BP.*

$$–$$$ 🏠 **Baladerry Inn.** During the Battle of Gettysburg, this 1812 home on the edge of the battlefield served as a field hospital. Today, it serves breakfast to the guests who overnight in the main house or the carriage house. The fully restored rooms are filled with antiques; many have fireplaces. Those on the ground floor of the carriage house have their own patios. Children over 12 welcome. ⊠ *40 Hospital Rd., 17325,* ☎ *717/337–1342,* WEB *www.baladerryinn.com. 8 rooms. Tennis court. AE, D, MC, V. BP.*

$–$$$ ⊞ **Best Western Gettysburg Hotel 1797.** The hotel is a pre–Civil War
★   structure in the heart of the downtown historic district; prominent guests
have included Carl Sandburg, Henry Ford, and General Ulysses S. Grant.
During the Cold War, the hotel served as President Eisenhower's national
operations center while he was recuperating at his nearby home. Rooms
are furnished in traditional style, and suites have fireplaces and whirl-
pool baths. Ask about the cannonball from the battle that is still em-
bedded in the brick wall across the street. In summer, the hotel uses an
adjacent college dormitory as family suites. ✉ *1 Lincoln Sq., 17325,* ☎
717/337–2000 or 800/528–1234, FAX *717/337–2075,* WEB *www.gettysburg-*
hotel.com. 48 rooms, 27 suites. Restaurant, bar, in-room data ports, micro-
waves, refrigerators, no-smoking rooms, room service, pool, business
services. AE, D, DC, MC, V.

$$ ⊞ **James Gettys Hotel.** Although it flourished as a hotel in the 1920s,
this four-story 1787 building just off the town square was later con-
verted into apartments and a youth hostel. Today it thrives as an af-
fordably priced, attractively furnished suites-only hotel. Each suite has
a sitting room with a kitchenette including a refrigerator, microwave
oven, and small dining table. A Continental breakfast is left in each suite
the night before. At the neighboring Thistlefields, you can relax with
full English afternoon tea. ✉ *27 Chambersburg St., 17325,* ☎ *717/337–*
1334 or 888/900–5275, FAX *717/334–2103,* WEB *www.jamesgettyshotel.*
com. 11 suites. Kitchenettes, laundry service. AE, D, MC, V. CP.

$ ⚠ **Artillery Ridge Campground.** You can pitch a tent or park an RV
a mile south of the Gettysburg National Military Park Visitor Center.
Horse owners can even bring their horses on vacation with them.
Families may enjoy the fishing pond. ✉ *610 Taneytown Rd., 17325,*
☎ *717/334–1288. 45 tent sites, 105 camper or RV sites. Pool, horse-*
back riding, fishing, bicycles. D, MC.

Shopping

Gallon Historical Art (✉ 9 Steinwher Ave., ☎ 717/334–8666) is an art
gallery showing original paintings and prints of Gettysburg battle
scenes by Dale Gallon, the town's artist-in-residence.

The Horse Soldier (✉ 777 Baltimore St., ☎ 717/334–0347) provides
a shopping experience that's more like visiting a museum. Carrying one
of the country's largest collections of military antiques—everything from
bullets to discharge papers—the shop focuses on the Civil War. It's Soldier Genealogical Research Service can help you find your ancestors'
war records prior to 1910. The store is closed Wednesday.

LANCASTER COUNTY A TO Z

BUS TRAVEL

Greyhound Lines has several daily runs between Philadelphia and
Lancaster's R&S Bus Terminal. The ride takes about 2½ hours.
➤ BUS INFORMATION: **Greyhound Lines** (✉ 22 W. Clay St., ☎ 800/231–
2222, WEB www.greyhound.com).

CAR TRAVEL

From Philadelphia take the Schuylkill Expressway (I–76) west to the
Pennsylvania Turnpike. Lancaster County sights are accessible from
Exits 20, 21, and 22. Another option is to follow U.S. 30 west from
Philadelphia, but be prepared for major highway construction on Rte.
30 in Lancaster. It's about 65 mi to the Pennsylvania Dutch Country.

EMERGENCIES

Lancaster County has four emergency rooms: Community Hospital of
Lancaster, Lancaster General Hospital, Lancaster Regional Medical Cen-

ter, and Ephrata Community Hospital. For nonemergency referrals, contact the Lancaster City & County Medical Society.

➤ CONTACTS: **Ambulance, fire, and police** (☎ 911). **Community Hospital of Lancaster** (✉ 1100 E. Orange St., ☎ 717/239–4000). **Lancaster General Hospital** (✉ 555 N. Duke St., ☎ 717/290–5511). **Lancaster Regional Medical Center** (✉ 250 College Ave., ☎ 717/291–8211). **Ephrata Community Hospital** (✉ 169 Martin Ave., Ephrata, ☎ 717/ 738–6420). **Lancaster City & County Medical Society** (☎ 717/393– 9588).

➤ PHARMACIES: **CVS Pharmacy** (✉ 1643½ Lincoln Hwy., Lancaster, ☎ 717/394–5121). **Weis Pharmacy** (✉ 1603 Lincoln Hwy. E, Lancaster, ☎ 717/394–9826).

LODGING
B&BS

Lancaster County Bed-and-Breakfast Inns Association is a group of 16 B&Bs in the area.

➤ RESERVATION SERVICES: **Lancaster County Bed-and-Breakfast Inns Association** (✉ 2835 Willow Street Pike, Willow Street 17548, ☎ 717/ 464–5588 or 800/848–2994).

TOURS

Amish Country Tours has large bus or minivan tours. Most popular is the two-hour Amish farmlands trip, with stops at a farmhouse, a wine tasting, and shopping for crafts; tours to Hershey are available on Tuesday. Brunswick Tours' private guides tour with you in your car. The company also has a self-guided auto audiotape tour with 28 stops that begins at the Pennsylvania Dutch Convention & Visitors Bureau and takes three or four hours. Glick Aviation, at Smoketown Airport, offers 18-minute flights in a four-seater plane (pilot plus three), that gives you a splendid aerial view of rolling farmlands. The Mennonite Information Center has local Mennonite guides who join you in your car. These knowledgeable escorts lead you to country roads, produce stands, and Amish crafts shops and also acquaint you with their religion.

➤ FEES & SCHEDULES: **Amish Country Tours** (✉ Rte. 340 at Plain & Fancy Farm, between Bird-in-Hand and Intercourse, ☎ 717/768–3600 or 800/441–3505). **Brunswick Tours** (✉ National Wax Museum, U.S. 30E, Lancaster, ☎ 717/397–7541 or 800/979–8687). **Glick Aviation** (✉ 311 Airport Dr., off Rte. 340, Smoketown, ☎ 717/394–6476). **Mennonite Information Center** (✉ 2209 Millstream Rd., Lancaster, ☎ 717/ 299–0954).

TRAIN TRAVEL

Amtrak has regular service from Philadelphia's 30th Street Station to the Lancaster Amtrak station. The trip takes 80 minutes.

➤ TRAIN INFORMATION: **Amtrak** (✉ 53 McGovern Ave., ☎ 215/824– 1600 or 800/872–7245, WEB www.amtrak.com).

TRANSPORTATION AROUND LANCASTER COUNTY

A car is the easiest way to explore the many sights in the area; it also lets you get off the main roads and into the countryside. Lancaster County's main arteries are U.S. 30 (also known as the Lincoln Highway) and Route 340 (sometimes called the Old Philadelphia Pike). Some pleasant back roads can be found between Routes 23 and 340. Vintage Road is a country road running north over U.S. 30 and then along Route 772 west to Intercourse. You get a look at some of the farms in the area and also see Amish schoolhouses, stores, and the Amish themselves. Remember that you must slow down for horse-drawn buggies when you're driving on country roads.

VISITOR INFORMATION

The Pennsylvania Dutch Convention & Visitors Bureau is the welcome center for Pennsylvania Dutch Country, with a wide selection of brochures, maps, and other materials, as well as direct connections to hotels. There's also a multi-image presentation, "Lancaster County: People, Places & Passions," that serves as a good introduction to the area. It's open daily 8:30–5, 8–6 in summer. The Mennonite Information Center serves mainly to "interpret the faith and practice of the Mennonites and Amish to all who inquire." It has information on local inns and Mennonite guest homes as well as a 20-minute video about the Amish and Mennonite people. It's open Monday through Saturday 8–5. The Susquehanna Heritage Tourist Information Center has information about visiting the Susquehanna River town of Columbia. The Gettysburg Convention and Visitors Bureau, in the former Western Maryland Railroad Passenger Depot, has free brochures and maps of area attractions. Be sure to pick up a self-guided walking tour map of the town's Historic District, centered on Baltimore Street. You'll find a number of museums along the route, as well as markers that point out homes and sites significant to the history of the town and to the battle.

➤ INFORMATION: **Pennsylvania Dutch Convention & Visitors Bureau** (✉ 501 Greenfield Rd., Lancaster 17601, ☎ 717/299–8901 or 800/735–2629, WEB www.padutchcountry.com). **Mennonite Information Center** (✉ 2209 Millstream Rd., Lancaster 17602-1494, ☎ 717/299–0954 or 800/858–8320, WEB www.mennoniteinfoctr.com). **Susquehanna Heritage Tourist Information Center** (✉ 445 Linden St., Box 510, Columbia 17512, ☎ 717/684–5249, WEB www.parivertowns.com). The **Gettysburg Convention and Visitors Bureau** (✉ 35 Carlisle St., ☎ 717/334–6274, WEB www.gettysburg.com).

10 PORTRAITS OF PHILADELPHIA AND THE PENNSYLVANIA DUTCH COUNTRY

Portrait

Books and Videos

Map of Philadelphia and Vicinity

Smart Travel Tips A to Z

PORTRAIT OF
AN AMISH FAMILY

You may spot Joseph Stoltzfus working his fields with a team of horses as you drive the back roads of Lancaster County. You will certainly encounter his somber black buggy on one of the traffic-choked highways. Perhaps you will exchange a few words with his wife, Becky, in her plain dark dress and white cap, if you stop by their farmhouse to buy fresh eggs or to inspect the homemade quilts she has for sale. You might see their younger children playing in the yard of a one-room schoolhouse. And on certain Sundays you may pass the farmhouse where the Stoltzfus family and other Amish people gather to worship.

Stoltzfus is the most common of a dozen Amish family names; Jacob and Becky and their seven children are fictitious but typical of the more than 22,000 Amish (pronounced *Ah*-mish) in this area. Their roots and religious traditions reach back to 16th-century Europe. Every detail of their lives, from their clothing to the way they operate their farms, is an expression of their faith in God and their separateness from "the world"; every detail is dictated by the *Ordnung,* the rules of their church.

Becky Stoltzfus, like Amish women of any age, wears a one-piece dress in a dark color. The sleeves are long and straight, and her full skirt is hemmed modestly halfway between knees and ankles. The high, collarless neck is fastened shut in front with straight pins; buttons and safety pins are forbidden, although the Ordnung of some church districts allow hooks and eyes. She wears black stockings rolled below the knee and black low-heeled oxfords. At home in warm weather Becky and her family go barefoot.

Soon after her daughters were born, Becky made sure they wore the white organdy prayer cap. When Katie turned 12, she changed to a black cap for the Sunday preaching; after she marries she will wear the white cap all the time. Subtle differences in the head covering tell the Amish a great deal about one another. The width of the front part, the length of the ties, the style of the seams, and the way the pleats are ironed indicate where the woman lives and how conservative or liberal her church district is.

Becky has never cut or curled her hair, nor has she let it hang loose. She pins it in a plain knot at the back of her neck. She parts little Hannah's hair in the middle, plaits it, and fastens the two little braids in the back. When Becky is away from home, she wears a black bonnet with a deep scoop brim over her prayer cap.

The clothes Jacob wears are also carefully dictated by the Ordnung of his church district. For Sunday preaching he wears a *Mutze,* a long black frock coat with split tails and hook-and-eye closings but no collar or lapels. His vest is also fastened with hooks and eyes. Jacob's broadfall or "barn-door" trousers have no zipper, just a wide front flap that buttons along the sides; they have no creases and no belt—homemade suspenders hold them up. There are buttons on his shirt, the number specified by the Ordnung. Colored shirts are permitted, but stripes and prints are out. Neckties are forbidden.

When he's not dressed up, Jacob hangs up his Mutze and puts on a *Wamus,* a black sack coat with either a high, round neck or V-neck but neither lapels nor outside pockets. Sometimes the Wamus has hooks and eyes, but more liberal church districts allow buttons.

In winter Jacob and his sons wear broad-brim black felt hats; in summer they switch to straw. Ben and Ezra, Jacob's younger boys, have been wearing hats with 3-inch brims since they were little. Sam, the oldest son, wears a hat with a crease around the top of the crown, a sign (along with his sprouting beard) that he is newly married. The hat is a status symbol among the Amish. The grandfather's hat is higher in the crown than the father's, and its brim is 4 inches wide. The width of an Amish man's hat brim also signifies his degree of conservatism: the broader the brim, the more conservative the wearer.

Jacob's long beard is as much the mark of an Amish man as a broad-brim hat. He shaves only his upper lip, since mustaches are against the rules. He cuts his hair straight around, well below the ears. Ben and Ezra have theirs parted in the middle, with bangs across the forehead. Cutting it short—up to the earlobe—is a form of rebellion.

The style of the Amish buggy is as carefully prescribed as the style of the hat. The Stoltzfus family owns a black carriage with a gray top and big wooden wheels. The battery-powered side lamps, reflectors, and bright orange triangles have been added as required by Pennsylvania state law. The iron-tire wheels are precisely set, toed in slightly, farther apart at the top than at the bottom. A gear assembly at the pivot of the front axle adds stability. The brakes are operated by hand, an iron block pressed hard against the rear tire. This kind of brake is prescribed by the Ordnung; different groups permit different kinds of brakes. The Ordnung tells the buggy owner whether or not he may have roll-up side curtains or sliding glass doors, and if he is allowed a dashboard, a whipsocket, or other variations. Incidentally, the Amish can—and do—ride in cars owned by non-Amish people and travel on trains, buses, and even airplanes and taxis. But they are not allowed to *own* a car.

No electric wires lead from the power lines along the road into the neat, well-kept buildings of the Stoltzfus farm, a difference that distinguishes Amish farms from those of their non-Amish neighbors. The farms are small, no more than 50 or 60 acres, which is all that can be handled by a farmer limited to horse power.

The Stoltzfus house is spacious and uncluttered. There is no wall-to-wall carpeting to vacuum; instead, plain and unpatterned linoleum covers the floor. There are no curtains to wash or draperies to clean; although some church districts allow plain curtains on the lower half of the windows, this district permits only dark-green roller shades. There are no slipcovers or upholstery because upholstered furniture is not allowed.

Becky has a large kitchen where the family eats around a big wooden table. Afterward Becky and Katie and Hannah clean up the kitchen, wash the dishes, and put away leftover food in the gasoline-operated refrigerator. A one-cylinder engine in the cellar chugs noisily, powering the water pump, but many Amish families still rely on windmills or water power. A creek that runs through a farm also supplies water. Although labor-saving devices are generally forbidden, Becky does have a washing machine that runs by gasoline. Her stove burns kerosene; she would prefer bottled gas, but that is forbidden by the Ordnung of her district. She uses a treadle sewing machine and sews by the bright and steady light of a gasoline lamp.

About once a year it is the Stoltzfuses' turn to host the every-other-Sunday preaching service. As many as 175 people may attend: There are 90 members in the district, and double that number when unbaptized children are counted. The removable partitions built into the downstairs walls are folded back and furniture moved aside. The district's backless oak benches are brought in and set up in rows.

Jacob and Becky Stoltzfus are fluent in English, but the language they speak among themselves is Pennsylvania Dutch, a German dialect related to the dialects spoken in the part of Germany from which their Amish ancestors came. It is primarily a spoken language and spelling varies with the writer. "Dutch" actually means *Deutsch,* or German, and some scholars call the dialect Pennsylvania German. Many Pennsylvanians of German descent speak the dialect, but among the Amish it is the mother tongue, the first language an Amish child learns to speak and another mark of separation from the world.

When Hannah, Becky's youngest child, starts school, she will learn to speak and read and write in the language of "the world." Jacob and Becky want their children to know English because their survival depends on good business relationships with English-speaking people.

About the same time Hannah Stoltzfus starts to learn English, she will also be taught High German, the language of religion. The family Bible is written in High German, and she and her brothers and sisters must learn to read it. By the time they are baptized, in their late teens, they will be able to understand most of the Sunday sermon and to join in the prayers and hymns. Most Amish can't carry on a conversation in High German and have no need to do so unless they are ordained church officials who must preach sermons and pray. But everyone needs to be able to read and to listen.

The outsider may not notice the inconspicuous building on a back road where Ben and Ezra and Annie Stoltzfus attend school, along with eight grades of children in one room. They are taught by a young Amish woman with only an eighth-grade education. Amish children are not sent to public school, and Amish schools continue only as far as the eighth grade. That's time enough to learn the basics of reading, writing, and arithmetic.

Schools are built to serve children within a 2-mi radius so that no one has far to walk. Some children go to old one-room schoolhouses once owned by the public school district. When districts consolidated, the Amish bought the obsolete schools and remodeled them—not modern-

izing them but ripping out the electric wiring. Since none was available near the Stoltzfus farm, the Amish fathers in that area built a plain cinder-block structure with big windows to take advantage of natural light.

Stepping into an Amish schoolhouse is like entering a time machine and emerging 80 or more years in the past. At 8:30 the teacher pulls the rope to ring the old-fashioned bell on the roof. Then the children line up and file through the big front door into the cloakroom. They hang their hats and jackets on pegs, line up their lunch boxes, and go quietly to their carefully refinished old-fashioned desks.

The school day begins with the roll call. During peak periods of farm work, the Amish close down the schools for a few days; they also stop earlier in the spring than the public schools. They make up for the time by taking only a short Christmas break and celebrating none of the national holidays.

Next, the teacher reads to the pupils from the German Bible, then everyone recites the Lord's Prayer in German. Except for the lessons in reading German Scriptures and prayers, the teacher speaks exclusively English in the classroom.

Beside the teacher's desk is a "recitation bench." There are more than 30 students in the eight grades, and each class of three or four or five comes forward by turns to recite its lessons. There is no competition to come up with the answer first, and they all respond in a singsong chorus.

Because it is essential to the work of a farmer, arithmetic is considered very important. Picking readers (books) for the pupils is not easy. The parents want the subject matter to be about farm living, not city life; and, they want the stories to teach a moral lesson; fairy tales, myths, and fantasies are taboo.

During the 15-minute morning recess, Ezra and Ben and the other boys play baseball. One of the rules of the Amish schoolyard is that children are never allowed to stand around by themselves; everyone must be included in the group. Annie and the older girls play blindman's bluff; the younger ones, joined by their teacher, race around in a game of tag.

The Amish want their children to learn to work together as a group, not to compete as individuals. Preserving tradition is a goal; reasoning abstractly is not. Asking too many questions is not acceptable. Discipline is strict; the only voices heard in the schoolroom are those of the teacher and the pupils who are reciting. The Amish expect pupils to master the material unquestioningly: Memorization replaces reasoning in a culture dominated by oral tradition. Thoroughness is valued more than rapid learning. Teachers believe that intellectual talents are a gift from God and that children should be encouraged to use the gift by helping others in the school.

Before the day is over, there is time for singing. Singing is a vital part of the Amish tradition, important in their religious life and in their social life as well. There are no songs with harmonization for the Amish; unaccompanied unison singing is the universal rule. The Amish have their own style of singing, in which the leader (*Vorsanger*) sings the first word and everybody else joins in for the rest of the line.

For years public school authorities were in conflict with the Amish. Truancy laws were enforced, and Amish fathers were often arrested and jailed for refusing to send older children to school. But in 1972 the United States Supreme Court ruled that the Amish are exempt from state compulsory education laws that require a child to attend beyond the eighth grade; they found that such laws violate Constitutional rights to freedom of religion.

Today the Amish accept the idea of sending their children to school for eight years to learn what they need to survive in the 20th-century rural economy. But what Amish children really need to know in order to survive in the Amish culture they learn from

their parents and from other adults in the community. Most of the practical knowledge of farmers and housewives is acquired not in books but in a family apprenticeship.

The marriage of Jacob and Becky Stoltzfus is a very practical affair. The Amish are quite realistic about their expectations. They do not marry for love or romance but out of mutual respect and the need for a partner in the kind of life they expect to live. The farmer needs a wife, and they both need children. Marriage is essential to the Amish community; divorce is unknown; separation is rare. Marriage is the climax of the rite of passage that begins with baptism, the signal of the arrival of adulthood and sober responsibility.

From the time they reach the age of *Rum Schpringe* (running around—about 16 for boys, a bit younger for girls) and for the next half-dozen years until each marries, Joe Stoltzfus and his sister Katie do much of their socializing at Sunday-night singings, usually held at the farm where the preaching service takes place in the morning. Singings are functions of the church district, which helps keep dating and eventually marriage, within the group.

Although outsiders believe that the social life of an Amish teenager begins with a singing and ends with a buggy ride home at a respectably early hour, Amish dating is actually much livelier. Among the more liberal groups, the old-fashioned singings can turn quickly into rowdy, foot-stomping hoedowns. A few bring out harmonicas, guitars, and other forbidden instruments; older boys haul in cases of beer. Few outsiders attend these events.

On the "off Sunday," when there is no preaching service, young unmarried people go courting—but always in secret. Before they marry, they are never seen together in public as a couple except as they leave a singing or a barn dance.

Bundling, the practice of courting in bed fully clothed, is usually attributed to the Amish. No one is quite sure whether the Amish do or don't, but the consensus is that the girl's parents, rather than the Ordnung, have the final say.

There is a saying that if a boy can persuade his girl to take off her prayer cap, she'll have sex with him. Evidently that doesn't happen often because the rate of premarital pregnancies among the Amish is quite low. Premarital sex is forbidden, birth control is taboo, and sex education is nonexistent.

When Jacob's son Sam married Sarah Beiler, their wedding was held after the harvest in November. December is the second most popular month for weddings, and there are traditionally only two possible days in the week for the ceremony: Tuesday and Thursday. Sarah chose Thursday. Now they're living on the Stoltzfus farm.

The average age at marriage of Amish couples has been rising because of the problems of accumulating enough money to establish a household and to acquire land. Many Amish parents retire while they are still relatively young, especially if they have a son who needs a farm. Sam and Sarah have moved into the "grandfather's house," a section of Jacob's farmhouse built to accommodate a second generation. In a few years, when Sam assumes full responsibility for the farm and has children, he and Sarah will move into the larger part of the house, and Jacob and Becky will move into the grandfather's house.

To understand the Amish as something more than a quaint anachronism, turn back the calendar to 16th-century Europe. The Roman Catholic Church wielded tremendous influence, and many blamed the church for society's ills. When Martin Luther launched the Protestant Reformation in 1517, he had many opponents in addition to the Roman Catholic Church. One was Ulrich Zwingli, a radical Swiss Protestant, who also opposed Conrad Grebel. Grebel's followers wanted to establish free congregations of believers baptized as adults who made a confession of faith and committed themselves freely to a Christian life. Backing Zwingli, the Great Council of Zurich announced that babies must be baptized within eight days after their birth or the parents would be exiled.

This marked the beginning of Anabaptism, which means "rebaptized." Regarded as radically left wing, the Anabaptist movement posed a threat to the Roman Catholic and Protestant establishments. Anabaptist leaders were imprisoned, beaten, and killed; by the end of the 16th century nearly all the Anabaptists of Switzerland and Germany had been put to death.

But the movement spread through Central and Western Europe. Menno Simons, a former Roman Catholic priest, became one of those persecuted for Anabaptist preaching. His followers were called Mennonites. And although they were hounded by Catholics and other Protestants, dissension began to grow among the Mennonites themselves. A principal source of disagreement was the interpretation of the *Meidung*, the practice of shunning church members who had broken a rule. Shunning was based on St. Paul's advice to the Corinthians to avoid keeping company and eating with sinners. The Mennonites interpreted this to mean the member was to be subjected to Meidung only at communion. But Jacob Amman, a young Mennonite bishop, insisted that the Meidung meant that the rule-breaker must be shunned totally, even by his family.

The controversy grew, and in 1697 the stubborn and fiery Jacob Amman broke from the Mennonites. His followers, known as the Amish, became known for their unwillingness to change. Although the difference in clothing detail was not a primary issue, it did become symbolic of the split. The Amish became known as the *Haftlers* (Hook-and-eyers), while the more worldly Mennonites were called the *Knopflers* (Buttoners).

Meanwhile, King Charles II of England granted a large province in the American colonies to William Penn.

A devout Quaker, Penn believed he could offer refuge, freedom, and equality to the persecuted. Penn arrived in 1682, and the following year Francis Daniel Pastorius of the Frankfort Land Company brought the first group of Mennonites to Pennsylvania. The first Amish immigrants left Switzerland and the Palatinate of Germany in 1727, settling near Hamburg north of Reading.

By the start of the Revolutionary War, about half of the 225,000 Pennsylvania colonists were German, but only a small minority were Amish and Mennonite. The English scorned the Germans and tried to anglicize them. But the Amish and Mennonites were determined to hold on to their religion.

The Amish of Pennsylvania were all of one conservative mind until 1850, when a schism divided the Amish into two main factions. The more progressive group built meeting houses, which earned them the label "Church Amish," to distinguish them from the stricter "House Amish," who continued to worship in their homes. Since then innumerable splits have been caused by various interpretations of the Meidung or by different details of the Ordnung.

Every society changes to some extent, and in every society there are a few people who cannot adjust. The Amish are no exception. Many leave; there is generally a shortage of young men in the Amish community because most of the dissidents who leave are male. But some exert pressure for changes in the Ordnung that result in splits. Today there are 8 Amish, 24 Mennonite, and 9 Brethren groups in the Lancaster area.

The ultimate control exerted by the Amish to keep the members in strict adherence to the Ordnung is the Meidung. No one will speak to the person, eat with him, conduct business with him, or have anything to do with him while he is under the ban. It can last for a lifetime, unless the sinner mends his ways, begs for forgiveness, and is readmitted to fellowship by a unanimous vote of the congregation.

Visitors are sometimes surprised to learn that "Pennsylvania Dutch" and "Amish" are not synonymous. Many of the early settlers of Pennsylvania came from Germany at Penn's invitation; many were farmers, most were Protestant, and they spoke the same dialect. Despite these similarities, the Amish refer to all non-Amish as "English." These English include the Pennsylvania Dutch who permit hex signs on their farms (the Amish do not) and whose ancestors decorated useful items such as furniture with colorful designs. The work of Amish craftsmen is competent but plain.

The Amish are generally friendly and hospitable people. Tape recorders and cameras are not welcome, but a visitor who is sincerely interested in the Amish people and does not act like an interrogator can quietly learn something about their unique way of life.

— Carolyn Meyer

Portrait

WHAT TO READ & WATCH BEFORE YOU GO

Fiction

"Writing fiction set in Philadelphia is tough," says novelist Steve Lopez. "There is nothing you can make up that is any more unbelievable than what actually happens here." Nonetheless, Lopez succeeded with *Third and Indiana,* a hard-edged story set in Philadelphia's "badlands;" *The Sunday Macaroni Club;* and *Land of Giants. God's Pocket,* by Pete Dexter; *South Street,* by David Bradley; and *Payback,* by Philip Harper, also capture the grittier side of the City of Brotherly Love.

Michael Shaara's Pulitzer Prize–winning *The Killer Angels* is a gripping account of the battle at Gettysburg.

History and Background

Philadelphia: A 300-Year History, with essays edited by Russell F. Weigley, is the best overall text. Ron Avery condenses those three centuries into the compact, easy-to-read *A Concise History of Philadelphia.* Catherine Drinker Bowen's *Miracle at Philadelphia* tells the story of the Constitution. In *Philly Firsts,* Janice L. Booker explores the unique ideas, products, and inventions that the city's natives have dreamed up—from Girl Scout cookies to the tranquilizing chair.

For biographies of seven Philadelphians, read *Philadelphia: Patricians and Philistines, 1900 to 1950,* by John Lukacs. *Puritan Boston and Quaker Philadelphia* by the late E. Digby Baltzell, is a scholarly work that compares the two cities. *Christopher Morley's Philadelphia* is edited by Ken Kalfus. Robert Lawson's *Ben and Me,* a classic children's story, gives a mouse's view of Ben Franklin's life.

Buzz Bissinger's *A Prayer for the City* assesses the struggles and achievements of Mayor Ed Rendell during the 1990s. *South Philadelphia,* by Philadelphia *Inquirer* reporter Murray Dubin, is both a memoir and an oral history that describes a well-known neighborhood. Harry D. Boonin's illustrated *The Jewish Quarter of Philadelphia: A History and Guide 1881–1930* traces the story of the area around South Street. Philip Stevick's *Imagining Philadelphia* looks at how visitors to Philadelphia since 1800 have perceived the city.

Sightseeing and Touring

The Foundation for Architecture's *Philadelphia Architecture: A Guide to the City* contains maps, photos, biographies of noted Philadelphia architects, and descriptions of almost 400 sites. *Historic Houses of Philadelphia,* by Roger W. Moss, includes stunning color photos and historical notes about 50 of the area's museum homes. Francis Morrone's 1999 *Architectural Guidebook to Philadelphia* is illustrated with photographs. *Cultural Connections, Museums and Libraries of Philadelphia and the Delaware Valley,* by Morris J. Vogel, has photos and text on sites throughout the region. *Frank Furness: The Complete Works,* by George E. Thomas, Jeffrey A. Cohen, and Michael J. Lewis, assesses one of Philadelphia's most original architects. *Eastern State Penitentiary: Crucible of Good Intentions,* by Norman Johnston, discusses the influence of the city's massive prison.

Guides to Philadelphia's spectacular collection of outdoor art include *Sculpture of a City,* by the Fairmount Park Art Association, with text and photos; *Philadelphia's Outdoor Art: A Walking Tour,* by Roslyn F. Brenner, describing more than 50 works of art along Benjamin Franklin Parkway; and the comprehensive *Public Art in Philadelphia,* by Penny Balkin Bach. Garden lovers will want to study *Gardens of Philadelphia and the Delaware Valley,* by William M. Klein

Jr., which has photographs. *Rediscovering the Wissahickon,* by Sarah West, gives mapped geology and history walks for this lovely area of Fairmount Park.

Other selections are *Country Walks and Bikeways in the Philadelphia Region,* by Alan Fisher; *Philadelphia and Its Countryside,* by Ruth Hoover Seitz, which has photographs; and *Around Philadelphia With Kids,* by Andrea Lehman, and *The Mid-Atlantic's Best Bed & Breakfasts,* both published Fodor's Travel Publications. *Pennsylvania,* a Compass America Guide by Douglas Root, has color photographs and historical and cultural information.

Videos

Rocky, with Sylvester Stallone (1976), and its four sequels describe the adventures of an underdog Philadelphia boxer. *Philadelphia* (1993) stars Tom Hanks as a lawyer who is dismissed from his job because he is battling AIDS. In *Witness* (1985) Philadelphia police detective Harrison Ford has to live undercover with the Amish. The four-hour movie *Gettysburg,* based on Michael Shaara's novel *The Killer Angels,* captures the intensity of the Civil War battle. Philadelphia filmmaker M. Night Shyamalan shot two recent movies in his hometown—*The Sixth Sense* (1999) and *Unbreakable* (2000). Both star Bruce Willis. The corner of 3rd and Arch streets in Old City, along with its closely surrounding blocks, was transformed into a mid-1880's Cincinnati shopping district, complete with horse-drawn carriages, for *Beloved* (1998).

Philadelphia and Vicinity

N

TO POCONOS

Zieglersville

Schwenksville

Kulpsville

Pottstown

Skippack

476

202

Evansburg
State Park

Center Square

73

100

Norristown

276

Valley Forge
National
Historic Park

Bridgeport

476

King of Prussia

Conshohe

PENNSYLVANIA

Pennsylvania Tnpk.

76

76

202

Radnor

Villanova

30

Devon

Mer

Paoli

Bryn Mawr

30

Haverford
Ardmore

Newtown Square

476

West Chester Pike

3

320

Upper
Darby

1

322

West
Chester

Springfield

13

100

252

202

Media

Swarthmore

BRANDYWINE

52

322

Wallingford

100

Chadds
Ford

322

1

Longwood
Gardens

Chester

VALLEY

52

Delaware River

100

Bridgeport

202

DELAWARE

95

Penns
Grove

295

322

495

Wilmington

Chalfont

Washington
Crossing

29

32

95

Warrington

232

Trenton

Montgomeryville

611

Yardley

Newtown

1

Warminster

Richboro

532

Horsham

132

Southampton

1

309

276

Feasterville

13

Willow
Grove

Bryn
Athyn

Pennsylvania

Tnpk.

Fort
Washington

95

Abington

Burlington

Jenkintown

13

Delaware River

541

Cheltenham

1

The
Wissahickon

73

Riverside

Schuylkill River

1

13

130

95

Bela-
Cynwyd

611

Betsy
Ross Br.

38

Fairmount
Park

PHILADELPHIA

76

Ben
Franklin Br.

73

Pennsauken

291

Camden

676

Cherry Hill

70

Walt
Whitman Br.

Gloucester
City

295

Marlton

95

Philadelphia
International
Airport

NEW JERSEY

30

Woodbury

130

New Jersey Tnpk.

0   10 miles

0   15 km

ESSENTIAL INFORMATION

ADDRESSES

Philadelphia is a city of distinct neighborhoods and some named streets (as opposed to numbered streets) repeat in more than one neighborhood. You will find several streets coming to an end at the Schuylkill River or Fairmount Park only to resume at the other side. It is important therefore to phone ahead for driving directions if you are traveling to destinations in neighborhoods beyond Center City.

AIR TRAVEL

BOOKING YOUR FLIGHT

When you book **look for nonstop flights** and **remember that "direct" flights stop at least once.** Try to avoid connecting flights, which require a change of plane. For more booking tips and to check prices and make on-line flight reservations, log on to www.fodors.com.

CARRIERS

All major airlines offer service to and from Philadelphia. It is a hub city for US Airways, which offers the most nonstop domestic flights. You can find discounted airfares on the smaller carriers Air Tran and Midwest Express. Both US Airways and British Airways offer daily nonstop service from London, while Air France frequently offers discounted fares from London with a stop in Paris.

➤ MAJOR AIRLINES: **American** (☎ 800/433–7300). **Continental** (☎ 800/523–3273). **Delta** (☎ 800/221–1212). **Northwest** (☎ 800/225–2525). **TWA** (☎ 800/221–2000). **United** (☎ 800/241–6522). **US Airways** (☎ 800/428–4322).

➤ SMALLER AIRLINES: **Air Tran** (☎ 800/825–8538). **Midwest Express** (☎ 800/452–2022).

➤ FROM CANADA: **Air Canada** (☎ 888/247–2262).

➤ FROM THE U.K.: **British Airways** (☎ 0345/222–111). **Air France** (☎ 0845/0845–111). **American** (☎ 0345/789-789), via Boston. **United** (☎ 0800/888–555), via New York. **Virgin Atlantic** (☎ 01293/747–747), via Washington, D.C. or New York.

CHECK-IN & BOARDING

For domestic flights, arrive at the airport at least two hours before your scheduled departure time. For international flights, plan on arriving at the airport at least 2½ hours before departure, but be sure to ask your carrier whether it requires an earlier check-in.

Assuming that not everyone with a ticket will show up, airlines routinely overbook planes. When everyone does, airlines ask for volunteers to give up their seats. In return, these volunteers usually get a certificate for a free flight and are rebooked on the next flight out. If there are not enough volunteers, the airline must choose who will be denied boarding. The first to get bumped are passengers who checked in late and those flying on discounted tickets, so **get to the gate and check in as early as possible,** especially during peak periods.

Always **bring a government-issued photo I.D. to the airport;** a passport is best. You will be asked to show it before you are allowed to check in.

CUTTING COSTS

The least-expensive airfares to Philadelphia and the Pennsylvania Dutch Country must usually be purchased in advance and are non-refundable. It's smart to **call a number of airlines, and when you are quoted a good price, book it on the spot**—the same fare may not be available the next day. Always **check different routings** and look into using different airports. The airlines' Web sites often offer reduced fares for tickets purchased via the Internet. Travel agents, especially low-fare specialists (☞ Discounts & Deals), are helpful.

Consolidators are another good source. They buy tickets for scheduled international flights at reduced rates from the airlines, then sell them at prices that beat the best fare available directly from the airlines, usually without restrictions. Sometimes you can even get your money back if you need to return the ticket. Carefully read the fine print detailing penalties for changes and cancellations, and **confirm your consolidator reservation with the airline.**

➤ CONSOLIDATORS: **Cheap Tickets** (☎ 800/377–1000). **Discount Airline Ticket Service** (☎ 800/576–1600). **Unitravel** (☎ 800/325–2222). **Up & Away Travel** (☎ 212/889–2345). **World Travel Network** (☎ 800/409–6753).

ENJOYING THE FLIGHT

For more legroom, **request an emergency-aisle seat.** Don't sit in the row in front of the emergency aisle or in front of a bulkhead, where seats may not recline. If you have dietary concerns, **ask for special meals when booking.** These can be vegetarian, low-cholesterol, or kosher, for example. On long flights, try to maintain a normal routine, to help fight jet lag. At night, **get some sleep.** By day, **eat light meals, drink water** (not alcohol), and **move around the cabin** to stretch your legs. For additional jet-lag tips consult *Fodor's FYI: Travel Fit & Healthy* (available at bookstores everywhere).

FLYING TIMES

Flying time from Boston is 1 hour; from Chicago, 2¼ hours; from Miami, 2½ hours; from Los Angeles, 6 hours; from London, 7 hours.

HOW TO COMPLAIN

If your baggage goes astray or your flight goes awry, complain right away. Most carriers require that you **file a claim immediately.**

➤ AIRLINE COMPLAINTS: U.S. Department of Transportation **Aviation Consumer Protection Division** (✉ C-75, Room 4107, Washington, DC 20590, ☎ 202/366–2220, WEB www.dot.gov/airconsumer). Federal Aviation Administration **Consumer Hotline** (☎ 800/322–7873).

The major gateway to Philadelphia is Philadelphia International Airport (PHL), 8 mi from downtown in the southwest part of the city. Renovations in the past few years have made the terminals more appealing; shops and more eating options are welcome additions.

➤ AIRPORT INFORMATION: **Philadelphia International Airport** (✉ 8900 Essington Ave., off I–95, ☎ 215/937–6800 for operator and lost and found; 800/745–4283 for arrival and departure times and gate assignments, WEB www.phl.org).

AIRPORT TRANSFERS

Allow at least a half hour, more during rush hour, for the 8-mi trip between the airport and Center City. By car the airport is accessible via I–95 south or I–76 east.

Taxis at the airport are plentiful but expensive—a flat fee of $20 plus tip. Follow the signs in the airport and wait in line for a taxi. Shuttle buses are also available. They cost $10 and up per person and will make most requested stops downtown as well as to the suburbs. You can make shuttle arrangements at the centralized ground transportation counter in the baggage claim areas.

SEPTA (Southeastern Pennsylvania Transportation Authority) runs the Airport Rail Line R1, which leaves the airport every 30 minutes from 6:10 AM to 12:10 AM. The trip to Center City takes about 20 minutes and costs $5. Trains serve the 30th Street, Suburban (Center City), and Market East stations.

➤ LIMOUSINES: **Carey Limousine Philadelphia** (☎ 215/492–8402). **London Limousine and Town Car Service** (☎ 800/834–0708).

➤ TRAIN: **Airport Information Desk** (☎ 800/745–4283, for schedules and information). **SEPTA** (☎ 215/580–7800).

Greyhound Lines operates long-haul service to Baltimore, Washington, DC, New York, Wilmington, and points

beyond out of the terminal at 10th and Filbert streets, just north of the Market East commuter rail station. NJ Transit stops at the Greyhound terminal and offers service between Philadelphia and Atlantic City and other New Jersey destinations.

➤ BUS INFORMATION: **Greyhound Lines** (☎ 215/931–4075 or 800/231–2222). **New Jersey Transit** (☎ 215/569–3752).

PAYING

You may purchase long-haul bus tickets from Greyhound and New Jersey Transit with cash, traveler's checks, or a major credit card.

BUS TRAVEL

AROUND PHILADELPHIA

Buses make up the bulk of the SEPTA system, with 110 routes extending throughout the city and into the suburbs. While the buses are comfortable and reliable, they should only be used when you are not in a hurry as traffic on the city's major thoroughfares can add some time to your trip. Bus 76, called the "Ben FrankLine," connects the zoo in West Fairmount Park with Penn's Landing at the Delaware River, stopping at major sights along the way, including the Pennsylvania Convention Center and the Philadelphia Museum of Art. Route 76 operates daily from around 9 to 6.

The distinctive purple minibuses you'll see around Center City are SEPTA's convenience line for visitors, the PHLASH. The 33 stops in the loop run from the Philadelphia Museum of Art on the Benjamin Franklin Parkway through Center City to Penn's Landing. Since a ride on the PHLASH costs $2 for a one-way ticket, **consider the handy all-day, unlimited-ride pass available for $4.** These buses run daily from 10 AM to midnight in summer, 10 to 6 September 15–May 14. There's service every 10 minutes.

FARES & SCHEDULES

The base fare for subways, trolleys, and buses is $2, paid with exact change or a token. Transfers cost 60¢. Senior citizens (with valid I.D.) ride free during off-peak hours and holidays. Tokens sell for $1.30 and can

be purchased in packages of 2, 5, or 10 from cashiers along the Broad Street subway and Market-Frankford lines and in many downtown stores (including some Rite Aid pharmacies).

If you plan to travel extensively within Center City, it's a good idea to **get a SEPTA pass.** The Day Pass costs $5 and is good for 24 hours of unlimited use on all SEPTA vehicles within the city, plus one trip on any regional rail line including the Airport Express train. A weekly transit pass costs $18.75. Tokens and transit passes are good on buses and subways but not on commuter rail lines.

You can purchase tokens and transit passes in the SEPTA sales offices in the concourse below the northwest corner of 15th and Market streets; in the Market East station (✉ 8th and Market Sts.); and in 30th Street Station (✉ 30th and Market Sts.)

Though SEPTA's automated answering system has cut down on your phone wait, **be prepared for a busy signal and a long time on hold.**

➤ BUS INFORMATION: **SEPTA** (☎ 215/580–7800; 215/580–7777 for a schedule, WEB www.septa.com). **PHLASH** (☎ 215/474–5274).

PAYING

You may purchase bus tokens and tickets with cash. Purchases of over $25 can also be made with traveler's checks, Visa or MasterCard.

SMOKING

There is a no smoking policy on SEPTA buses.

BUSINESS HOURS

Banks are open weekdays 9–3; a few are open Saturday 9–noon. The main post office is open 24 hours daily; some branches are open 9 to 5 weekdays, and Saturday 9 to noon. All banks and post offices are closed on national holidays.

MUSEUMS & SIGHTS

Many museums and sights are open 10–5; a few stay open late one or two evenings a week, and a number are closed on Monday. Historic Area sights are open daily, with longer hours in summer, but it's wise to check ahead.

PHARMACIES

Most Center City pharmacies are open 9–6. Hours vary in the outlying neighborhoods and suburbs.

SHOPS

Downtown shopping hours are generally 9:30 or 10 to 5 or 6. Many stores are open until 9 PM on Wednesday. Most downtown stores are closed on Sunday, but the Gallery, the Shops at Liberty Place, and some stores in the Bellevue are open noon–5 or 6. The Bourse is open Sundays 11–5 from spring to fall. Antiques stores and art galleries may be closed some mornings or weekdays; it's wise to call ahead for hours.

CAMERAS & PHOTOGRAPHY

The *Kodak Guide to Shooting Great Travel Pictures* (available at bookstores everywhere) is loaded with tips.

➤ PHOTO HELP: **Kodak Information Center** (☎ 800/242–2424).

EQUIPMENT PRECAUTIONS

Don't pack film and equipment in checked luggage, where it is much more susceptible to damage. X-ray machines used to view checked luggage are becoming much more powerful and therefore are much more likely to ruin your film. Always **keep film and tape out of the sun.** Carry an extra supply of batteries, and **be prepared to turn on your camera or camcorder** to prove to security personnel that the device is real. Always **ask for hand inspection of film,** which becomes clouded after repeated exposure to airport X-ray machines, and **keep videotapes away from metal detectors.**

CAR RENTAL

Rates in Philadelphia begin at $25 a day and $176 a week for an economy car with air-conditioning, an automatic transmission, and unlimited mileage. This does not include airport surcharges and the tax on car rentals, which is 9%.

➤ MAJOR AGENCIES: **Alamo** (☎ 800/327–9633; 020/8759–6200 in the U.K.). **Avis** (☎ 800/331–1212; 800/879–2847 in Canada; 02/9353–9000 in Australia; 09/525–1982 in New Zealand; 0870/606–0100 in the U.K.). **Budget** (☎ 800/527–0700; 0144/227–6266 in the U.K., through affiliate Europcar). **Dollar** (☎ 800/800–4000; 0124/622–0111 in the U.K., where it is known as Sixt Kenning; 02/9223–1444 in Australia). **Hertz** (☎ 800/654–3131; 800/263–0600 in Canada; 020/8897–2072 in the U.K.; 02/9669–2444 in Australia; 09/256–8690 in New Zealand). **National Car Rental** (☎ 800/227–7368; 0845/722–2525 in the U.K., where it is known as National Europe).

CUTTING COSTS

To get the best deal, **book through a travel agent who will shop around.** Also **price local car-rental companies,** although the service and maintenance may not be as good as those of a major player. Remember to ask about required deposits, cancellation penalties, and drop-off charges if you're planning to pick up the car in one city and leave it in another. If you're traveling during a holiday period, also make sure that a confirmed reservation guarantees you a car.

➤ LOCAL AGENCIES: **Ace Rent-a-Car** (☎ 215/492–8554 or 888/386–7368). **Enterprise Rent-a-Car** (☎ 800/736–8222).

INSURANCE

When driving a rented car you are generally responsible for any damage to or loss of the vehicle as well as for any property damage or personal injury that you may cause. Before you rent, see what coverage your personal auto-insurance policy and credit cards provide.

For about $15 to $20 per day, rental companies sell protection, known as a collision- or loss-damage waiver (CDW or LDW), that eliminates your liability for damage to the car. In most states you don't need a CDW if you have personal auto insurance or other liability insurance. However, **make sure you have enough coverage to pay for the car.** If you do not have auto insurance or an umbrella policy that covers damage to third parties, purchasing liability insurance and a CDW or LDW is highly recommended.

REQUIREMENTS & RESTRICTIONS

In Philadelphia and the Pennsylvania Dutch Country you must be 21 to rent a car, and rates may be higher if you're under 25. You'll pay extra for child seats (about $3 a day), which are compulsory for children under five, and for additional drivers (about $2 per day). Non-U.S. residents need a reservation voucher (for prepaid reservations that were made in the traveler's home country), a passport, a driver's license, and a travel policy that covers each driver, when picking up a car.

SURCHARGES

Before you pick up a car in one city and leave it in another, **ask about drop-off charges or one-way service fees,** which can be substantial. Note, too, that some rental agencies charge extra if you return the car before the time specified in your contract. To avoid a hefty refueling fee, **fill the tank just before you turn in the car,** but be aware that gas stations near the rental outlet may overcharge.

CAR TRAVEL

Getting to and around Philadelphia by car can be difficult and at rush hour can be a nightmare. The main east–west freeway through the city, the Schuylkill Expressway (I–76), is often tied up for miles.

The main north–south highway through Philadelphia is the Delaware Expressway (I–95). To reach Center City heading southbound on I–95, take the Vine Street exit.

From the west the Pennsylvania Turnpike begins at the Ohio border and intersects the Schuylkill Expressway (I–76) at Valley Forge. The Schuylkill Expressway has several exits in Center City. The Northeast Extension of the turnpike, renamed I–476, runs from Scranton to Plymouth Meeting, north of Philadelphia. From the east the New Jersey Turnpike and I–295 access U.S. 30, which enters the city via the Benjamin Franklin Bridge, or New Jersey Route 42 and the Walt Whitman Bridge into South Philadelphia.

With the exception of a few wide streets (notably the Benjamin Franklin Parkway, Broad Street, Vine Street,

and part of Market Street), streets in Center City are narrow and one-way. Philadelphia's compact 2-square-mi downtown is laid out in a grid. The traditional heart of the city is Broad and Market streets, where City Hall stands. Market Street divides the city north and south; 130 South 15th Street, for example, is in the second block south of Market Street. North–south streets are numbered, starting with Front (1st) Street, at the Delaware River, and increasing to the west. Broad Street, recently renamed the Avenue of the Arts, is the equivalent of 14th Street. The diagonal Benjamin Franklin Parkway breaks the grid pattern by leading from City Hall out of Center City into Fairmount Park.

EMERGENCY SERVICES

If you have a AAA membership card, you can dial the group's toll-free number for emergency road service. If not, call the mechanics at Philadelphia Motorworld for round-the-clock service.

➤ CONTACTS: **AAA Mid-Atlantic** (✉ 2040 Market St., ☎ 215/864–5000; 800/222–4357 for emergency service). **Philadelphia Motorworld** (✉ Washington La. and Ogontz Ave., ☎ 215/425–2331).

PARKING

Parking in Center City can be tough. A spot at a parking meter, if you're lucky enough to find one, costs 25¢ per 15 minutes. Parking garages are plentiful, especially around Independence Hall, City Hall, and the Pennsylvania Convention Center, but can charge up to $1.50 per 15 minutes and up to $20 or so for the day. Police officers are vigilant about ticketing illegally parked cars and fines begin at $25. Fortunately the city is compact, and you can easily **get around downtown on foot or by bus after you park your car.**

ROAD CONDITIONS

Use extra caution when maneuvering the narrow one-way streets of Center City. Drivers on the Philadelphia stretch of the Schuylkill Expressway (I–76) routinely drive well over the speed limit (and the many accidents on this highway attest to this). If you can, choose gentler routes to your destination, such as Kelly Drive or West River Drive.

RULES OF THE ROAD

Always **strap children 4 and under into approved child-safety seats.** Pennsylvania law requires all passengers to wear seat belts. In Pennsylvania, unless otherwise indicated, you may turn right at a red light after stopping if there is no oncoming traffic. When in doubt, wait for the green. Speed limits in Philadelphia are generally 35–40 mph, 55 mph on the surrounding highways.

CHILDREN IN PHILADELPHIA

Philadelphia has many attractions and activities for young ones. The Please Touch Museum is designed for youngsters ages 1–7. Several museums, including the Franklin Institute, Academy of Natural Sciences, and the Independence Seaport Museum, are entertaining for children of all ages. Others, such as the Philadelphia Museum of Art, offer weekly children's activities and entertainment. Playgrounds abound in Center City and in the outlying neighborhoods. Many restaurants offer children's menus. If you are renting a car, don't forget to **arrange for a car seat** when you reserve.

Pick up copies of the free monthly publications *Parents Express* and *Metrokids,* which include up-to-date listings of museum exhibitions, festivals, films, and bookstore readings for children. These are available in bookstores, cafés, and libraries. *Fodor's Around Philadelphia with Kids* can help you plan your days together. For general advice about traveling with children, consult *Fodor's FYI: Travel with Your Baby.* Both Fodor's titles are available in bookstores everywhere.

➤ LOCAL INFORMATION: **Metrokids** (✉ ☎ 215/291–5560, WEB www. metrokids.com). **Parents Express** (✉ ☎ 215/629–1774).

BABY-SITTING

Baby-sitting services are offered at several upscale hotels. In hotels where they are not offered, the front desk or concierge may provide referrals.

FLYING

If your children are two or older, **ask about children's airfares.** As a general rule, infants under two not occupying a seat fly at greatly reduced fares or even for free. Experts agree that it's a good idea to use safety seats aloft for children weighing less than 40 pounds. Airlines set their own policies: U.S. carriers usually require that the child be ticketed, even if he or she is young enough to ride free, since the seats must be strapped into regular seats. Do **check your airline's policy about using safety seats during takeoff and landing.** And since safety seats are not allowed everywhere in the plane, get your seat assignments early.

When reserving, **request children's meals or a freestanding bassinet** if you need them. But note that bulkhead seats, where you must sit to use the bassinet, may lack an overhead bin or storage space on the floor.

LODGING

Most hotels in Philadelphia allow children under a certain age to stay in their parents' room at no extra charge, but others charge for them as extra adults; be sure to **find out the cutoff age for children's discounts.** The Loews Hotel offers ½ price for adjoining rooms, book and game rentals, and supervised children's recreation activities. The Four Seasons caters to young people with child-size robes and children's toiletries, babysitting referrals, and special room-service menus for children.

➤ BEST CHOICES: **Loews Philadelphia Hotel** (☎ 215/627–1200 or 800/235–6397). **Four Seasons Hotel** (☎ 215/963–1500).

SIGHTS & ATTRACTIONS

Places that are especially appealing to children are indicated by a rubber-duckie icon (🦆) in the margin.

TRANSPORTATION

Up to two children under 42 inches tall ride free with a paying adult on SEPTA buses, subways, and trolleys at any time. On weekends, all children under 11 can ride free. Children under 5 ride free on SEPTA regional rail lines.

CONCIERGES

Concierges, found in many hotels, can help you with theater tickets and dinner reservations: a good one with connections may be able to get you seats for a hot show or prime-time dinner reservations at the restaurant of the moment. You can also turn to your hotel's concierge for help with travel arrangements, sightseeing plans, baby-sitting, services ranging from aromatherapy to zipper repair, and emergencies. Always, **always tip** a concierge who has been of assistance (☞ Tipping).

CONSUMER PROTECTION

Whenever shopping or buying travel services in Philadelphia, **pay with a major credit card,** if possible, so you can cancel payment or get reimbursed if there's a problem. If you're doing business with a particular company for the first time, **contact your local Better Business Bureau and the attorney general's offices** in your state and (for U.S. businesses) the company's home state as well. Have any complaints been filed? Finally, if you're buying a package or tour, always **consider travel insurance** that includes default coverage (☞ Insurance).

➤ BBBs: **Council of Better Business Bureaus** (✉ 4200 Wilson Blvd., Suite 800, Arlington, VA 22203, ☎ 703/276–0100, FAX 703/525–8277, WEB www.bbb.org).

CUSTOMS & DUTIES

When shopping, **keep receipts** for all purchases. Travelers from outside the United States may be required to show their purchases to customs officials.

IN AUSTRALIA

Australian residents who are 18 or older may bring home $A400 worth of souvenirs and gifts (including jewelry), 250 cigarettes or 250 grams of tobacco, and 1,125 ml of alcohol (including wine, beer, and spirits). Residents under 18 may bring back $A200 worth of goods. Prohibited items include meat products. Seeds, plants, and fruits need to be declared upon arrival.

➤ INFORMATION: **Australian Customs Service** (Regional Director, ✉ Box 8,

Sydney, NSW 2001, Australia, ☎ 02/9213–2000, FAX 02/9213–4000, WEB www.customs.gov.au).

IN CANADA

Canadian residents who have been out of Canada for at least seven days may bring home C$500 worth of goods duty-free. If you've been away fewer than seven days but more than 48 hours, the duty-free allowance drops to C$200; if your trip lasts 24–48 hours, the allowance is C$50. You may not pool allowances with family members. Goods claimed under the C$500 exemption may follow you by mail; those claimed under the lesser exemptions must accompany you. Alcohol and tobacco products may be included in the seven-day and 48-hour exemptions but not in the 24-hour exemption. If you meet the age requirements of the province or territory through which you reenter Canada, you may bring in, duty-free, 1.14 liters (40 imperial ounces) of wine or liquor *or* 24 12-ounce cans or bottles of beer or ale. If you are 16 or older you may bring in, duty-free, 200 cigarettes and 50 cigars. Check ahead of time with Revenue Canada or the Department of Agriculture for policies regarding meat products, seeds, plants, and fruits.

You may send an unlimited number of gifts worth up to C$60 each duty-free to Canada. Label the package UNSOLICITED GIFT—VALUE UNDER $60. Alcohol and tobacco are excluded.

➤ INFORMATION: **Revenue Canada** (✉ 2265 St. Laurent Blvd. S, Ottawa, Ontario K1G 4K3, Canada, ☎ 613/993–0534; 800/461–9999 in Canada, FAX 613/991–4126, WEB www.ccra-adrc.gc.ca).

IN NEW ZEALAND

Homeward-bound residents 17 or older may bring back $700 worth of souvenirs and gifts. Your duty-free allowance also includes 4.5 liters of wine or beer; one 1,125-ml bottle of spirits; and either 200 cigarettes, 250 grams of tobacco, 50 cigars, or a combination of the three up to 250 grams. Prohibited items include meat products, seeds, plants, and fruits.

➤ INFORMATION: **New Zealand Customs** (Custom House, ✉ 50 Anzac

Ave., Box 29, Auckland, New Zealand, ☎ 09/300–5399, 𝖥𝖠𝖷 09/359–6730, 𝖶𝖤𝖡 www.customs.govt.nz).

IN THE U.K.

From countries outside the EU, including the United States, you may bring home, duty-free, 200 cigarettes or 50 cigars; 1 liter of spirits or 2 liters of fortified or sparkling wine or liqueurs; 2 liters of still table wine; 60 ml of perfume; 250 ml of toilet water; plus £136 worth of other goods, including gifts and souvenirs. If returning from outside the EU, prohibited items include meat products, seeds, plants, and fruits.

➤ INFORMATION: **HM Customs and Excise** (✉ Dorset House, Stamford St., Bromley, Kent BR1 1XX, U.K., ☎ 020/7202–4227, 𝖶𝖤𝖡 www.hmce.gov.uk).

IN THE U.S.

Non-U.S. residents ages 21 and older may import into the United States 200 cigarettes or 50 cigars or 2 kilograms of tobacco, 1 liter of alcohol, and gifts worth $100. Meat products, seeds, plants, and fruits are prohibited.

➤ INFORMATION: **U.S. Customs Service** (✉ 1300 Pennsylvania Ave. NW, Washington, DC 20229, 𝖶𝖤𝖡 www.customs.gov; inquiries ☎ 202/354–1000; complaints c/o ✉ 1300 Pennsylvania Ave. NW, Room 5.4D, Washington, DC 20229; registration of equipment c/o ✉ Resource Management, ☎ 202/927–0540).

DINING

Philadelphia and the surrounding area offers a wide range of eateries from cheese steak shops to elegant three-star restaurants; from brew pubs to Chinese take-out establishments. The restaurants we list are the cream of the crop in each price category. In Chapters 7, 8, and 9, properties indicated by an ✕🏠 are lodging establishments whose restaurant warrants a special trip.

CATEGORY	COST*
$$$$	over $26
$$$	$18–$26
$$	$9–$17
$	under $9

*per person for a main course at dinner

RESERVATIONS & DRESS

Reservations are always a good idea: we mention them only when they're essential or not accepted. Some places that don't accept reservations for one to four people will require them for larger parties. Book as far ahead as you can, and reconfirm as soon as you arrive. We mention dress only when men are required to wear a jacket or a jacket and tie.

SPECIALTIES

While Philadelphia is home to some of the most highly praised gourmet restaurants in the country, its best-known specialties remain the Philly cheese steak, the Italian hoagie, plump salted soft pretzels (with mustard), and snapper (turtle) soup.

WINE, BEER, & SPIRITS

The legal drinking age in Pennsylvania is 21. Most restaurants are licensed to served liquor, while smaller ones may have a bring-your-own policy. State-run package stores, called state stores, sell wine and other spirits. Beer is sold on a take-out basis by some restaurants but is otherwise available only by the case from certain distribution centers. State stores and beer distribution centers are closed on Sunday.

DISABILITIES & ACCESSIBILITY

People with disabilities will find that most attractions and the larger hotels in Philadelphia will accommodate their needs. Theaters and stadiums contain ramps and/or elevators. Some of Philadelphia's older, bumpier sidewalks and walkways may be difficult to navigate with wheelchairs, but all of the major streets in Center City have curb cuts. Handicapped parking is available on streets in front of major attractions and in parking lots.

An 80-page booklet from ART-REACH, Inc., *Access the Arts: A Guide for People with Disabilities,* contains information on more than 75 of the region's theaters, performing-arts centers, and museums for people with physical disabilities. Listings include wheelchair accessibility of entrances and restrooms; phone and TTY numbers; and large-print or Braille materials or assistive listening devices. The book is available on audio cassette for individuals who are blind.

➤ LOCAL RESOURCES: **Artreach, Inc.** (☎ 215/951–0316, WEB www.art-reach. org).

LODGING

When discussing accessibility with an operator or reservations agent, **ask hard questions.** Are there any stairs, inside *or* out? Are there grab bars next to the toilet *and* in the shower/ tub? How wide is the doorway to the room? To the bathroom? For the most extensive facilities meeting the latest legal specifications, **opt for newer accommodations.**

SIGHTS & ATTRACTIONS

Museums and theaters have brought their facilities in line with federal regulations and all include wheelchair access, barrier-free entrances, and accessible rest rooms and elevators. Some, such as the Philadelphia Museum of Art and the Pennsylvania Academy of the Fine Arts, offer wheelchair rentals. The Philadelphia Museum of Art also offers an audio tour for its major exhibitions. Infrared headsets may be obtained at the Academy of Music and the Kimmel Center for the Performing Arts. Some of the attractions in Independence National Historical Park may pose obstacles to people with disabilities as their historic designation occasionally precludes structural improvements. The Independence Visitor Center and Liberty Bell Pavilion are entirely accessible. A captioned version of a film shown at the visitor center and a printed script of an audio program may be obtained on request.

TRANSPORTATION

More than half of SEPTA's buses are wheelchair accessible and one-third have wheelchair lifts and computerized, recorded announcements of stops. Fares for travelers with disabilities are reduced for off-peak travel. Specialized pick-up and drop-off service is available by calling SEPTA Paratransit. A complete list of accessible bus routes and times is available on SEPTA's Web site. Route 76 and the PHLASH buses are accessible.

For general complaints, call the Disability Rights Section. The Aviation Consumer Protection Division handles airline-related problems and the Civil Rights Office deals with problems with surface transportation.

➤ INFORMATION: **SEPTA Paratransit** (☎ 215/580–7700 TTY).

➤ COMPLAINTS: **Aviation Consumer Protection Division** (✉ C-75, Room 4107, Washington, DC 20590. **Civil Rights Office** (✉ U.S. Department of Transportation, Departmental Office of Civil Rights, S-30, 400 7th St. SW, Room 10215, Washington, DC 20590, ☎ 202/366–4648, FAX 202/ 366–9371, WEB www.dot.gov/ost/docr/ index.htm). **Disability Rights Section** (✉ U.S. Department of Justice, Civil Rights Division, Box 66738, Washington, DC 20035-6738, ☎ 202/514– 0301 or 800/514–0301; 202/514– 0383 TTY; 800/514–0383 TTY, FAX 202/307–1198, WEB www.usdoj. gov/crt/ada/adahom1.htm).

TRAVEL AGENCIES

In the United States, the Americans with Disabilities Act requires that travel firms serve the needs of all travelers. Some agencies specialize in working with people with disabilities.

Access Adventures is run by a former physical-rehabilitation counselor. CareVacations handles group tours and cruises.

➤ TRAVELERS WITH MOBILITY PROBLEMS: **Access Adventures** (✉ 206 Chestnut Ridge Rd., Scottsville, NY 14624, ☎ 716/889–9096, dltravel@ prodigy.net). **Accessible Vans of America** (✉ 9 Spielman Rd., Fairfield, NJ 07004, ☎ 877/282–8267, FAX 973/ 808–9713, WEB www.accessiblevans. com). **CareVacations** (✉ 5-5110 50th Ave., Leduc, Alberta T9E 6V4, Canada, ☎ 780/986–6404 or 877/478– 7827, FAX 780/986–8332, WEB www. carevacations.com). **Flying Wheels Travel** (✉ 143 W. Bridge St., Box 382, Owatonna, MN 55060, ☎ 507/451– 5005 or 800/535–6790, FAX 507/451– 1685, WEB www.flyingwheelstravel.com).

➤ TRAVELERS WITH DEVELOPMENTAL DISABILITIES: **Sprout** (✉ 893 Amsterdam Ave., New York, NY 10025, ☎ 212/222–9575 or 888/222–9575,

FAX 212/222–9768, WEB www.
gosprout.org).

DISCOUNTS & DEALS

Be a smart shopper and **compare all
your options** before making decisions.
A plane ticket bought with a promotional coupon from travel clubs,
coupon books, and direct-mail offers
or on the Internet may not be cheaper
than the least expensive fare from a
discount ticket agency. And always
keep in mind that what you get is just
as important as what you save.

If you're planning to visit some of
the city's top museums, **look into
CityPass,** which offers 50% savings
on admission to five attractions and
is valid for nine days. The pass costs
$28.50 (less for senior citizens and
children) and covers the Academy
of Natural Sciences, the Franklin
Institute Science Museum, the Independence Seaport Museum, the
Philadelphia Zoo, and the Philadelphia Trolley Tour. You can buy the
pass at any of the attractions; because
the passes are tickets, you also avoid
any ticket lines.

➤ CONTACT: **CityPass** (☎ 707/256–
0490, WEB www.citypass.com).

DISCOUNT RESERVATIONS

To save money, **look into discount
reservations services** with toll-free
numbers, which use their buying
power to get a better price on hotels,
airline tickets, even car rentals. When
booking a room, always **call the
hotel's local toll-free number** (if one
is available) rather than the central
reservations number—you'll often
get a better price. Always ask about
special packages or corporate rates.

➤ AIRLINE TICKETS: ☎ **800/FLY–
ASAP.**

➤ HOTEL ROOMS: **Accommodations
Express** (☎ 800/444–7666, WEB www.
accommodationsexpress.com). Players Express Vacations (☎ 800/458–
6161, WEB www.playersexpress.com).
Quikbook (☎ 800/789–9887,
WEB www.quikbook.com). **RMC
Travel** (☎ 800/245–5738, WEB www.
rmcwebtravel.com). **Turbotrip.com**
(☎ 800/473–7829, WEB www.
turbotrip.com).

PACKAGE DEALS

Don't confuse packages and guided
tours. When you buy a package, you
travel on your own, just as though
you had planned the trip yourself.
Fly/drive packages, which combine
airfare and car rental, are often a
good deal. In cities, ask the local
visitors' bureau about hotel packages
that include tickets to major museum
exhibits or other special events.

EMERGENCIES

Get doctor and dentist referrals from
the Philadelphia County Medical
Society and the Philadelphia County
Dental Society.

Pennsylvania Hospital is near the
historic district, Hahnemann Hospital
is near City Hall, and Graduate
Hospital is near Rittenhouse Square.

➤ DOCTORS & DENTISTS: **Philadelphia
County Medical Society** (☎ 215/563–
5343). **Philadelphia County Dental
Society** (☎ 215/925–6050).

➤ EMERGENCY SERVICES: **Ambulance,
fire, police** (☎ 911).

➤ HOSPITALS: **Pennsylvania Hospital**
(✉ 8th and Spruce Sts., ☎ 215/829–
3000 information; 215/829–3350
emergency room). **Hahnemann**
(✉ Broad and Vine Sts., ☎ 215/762–
7000 information; 215/762–7963
emergency room). **Graduate Hospital**
(✉ 1800 Lombard St., ☎ 215/893–
2000 information; 215/893–2350
emergency room).

➤ HOT LINES: **Poisoning Control
Center** (☎ 215/386–2100). **Suicide
and Crisis Intervention Center**
(☎ 215/686–4420). **Women Against
Abuse** (☎ 215/386–7777).

➤ 24-HOUR PHARMACIES: **CVS Pharmacy** (✉ 1826–30 Chestnut St.,
☎ 215/972–1401). **Rite Aid** (✉ 2017–
2023 S. Broad St., ☎ 215/467–0850).

ETIQUETTE & BEHAVIOR

When you are visiting among the
Amish in Lancaster County, **remember to respect their values.** They
believe that photographs and videos
with recognizable reproductions of
them violate the biblical commandment against making graven images.
You will be asked to refrain from

photographing or making videos of the Amish, and you should comply.

FERRY TRAVEL

The RiverLink Ferry, a seasonal (April–mid-November) passenger ferry, offers service between Philadelphia and Camden, site of the New Jersey State Aquarium, the Tweeter Center, Battleship New Jersey, and Campbell's Field. There are departures from Penn's Landing and from Camden's waterfront every 20 minutes, daily 9:40–5:40, with extended hours and continuous service for Penn's Landing and Tweeter Center concerts, and Camden Riversharks baseball games. The cost is $5 round-trip and the ride takes 12 minutes.

FARES & SCHEDULES

RiverLink Ferry tickets must be purchased at Penn's Landing at Walnut Street and Columbus Avenue, outside the Independence Seaport Museum. Payment can be made by cash only.

➤ FERRY INFORMATION: **RiverLink Ferry** (⊠ Penn's Landing near Walnut St., ☎ 215/925–5465, WEB www.drpa. org).

GAY & LESBIAN TRAVEL

Attitudes are most accepting in Center City, University City, and in the Mt. Airy and Chestnut Hill neighborhoods. Stares or rudeness may greet same-sex couples in the more conservative neighborhoods and suburbs of Philadelphia. For details about the gay and lesbian scene, consult *Fodor's Gay Guide to the USA* (available in bookstores everywhere).

➤ GAY- & LESBIAN-FRIENDLY TRAVEL AGENCIES: **Different Roads Travel** (⊠ 8383 Wilshire Blvd., Suite 902, Beverly Hills, CA 90211, ☎ 323/651–5557 or 800/429–8747, FAX 323/651–3678, lgernert@tzell.com). **Kennedy Travel** (⊠ 314 Jericho Turnpike, Floral Park, NY 11001, ☎ 516/352–4888 or 800/237–7433, FAX 516/354–8849, WEB www.kennedytravel.com). **Now Voyager** (⊠ 4406 18th St., San Francisco, CA 94114, ☎ 415/626–1169 or 800/255–6951, FAX 415/626–8626, WEB www.nowvoyager.com). **Skylink Travel and Tour** (⊠ 1006 Mendocino Ave., Santa Rosa, CA 95401, ☎ 707/546–9888 or 800/225–5759, FAX 707/546–9891, WEB www. skylinktravel.com), serving lesbian travelers.

GUIDEBOOKS

Plan well and you won't be sorry. Guidebooks are excellent tools—and you can take them with you. You may want to check out color-photo-illustrated *Compass American Guide: Pennsylvania*, thorough on culture and history, and *Fodor's Road Guide USA: Delaware, District of Columbia, Maryland, Pennsylvania, Virginia,* with comprehensive restaurant, hotel, and attractions listings for driving vacations. Both are available at on-line retailers and bookstores everywhere.

HOLIDAYS

Major national holidays include New Year's Day (Jan. 1); Martin Luther King, Jr., Day (3rd Mon. in Jan.); President's Day (3rd Mon. in Feb.); Memorial Day (last Mon. in May); Independence Day (July 4); Labor Day (1st Mon. in Sept.); Thanksgiving Day (4th Thurs. in Nov.); Christmas Eve and Christmas Day (Dec. 24 and 25); and New Year's Eve (Dec. 31).

INSURANCE

The most useful travel-insurance plan is a comprehensive policy that includes coverage for trip cancellation and interruption, default, trip delay, and medical expenses (with a waiver for pre-existing conditions).

Without insurance you will lose all or most of your money if you cancel your trip, regardless of the reason. Default insurance covers you if your tour operator, airline, or cruise line goes out of business. Trip-delay covers expenses that arise because of bad weather or mechanical delays. Study the fine print when comparing policies.

Always **buy travel policies directly from the insurance company**; if you buy them from a cruise line, airline, or tour operator that goes out of business you probably will not be covered for the agency or operator's default, a major risk. Before making any purchase, **review your existing health and home-owner's policies** to find what they cover away from home.

➤ TRAVEL INSURERS: In the U.S.: **Access America** (⊠ 6600 W. Broad St., Richmond, VA 23230, ☎ 804/285–3300 or 800/284–8300, FAX 804/673–1586, WEB www.previewtravel.com). **Travel Guard International** (⊠ 1145 Clark St., Stevens Point, WI 54481, ☎ 715/345–0505 or 800/826–1300, FAX 800/955–8785, WEB www.noelgroup.com).

FOR INTERNATIONAL TRAVELERS

For information on customs restrictions, *see* Customs & Duties.

CAR TRAVEL

Gasoline costs about $1.27 to $1.67 per gallon in Philadelphia. Most Center City (downtown) gas stations can be found on Broad Street. Most gas stations in the area stay open late (24 hours along large highways and in big cities), except in rural areas, where Sunday hours are limited and where you may drive long stretches without a refueling opportunity. Highways are well paved. Interstate highways—limited-access, multilane highways whose numbers are prefixed by "I–"—are the fastest routes. Interstates with three-digit numbers encircle urban areas, which may have other limited-access expressways, freeways, and parkways as well. Tolls may be levied on limited-access highways. So-called U.S. highways and state highways are not necessarily limited-access but may have several lanes.

Along larger highways, roadside stops with rest rooms, fast-food restaurants, and sundries stores are well spaced. State police and tow trucks patrol major highways and lend assistance. If your car breaks down on an interstate, pull onto the shoulder and wait for help, or have your passengers wait while you walk to an emergency phone. If you carry a cell phone, dial *55, noting your location on the small green roadside mileage markers.

Driving in the United States is on the right. Do **obey speed limits** posted along roads and highways. Watch for lower limits in small towns and on back roads. **Pennsylvania requires all passengers to wear seat belts.** On weekdays between 6 and 10 AM and

again between 4 and 7 PM, **expect heavy traffic.** To encourage carpooling, some freeways have special lanes for so-called high-occupancy vehicles (HOV)—cars carrying more than one passenger.

Book stores, gas stations, convenience stores, and rest stops sell maps (about $3) and multiregion road atlases (about $10).

CONSULATE

➤ UNITED KINGDOM: **British Consulate** (⊠ 1818 Market St., 33rd Floor, Philadelphia 19103, ☎ 215/557–7665.

CURRENCY

The dollar is the basic unit of U.S. currency. It has 100 cents. Coins include the copper penny (1¢); the silvery nickel (5¢), dime (10¢), quarter (25¢), and half-dollar (50¢); and the golden $1 coin, replacing a now-rare silver dollar. Bills are denominated $1, $5, $10, $20, $50, and $100, all green and identical in size; designs vary. The exchange rate at press time was $1.42 per British pound, 65¢ per C$1, 51¢ per A$1, and 43¢ per NZ$1.

ELECTRICITY

The U.S. standard is AC, 110 volts/60 cycles. Plugs have two flat pins set parallel to each other.

EMERGENCIES

For police, fire, or ambulance, **dial 911** (0 in rural areas).

INSURANCE

Britons and Australians need extra medical coverage when traveling overseas.

➤ INSURANCE INFORMATION: In the U.K.: **Association of British Insurers** (⊠ 51–55 Gresham St., London EC2V 7HQ, U.K., ☎ 020/7600–3333, FAX 020/7696–8999, WEB www.abi.org.uk). In Australia: **Insurance Council of Australia** (⊠ Level 3, 56 Pitt St., Sydney NSW 2000, ☎ 03/9614–1077, FAX 03/9614–7924). In Canada: **RBC Insurance** (⊠ 6880 Financial Dr., Mississauga, Ontario L5N 7Y5, Canada, ☎ 905/816–2400 or 800/668–4342 in Canada, FAX 905/816–2498, WEB www.royalbank.com). In New Zealand: **Insurance Council of**

New Zealand (✉ Box 474, Wellington, New Zealand, ☎ 04/472–5230, FAX 04/473–3011, WEB www.icnz.org.nz).

MAIL & SHIPPING

You can buy stamps and aerograms and send letters and parcels in post offices. Stamp-dispensing machines can occasionally be found in airports, bus and train stations, office buildings, drugstores, and the like. You can also deposit mail in the stout, dark blue, steel bins at strategic locations everywhere and in the mail chutes of large buildings; pickup schedules are posted.

For mail sent within the United States, you need a 34¢ stamp for first-class letters weighing up to 1 ounce (23¢ for each additional ounce) and 21¢ for domestic postcards. For overseas mail, you pay 80¢ for 1-ounce airmail letters, 70¢ for airmail postcards, and 35¢ for surface-rate postcards. For Canada and Mexico you need a 60¢ stamp for a 1-ounce letter and 50¢ for a postcard. For 70¢ you can buy an aerogram—a single sheet of lightweight blue paper that folds into its own envelope, stamped for overseas airmail.

To receive mail on the road, have it sent c/o General Delivery at your destination's main post office (use the correct five-digit zip code). You must pick up mail in person within 30 days and show a driver's license or passport.

PASSPORTS & VISAS

When traveling internationally, **carry your passport** even if you don't need one (it's always the best form of I.D.) and **make two photocopies of the data page** (one for someone at home and another for you, carried separately from your passport). If you lose your passport, promptly call the nearest embassy or consulate and the local police.

Visitor visas are not necessary for Canadian citizens, or for citizens of Australia and the United Kingdom who are staying fewer than 90 days.

➤ AUSTRALIAN CITIZENS: **Australian Passport Office** (☎ 131–232). U.S. **Office of Australia Affairs** (✉ MLC Centre, 19–29 Martin Pl., 59th floor, Sydney NSW 2000, Australia).

➤ CANADIAN CITIZENS: **Passport Office** (☎ 819/994–3500; 800/567–6868 in Canada).

➤ NEW ZEALAND CITIZENS: **New Zealand Passport Office** (☎ 04/494–0700 for application procedures; 0800/225–050 in New Zealand for application-status updates). U.S. **Office of New Zealand Affairs** (✉ 29 Fitzherbert Terr., Thorndon, Wellington, New Zealand).

➤ U.K. CITIZENS: **London Passport Office** (☎ 0870/521–0410) for application procedures and emergency passports. U.S. Embassy Visa Information Line (☎ 01891/200–290). U.S. Embassy Visa Branch (✉ 5 Upper Grosvenor Sq., London W1A 1AE, U.K.); send a self-addressed, stamped envelope. U.S. Consulate General (✉ Queen's House, Queen St., Belfast BTI 6EO, Northern Ireland).

TELEPHONES

All U.S. telephone numbers consist of a three-digit area code and a seven-digit local number. Within most local calling areas, dial only the seven-digit number. Within the same area code, dial "1" first. To call between area-code regions, dial "1" then all 10 digits; the same goes for calls to numbers prefixed by "800," "888," and "877"—all toll-free. For calls to numbers preceded by "900" you must pay—usually dearly.

For international calls, dial "011" followed by the country code and the local number. For help, dial "0" and ask for an overseas operator. The country code is 61 for Australia, 64 for New Zealand, 44 for the United Kingdom. Calling Canada is the same as calling within the United States. Most local phone books list country codes and U.S. area codes. The country code for the United States is 1.

For operator assistance, dial "0". To obtain someone's phone number, call directory assistance, 555–1212 or occasionally 411 (free at public phones). To have the person you're calling foot the bill, phone collect; dial "0" instead of "1" before the 10-digit number.

At pay phones, instructions are usually posted. Usually you insert coins in a slot (10¢–35¢ for local calls) and

wait for a steady tone before dialing.
When you call long-distance, the
operator will tell you how much to
insert; prepaid phone cards, widely
available in various denominations,
are easier. Call the number on the
back, punch in the card's personal
identification number when prompt-
ed, then dial your number.

LODGING

Philadelphia has been undergoing a
lodging boom, and you have a choice
of everything from homey Victorian
bed-and-breakfasts to luxurious modern hotels. The lodgings we list are
the cream of the crop in each price
category. We always list the facilities
that are available—but we don't
specify whether they cost extra: when
pricing accommodations, always ask
what's included and what is extra.
Assume that all rooms have private
baths unless otherwise noted. At bed-
and-breakfasts, ask if there are special
rates for business travelers. Lodging is
denoted in the text by a little house,
🏠 . In Chapters 7, 8, and 9, properties indicated by an ✕🏠 are lodging
establishments whose restaurant
warrants a special trip.

Assume that hotels operate on the
European Plan (EP, with no meals)
unless we specify that they use the
Continental Plan (CP, with a Conti-
nental breakfast), **Breakfast Plan**
(BP, with a full breakfast), **Modified
American Plan** (MAP, with breakfast
and dinner), or the **Full American
Plan** (FAP, with all meals).

CATE-GORY	PHILA-DELPHIA*	OTHER AREAS*
$$$$	over $260	over $220
$$$	$190–$260	$150–$220
$$	$130–$190	$100–$150
$	under $130	under $100

*All prices are for a standard double
room, excluding tax (14% in Philadelphia, 8% in Bucks County, and 6% in
Lancaster County).

APARTMENT RENTALS

If you want a home base that's roomy
enough for a family and comes with
cooking facilities, **consider a furnished
rental.** These can save you money,
especially if you're traveling with a
group. Home-exchange directories

sometimes list rentals as well as
exchanges.

➤ LOCAL AGENTS: **Almost Like
Home** (☎ 610/935–0935, WEB www.
almostlikehome.net). **Bed and Breakfast Connections of Philadelphia**
(☎ 610/687–3565 or 800/448–3619,
WEB www.bnbphiladelphia.com).

B&BS

A wide variety of intimate accommodations can be found in Philadelphia
and the surrounding areas, from small
historic homes in the city with two or
three guest rooms, to elegant country
inns and rambling estates in the
Brandywine Valley, to farmsteads in
Lancaster County.

For information about bed-and-
breakfasts and reservation services
in Philadelphia, Bucks County, and
Lancaster County, *see* Chapters 3, 8,
and 9.

HOME EXCHANGES

If you would like to exchange your
home for someone else's, **join a home-
exchange organization,** which will
send you its updated listings of available exchanges for a year and will
include your own listing in at least
one of them. It's up to you to make
specific arrangements.

➤ EXCHANGE CLUBS: **HomeLink International** (✉ Box 47747, Tampa, FL
33647, ☎ 813/975–9825 or 800/638–
3841, FAX 813/910–8144, WEB www.
homelink.org; $98 per year). **Intervac
U.S.** (✉ Box 590504, San Francisco,
CA 94159, ☎ 800/756–4663, FAX 415/
435–7440, WEB www.intervacus.com;
$93 yearly fee includes one catalogue
and on-line access).

HOSTELS

No matter what your age, you can
**save on lodging costs by staying at
hostels.** In some 5,000 locations in
more than 70 countries around the
world, Hostelling International (HI),
the umbrella group for a number of
national youth-hostel associations,
offers single-sex, dorm-style beds and,
at many hostels, rooms for couples
and family accommodations. Membership in any HI national hostel
association, open to travelers of all
ages, allows you to stay in HI-affili-
ated hostels at member rates; one-

year membership is about $25 for adults (C$26.75 in Canada, £9.30 in the U.K., $30 in Australia, and $30 in New Zealand); hostels run about $10–$25 per night. Members have priority if the hostel is full; they're also eligible for discounts around the world, even on rail and bus travel in some countries.

➤ BEST OPTIONS: For information about hostels in the Philadelphia area, *see* Chapter 3.

➤ ORGANIZATIONS: **Hostelling International—American Youth Hostels** (⊠ 733 15th St. NW, Suite 840, Washington, DC 20005, ☎ 202/783–6161, FAX 202/783–6171, WEB www. hiayh.org). **Hostelling International—Canada** (⊠ 400–205 Catherine St., Ottawa, Ontario K2P 1C3, Canada, ☎ 613/237–7884, FAX 613/237–7868, WEB www.hostellingintl.ca). **Youth Hostel Association of England and Wales** (⊠ Trevelyan House, 8 St. Stephen's Hill, St. Albans, Hertfordshire AL1 2DY, U.K., ☎ 0870/8708808, FAX 01727/844126, WEB www.yha. org.uk). **Australian Youth Hostel Association** (⊠ 10 Mallett St., Camperdown, NSW 2050, Australia, ☎ 02/9565–1699, FAX 02/9565–1325, WEB www.yha.com.au). **Youth Hostels Association of New Zealand** (⊠ Box 436, Christchurch, New Zealand, ☎ 03/379–9970, FAX 03/365–4476, WEB www.yha.org.nz).

HOTELS

All hotels listed have private bath unless otherwise noted.

➤ TOLL-FREE NUMBERS: **Adam's Mark** (☎ 800/444–2326, WEB www. adamsmark.com). **Best Western** (☎ 800/528–1234, WEB www. bestwestern.com). **Choice** (☎ 800/221–2222, WEB www.hotelchoice. com). **Clarion** (☎ 800/252–7466, WEB www.hotelchoice.com). **Colony** (☎ 800/777–1700, WEB www.colony. com). **Comfort** (☎ 800/228–5150, WEB www.comfortinn.com). **Days Inn** (☎ 800/325–2525, WEB www.daysinn. com). **Doubletree and Red Lion Hotels** (☎ 800/222–8733, WEB www. doubletree.com). **Embassy Suites** (☎ 800/362–2779, WEB www. embassysuites.com). **Fairfield Inn** (☎ 800/228–2800, WEB www.marriott.

com). **Four Seasons** (☎ 800/332–3442, WEB www.fourseasons.com). **Hilton** (☎ 800/445–8667, WEB www. hilton.com). **Holiday Inn** (☎ 800/465–4329, WEB www.holiday-inn. com). **Howard Johnson** (☎ 800/654–4656, WEB www.hojo.com). **Hyatt Hotels & Resorts** (☎ 800/233–1234, WEB www.hyatt.com). **La Quinta** (☎ 800/531–5900, WEB www.laquinta. com). **Marriott** (☎ 800/228–9290, WEB www.marriott.com). **Omni** (☎ 800/843–6664, WEB www. omnihotels.com). **Radisson** (☎ 800/333–3333, WEB www.radisson.com). **Ramada** (☎ 800/228–2828, WEB www. ramada.com). **Ritz-Carlton** (☎ 800/241–3333, WEB www.ritzcarlton.com). **Sheraton** (☎ 800/325–3535, WEB www. sheraton.com). **Wyndham Hotels & Resorts** (☎ 800/822-4200, WEB www. wyndham.com).

MAIL & SHIPPING

➤ POST OFFICES: **Main Post Office** (⊠ 2970 Market St., ☎ 215/895–8000).

University City Branch (⊠ 228 S. 40th St., ☎ 215/387–7755).

Middle City Branch (⊠ 2037 Chestnut St., ☎ 215/567–3772).

MEDIA

NEWSPAPERS & MAGAZINES

The *Philadelphia Inquirer* and the *Philadelphia Daily News* are the city's main daily newspapers. They share a Web site (www.phillynews.com) with the alternative weekly *City Paper.* The monthly *Philadelphia* magazine (www.phillymag.com) contains listings and advertisements of interest to visitors as well as residents.

RADIO & TELEVISION

AM radio: KYW 1060, news and weather. FM radio: WXPN 88.5, University of Pennsylvania, news and music, including jazz; WHYY 90.1, National Public Radio; WMMR 93.3, album rock; WYTU 92, country.

The local affiliates of the major networks are channel 3, which is CBS; channel 6, which is ABC; channel 10, which is NBC; channel 12, which is PBS; and channel 29, which is FOX.

MONEY MATTERS

Philadelphia is a major city and can be expensive, although it is less so than New York. A cup of coffee will cost $1 at a diner but $2–$3 at an upscale restaurant; a sandwich will set you back $4–$8. Taxi rides begin at $1.80 and can quickly add up to $6 or more for a ride across Center City. Most sites in Independence National Historical Park are free; museums in the city cost $3–$9. Prices throughout this guide are given for adults. Substantially reduced fees are almost always available for children, students, and senior citizens. For information on taxes, *see* Taxes.

ATMS

Automatic teller machines are available in the lobbies or on the outside walls of most banks. They can also be found at branches of the local convenience store chain, WAWA, and in larger grocery stores.

➤ ATM LOCATIONS: **Cirrus** (☎ 800/424–7787). **Plus** (☎ 800/843–7587).

CREDIT CARDS

Throughout this guide, the following abbreviations are used: **AE**, American Express; **D**, Discover; **DC**, Diners Club; **MC**, MasterCard; and **V**, Visa.

➤ REPORTING LOST CARDS: **American Express** (☎ 800/300–8765). **Diners Club** (☎ 800/234–6377). **Discover** (☎ 800/347–2683). **MasterCard** (☎ 800/826–2181). **Visa** (☎ 800/336–8472).

PACKING

Portage and luggage trolleys are hard to find, so **pack light.** Philadelphia is a fairly casual city, although men will need a jacket and tie in some of the better restaurants. Jeans and sneakers or other casual clothing is fine for sightseeing. You'll need a heavy coat for winter, which can be cold and snowy. Summers are hot and humid, but you'll need a shawl or jacket for air-conditioned restaurants. Many areas are best explored on foot, so **bring good walking shoes.**

In your carry-on luggage, **pack an extra pair of eyeglasses or contact lenses** and **enough of any medication you take** to last the entire trip. You may also ask your doctor to write a spare prescription using the drug's generic name, since brand names may vary from country to country. In luggage to be checked, **never pack prescription drugs or valuables.** To avoid customs delays, carry medications in their original packaging. And don't forget to carry with you the addresses of offices that handle refunds of lost traveler's checks. *Fodor's How to Pack* (available in bookstores everywhere) has more tips.

CHECKING LUGGAGE

You are allowed one carry-on bag and one personal article, such as a purse or a laptop computer. Make sure that everything you carry aboard will fit under your seat or in the overhead bin. Get to the gate early, so you can board as soon as possible. Note that if you have a seat at the back of the plane, you'll probably board first, while the overhead bins are still empty.

If you are flying internationally, note that baggage allowances may be determined not by piece but by weight—generally 88 pounds (40 kilograms) in first class, 66 pounds (30 kilograms) in business class, and 44 pounds (20 kilograms) in economy.

Airline liability for baggage is limited to $1,250 per person on flights within the United States. On international flights it amounts to $9.07 per pound or $20 per kilogram for checked baggage (roughly $640 per 70-pound bag) and $400 per passenger for unchecked baggage. You can buy additional coverage at check-in for about $10 per $1,000 of coverage, but it excludes a rather extensive list of items, shown on your airline ticket.

Before departure, **itemize your bags' contents** and their worth, and label the bags with your name, address, and phone number. (If you use your home address, cover it so potential thieves can't see it readily.) Inside each bag, **pack a copy of your itinerary.** At check-in, **make sure that each bag is correctly tagged** with the destination airport's three-letter code. If your bags arrive damaged or fail to arrive at all, file a written report with the airline before leaving the airport.

SAFETY

As in many other major cities, sections of Philadelphia range from posh old-money enclaves to inner-city slums. Center City and the major tourist destinations are generally safe during the day but it is wise to take certain precautions. Avoid wearing flashy jewelry and leave all valuables in your hotel's safe. Wear a money belt; if you bring a handbag, keep it on your lap—not on the floor or dangling on the back of your chair—in restaurants and theaters. Exercise caution, particularly after dark, in the areas north of Center City and west of University City; avoid deserted streets. You can **ask hotel personnel or guides at the Independence Visitor Center about the safety of places** you're interested in visiting. As you would in any city, **keep your car locked and watch your possessions carefully.** Remember to **remove items from your car.**

Subway crime has diminished in recent years. During the day cars are crowded and safe. However, platforms and cars can be relatively empty in the late evening hours. SEPTA train travelers should **avoid North Philadelphia Station,** which is in an economically depressed neighborhood. Instead of waiting for a subway or train in off hours, **take a cab late at night.**

SENIOR-CITIZEN TRAVEL

Most museums and attractions in and around Philadelphia, including the Philadelphia Museum of Art, the Franklin Institute, and the Pennsylvania Academy of the Fine Arts, offer reduced rates for seniors. Many hotels and restaurants offer discounts as well. Seniors can ride free on the SEPTA system during off-peak hours.

To qualify for age-related discounts, **mention your senior-citizen status up front** when booking hotel reservations (not when checking out) and before you're seated in restaurants (not when paying the bill). When renting a car, ask about promotional car-rental discounts, which can be cheaper than senior-citizen rates.

➤ EDUCATIONAL PROGRAMS: **Elderhostel** (⊠ 11 Ave. de Lafayette, Boston, MA 02111-1746, ☎ 877/426–8056, FAX 877/426–2166, WEB www.elderhostel.org).

SIGHTSEEING TOURS

Following are some sightseeing options for Philadelphia. For information about special tours in the Brandywine Valley, Bucks County, and Lancaster County, *see* the A to Z sections at the end of Chapters 7, 8, and 9.

BOAT TOURS

Liberty Belle Cruises, aboard a new 600-passenger Mississippi paddle-wheel riverboat, offers lunch, dinner, and Sunday brunch cruises with a banjo player, sing-alongs, and a buffet. Board at Penn's Landing (⊠ Columbus Blvd. at Lombard Circle).

The *Spirit of Philadelphia* runs lunch and dinner cruises along the Delaware River. This three-deck ship leaves Penn's Landing at Lombard Circle and Columbus Boulevard for lunch, dinner, and starlight cruises. Dinner cruises include a live musical revue and dance music.

➤ FEES & SCHEDULES: *Liberty Belle* Cruises (☎ 215/629–1131, WEB www.libertybelle.com). *Spirit of Philadelphia* (☎ 215/923–1419, WEB www.spiritcruises.com).

BUS TOURS

Two companies offer narrated tours in buses designed to resemble Victorian-style trolleys. With both companies, the fare is an all-day pass, allowing unlimited on/offs. Board at any stop, including the Pennsylvania Convention Center and the Liberty Bell.

American Trolley Tours offers free pickup at major hotels as well as historic sites and the Pennsylvania Convention Center. Tours run every 45 minutes between 9 and 3:45 and take approximately two hours; the cost is $14.

The Philadelphia Trolley Works tour takes about 90 minutes and costs $18. The tour makes 20 stops on a route covering the historic area, the Benjamin Franklin Parkway, the Avenue of the Arts (South Broad Street), Fairmount Park, the Philadelphia Zoo, Eastern State Penitentiary, and Penn's Landing.

➤ FEES & SCHEDULES: **American Trolley Tours** (☎ 215/333–2119). **Philadelphia Trolley Works** (☎ 215/925–8687, WEB www.phillytour.com).

CARRIAGE RIDES

Numerous horse-drawn carriages wind their way through the narrow streets of the historic area. Tours last anywhere from 15 minutes to an hour and cost from $20 to $70. Carriages line up on Chestnut and 6th streets near Independence Hall between 10 AM and 6 PM and at South Street and 2nd Street between 7 PM and midnight. You can reserve a carriage and be picked up anywhere downtown. Carriages operate year-round, except when the temperature is below 20°F or above 92°F.

➤ FEES & SCHEDULES: **'76 Carriage Company** (☎ 215/923–8516, WEB www.phillytour.com).

MULTILINGUAL TOURS

Centipede Tours can supply German-, French-, Spanish-, or Italian-speaking guides for all parts of Philadelphia.

➤ FEES & SCHEDULES: **Centipede Tours** (☎ 215/735–3123).

SPECIAL-INTEREST TOURS

Year-round special walking tours offer opportunities to discover the unique and varied cultural heritage of the city. You can sample ethnic fare and listen to experts recount the history of particular areas and peoples. Tours can be arranged by appointment only.

Great American Tours leads a 3½-hour Saturday morning walking tour of Old City's many landmarks of African-American history. Stops include an underground railroad station, the African American Museum, and the Liberty Bell, where you'll hear tales of what happened to Africans who were being held as slaves in Pennsylvania.

Italian Market Tours gives an afternoon's introduction to this vibrant area's cultural and historic sites with visits to cheese, meat, and pastry shops for foodmaking demonstrations and tastings. Celeste Morello, author

of the *Italian Market Cookbook,* leads the walking tour, with a six-person minimum.

Harry Boonin, historian and author of *The Jewish Quarter of Philadelphia: A History and Guide, 1881–1930,* heads up Jewish Walking Tours of Philadelphia; two mornings a week he guides visitors through Society Hill and Queen Village, the old Jewish quarter where Eastern European Jews settled at the turn of the last century.

➤ FEES & SCHEDULES: **Great American Tours** (☎ 215/768–8157). **Italian Market Tours** (☎ 215/334–6008). **Jewish Walking Tours of Philadelphia** (☎ 215/934–7184, WEB www.boonin. com).

WALKING TOURS

Centipede Tours offers a candlelight stroll through Society Hill led by guides in Colonial dress. Tours begin at Welcome Park, at Walnut and Second streets, Friday and Saturday at 6:30 PM, May through October.

The Foundation for Architecture tours focus on architecture and history. Neighborhood tours include Manayunk, Chestnut Hill, and Spruce Hill; theme tours include art deco, skyscrapers, and Judaic architecture and influence. Most tours begin at 2.

➤ FEES & SCHEDULES: **Centipede Tours** (☎ 215/735–3123, WEB www.centipedeinc.com). **Foundation for Architecture** (☎ 215/569–3187).

STUDENTS IN PHILADELPHIA

The majority of museums and attractions in and around Philadelphia offer reduced rates to students presenting a valid student I.D.

➤ I.D.s & SERVICES: **Council Travel** (CIEE; ✉ 205 E. 42nd St., 15th floor, New York, NY 10017, ☎ 212/822–2700 or 888/268–6245, FAX 212/822–2699, WEB www.councilexchanges.org) for mail orders only, in the U.S. **Travel Cuts** (✉ 187 College St., Toronto, Ontario M5T 1P7, Canada, ☎ 416/979–2406 or 800/667–2887 in Canada, FAX 416/979–8167, WEB www.travelcuts.com).

SUBWAY TRAVEL

The Broad Street Subway runs from Fern Rock station in the northern part of the city to Pattison Avenue and the sports complex (First Union Center and Veterans Stadium) in South Philadelphia. The Market-Frankford line runs across the city from the western suburb of Upper Darby to Frankford in Northeast Philadelphia. Both lines shut down from midnight to 5 AM, during which time "Night Owl" buses operate along the same routes. Tickets may be purchased at all subway stations. The one-way fare within the city is $2 with transfers costing 60¢.

➤ FARES & SCHEDULES: SEPTA (☎ 215/580–7800).

TAXES

SALES TAX

The main sales tax in Philadelphia and the surrounding areas is 7%. This tax also applies to restaurant meals. Various other taxes—including a liquor tax—may apply. There is no sales tax on clothing. Hotel taxes are 14% in Philadelphia, 8% in Bucks County, and 6% in Lancaster County.

TAXIS

Cabs cost $1.80 at the flag throw and then $1.80–$2.30 per mile. They are plentiful during the day downtown— especially along Broad Street and near hotels and train stations. At night and outside Center City, taxis are scarce. Your best bet is to go to a hotel and have the doorman hail a taxi for you. Or, you can call for a cab, but they frequently show up late and occasionally never arrive. Be persistent: calling back if the cab is late will often yield results. The standard tip for cabdrivers is 15% of the total fare.

➤ TAXI COMPANIES: Olde City Taxi (☎ 215/338–0838). Quaker City Cab (☎ 215/728–8000). Yellow Cab (☎ 215/922–8400).

TELEPHONES

Philadelphia has two area codes: 215 and 267, which is being assigned to new numbers. Because of this, the city now requires that you dial "1" followed by all ten digits of a telephone number even for local calls.

TIME

Philadelphia and the Pennsylvania Dutch Country are in the eastern time zone. Daylight Savings Time is in effect from early April through late October; Eastern Standard Time, the rest of the year. Clocks are set ahead one hour when Daylight Savings Time begins, back one hour when it ends. Philadelphia is 3 hours ahead of Los Angeles, 1 hour ahead of Chicago, 6 hours behind London, and 15 hours behind Sydney.

TIPPING

At restaurants, a 15% tip is standard for servers; up to 20% may be expected at more expensive establishments. The same goes for taxi drivers, bartenders, and hairdressers. Coat checkers usually expect $1–$2; bellhops and hotel and airport porters should get $1 per bag. Hotel maids in upscale hotels should get about $1 per day of your stay. For local sightseeing tours, you may individually tip the driver-guide $1–$5, depending on the length of the tour and the number of people in your party, if he or she has been helpful or informative. Ushers in theaters do not expect tips.

A concierge typically receives a tip of $5–$10, with an additional gratuity for special services or favors.

TOURS & PACKAGES

Because everything is prearranged on a prepackaged tour or independent vacation, you spend less time planning—and often get it all at a good price.

BOOKING WITH AN AGENT

Travel agents are excellent resources. But it's a good idea to collect brochures from several agencies as some agents' suggestions may be influenced by relationships with tour and package firms that reward them for volume sales. If you have a special interest, **find an agent with expertise in that area**; ASTA (☞ Travel Agencies) has a database of specialists worldwide.

Make sure your travel agent knows the accommodations and other services of the place they're recommending. Ask about the hotel's location, room size, beds, and whether it has a pool, room service, or programs for children, if you care about these. Has your agent been there in person or sent others whom you can contact?

Do some homework on your own, too: local tourism boards can provide information about lesser-known and small-niche operators, some of which may sell only direct.

BUYER BEWARE

Each year consumers are stranded or lose their money when tour operators—even large ones with excellent reputations—go out of business. So **check out the operator.** Ask several travel agents about its reputation, and try to **book with a company that has a consumer-protection program.** (Look for information in the company's brochure.) In the United States, members of the National Tour Association and the United States Tour Operators Association are required to set aside funds to cover your payments and travel arrangements in the event that the company defaults. It's also a good idea to choose a company that participates in the American Society of Travel Agents' Tour Operator Program (TOP); ASTA will act as mediator in any disputes between you and your tour operator.

Remember that the more your package or tour includes the better you can predict the ultimate cost of your vacation. Make sure you know exactly what is covered, and **beware of hidden costs.** Are taxes, tips, and transfers included? Entertainment and excursions? These can add up.

➤ TOUR-OPERATOR RECOMMENDATIONS: **American Society of Travel Agents** (☞ Travel Agencies). **National Tour Association** (NTA; ⌧ 546 E. Main St., Lexington, KY 40508, ☎ 859/226–4444 or 800/682–8886, WEB www.ntaonline.com). **United States Tour Operators Association** (USTOA; ⌧ 342 Madison Ave., Suite 1522, New York, NY 10173, ☎ 212/599–6599 or 800/468–7862, FAX 212/599–6744, WEB www.ustoa.com).

TRAIN TRAVEL
TO AND FROM PHILADELPHIA

Philadelphia's 30th Street Station (⌧ 30th and Market Sts.) is a major stop on Amtrak's Northeast Corridor line. The 90-minute Philadelphia to New York trip is $44 one way. Amtrak's new high-speed Acela trains run three times a day, Monday through Friday, between Washington, D.C. and Boston, and twice a day on the weekends. You can shave 20 minutes off the Philadelphia–New York trip, but it'll cost you $91. The trains cater to the business traveler and are equipped with conference tables and phone jacks at every seat.

You can **travel by train between Philadelphia and New York City on the cheap** by taking the SEPTA commuter line R7 to Trenton, New Jersey, and transferring to a NJ Transit commuter line to Manhattan. Ask for the excursion rate. The trip takes an extra 30 minutes, but costs about $12.

Amtrak also serves Philadelphia from points west, including Harrisburg, Pittsburgh, and Chicago.

Philadelphia's fine network of commuter trains, operated by SEPTA, serves both the city and the suburbs. The famous Main Line, a cluster of affluent suburbs, got its start—and its name—from the Pennsylvania Railroad route that ran westward from Center City. All SEPTA commuter trains stop at 30th Street Station and connect to Suburban Station (⌧ 16th St. and John F. Kennedy Blvd., near major hotels), and Market East Station (⌧ 10th and Market Sts.), near the historic section and beneath the Gallery at Market East shopping complex. Fares, which vary according to route and time of travel, range from $2.50 to $5 one way. These trains are your best bet for reaching Germantown, Chestnut Hill, Merion (site of the Barnes Foundation), and other suburbs.

PATCO (Port Authority Transit Corporation) High Speed Line trains run underground from 16th and Locust streets to Lindenwold, New Jersey. Trains stop at 13th and Locust, 9th and Locust, and 8th and Market streets, then continue across the Benjamin Franklin Bridge to Camden. It's one way to get to the New Jersey State Aquarium or the Tweeter Center; NJ Transit has a shuttle bus from the Broadway stop to the aquarium on weekends and to the center during concerts. Fares run from $1 to $2.10. **Sit in the very front seat for a great view going across the bridge.**

For information on train service for the Brandywine Valley, Bucks County, and the Pennsylvania Dutch Country, *see* Arriving and Departing *in* the A to Z sections at the end of Chapters 7, 8, and 9.

FARES & SCHEDULES

You can obtain SEPTA train schedules and purchase tickets at the 30th Street, Market East, and Suburban stations or online from the SEPTA Web site. Several smaller stations are open for tickets sales in the morning. You may also purchase tickets on the train but will pay a surcharge if you are departing from a station that sells tickets. PATCO schedules can be obtained from their station at 16th and Locust streets. Tickets for both SEPTA and PATCO train travel may be purchased with cash or a major credit card.

➤ TRAIN INFORMATION: **Amtrak** (☎ 215/824–1600 or 800/872–7245, WEB www.amtrak.com). **New Jersey Transit** (☎ 215/569–3752, WEB www. njtransit.state.nj.us). **PATCO** (☎ 215/ 922–4600). **SEPTA** (☎ 215/580– 7800, WEB www.septa.com).

RESERVATIONS

While reservations are not always necessary for Amtrak travel, it is a good idea to purchase tickets in advance, particularly for travel during peak holiday times. SEPTA and PATCO reservations are not necessary.

TRANSPORTATION
AROUND PHILADELPHIA

If you are staying in Center City, the best way to get around is on foot or by taking the PHLASH bus, which stops at all of the major museums and attractions. The subway system services the four ends of the city but is not a good choice for stops in between because it does not service the main areas of Center City.

Taxis are also plentiful around tourist destinations. SEPTA's commuter trains service most attractions in the Philadelphia suburbs; PATCO will get you to the Camden attractions. You'll want a car to get to the Brandywine Valley, Lancaster, and Bucks County attractions.

TRAVEL AGENCIES

A good travel agent puts your needs first. Look for an agency that has been in business at least five years, emphasizes customer service, and has someone on staff who specializes in your destination. In addition, **make sure the agency belongs to a professional trade organization.** The American Society of Travel Agents (ASTA)—the largest and most influential in the field with more than 26,000 members in some 170 countries—maintains and enforces a strict code of ethics and will step in to help mediate any agent-client disputes if necessary. ASTA (whose motto is "Without a travel agent, you're on your own") also maintains a Web site that includes a directory of agents. (If a travel agency is also acting as your tour operator, *see* Buyer Beware *in* Tours & Packages).

➤ LOCAL AGENT REFERRALS: **American Society of Travel Agents** (ASTA; ☎ 800/965–2782 24-hr hot line, FAX 703/739–7642, WEB www.astanet. com). **Association of British Travel Agents** (✉ 68–71 Newman St., London W1T 3AH, U.K., ☎ 020/7637– 2444, FAX 020/7637–0713, WEB www. abtanet.com). **Association of Canadian Travel Agents** (✉ 130 Albert St., Ste. 1705, Ottawa, Ontario K1P 5G4, Canada, ☎ 613/237–3657, FAX 613/ 237–7502, WEB www.acta.net). **Australian Federation of Travel Agents** (✉ Level 3, 309 Pitt St., Sydney NSW 2000, Australia, ☎ 02/9264–3299, FAX 02/9264–1085, WEB www.afta. com.au). **Travel Agents' Association of New Zealand** (✉ Box 1888, Wellington 10033, New Zealand, ☎ 04/ 499–0104, FAX 04/499–0827, WEB www.taanz.org.nz).

TROLLEYS

Philadelphia once had an extensive trolley network, and a few trolley lines are still in service and run by SEPTA. Routes 10 and 13 begin west and north of Center City and end on Market Street. Due to the frequent construction along these routes, these are not a reliable source of transportation. For privately run trolleys, *see* Bus Tours *in* Sightseeing Tours.

VISITOR INFORMATION

For general information before you go, call or check the Web sites of the Greater Philadelphia Tourism Marketing Corporation and the Pennsylvania Office of Travel and Tourism. When you arrive, stop by the new Independence Visitor Center on 6th Street between Market and Arch streets.

If you are planning to make side trips from Philadelphia or are traveling on to Bucks County or Lancaster County, you should also *see* Visitor Information *in* the A to Z sections of Chapters 7, 8, and 9.

➤ TOURIST INFORMATION: **Greater Philadelphia Tourism Marketing Corporation** (☎ 215/599–0776 or 888/467–4452, WEB www.gophila.com). **Independence Visitor Center** (✉ 6th St. between Market and Arch Sts., ☎ 215/965–7676 or 800/537–7676, WEB www.independencevisitorcenter.com). **Pennsylvania Office of Travel and Tourism** (☎ 717/787–5453; 800/847–4872 for brochures, WEB www.experiencepa.com). **Philadelphia Convention and Visitors Bureau** (✉ 1515 Market St., Suite 2020, 19102, ☎ 215/636–3300 or 800/537–7676, FAX 215/636–3327, WEB www.pcvb.org). In the U.K.: **Pennsylvania Tourism Office** (✉ Suite 302, 11–15 Betterton St. Covent Garden, London WC2H 9BP, ☎ 020/7470–8801, FAX 020/7470–8810).

WEB SITES

Do check out the World Wide Web when planning your trip. You'll find everything from weather forecasts to virtual tours of famous cities. Be sure to **visit Fodors.com** (www.fodors.com), a complete travel-planning site. You can research prices and book plane tickets, hotel rooms, rental cars, vacation packages, and more. In addition, you can post your pressing questions in the Travel Talk section. Other planning tools include a currency converter and weather reports, and there are loads of links to travel resources.

WHEN TO GO

Any time is right to enjoy the area's attractions, and a variety of popular annual events takes place throughout the year (☞ Festivals and Seasonal Events). The period around July 4th is particularly festive; there are special activities in the historic area throughout the summer. Concert and theater seasons run from October through the beginning of June. You may find some better lodging deals in the winter. In spring, the city's cherry blossoms bloom, and they rival those of Washington, DC.

CLIMATE

Like other northern American cities, Philadelphia can be hot and humid in the summer and cold in winter (winter snowfall averages 21 inches).

➤ FORECASTS: **Weather Channel Connection** (☎ 900/932–8437), 95¢ per minute from a Touch-Tone phone.

Climate in Philadelphia

Jan.	40F	4C	May	72F	22C	Sept.	76F	24C
	27	– 3		54	12		61	16
Feb.	41F	5C	June	81F	27C	Oct.	67F	19C
	27	– 3		63	17		50	10
Mar.	49F	9C	July	85F	29C	Nov.	54F	12C
	34	– 1		68	20		40	– 4
Apr.	61F	16C	Aug.	83F	28C	Dec.	43F	6C
	43	6		67	19		31	– 1

FESTIVALS AND SEASONAL EVENTS

For exact dates and other information about the following events, contact the Independence Visitor Center (☞ Visitor Information).

➤ JAN. 1: The day-long **Mummers Parade** (☎ 215/965–7676 or 800/537–7676) kicks off the New Year as some 30,000 sequined and feathered paraders—members of string bands, "fancies," comics, and fancy brigades—march west on Market Street to City Hall. The Fancy Brigade Finale is a ticket-only event at the Pennsylvania Convention Center.

➤ FEB.: **Black History Month** is celebrated with exhibits, lectures, and music at the African American Museum in Philadelphia (⊠ 701 Arch St., ☎ 215/574–0380), plus related events around the city.

➤ FEB.–MAY: **Chinese New Year** (⊠ Chinese Cultural Center, 125 N. 10th St., ☎ 215/923–6767) celebrations include 10-course banquets from Tuesday through Sunday nights beginning at 6:30.

➤ EARLY MARCH: The **Philadelphia Flower Show** (⊠ Pennsylvania Convention Center, 12th and Arch Sts., ☎ 215/988–8800, ᴡᴇʙ www.phi-laflowershow.com), the nation's largest and most prestigious indoor flower show, has acres of exhibits and themed displays. Other events for gardening enthusiasts are part of Flower Show Week.

➤ MAR.: The **St. Patrick's Day Parade** (☎ 215/965–7676 or 800/537–7676) brings the wearing of the green to Benjamin Franklin Parkway.

➤ MAR.: The **Food Network's The Book and the Cook** (☎ 215/965–7676 or 800/537–7676) teams the city's best chefs and the world's top cookbook authors in a weeklong event held in 60 restaurants. Festivities include wine tastings, market tours, and food sampling. It kicks off with the Book and the Cook Fair, at the Pennsylvania Convention Center.

➤ APR.: The **Philadelphia Antiques Show** (⊠ 103rd Engineers Armory, 33rd St. above Market St., ☎ 215/387–3500) showcases museum-quality antiques, lectures, and appraisals.

➤ LATE APR.: **Penn Relays** (⊠ Franklin Field, 33rd and Spruce Sts., ☎ 215/898–6145) is one of the world's oldest and largest amateur track meets with more than 350 races and events.

➤ LATE APR.: **Valborgsmässoafton** (⊠ American-Swedish Historical Museum, 1900 Pattison Ave., ☎ 215/389–1776), the traditional Swedish welcome to spring, has food, song, dance, and bonfires.

➤ LATE APR.–MAY: **Philadelphia Open House** (☎ 215/928–1188) is a three-week period when selected private homes, gardens, and historic buildings in neighborhoods around the city open their doors to the public.

➤ LATE APR.–MAY: **PrideFest Philadelphia** (☎ 215/732–3378) is the nation's most comprehensive gay and lesbian symposium and festival, with a street fair and meetings and parties at locations around the city.

➤ EARLY MAY: International House's **Philadelphia Festival of World Cinema** (☎ 800/969–7392) presents more than 100 features, documentaries, and short films from more than 30 countries at venues throughout the city during the first two weeks of May.

➤ MID-MAY–EARLY JUNE: The Pennsylvania Academy of the Fine Arts annual **Student Art Exhibition** (⊠ Broad and Cherry Sts., ☎ 215/972–7600) presents the work of this talented student body for viewing and purchase.

➤ MOTHER'S DAY WEEKEND: The **Dad Vail Regatta** (☎ 215/248–2600) is the largest collegiate rowing event in the country. Up to 500 shells from more than 100 colleges race on a 2,000-meter course on the Schuylkill River in Fairmount Park.

➤ THIRD WEEK IN MAY: For more than 80 years, the **Rittenhouse Square Flower Market** (⊠ 18th and Walnut Sts., ☎ 215/271–7149) has held this two-day sale of plants, flowers, and food, including the traditional candy lemon stick.

➤ MEMORIAL DAY WEEKEND: **First Union Jam on the River** (⊠ Penn's Landing, ☎ 215/965–7676 or 800/537–7676) is Philadelphia's kickoff to summer, showcasing the best of the bayou with a weekend of music, food, and crafts from New Orleans, in a family-oriented event.

➤ MEMORIAL DAY–SEPT.: At the **Head House Crafts Fair** (✉ 2nd and Pine Sts., ☎ 215/790–0782), more than 30 artisans exhibit jewelry, stained glass, leather, and quilts on summer weekends, noon–11 Saturday and noon–6 Sunday.

➤ LATE MAY–EARLY JUNE: The **Devon Horse Show and Country Fair** (✉ Devon Fairgrounds, U.S. 30, Devon, ☎ 610/964–0550), first held in 1896, is a nine-day event in which top riders compete for more than $200,000 in prize money.

➤ LATE MAY–AUG.: Longwood Gardens's **Summer Festival of Fountains** (✉ U.S. 1, Kennett Square, ☎ 610/388–1000) includes fountain displays during the day and fountain light shows set to music several nights a week.

➤ EARLY JUNE: The **Rittenhouse Square Fine Arts Annual** (✉ Rittenhouse Sq., 18th and Walnut Sts., ☎ 877/689–4112), America's oldest (1931) and largest outdoor juried art show, exhibits works by more than 100 Delaware Valley artists.

➤ EARLY JUNE: The **First Union U.S. Pro Cycling Championship** (WEB www.firstunioncycling.com), the country's premier bicycle race, attracts the world's top cyclists to its 156-mi course, including the grueling Manayunk Wall. On Friday night before the race, Manayunk hosts the Main Street Stroll, a Victorian street festival with a costume parade.

➤ SECOND WEEKEND IN JUNE: **Elfreth's Alley Fete Days** (✉ Elfreth's Alley, between Front, 2nd, Arch, and Race Sts., ☎ 215/574–0560) is the time for open houses on America's oldest continuously occupied street, along with food and fife-and-drum music.

➤ MID-JUNE: The **Mellon Jazz Festival** (☎ 610/667–3559) presents music from local talent to the top names in jazz in a weeklong series of concerts (many free) at locations around town.

➤ LAST WEEKEND IN JUNE: The **Manayunk Annual Arts Fest** (✉ Main St., ☎ 215/482–9565) lines this neighborhood's main drag with more than

250 artists from all over the country displaying arts and crafts.

➤ JUNE–JULY: The **Philadelphia Orchestra's Summer Season** (✉ Mann Center for the Performing Arts, 52nd St. and Parkside Ave., ☎ 215/893–1999) showcases noted guest conductors and soloists in six weeks of outdoor concerts.

➤ LATE JUNE–JULY 4: Philadelphia's premier event, the **Sunoco Welcome America Festival** (☎ 215/683–2201) celebrates America's birthday in America's birthplace. Highlights of the more than 80 free happenings are three big-name outdoor concerts; two are at Penn's Landing (one followed by fireworks, the other by a lighted boat parade on the Delaware). The third, the July 4th finale, concludes with fireworks and music in front of the Philadelphia Museum of Art. Among the other events are a patriotic parade on the Parkway, the awarding of the Philadelphia Liberty Medal, a Family Festival, a Summer Mummers Parade, and a costumed reenactment at Ft. Mifflin.

➤ SUNDAY BEFORE JULY 14: The Eastern State Penitentiary (✉ 22nd St. and Fairmount Ave., ☎ 215/236–3300) reenacts the storming of the Bastille at a **Bastille Day Celebration**, which includes an appearance by Marie Antoinette.

➤ MID-AUG.–MID-OCT.: In Lancaster County, the **Pennsylvania Renaissance Faire** (✉ Mount Hope Estate and Winery, Manheim, ☎ 717/665–7021) is a re-creation of Elizabethan England, with 11 stages and a jousting area. There are magicians, storytellers, and performers; craftspeople demonstrating ancient arts; a human chess game; and food of the period. It's open on Saturday and Sunday, 10 to 6:30.

➤ WEEKEND BEFORE LABOR DAY: The **Philadelphia Folk Festival** (✉ Old Pool Farm, Schwenksville, ☎ 215/242–0150 or 800/556–3655), America's oldest (1962) continuous folk festival, lasts three days. Performers range from the relatively new to folk superstars. There's also food, folk dancing, and sing-alongs.

➤ LABOR DAY WEEKEND: The big **Long's Park Art & Craft Festival**

(☎ 717/295–7054) in Lancaster offers three days of contemporary fine art and crafts, a food fair, and children's activities.

➤ SEPT.: The **Philadelphia Distance Run** (☎ 610/526–9188) is the country's premier half-marathon, with more than 7,000 runners completing a 13-mi course through downtown and along the Schuylkill River. Other competitions include a walk and children's run.

➤ EARLY–MID-SEPT.: The **Philadelphia Fringe Festival** (☎ 215/413–9001) presents 11 days of avant-garde performances—dance, music, theater, poetry, puppetry, and performance art—by performers from all over the world at various sites in Old City.

➤ LATE SEPT.: The **Von Steuben Day Parade** (☎ 215/965–7676 or 800/537–7676), along Benjamin Franklin Parkway, honors the Prussian general who trained the Continental soldiers at Valley Forge.

➤ OCT.: The **Pulaski Day Parade** (☎ 215/965–7676 or 800/537–7676) marches up Broad Street; the Polish-American Congress honors this Polish general, a hero of the Revolutionary War.

➤ SECOND MON. IN OCT.: The **Columbus Day Parade** (☎ 215/965–7676 or 800/537–7676) includes both a parade on South Broad Street and a festival at Marconi Plaza.

➤ OCT.: **Candlelight Tours of the Edgar Allan Poe National Historic Site** (⊠ 532 N. 7th St., ☎ 215/597–8780) celebrate Halloween and Poe with "ghostly" weekend walks through the house.

➤ LAST TWO WEEKS IN OCT.: The Eastern State Penitentiary (⊠ 22nd St. and Fairmount Ave., ☎ 215/236–3300) presents **Terror Behind the Walls,** a Halloween-theme tour through its cells and corridors featuring costumed actors and ghoulish tales.

➤ EARLY NOV.: The **Philadelphia Museum of Art Craft Show** (⊠ Penn-sylvania Convention Center, 12th and Arch Sts., ☎ 215/763–8100) is four days of exhibits by 100 top national craftspeople.

➤ LATE NOV.: The **Thanksgiving Day Parade** (⊠ Benjamin Franklin Pkwy., ☎ 215/965–7676 or 800/537–7676) has thousands of marchers, floats, and local personalities.

➤ NOV. OR DEC.: The **Philadelphia Dog Show** (⊠ Pennsylvania Convention Center, 12th and Arch Sts., ☎ 215/947–1677), sponsored by the Kennel Club of Philadelphia, includes 2,500 entries.

➤ SECOND FRI. EVENING IN DEC.: During **Elfreth's Alley Christmas Open House** (⊠ Elfreth's Alley, between Front, 2nd, Arch, and Race Sts., ☎ 215/574–0560), the community opens its early 18th century homes to the public for tours.

➤ DEC.: **Christmas House Tours** (☎ 215/235–7469) take you around the Colonial and Federal mansions in Fairmount Park, which are decorated for Christmas.

➤ DEC.: *The Nutcracker* (⊠ Academy of Music, Broad and Locust Sts., ☎ 215/893–1999), the Pennsylvania Ballet's production of the Tchaikovsky classic, is a Philadelphia Yuletide tradition.

➤ DEC. 25: **Washington Crossing the Delaware** (⊠ Washington Crossing Historic Park, Washington Crossing, ☎ 215/493–4076) is reenacted with four 40-ft replicas of Durham boats. On Christmas Day 1776, George Washington and his troops took the Hessian camp at Trenton by surprise.

➤ DEC. 27–JAN. 1: **Neighbors in the New Year** (⊠ Penn's Landing, ☎ 215/965–7676 or 800/537–7676) is six days of entertaining events, including a Mummers Fest at the Pennsylvania Convention Center. The culmination is a New Year's Eve celebration with fireworks over the Delaware River.

INDEX

FODOR'S PHILADELPHIA AND THE PENNSYLVANIA DUTCH COUNTRY

EDITOR: Joyce Eisenberg

Editorial Contributors: Anne Dubuisson Anderson, Laura Knowles Callanan, Robert DiGiacomo, Shannon Kelly, Barbara Ann Rosenberg, Melissa Solomon Rosten, Helayne Schiff, Chris Swiac

Editorial Production: Taryn Luciani

Maps: David Lindroth, *cartographer;* Rebecca Baer, Robert Blake, *map editors*

Design: Fabrizio La Rocca, *creative director;* Guido Caroti, *art director;* Jolie Novak, *senior picture editor;* Melanie Marin, *photo editor*

Cover Design: Pentagram

Production/Manufacturing: Yexenia (Jessie) Markland

Cover Photograph: H. Mark Weidman

COPYRIGHT

12th Edition

ISBN 0-679-00893-4

ISSN 1098-9358

SPECIAL SALES

Fodor's Travel Publications are available at special discounts for bulk purchases for sales promotions or premiums. Special editions, including personalized covers, excerpts of existing guides, and corporate imprints, can be created in large quantities for special needs. For more information, contact your local bookseller or write to Special Markets, Fodor's Travel Publications, 280 Park Ave., New York, NY 10017. Inquiries from Canada should be directed to your local Canadian bookseller or sent to Random House of Canada, Ltd., Marketing Department, 2775 Matheson Boulevard East, Mississauga, Ontario L4W 4P7. Inquiries from the United Kingdom should be sent to Fodor's Travel Publications, 20 Vauxhall Bridge Road, London SW1V 2SA, England.

PRINTED IN THE UNITED STATES OF AMERICA

10 9 8 7 6 5 4 3 2 1

IMPORTANT TIP

Although all prices, opening times, and other details in this book are based on information supplied to us at press time, changes occur all the time in the travel world, and Fodor's cannot accept responsibility for facts that become outdated or for inadvertent errors or omissions. So always confirm information when it matters, especially if you're making a detour to visit a specific place.

PHOTOGRAPHY

Bob Krist, *cover. (Pennsylvania Hospital).*

©The Barnes Foundation, *14G.*

Brandywine River Museum, *3 bottom right, 14B.*

Corbis: *2 top left, 2 top right, 2 bottom left, 2 bottom center. Richard T. Nowitz, 13C. Lee Snider, 6B. Ted Spiegel, 11A. Joseph Sohm/Visions of America, 7D. David H. Wells, 8A, 8C.*

Lee Foster, *7E.*

Good N' Plenty, *14C.*

G.P.T.M.C.: *Bob Krist, 14F.*

Green Dragon Farmer's Market & Auction, *3 top right.*

Houserstock: *Dave G. Houser, 11B. 11C.*

The Image Bank: *Gary Cralle, 8B. Andrea Pistolesi, 16.*

Jake's, *14A.*

Bob Krist, *9D, 9F, 10A, 10C, 12A, 12B, 12C.*

Liaison Agency: *Stan Godlewski, 10B.*

Lights of Liberty Show, *2 bottom right.*

Longwood Gardens: *Larry Albee, 3 top left, 14H.*

Richard T. Nowitz, *1, 9E.*

Penn's View Inn, *14E.*

PhotoDisc, *3 bottom left.*

Stone: *David E. Myers, 13A. Joseph Nettis, 4–5, 6A. Larry Ulrich, 13B. .*

The Viesti Collection: *Joe Viesti, 7C.*

Westin Philadelphia Hotel, *14D.*

ON THE ROAD WITH FODOR'S

The more you know before you go, the better your trip will be. Philadelphia's most fascinating small museum (or its most creative restaurant or hippest clothing boutique) could be just around the corner from your hotel, but if you don't know it's there, it might as well be on the other side of the globe. That's where this book comes in. It's a great step toward making sure your next trip lives up to your expectations. As you plan, check out the Web as well. Guidebooks have been helping smart travelers find the special places for years; the Web is one more tool. Whatever reference you consult, be savvy about what you read, and always consider the source. Images and language can be massaged to make places appear better than they are. And one traveler's quaint is another's grimy. Here at Fodor's, and at our on-line arm, Fodors.com, our focus is on providing you with information that's not only useful but accurate and on target. Every day Fodor's editors put enormous effort into getting things right, beginning with the search for the right contributors—people who have objective judgment, broad travel experience, and the writing ability to put their insights into words. There's no substitute for advice from a like-minded friend who has just come back from where you're going, but our writers, having seen all corners of Philadelphia and the Pennsylvania Dutch Country, are the next best thing. They're the kind of people you'd poll for tips yourself if you knew them.

Anne Dubuisson Anderson is pleased to call Philadelphia home after 10 years as a literary agent in New York. In between visits to the Philadelphia Museum of Art and Longwood Gardens, she works as a writing and publishing consultant. She has served as both a writer and editor for books and articles on travel and parenting, including the *Compass American Guide: Alaska*. She updated Side Trips from Philadelphia and Smart Travel Tips A to Z.

New Jersey native **Laura Knowles Callanan** has lived in the Lititz area for more than 20 years, yet she can still remember when she first saw Lancaster County and her initial fascination with the Amish and their unique way of life. She is pleased to share some of the best of the traditional experiences of Pennsylvania Dutch Country, along with the innovative cuisine and multifaceted cultural offerings of the region.

Freelance writer and regular Fodor's contributor **Robert DiGiacomo** updated the Exploring, Nightlife and the Arts, Outdoor Activities and Sports, and Bucks County chapters. A Philadelphia resident, he has written for many national and regional publications, including *Travel Holiday*, *Woman's Day*, and *Elegant Wedding*.

Philadelphia native **Joyce Eisenberg,** who has contributed to Fodor's guides for more than 15 years, edited this edition of the guide. The author of the *JPS Dictionary of Jewish Words* defines herself as a travel maven and recently took her family to Iceland, Japan, and Costa Rica.

Barbara Ann Rosenberg, who revised the Dining and Lodging chapters, is a Center City–based food and travel writer. She is the Dateline correspondent for the James Beard House, a columnist for *Cuizine* magazine, and a frequent contributor to the *Robb Report,* as well as an advisory-board member for the Culinary Institute, and the mid-Atlantic bureau chief for the East-West News Bureau.

Our Shopping updater, freelance writer **Melissa Solomon Rosten,** is a Philadelphia native who's well-versed in the city's most exciting retail areas—she has lived in Manayunk and Rittenhouse Square, and now calls Society Hill home.

Don't Forget to Write

Your experiences—positive and negative—matter to us. If we have missed or misstated something, we want to hear about it. We follow up on all suggestions. Contact the Philadelphia editor at editors@fodors.com or c/o Fodor's, 280 Park Avenue, New York, New York 10017. And have a fabulous trip!

Karen Cure

Karen Cure
Editorial Director